Advanced Textbooks in Economics

Series Editors: C.J. Bliss *and* M.D. Intriligator

Currently Available:

K.J. ARROW, F.H. HAHN	General Competitive Analysis
D. BÖS	Public Enterprise Economics
R.R. CORNWALL	Introduction to the Use of General Equilibrium Analysis
P.J. DHRYMES	Distributed Lags
P.D. DIXON ET AL.	Notes and Problems in Microeconomic Theory
J.W. FRIEDMAN	Oligopoly and the Theory of Games
G. GANDOLFO	Economic Dynamics: Methods and Models
J.D. HESS	The Economics of Organization
W. HILDENBRAND, A.P. KIRMAN	Introduction to Equilibrium Analysis
M.D. INTRILIGATOR	Econometric Models, Techniques, and Applications
L.R. KLEIN, W. WELFE	Lectures in Econometrics
C.G. KROUSE	Capital Markets and Prices: Valuing Uncertain Income Streams
E. MALINVAUD	Lectures on Microeconomic Theory
A.G. MALLIARIS	Stochastic Methods in Economics and Finance
L. PHILIPS	Applied Consumption Analysis
A. SEIERSTAD, K. SYDSÆTER	Optimal Control Theory with Economic Applications
A.K. SEN	Collective Choice and Social Welfare
A.D. WOODLAND	International Trade and Resource Allocation

HISTORY OF ECONOMIC THEORY

ADVANCED TEXTBOOKS IN ECONOMICS

VOLUME 26

Editors:

C.J. BLISS

M.D. INTRILIGATOR

Advisory Editors:

W.A. BROCK

D.W. JORGENSON

M.C. KEMP

J.-J. LAFFONT

J.-F. RICHARD

NORTH-HOLLAND
AMSTERDAM · NEW YORK · OXFORD · TOKYO

HISTORY OF ECONOMIC THEORY

TAKASHI NEGISHI

University of Tokyo

1989
NORTH-HOLLAND
AMSTERDAM · NEW YORK · OXFORD · TOKYO

ISBN: 0 444 70437 X

Publishers
ELSEVIER SCIENCE PUBLISHERS B.V.
P.O. BOX 1991
1000 BZ AMSTERDAM
THE NETHERLANDS

Sole distributors for the U.S.A. and Canada
ELSEVIER SCIENCE PUBLISHING COMPANY, INC.
655 AVENUE OF THE AMERICAS
NEW YORK, N.Y. 10010
U.S.A.

Library of Congress Cataloging in Publication Data

Negishi, Takashi, 1933–
  History of economic theory/Takashi Negishi.
  p. cm. — (Advanced textbooks in economics; v. 26)
  Includes bibliographies and indexes.
  ISBN 0-444-70437-X (U.S.)
  1. Economics—History. I. Title. II. Series.
HB75.N423 1988
330'.09—dc19   88-25139
                                                CIP

PRINTED IN THE NETHERLANDS

INTRODUCTION TO THE SERIES

The aim of the series is to cover topics in economics, mathematical economics and econometrics, at a level suitable for graduate students or final year undergraduates specializing in economics. There is at any time much material that has become well established in journal papers and discussion series which still awaits a clear, self-contained treatment that can easily be mastered by students without considerable preparation or extra reading. Leading specialists will be invited to contribute volumes to fill such gaps. Primary emphasis will be placed on clarity, comprehensive coverage of sensibly defined areas, and insight into fundamentals, but original ideas will not be excluded. Certain volumes will therefore add to existing knowledge, while others will serve as a means of communicating both known and new ideas in a way that will inspire and attract students not already familiar with the subject matter concerned.

The Editors

To my Aiko,
for our silver wedding anniversary

CONTENTS

Introduction to the Series   v

Preface   xi

Chapter 1.   A bird's-eye view of the history of economics   1

   1.   Why do we study the history of economics?   1
   2.   The dawn of economics   5
   3.   The classical school of economics   11
   4.   The historical school and institutionalism   16
   5.   Marxian economics   21
   6.   Marginal revolution and after   24
        References   29

Chapter 2.   Some pioneers in economic theory   31

   1.   Locke's microfoundation of quantity theory   31
   2.   Hume and specie-flow mechanism   40
   3.   Quesnay's *Tableau Économique*   48
   4.   Expenditure patterns in the *Tableau Économique*   59
        References   68

Chapter 3.   Adam Smith and the formation of classical economics   71

   1.   *The Wealth of Nations*   71
   2.   Samuelson's mathematical model   77
   3.   Wages and profit in a growing economy   83
   4.   Division of labor and market   89
   5.   Division of labor and capital accumulation   95
        References   102

Chapter 4.   Ricardo, Malthus and the development of classical
economics   105

1.   Ricardo and the moderns   105
2.   Some mathematical models   109
3.   Value and distribution   124
4.   Dichotomy in the theory of international trade   131
5.   Malthus as a precursor of Keynes   138
6.   The motives to produce   145
      References   152

Chapter 5.   J.S. Mill and the close of classical economics   155

1.   Equilibrium of demand and supply   155
2.   Recantation of the wages fund doctrine   162
3.   Say's law and business cycles   170
4.   The existence of a trade equilibrium   176
5.   Equilibrium and disequilibrium   181
      References   189

Chapter 6.   Marx's economics   191

1.   *Das Kapital*   191
2.   Some linear models   200
3.   On exploitations   206
4.   Marx's dichotomy of distribution   213
5.   The falling rate of profit   221
6.   On market values   229
      References   237

Chapter 7.   Walras and the general equilibrium theory   241

1.   Augustin Cournot   241
2.   *Eléments d'économie politique pure*   246
3.   The existence of a general equilibrium   254
4.   The stability of a general equilibrium   263
5.   Capital and money   268
      References   276

Chapter 8.   Menger and the Austrian school   279

  1.   Menger's marketability   279
  2.   Wieser's welfare economics   289
  3.   Böhm-Bawerk and the positive rate of interest   297
  4.   Böhm-Bawerk versus Schumpeter   307
      References   315

Chapter 9.   Jevons and Edgeworth   319

  1.   Hermann Heinrich Gossen   319
  2.   Jevons's theory of exchange   324
  3.   Edgeworth's *Mathematical Psychics*   330
  4.   Reflections on Edgeworth's theorem   338
      References   343

Chapter 10.   Marshall's economics   345

  1.   *Principles of Economics*   345
  2.   Consumers' and producers' surplus   355
  3.   Life-cycle theory and internal economies   363
  4.   From Marshall to Keynes   375
      References   382

Postscript   385

Author index   387

Subject index   393

PREFACE

As a book in the series of Advanced Textbooks in Economics, this volume aims to interest students of modern economic theory in the history of economics. For this purpose, past economic theories are considered from the point of view of current economic theories and translated, if possible and necessary, into mathematical models.

When he reformulated Wicksell's theory of capital mathematically, R. Frisch tried to justify his purpose by emphasizing that nowadays the younger generation of economists are not induced to spend time and trouble discussing problems in economic theory unless the details of the problem are rigorously formulated in mathematical terms, while in the days of Wicksell, on the contrary, one had to write literally if one wished to be read by more than a very minor group of specialists.[1] What was true for Wicksell in this respect is all the more true for much earlier economic theories, i.e., those of the mercantilists, physiocrats, classical economists, Marx and the Marxians, and some economists of the marginal revolution. While Wicksell merely explained literally what he himself considered mathematically, some earlier economists did not employ mathematical method at all. Those economists used at best numerical examples not only for explanatory purposes but also as the only weapon available to analyze their problems. The result is that they sometimes insisted on the unwarranted generality of their propositions derived from numerical examples, since numerical examples, unlike the mathematical method, cannot reveal the implicit assumptions on which the derived propositions are based.

In view of these circumstances, it is necessary to use mathematical models of contemporary economic theory to explain the problems economists had to face in the past and to analyze the theories they developed to solve them in their own ways, i.e., literally and by using numerical examples. By doing so we can see their historically celebrated and still interesting problems in a new light and the problems they could not solve by their techniques are easily solved using modern techniques. We should not, however, indulge ourselves in an easy victory like a modern army in a science fiction, slipping through time to overcome a band of medieval knights. We hope we can find in the works of past economists clues to questions of present interest or theories and techniques of analysis that might be applied to modern problems. It is this possibility that is

---

[1] See R. Frisch, "Wicksell", in *The Development of Economic Thought*, H.W. Spiegel, ed., John Wiley, 1952.

the motivation for our studying the history of economics from the point of view of contemporary theory. Although it cannot be denied that, by studying mathematical models, we can understand more easily what economists in earlier times really meant, we must admit that something of the original content is always lost by the mathematical translation of the classical works of past economists. Translation is treason. We have to study critically and carefully, therefore, those mathematical models of classical works constructed by contemporary economists, by always referring to the content of the original literature.

After a brief discussion of why we have to study the history of economics from the point of view of contemporary economic theory, a bird's-eye view of the historical development of economics is given in Chapter 1 so that readers can see the significance of the topics to be discussed in subsequent chapters from a proper historical perspective. These topics are carefully chosen to show not only what great economists in the past contributed to the development of economics, but also what suggestions for solving our own current problems we can obtain by reworking the problems they had to face. It is our great pleasure if readers can find there some useful hints for their researches to develop modern theories further. Alternatively, we are also happy if some readers conclude that something is wrong with the current mainstream theory and that economics should be developed under different paradigms.

This book can be used in advanced undergraduate as well as graduate classes on the history of economics, since each chapter is developed from my undergraduate lectures for senior students at the University of Tokyo and the International Christian University and from my hand-outs for graduate seminars at the University of Tokyo and Kyoto University. Mathematical techniques used can be easily understood by advanced undergraduates of economics major, since some models constructed originally by contemporary mathematical economists are carefully reformulated without losing their essence, so that only basic calculus and the rudiments of linear algebra are necessary to understand them[2].

Since this is a text book, we tried to be as objective and eclectic as possible, at least in the introductory chapter and in the introductory parts of all the chapters. In this respect, we owe greatly to standard and authoritative histories of economics, such as those of Schumpeter, Blaug, Ekelund and Hébert, as well as to other secondary literature on the history of economics. It is our pleasant

---

[2] Readers of, for example, J.M. Henderson, and R.E. Quandt, *Microeconomic Theory, A Mathematical Approach*, McGraw-Hill, 1958, can understand the techniques used in this book, and readers of the first half of M.D. Intriligator, *Mathematical Optimization and Economic Theory*, Prentice-Hall, 1971, will find them easy.

duty to acknowledge our debt to them, although, of course, it is possible that we misunderstood some of their arguments. Materials developed in our articles published in *Manchester School, History of Political Economy, Economic Studies Quarterly*, and *Zeitschrift für Nationalökonomie*, as well as those in our three collections of essays[3] are used freely in completely revised and abridged forms. We are grateful to the editors and referees of these journals and the reviewers of these books.

We owe thanks for valuable comments and warm encouragement to our colleagues in the University of Tokyo, members of the Japanese History of Political Economy (HOPE) Association, and participants of seminars where some of the chapters were read. Although some of them are mentioned in the relevant chapters below, we regret that we cannot include the names of many others to whom we are greatly indebted. Our research activities have been supported financially by the Foundation for Promoting Economics of the University of Tokyo, and by Grant-in-Aid for Scientific Research of the Japanese Ministry of Education, Science and Culture. Last, but not least, we would like to thank Professors C.J. Bliss and M.D. Intriligator, and the North-Holland editors for their valuable suggestions and editorial efforts, and Miss Tomoko Kiyama, Miss Toshiko Hutatsuishi and Miss Keiko Mizuno for their excellent typing.

Tokyo, December, 1987   Takashi Negishi

---

[3] *Kotenhakeizaigaku to Kindaikeizaigaku* (Classical Economics and Modern Economics), Iwanami-shoten, 1981, *Economic Theories in a Non-Walrasian Tradition*, Cambridge University Press, 1985, and *Keizaigaku niokeru Koten to Gendairiron* (Classics and Contemporary Theory in Economics), Yuhikaku, 1985.

CHAPTER 1

A BIRD'S-EYE VIEW OF THE HISTORY OF ECONOMICS

1. Why do we study the history of economics?

Of course, it is interesting to learn how several men of genius and many earnest scholars faced the economic problems of their days and what kind of economic theories have been developed in the past to solve them. However, we now have our own economic problems which are more diversified and more complex than theirs, and contemporary economic theories to be applied to them are highly developed, so that they are very difficult and time consuming to learn. One may naturally feel that there is no time left to study old problems and old theories. Why, then, do we study the history of economic theory?

To reply to this question, let us first consider how theories should be, or have actually been, developed in economics as a positive science. A standard explanation may run as follows. To explain phenomena which are either collective or recurrent, a theoretical model is constructed. It is a system of hypotheses in which we introduce only such elements or factors as can be considered essential. By the use of the model, we logically derive predictions or conjectures on phenomena to be explained. It is, then, necessary to see whether conjectures obtained from the theoretical model can explain the behavior of phenomena actually observed. This is the test of the theory through experiments or observation. A theory which is not refuted in the test is retained for the time being, to obtain further conjectures and to be tested again by new experiments and new observation. If a theory is refuted in the test, it implies that the hypotheses adopted are wrong and the factors or elements introduced in the model are not properly chosen. Through such a cycle of the construction of a model, the making of conjectures, the empirical test, the refutations, and the construction of a new model, economic theories are developed, step by step, toward the truth.

If economic theories have actually developed in this way, however, the history of economics is not necessary to study theories of present day economics. Economic theories of the past which are no longer included in the theoretical system of contemporary economics are those theories which have once been refuted by the empirical test in the past. Revisiting past theories which are false is not necessary either to understand contemporary theories which are currently regarded as valid, or to develop them further into more generalized or refined ones. Consideration of why economists made mistakes in the past may be left to psychological or sociological studies of research activities.

The continuous process of conjectures and refutations described above is a popularized text-book version of Popper's theoretical model of the development of sciences. As Popper himself recognized, however, the actual development of a science has never been such a rational process even in the case of natural sciences, let alone the case of economics. Even if a theory is refuted by the test, "it is always possible to say that the experimental results are not reliable, or that the discrepancies which are asserted to exist between the experimental results and the theory are only apparent and that they will disappear with the advance of our understanding" (Popper [27, p. 50]). Refuted theories have not been continuously replaced, since it is not so easy to construct new theoretical models. Although *ad hoc* assumptions are added, such theories are retained without any changes being made in the essential part.

From his study of the Copernican revolution in astronomy [14], Kuhn [15] developed a theoretical model of the development process of sciences which describes the real history of science faithfully, rather than insisting on rational rules of scientific discovery. The history of science is not the history of continuous conjectures and refutations à la Popper. It is marked by long periods of steady refinement, normal science or problem-solving activity in the context of an accepted theoretical framework, a paradigm, interrupted on occasion by scientific revolutions, discontinuous jumps from one ruling paradigm to another, with no bridge for communicating between them. It should be emphasized that a paradigm cannot be overthrown by one single empirical refutation. It is overthrown as a consequence of repeated refutations and mounting anomalies only when a competing, alternative paradigm is ready.

As the study of Ptolemaic astronomy is not necessary to understand the modern theory of astronomy, however, Kuhn's theory of scientific revolution does not persuade us that the study of the history of economics is necessary to understand the modern theory of economics. In the history of economics there were several revolutions, such as the marginal revolution and the Keynesian revolution. If these revolutions in the history of economics are scientific revolutions in the sense of Kuhn, the study of a pre-Keynesian paradigm, say, is not necessary to understand a post-Keynesian paradigm, since there is no bridge for communicating between two paradigms. Fortunately, however, Kuhn's theory cannot be applied to the case of economics.

A typical reaction of economists to Kuhn's theory can be seen in Bronfenbrenner's [2] interpretation that Kuhn's theory is a catastrophic theory. Bronfenbrenner does not deny the existence of scientific revolutions in the sense of Kuhn, but thinks that the catastrophic theory of Kuhn does not explain the facts very well in the history of economics, because some special features distinguish the history of economics from that of other sciences. Firstly, the catastrophic theory maintains that paradigms, once displaced, are displaced definitely. But, according to Bronfenbrenner, outmoded ideas are never definitely displaced in economics. Secondly, advances in economics tend to be major accretions without a rejection of existing paradigms, which Bronfenbrenner argues is inconsistent with a catastrophic theory. Two examples given by Bronfenbrenner of outmoded and displaced ideas that still continue to exist in economics are elements of the medieval notion of just price, on which modern income policy proposals are based, and mercantilist notions, which continue to exist in spite of their displacement by classical economics.

Mehta [24, pp. 198–201] defends Kuhn and criticizes Bronfenbrenner to the effect that Kuhn's theory is not the catastrophic theory that Bronfenbrenner claims it to be. Kuhn's theory is not a theory of scientific revolutions that are complete and unaccountable breaks with the past, since Kuhn himself admits that new paradigms usually preserve a great deal of the most concrete parts of past achievement. In other words, in the later and weaker version of Kuhn's theory, any period of scientific development is marked by a large number of overlapping and interpenetrating paradigms, some of which may be incommensurable but certainly not all of which are (Kuhn [15, pp. 199–200]. Paradigms are not considered to be replaced by each other immediately. In economics as well as in other sciences, then, outmoded ideas continue to exist, since outmodedness can be defined, as was emphasized by Mehta, only relatively to a given paradigm. From this point of view, the study of the history of economics is very important to promote the progress of economics, since an idea that is outmoded relative to one of the currently dominating paradigms may be useful for the development of another, possibly new, paradigm. The study of mercantilism, which has been outmoded since the dominance of classical economics, may suggest to us a perspective on the current problem of frictions among trading nations which classical and post-classical economics cannot (Schmitt [29]).

Perhaps it is the theory of Lakatos [17, pp. 91–196] which explains the development process of economics best. It is a halfway house between Popper and Kuhn. Lakatos [17, p. 155] considered that *"the history of science has been and should be a history of competing research programs (or, if you wish, 'paradigms') but it has not been and not become a succession of periods of normal sciences,"* the monopolies of a research program. All scientific research programs may be characterized as having an immutable hard core that is irrefutable and that is surrounded by a changeable protective belt of refutable auxiliary hypotheses that has to bear the brunt of tests. Let us note that scientific research programs are not competing theories but competing series of changing theories. If changes increase content, they are called progressive, whereas if they are *ad hoc* and decrease content, they are called degenerating.

When two research programs, R_1 and R_2, compete, their first models usually deal with different aspects of the domain. As the rival research programs expand, however, they gradually encroach on each other's territory. In other words, they are commensurable. This overlapping of R_1 and R_2 eventually results in the first battle between the two programs in which, say, the nth version of R_1 will be bluntly, dramatically inconsistent with the mth version of R_2. Suppose the battle is won by R_1, as the result of an experiment. But the war is not yet over, since any research program is allowed a few such defeats. All it needs for a comeback is to produce an $m+1$ content-increasing version and a verification of some of its novel content (Easlea [5, pp. 21–22]). It is difficult to see why an apparently defeated research program cannot make a triumphal return with its hard core the same as before but with a better articulated or different protective belt. But, to make a triumphal return, there must be some scientists seeking to develop it while it is in a state of hibernation. In other words, it is necessary to study theories that are regarded as past ones from the point of view of other research programs.[1]

We may perhaps consider that Marxian and non-Marxian economics are different research programs. In the latter, of course, there are several different competing research programs. From the Keynesian point of view, the theories of mercantilism, Malthus, the underconsumptionists, Kalecki and Keynes are a series of theories which belongs to the same research program with the common hard core of the possibility of general glut (overproduction) and deficiency of effective demand. Similarly, the pre-Keynesian quantity theory of money and the recent theory of monetarism belong to the same research program, which has the reliable automatic market adjustments as a hard core. The latter theory has, however, a new protective belt, that is, a new theory to explain changes in employment which the former did not have. This is the reason why the quantity theory made a triumphal return from its state of hibernation after the Keynesian revolution. The so-called neo-classical, or

---

[1] For further development of recent theories of science "beyond positivism", see Feyerabend [7] and Caldwell [3].

neo-Walrasian paradigm is currently dominating but is being challenged by neo-Austrians who succeeded the Menger–von Mises tradition. Finally, the Ricardian research program, which was in a state of hibernation after the marginal revolution, was revived by Sraffa's theory, and is now developing as the economics of neo-Ricardians.

The historical development of economic theories is not a unidirectional progression toward the truth and the currently influential theory is not necessarily superior, in every respect, to past theories, which have been neglected so far (Cesarano [4]). With a new protective belt theory, even a currently hibernating research program can make a triumphal return. The outmoded ideas of such a research program are, however, not well reflected in the currently dominating economic theories, so that one cannot understand the possibility of the return of the former ideas simply by studying the latter theories only. This is why we should study the history of economics. It is evident that the study of the economics of mercantilism and Malthus was important for the development of the economics of Keynes (Keynes [12, pp. 333–371]). The fact that Sraffa himself was the editor of the works of Ricardo shows that the historical study of the economics of Ricardo was indispensable for the development of neo-Ricardian economics. Since currently competing different research programs are succeeding different past theories in this way, the study of the history of economics is essential to maintain commensurability among such research programs. The study of comparative economic theories in the present is possible only on the basis of the study of how different theories have been developed from the different traditions which were dominant in the past. Profitable competition among paradigms is made possible only by the study of the history of economics.

2. The dawn of economics

As we saw in the previous section, Bronfenbrenner [2] pointed out that the medieval notion of just price and the mercantilist notions are two examples of outmoded and once displaced ideas that still continue to exist in economics. According to Schumpeter [30, pp. 9–10], the construction of scientific economics was started in the late eighteenth century on two different foundations made in earlier periods. The first one is the ancient and medieval economic thought of philosophers, while the second one is popular arguments of current practical economic problems in the sixteenth to eighteenth centuries. The medieval theory of just price can be considered as a representative example of the former. The latter is, of course, what is called mercantilism. Let us, therefore, start our brief history of economics with a consideration of the modern significance of the theory of just price and mercantilism.

The greatest medieval philosopher St. Thomas Aquinas (1225–1274), author of the great *Summa Theologica*, developed his theory of just price following the greatest Greek philosopher Aristotle (384–322 B.C.). In his *Nicomachean Ethics*, Aristotle argued that commutative or contractual justice requires an exchange of equivalents. Aquinas considered that this equivalence should be interpreted in terms of costs, chiefly labor costs. Karl Marx, who was called the last of the schoolmen by Tawney, also followed Aristotle to consider that two commodities to be exchanged have to be of equal value and insisted that this value should be measured in terms of embodied labor, since the only one common property of two commodities is that of being products of labor. It may seem, therefore, that Aquinas as well as Marx insisted on the labor theory of value. Aquinas, however, also insisted that all goods are valued only in relation to human wants.[2]

The greatest difference between the classical and the Marxian labor theory of value and the theory of just price considered by Aquinas and medieval philosophers lies in the fact that the former is to be applied to competitive markets, while the latter is mainly concerned with cases in which markets do not exist or competitions are imperfect. In the case of bilateral monopoly and isolated exchange, the equilibrium price is indeterminate in the sense that it is influenced by non-market factors such as the social status of traders. The just theory of price is a normative theory to determine the price in such non-competitive situations, so that gains from trade are assured even to the traders whose position is weaker.

A case discussed often by medieval philosophers was that of a stranger entering a village whose inhabitants could and would charge him cartel prices. The theory of just price arbitrated between the stranger and the village inhabitants so that the former was charged no more than local market prices. In other words, if there exists a competitive market price, it is the just price, even if it is higher than the cost of production. The theory of just price is, therefore, unnecessary in the world of perfect competition which is presupposed by classical, Marxian and neo-classical economics. The theory of just price is concerned with the case where competitive market price does not exist.[3]

Aquinas and medieval philosophers insist in general on the unlawfulness of interest on loans of money. Following Aristotle, Aquinas argued that money was invented chiefly for the purpose of exchange and that it is by its very nature

[2] See Marx [20, pp. 45, 65, 727], Blaug [1, p. 29], Tawney [34, p. 36], and Viner [36, pp. 68, 84].
[3] For the theory of just price, see Friedman [8] and Viner [36, pp. 81–85].

unlawful to take payment for the use of money lent, which payment is known as usury. Taken from Roman law was the distinction between fungibles, which lose their identity in or are destroyed or transformed by use, and non-fungibles, which are not destroyed or transformed by use. It was insisted that non-fungibles (like a horse or a house) could be the subject of a lease (transfer of possession with right of use without transfer of ownership), whereas fungibles (like grain) could not be the subject of a lease as distinguished from a sale, since transfer of possession (with right of use) is inseparable from transfer of ownership. Money, which is a fungible, could be loaned, but not leased. In other words, it is unlawful to take interest payment on money lent (Viner [36, pp. 86–89]). It is hardly possible to be persuaded by these arguments against interest. It may, however, be conjectured that one purpose of these arguments was, like that of the theory of just price, to interfere with imperfect loan markets in which the lenders are rich men and the borrowers are the needy poor.

Let us return to Bronfenbrenner [2], who pointed out the modern significance of the theory of just price in its relation to modern income policy proposals. If wages are determined not by a competitive labor market but by collective bargaining between employers and employees, the situation is similar to that of bilateral monopoly or isolated exchange, where the equilibrium price is indeterminate. A criterion is necessary to arbitrate two parties in a wage dispute. It cannot be denied, therefore, that the theory of just price and income policy face similar problems in the sense that the problems are not solved automatically in competitive markets.

The labor productivity criterion is often used as a guideline for the rate of wage in income policy proposals. By definition,

$$w = s \, p \, (V/L),$$

where w, V, p, L and s denote, respectively, the money rate of wage, the real national product, the average price level, the total employment and the relative share of labor. The labor productivity criterion insists that the rate of increase in wages should be equal to the rate of increase in labor productivity V/L, so that the price level is stabilized and the relative share is kept unchanged. Why should the relative share be kept unchanged? The reason is that, according to the stylized facts of economic growth in developed capitalist economies since the second half of the 19th century,[4] the relative share of labor remained almost constant even though wages were largely determined in competitive labor markets. The philosophy of the labor productivity criterion is, therefore, similar to that of the theory of just price, which insists that the competitive

[4] See Chapter 8, section 4 and the literature cited there for the stylized facts of economic growth.

market price available in a similar condition should be the just price in the case where no such price is available.

Mercantilism is a system of policies which aimed to create strong and centralized nation-states in European countries after the break-up of the medieval organization of industry and commerce. Mercantilism literature, which discussed such policies and went beyond it to consider economic principles, is highly diversified and heterogeneous so that it is not possible to call mercantilism a school in the history of economics. "Mercantilism was neither a scientific school nor a scientific theory – there were then no schools at all in our sense of the word – and we distort the picture if we seek already in this period what was in fact the consequence of a specialized discipline after it had properly constituted itself" (Schumpeter [30, p. 39]). We cannot discuss here the details of such diversified literature. From our point of view, however, we may raise the following four points.

Firstly, Adam Smith, who first criticized mercantilism systematically, defined it as a system of commerce.

> The two principles being established,..., that wealth consisted in gold and silver, and that those metals could be brought into a country which had no mines only by the balance of trade, or by exporting to a greater value than it imported; it necessarily became the great object of political economy to diminish as much as possible the importation of foreign goods for home-consumption, and to increase as much as posssible the exportation of the produce of domestick industry. Its [mercantilism's] two great engines for enriching the country, therefore, were restraints upon importation, and encouragements to exportation. (Smith [32, p. 450].)

According to the theory of price-specie-flow mechanism, however, it is impossible to keep the result of such a favorable balance of trade in a country. If a country, as a result of an export surplus, gains specie, her price level will rise, while the opposite effect will take place in the rest of the world, which has lost specie on account of its import surplus. Prices in the country are now too high to enable the country to maintain her export surplus. Her high price level attracts imports from the rest of the world while reducing her exports. The opposite will happen in the rest of the world, to which there will be a reversal of the flow of specie. Thomas Mun (1571–1641), a representative mercantilist thinker, realized that "all men do consent that plenty of money in a Kingdom doth make the native commodities dearer,..., so is it directly against the benefit of the Publique in the quantity of the trade; for as plenty of money makes wares dearer, so dear wares decline their use and consumption" (McCulloch [19, p. 138]). However, he did not hesitate to advocate the indefinite accumulation of hard money. This is the so-called mercantilist dilemma. Even if mercantilists thought that an increase in the supply of money is attended by a rise in the demand for money and hence the volume of trade and not prices would be directly affected by a specie inflow (Blaug [1, p. 18]), specie-flow mechanism still works, since the imports of a country depend positively on the level of her real national product.[5]

The second issue is Keynes's view of mercantilism as a monetary economics. In his *General Theory*, he considered that mercantilism is "a doctrine which the classical school has repudiated as childish but which deserves rehabilitation and honour" [12, p. 351]. For a country which has no mines, it is impossible to increase the supply of money so that the economy can grow without deficiency of effective demand, which causes unemployment, unless she has the positive balance of trade, which causes a specie inflow.

At a time when the authorities had no direct control over the domestic rate of interest or the other inducements to home investment, measures to increase the favourable balance of trade were the only *direct* means at their disposal for increasing foreign investment; and, at the same time, the effect of a favourable balance of trade on the influx of the precious metals was their only *indirect* means of reducing the domestic rate of interest and so increasing the inducement to home investment. [12, p. 336.]

It is impossible to study the notions to which the mercantilists were led by their actual experiences, without perceiving that there has been a chronic tendency throughout human history for the propensity to save to be stronger than the inducement to invest. The weakness of the inducement to invest has been at all times the key to the economic problem. To-day the explanation of the weakness of this inducement may chiefly lie in the extent of existing accumulations; whereas, formerly, risks and hazards of all kinds may have played a large part. [12, p. 347–348.]

Keynes's exposition of the mercantilist interpretation of economic phenomena is to a very large extent based on the first edition of Heckscher's *Mercantilism*. In an appendix in the new edition (1955), however, Heckscher criticized Keynes's view on mercantilism. For example, Heckscher points out that the basic flaw in Keynes's interpretation is the belief that unemployment in the mercantilist era was similar in character to unemployment recurring in industrialized economies. Unemployment caused by a fall in fixed investment was virtually unknown before the Industrial Revolution. The predominant type of industrial unemployment before the Industrial Revolution was mainly,

[5] See Chapter 2, section 2 and section 3.1 for the theory of specie-flow mechanism.

if not wholly, of the classical type which Keynes called voluntary on frictional.[6] The issue is, however, not completely settled yet, since there are a number of economic historians who maintain that involuntary industrial unemployment, due to the deficiency of effective demand, which was to a serious extent of monetary origin, was a major problem in seventeenth century England (Hutchison [10, p. 130]).

The next issue is so-called primitive accumulation. Marx defines it as the accumulation "preceding capitalistic accumulation; an accumulation not the result of the capitalist mode of production, but its starting-point" [20, p. 667]. It is

> the historical process of divorcing the producer from the means of production. It appears as primitive, because it forms the pre-historic stage of capital and of the mode of production corresponding with it. The economic structure of capitalistic society has grown out of the economic structure of feudal society. The dissolution of the latter set free the element of the former. [20, p. 668.]

In other words, it is necessary to set up by exogenous forces a starting point of a market economy which, once set up, can grow endogenously. It is believed by many Marxian economists that the absence of primitive accumulation is a principal cause of the current difficulties of underdeveloped countries.

After his life-long studies of mercantilism, Kobayashi [13, pp. 335–425] concluded that mercantilism is to be defined as economic theories of primitive accumulation. As a matter of fact, Marx called James Steuart (1713–1780), the author of *An Inquiry into the Principles of Political Economy* (1767), the *rational* expression of the monetary and mercantile systems and argued as follows.

> His service to the theory of capital is that he shows how the process of separation takes place between the conditions of production, as the property of a definite class, and labour-power. He gives a great deal of attention to this *genesis* of capital – without as yet seeing it directly as the genesis of capital, although he sees it as a condition for large-scale industry. He examines the process particularly in agriculture; and he rightly considers that manufacturing industry proper only came into being through this process of separation in agriculture. In Adam Smith's writings this process of separation is assumed to be already completed. [21, p. 43.][7]

---

[6] See Heckscher [9, pp. 340–358, especially, 354–356], and Blaug [1, pp. 14–16, 31].

[7] Since Steuart entertains a strong view of the influence which statesmen can exercise on the process of primitive accumulation, he influenced the theory of economic policies and the interpretation of the mercantilism of the German historical school (e.g., List and Schmoller).

Finally, we have to discuss a recent interpretation of mercantilism in terms of the theory of the rent-seeking society (Ekelund and Tollison [6]). In this view, the positive balance of trade, for example, is not the direct objective of mercantilism, but merely a result of the interactions of projectors seeking monopoly rents from the sole rights to produce particular goods and services and a revenue-seeking absolute monarchy that satisfies its fiscal needs by the sale of protective legislation and granting monopoly rights. In England, then, the decline of mercantilism can be explained by struggles evolved between the King and the newly rising Parliament and between the King's courts and the common law courts allied to parliamentary interests. In France, on the other hand, the absence of representative institutions or conditions that would facilitate their emergence can explain the growth and persistence of mercantilism.[8]

From the point of view of the welfare of a country as a whole, the positive balance of trade is a decrease in the gains from trade, since it implies to give commodities and services to foreigners more than to receive from them. As in the days of mercantilism, however, even nowadays the economic policies of a government do not necessarily aim to increase the welfare of a country as a whole, since they are strongly influenced by the interest of big industries. Furthermore, as is insisted by Schmitt [29], mercantilist policies to increase the extent of the market for exporting and import-competing industries of a country do not necessarily decrease the gains from trade, if these industries are subject to increasing returns or diminishing costs. It may be possible that gains from increasing returns due to large markets outweigh losses from the positive balance of trade, from the point of view of a country as a whole. The problem of mercantilism is, therefore, not that of past history, but it still has significance today.

3. The classical school of economics

Since mercantilism cannot be called a school in the history of economics, the honor of the first school of economics in history should be given to physiocracy, which was developed in France. The physiocrats criticized the mercantilist policies of Colbert, by which manufactures were protected but agriculture was consistently neglected. Being based on the doctrine of natural law, they insisted on *laissez-faire* and emphasized the importance of agricul-

[8]This view contradicts, therefore, that of Kobayashi [13, pp. 339–356], who called the mercantilism after the English revolution the proper mercantilism and did not regard Colbertism as the proper one.

ture which they considered is only productive in the sense that *produit net* (surplus) can be generated. To encourage the accumulation of capital, which is necessary to improve agriculture, they argued for tax reform and free trade. A single tax on land rent was proposed, since rent is the only possible form of *produit net* in the economics of physiocracy. The removal of the mercantilist restrictions on free trade in the agricultural product was insisted on to keep farm prices and therefore land rents high.

The founder of physiocracy was François Quesnay (1694–1774), who wrote the famous *Tableau Économique* (1758). In his *Tableau*, Quesnay assumed that the then French economy was developed into the optimal state called *ordre naturel* and skilfully described the circular flow of commodities and money among agriculture, manufacture, and landowners. In the economics of physiocracy, the concept of capitals is firmly established as advances, i.e., original advances (fixed capital) and annual advances (working capital). In the *Tableau* as well as Quesnay's other writings which discussed the dynamic processes towards the optimal state, however, profit is not considered as a permanent source of income. We have to wait for the emergence of the classical school to see profit treated symmetrically with wage and rent in the distribution of national income (see Chapter 2, sections 3 and 4).

The founder of the classical school of economics is Adam Smith (1723–1790), the author of *The Wealth of Nations* (1776), who insisted on *laissez-faire* and criticized mercantilism, like physiocrats, on the basis of the doctrine of natural law. The pursuit of private interests can, through the guidance of the invisible hands of market mechanism based on the social division of labor, promote public benefits. Smith criticized the physiocracy too, however, since it insists that only agriculture is productive. Profits are considered by Smith as a permanent source of income, equally with wages and rents in his theory of income distributions. Classical economics was developed further by, among others, David Ricardo (1772–1823), the author of *On the Principles of Political Economy and Taxation* (1817), and Thomas Malthus (1766–1834) who wrote *Essay on Population* (1798) and *Principles of Political Economy* (1820). The last great economist of the classical school is John Stuart Mill (1806–1873). His *Principles of Political Economy* (1848) is a monument of the final stage of classical economics.

Smith admitted the embodied labor theory of value in the "early and rude state of society which precedes both the accumulation of stock and the appropriation of land. ... If among a nation of hunters, for example, it usually costs twice the labour to kill a beaver which it does to kill a deer, one beaver should naturally exchange for or be worth two deer" (Smith [32, p. 65]). He insisted, however, that the natural price, i.e., the long-run equilibrium price, of a commodity consists of three parts, wages, rents and profits, all at their natural level, in a modern society where all the lands are private properties and stocks (capitals) are used in production. The existence of profit implies that the commanding labor is not identical to the embodied labor and the latter is no longer the determinant of the price. Natural prices are by no means independent of demands, since the natural rate of wage, for example, is higher in a growing economy, such as that of new colonies where demands expand rapidly, than in a stationary economy or in a declining one (see Chapter 3, section 3).

Unlike Adam Smith, Ricardo tried to apply the theory of embodied labor value to a modern economy with the appropriation of land and accumulated capital. Unless the rate of profit is zero, of course, the simple embodied labor theory of value has to be modified, since the time necessary to transfer the labor bestowed on the fixed capital to the final products must be rewarded by the rate of profit. The modification has to be done in view of the differences among commodities in the ratio of the fixed and circulating capitals, the durability of the fixed capital and the rate of turnover of capital. As is argued by Stigler [33, pp. 326–342], one may say that this is still the 93 per cent labor theory of value, since the modification is within 7 per cent if the rate of profit is 7 per cent. The value of the commodity does, however, vary with the rise or fall of wages (and, therefore, of the rate of profit). Ricardo's life-long problem was the search for an invariable measure of value (see Chapter 4, section 3).

J.S. Mill argued that we have to fall back on an antecedent law, that of supply and demand if the law of cost of production is not applicable, let alone the law of embodied labor value, as in the case of international trade, where labor is not mobile among countries. This implies, however, that even Mill admitted the law of cost of production and the labor theory of value in some special cases where labor is perfectly mobile. In other words, a special feature of the classical value theory lies in its emphasis on the possibility of the determination of values exclusively by costs and independently of demands. This tradition is revived by Piero Sraffa's (1898–1983) *Production of Commodities by Means of Commodities* (1960), which challenged the Ricardian problem of the invariable measure of value, and is succeeded by the so-called neo-Ricardian economists.

The idea of the value or the natural price independent of the level of demand is also applied by Ricardo to the natural price of labor or the natural wage. The natural wage is equalized to the reproduction cost of labor, which is historically determined by habit and custom in each society. Behind this supposition is a dynamic adjustment process of classical economics, which is based on the Malthusian principle of the population. If the market wage is higher than the natural wage, the population is increased so that the market wage declines toward the natural wage through an increase in the supply of labor. Similarly, if the market wage is lower than the natural, the population and the labor supply decrease and the market wage rises to the level of the natural one. In modern economics, the population is considered as an exogenously given data and not explained endogenously. In advanced industrial countries, economic growth has not been dissipated by the population increase and the rate of real wage has been rising, so that one may rightly deny the relevance of the Malthusian population theory. In some underdeveloped countries, however, even now the possiblity of economic growth is ruthlessly killed by the pressure of increases in population. The dynamic Malthusian process of classical economics is, therefore, still relevant in the theory of economic development.

According to W. Petty (1623–1687), a precursor of the classical school, "labour is the father of wealth, as lands are the mother" [26, p. 68]. Ricardo's theory of differential rent is necessary to reduce the pluralism of Petty to the monism of the labor theory of value. The supply of rich and fertile lands with high productivity is limited, and the marginal productivity of labor and capital declines as they are increasingly applied on the given land. On the marginal land whose productivity is the lowest among lands utilized, or for the marginal dose of capital-and-labor applied on the given land, there is no rent at all. There the price of the product is composed of wage cost and the average profit on it. On lands with productivity higher than the marginal land, or for intra-marginal doses of capital-and-labor, the price of the product exceeds the sum of wage cost and the average profit on it. The difference is the rent of the land. Ricardo's theory of differential rent is generalized by latter-day economists into the marginal productivity theory and is applied to the theories of wages and profits as well as to the theory of rents. In classical economics, however, it is insisted that rent is not the cause, but the effect of high price and that, unlike wages and profits, it is not a component part of price. The theory of differential rent is used to show that the role of land is different from the roles of labor and capital in the production.

If we assume a limited supply of lands and diminishing marginal productivity, and dismiss the possibility of technological progress, the productivity of marginal land or marginal capital-and-labor diminishes and rent is increased as capital is accumulated and the population increases. Since the rate of the natural wage is unchanged, this implies the fall of the rate of profit, which reduces the rate of economic growth. Eventually, the economy approaches the stationary state. If we generalize the concept of land so that it includes environments and resources and their shadow prices are signified by rents, the modern significance of this dynamic model of classical economics is much greater than that of the so-called neo-classical growth model which permits unlimited growth of the economy.

By the use of the specie-flow mechanism, classical economics criticized the mercantilist doctrine of international trade, which aims to obtain surplus in the balance of trade. On the basis of the assumption of the equilibrium balance of trade, the gains from trade are demonstrated by the theory of comparative costs. In Ricardo's numerical example, it requires the labor of 100 men for one year to produce cloth and the labor of 120 men to make wine in England, while it requires the labor of 80 men for one year to make wine and the labor of 90 men to produce cloth in Portugal. Though the cost of cloth in labor units is higher in England than in Portugal, it is relatively cheaper in comparision with wine. If each country specializes in the production of the commodity which is relatively cheaper than in the other country and imports the other commodity, both countries can gain from trade and consume greater amounts of both commodities than in the case of the autarky.

The reason why England can export cloth to Portugal is that the cost of cloth in terms of money is higher in Portugal than in England, as a result of specie-flow from the latter into the former. Since international trade is the exchange of commodities at the ratio of prices in terms of gold, the product of the labor of 90 Portuguese is valued higher than that of the labor of 100 Englishmen. The labor theory of value is, therefore, not applicable in the case of international trade. The reason is, of course, immobility of labor and capital between countries.

How, then, can we explain the determination of the terms of trade, i.e., the ratio of exchange between English cloth and Portuguese wine? Since we cannot apply the labor theory of value, argued J.S. Mill, we have to fall back upon an antecedent law, that of supply and demand. According to Mill's theory of reciprocal demands, terms of trade should be determined by the relation of demand for wine of England that offers cloth and demand for cloth of Portugal that offers wine. Since supply is negative demand, the theory of reciprocal demands is nothing but the theory of demand and supply. The theory of reciprocal demands, as well as the theory of comparative costs, are examples of the great legacy of classical economics and they are essential parts of the contemporary theory of international trade.[9]

While the theory of a natural wage is a long-run theory, classical economics has the doctrine of wages fund as a short-run theory of wage. Suppose the only wage good is an agricultural product such as wheat. The period of production is one year and there must be a given stock of wheat to support laborers for one

---

[9] For Ricardo's and Mill's theory of international trade, see Chapter 4, section 4 and Chapter 5, section 4.

year. Since the labor population is given in the short-run, the real wage is determined as the ratio of the stock of wheat, i.e., the wages fund, and the labor population. In other words, the demand for labor has a unitary elasticity with respect to the rate of the real wage. The demand for labor is determined by the wages fund and, according to J.S. Mill (see Chapter 5, section 1), "the demand for commodities is not demand for labour." Of course, this is the story of the world of Say's law, where supply creates demand and there is no possibility of glut.[10] If the wages fund is given, furthermore, an increase in the real wage necessarily reduces employment. In this sense, trade unions are powerless to improve the conditions of the labor class in the world of wages fund doctrine. When J.S. Mill recanted this important theory of classical economics in 1869, it was natural that people regarded it as the sign of the decline and fall of classical economics.[11]

4. The historical school and institutionalism

Unlike English classical economics, which was developed in an advanced capitalist country, the historical school of economics was formed in Germany, a less developed capitalist country in the second half of the 19th century. Being based on the doctrine of natural law and the Enlightenment, classical economics aimed to establish a general and universal theory by the abstract and deductive method. In contrast to it, the historical school emphasized the importance of the concrete and inductive method and of the descriptive work on historical details, under the influence of the romantic movement of historicism.

Friedrich List (1789–1846), a precursor of the German historical school, criticized the free trade policy of classical economics, and insisted on mercantilist and protectionist policies for Germany. The older school is represented by Wilhelm Roscher (1817–1894), Karl Knies (1821–1898) and Bruno Hildenbrand (1812–1878). The younger school is dominated by Gustav Schmoller (1838–1917). While the former school involves ideas in the field of the philosophy of history, the latter school eliminates such philosophical conceptions and aims at unbiased and detailed historical study. The methodological studies on Idealtypus and Wertfreiheit of Max Weber (1864–1920), the author of *Die Protestantische Ethik und der Geist des Kapitalismus* (1904–1905),

---

[10] Jean-Baptiste Say (1767–1832) is a French classical economist who wrote *Traite d'économie politique* (1803). For Say's law, see Chapter 5, section 3. Among classical economists, Malthus was against Say's law. See Chapter 4, sections 5 and 6.

[11] For Mill's recantation of wages fund doctrine, see Chapter 5, sections 2 and 5.

may be considered as a self-criticism of the German historical school in its final stage (Weber [38]).

Schumpeter [30, pp. 175–180] raised the following six points as the essential points of view which resulted from detailed historical research of the historical school.

(1) The point of view of relativity. Detailed historical research teaches us how untenable the idea is that there are generally valid practical rules in the field of economic policy. The possibility of general laws is, furthermore, challenged by the argument of the historical causation of social events.
(2) The point of view of the unity of social life and of the inseparable correlation between its elements. The tendency to go beyond the confines of a mere economic doctrine.
(3) The anti-rationalist point of view. The multiplicity of motives and the small importance of a merely logical insight of human actions. This is established in the form of an ethical argument and in the form of a desire for a psychology of the individual and the masses.
(4) The point of view of evolution. Evolutionary theories are bound to make such use of historical material.
(5) The point of view of the interest in individual correlations. What matters is how concrete events and conditions establish themselves and what their concrete causes are, not the general causes of social events altogether.
(6) The organic point of view. The analogy of the social body to a physical one. The original organic conception that the national economy exists outside and above the various individual economies is later replaced by a conception that the individual economies, which comprise the national economy, stand in intimate mutual relations with each other.

The German historical school criticized classical economics on the grounds that the variety and diversity of economic institutions in different societies and centuries makes it impossible to explain all the variety of economic action by the single universal theory of the market economy which lies at the heart of classical economics. In the *Methodenstreit* (battle of methods) against the historical school, Carl Menger, one of the founding fathers of the marginalist school (see section 6 of this Chapter and Chapter 8, section 1), admitted the importance of institutions for economic actions and developed the organic theory of institutions which states that they are the unintended social results of efforts in pursuit of rational individual interests. In other words, institutions can be explained by the universal theory of rational behavior of individuals, just as such strictly economic phenomena as market prices, wage rates, etc. are explained by the universal theory of the market economy (Lachmann [16, pp. 55–57]).

Max Weber, who was a disciple of Schmoller and trained in the historical school, tried eagerly to bring the *Methodenstreit* to an end. He was willing to agree that all historical explanation requires causal schemes which are of a general nature. In other words, he recognized that there is a need for abstract economic theory, though he regarded Menger's own view of the nature of theory as a naturalistic fallacy. Weber remained, however, the heir of the historical school and objected to the artificial separation of economic from other social activity. He saw no reason why abstract schemes should have to be confined to schemes of rational economic conduct. He devised, therefore, the famous notion of the *Idealtypus*, an abstract model of the reality which is for him the chief instrument of causal analysis in society. This enables us to go beyond the rational schemes of economics and grasp the meaning of irrational action, for example, that of the action of a crowd in a state of mass emotion (Lachmann [16, pp. 24–26]).

In the period under discussion, the German economists' zeal for social reform can be seen in their deep, even passionate interest in *Sozialpolitik*. The *Verein für Sozialpolitik* was formed in 1873. The German historical school was in fact in most cases united with the *Verein*, though it can be separated from it in principle and is of much greater scientific importance. Certainly the interest in questions of *Sozialpolitik* stimulated related investigation and it led people to collect and to discuss material for questions such as industrial organization, the living conditions of the working class, and the effectiveness of social administration. Preoccupation with practical questions, however, pushed into the background the kind of analysis which does not carry with it immediately practical solutions of the problems concerned. From a political standpoint it is not always possible to do justice even to the work of the historian. In these circumstances it becomes increasingly difficult to carry out purely scientific discussions (Schumpeter [30, pp. 153–154]).

Concern about the future of economics developed a reaction to this trend and a desire to shape the *Verein* into something more like a scientific society, which manifests itself in particular in the controversy about whether scientific value judgements (*Werturteil*) about social events and practical proposals are admissible, or even possible. Heated discussions culminated in a row at the *Verein's* Vienna meeting of 1909. The most prominent leaders in the campaign for freedom from evaluation (*Wertfreiheit*) were Max Weber and Werner Sombart (1863–1941), the author of *Der Moderne Kapitalismus* (1902), both of whom belonged to the radical wing of the *Verein* and to the youngest historical school (Schumpeter [31, pp. 804–805, 815–816]).

Institutionalism is the American version of the historical school. Representative scholars of institutionalism are Thorstein B. Veblen (1857–1929), the author of *The Theory of the Leisure Class* (1899) and *The Theory of Business Enterprise* (1904), J.R. Commons (1862–1945), who wrote *Legal Foundations of Capitalism* (1924) and *Institutional Economics* (1934), and W.C. Mitchell (1874–1948), who is well known for his quantitative studies of business cycles and as the founder of the National Bureau of Economic Research. This tradition is succeeded by such contemporary economists critical of modern industrial economy and neo-classical economics as J.K. Galbraith, the author of *The Affluent Society* (1958), and Gunnar Myrdal, who wrote *Asian Drama, An Inquiry into the Poverty of Nations* (1968).

Being influenced by the evolutionism of Darwin and Spencer, Veblen insisted that economics should be an evolutionary science which examines the emergence and modification through time of economic instructions.[12] He defined institutions as the widely prevalent habits of thought or the widespread social habits, which should be regarded as the current outcome of an age-long accumulation of human experience. Veblen's view of modern industrial society is based on the dichotomy between production, serviceability, industrial employments, the machine process, and engineers, on the one hand, and acquisition, vendibility, pecuniary employments, business enterprises, and businessmen, on the other.

> These institutions ... the economic structure ... may be roughly distinguished into two classes or categories, according as they serve one or the other of two divergent purposes of economic life. To adopt the classical terminology, they are institutions of acquisition or of production; or ... they are pecuniary or industrial institutions; or in still other terms, they are institutions serving either the invidious or the non-invidious economic interest. The former category have to do with "business," the latter with industry, taking the latter word in the mechanical sense. ... The relation of the leisure (that is, propertied nonindustrial) class to the economic process is a pecuniary relation ... a relation of acquisition, not of production; of exploitation, not of serviceability. (Veblen [35, pp. 208–209].)

According to Veblen, there is a struggle under capitalism, not between capitalists and proletariate, but between businessmen and engineers. Two great conflicting institutions are business enterprise, the art of making money, and the machine process which is the modern art of making goods. Veblen emphasized that the businessmen's goal of making money is in conflict with the

---

[12] For Veblen, see Blaug [1, p. 709], Mitchell [25, pp. 599–699], and Walker [37].

industrial pursuits of engineers, which aim at the efficient production of commodities. To make money, businessmen restrict output in order to raise prices, and waste resources by conducting sales promotion campaigns and by producing superfluities and spurious goods. Unemployment and business fluctuations are caused, according to Veblen, by businessmen's search for profits at the expense of industrial efficiency.

Although Veblen's arguments provided a number of suggestive insights into the problems of market failures, pollution and unemployment, he went too far with his emotional bias against business and formed the absurd proposition that all business behavior is destructive to the economy. Industrial efficiency can be defined only in economic terms and not in technological terms. Although Veblen believed that pecuniary criteria lead to wastefulness and that the optimum level of production can be determined by technological rule alone, the optimum volume of output and the optimum technique of production are determined only by the condition of profit maximization, under socialism as well as capitalism, that is, whether the profit accrues to businessmen or not (Walker [37]). In spite of Veblen, therefore, the role of businessmen cannot be replaced by that of engineers.

The main features of institutionalism are (see Blaug [1, pp. 708–709]), (1) dissatisfaction with neo-classical economics which is abstract, static and based on a hedonistic and atomistic conception of human nature, (2) a demand for the integration of economics with other social sciences, such as sociology, psychology, anthropology and legal studies, or what might be described as faith in the advantages of the interdisciplinary approach, (3) discontent with the causal empiricism of classical and neo-classical economics, expressed in the proposal to pursue detailed quantitative investigations, and (4) the plea for more social control of business, in other words, a favorable attitude to state intervention.

The historical school and institutionalism are paradigms or research programs clearly different from classical and neo-classical economics. Their criticism of classical economics was highly relevant and strongly influenced the development of neo-classical economics. This can be seen, for example, in the fact that the British historical school was evaluated highly by Marshall, who succeeded the classical school and developed it into a school of neo-classical economics (see Chapter 10, section 1). It is also expected that the historical school and institutionalism may provide suggestive insights into the difficult problems which remain unsolved in the neo-classical school. As a matter of fact, Veblen's concept of conspicuous consumption was already utilized to show the possibility of an upwardly sloping demand curve, which the neo-classical theory of consumer behavior cannot do, unless the income effect is assumed to be strong and to work against the substitution effect (Leibenstein [18]).

5. Marxian economics

Marxism succeeded three great intellectual achievements in the 19th century, classical German philosophy, English classical economics and French socialism. The labor theory of value of classical economics was developed into the Marxian value theory, to explain the existence of the exploitation of labor by capital through the equal value exchange between capital and labor-power in a capitalist society. The classical school of economics was ahistoric in the sense that it aimed to find a universal law of capitalist economy which continues to exist indefinitely. Marxism emphasized, however, that the capitalist mode of production is historical and transitive, from the point of view of the materialist interpretation of history, which is Hegel's idealistic interpretation of history turned upside down, so that it is now right side up again. Utopian socialism should be replaced by the scientific socialism which is based on the Marxian interpretation of history and the Marxian theory of economics.

Das Kapital by Karl Marx (1818–1883) consists of three volumes. The first volume, *The Process of Production of Capital* (1867), starts with a discussion of commodity circulation and the labor theory of value, and concentrates on the theory of production to explain how surplus values are exploited by capital from labor. The second volume, *The Process of Circulation of Capital* (1885), is concerned with the realization of surplus value, and discusses the turnover of capital and the reproduction schema which is Marx's own "tableau économique". The third volume, *The Process of Capitalist Production as a Whole* (1894), considers the law of falling rate of profit, the transformation of values into prices, market values, commercial capital, the rate of interest and land rents. In other words, it is concerned with how surplus values are distributed among different capitalists and landowners.[13]

Das Kapital does not, however, cover the whole system of economics Marx planned in 1857. According to the original outline, the structure of Marx's work was as follows.

I. The Book on Capital
   (a) Capital in general

---

[13] See Chapter 6, section 1. Only the first volume of *Das Kapital* was published before Marx died in 1883. The second and third volumes were published by F. Engels. What corresponds to the fourth volume of *Das Kapital* is *Theorien über den Mehrwert*, which is Marx's own history of economics and was first published by K. Kautsky in 1905–1910.

    1. Production process of capital
    2. Circulation process of capital
    3. Profit and interest
  (b) Section on Competition
  (c) Section on the Credit System
  (d) Section on Share-Capital
 II. The Book on Landed Property
III. The Book on Wage-Labour
IV. The Book on the State
 V. The Book on Foreign Trade
VI. The Book on the World Market and Crises

It might seem that *Das Kapital* covers only section (a), Capital in general, of Book I, The Book on Capital. However, the first volume of *Das Kapital* contains chapters on wages and their forms, the working day, the exploitative practices of capital, and labor legislation, which would have come under the scope of The Book on Wage-Labour. Furthermore, in the third volume of *Das Kapital* we can clearly see that Marx dropped the separation of the analysis of capital in general and that of competition. The question of the sections on credit and share-capital may not be resolved so definitely, since Marx did not have the chance to draft the related part of the manuscript in a form ready for publication, particularly Part 5 (on interest and interest-bearing capital) of the third volume of *Das Kapital*. Finally, the crucial themes of The Book on Landed Property are exhaustively discussed in Part 6 of the third volume of *Das Kapital*. We can conclude, therefore, that the first three Books of the original outline are somehow covered by the present three volumes of *Das Kapital*. The position is quite different, however, in the case of Books IV–VI. The problems of the state, international trade, crises and the world market are left to be solved by the follower of Karl Marx.[14]

It is natural that the main contributions of post-Marxian economists are concerned with these problems Marx left unsolved, and reflect the development of world capitalism after the death of Marx. In his book *Das Finanzkapital* (1910), Rudolf Hilferding (1877–1941) argued that finance capital, unlike industrial capital, abhors the anarchy of competition, needs the state to guarantee the home market through protection, and requires a politically powerful state which can exert its influence all over the world in order to be able to turn the entire world into a sphere for investment. Hilferding's book was followed in 1913 by *Die Akkumulation des Kapitals* by Rosa Luxemburg (1871–1919), who interpreted Marx's reproduction schema

---

[14] See Marx [22, pp. 52–55], and Rosdolsky [28, pp. 10–23].

that the capitalist economy was unable to dispose of its output at home and was forced into overseas expansion to realize surplus value. Finally, V.I. Lenin (1870–1924) published *Imperialism, the Highest Stage of Capitalism* (1917) and argued that capitalists of advanced countries desire to divide up the world to wrestle from the underdeveloped countries superprofits with which they bribe domestic labor. It is interesting to see that representative Marxian scholars before World War II were also influential leaders of the socialist and communist parties.

After World War II, the situation of Japan as a non-communist country is unique in the sense that almost half of its academic economists are Marxian, explicitly or implicitly, though they are split into several different sects. Among different sects of Marxian economists in Japan, one of the most interesting is perhaps the so-called "Uno school", the followers of Kozo Uno (1897–1977).[15] Against those who insist that the correctness of Marxian economics cannot be understood by people without socialist views or without class consciousness and that the communist party is the judge of truth, Uno insisted that Marxian economics should be a science, independent of ideology and political claims. He warned against too hasty applications of the basic theories of *Das Kapital* to the development of Japanese capitalism. Instead, he proposed the three-level approach of principles, stage theory and empirical analysis.

According to Uno, the first level of research is concerned with principles and to deal with the economic laws of motion of an autonomous, pure capitalist society, an abstract model of an economy, to which the mid-nineteenth century British economy was approaching. *Das Kapital* should be regarded as a work clarifying the principles of this pure capitalist economy. The next level of research develops a stage theory of world capitalist development. Uno proposed three stages of capitalist development, mercantilism, liberalism and imperialism, the leading capital of which are, respectively, merchant capital, industrial capital and finance capital. He excludes the world economy after World War I from his stage theory, since in this period the economic policies of capitalist countries are no longer directed exclusively by the economic interests of the leading capitals. In other words, this period is a transitional one from capitalism to socialism and should be studied as a research of the third level, the empirical analysis of the current situation.

Following the pioneering works of Bortkiewicz (1868–1931) and Kei Shibata (1902–1986), mathematical models of Marxian economics have been constructed and analyzed by such economists as, among others, Okishio, Morishima, Seton, Nikaido, Steedman, Samuelson and Roemer, some of

[15] Uno's representative work was translated from Japanese as *Principles of Political Economy* (1980). For the Uno school, see Itoh [11, pp. 37–45], and Mawatari [23].

whom are Marxian economists while others are critical to Marx (see Chapter 6, sections 2 and 5). We may perhaps say that the representative contribution is Morishima's *Marx's Economics* (1973). It is interesting to see the similarity, at least formally, between these models of Marxian economics and the models of the neo-Ricardian economists who follow Sraffa. These models are largely applications of the linear economic models of neo-classical economics, developed in the theory of general equilibrium, input–output analysis and linear-programming. It is certainly true that, by these models, some aspects of Marxian economics can now be rather easily approached by non-Marxian economists. It must, however, also be admitted that there are many other aspects of Marxian economics which cannot be expressed by these mathematical models of economic equilibrium.

Although Marx's own theory of international trade is highly interesting (see Chapter 6, section 3), it remains fragmentary, since the problem itself was the beyond scope of *Das Kapital*, according to the plan of Marx's system of economics. Contemporary Marxian economists are, however, succeeding it and developing the so-called dependency theory. The pioneering contribution is *L'échange inégal* (1969) by A. Emmanuel. Emmanuel rightly criticizes the neo-classical theory of international trade and tries to replace it. He emphasizes the importance of the international difference of the real wage between developed and underdeveloped countries and that of capital movements between such countries. We have to admit that Emmanuel's arguments do fit present day reality much more than the so-called Heckscher–Ohlin model with international factor price (including real wage) equalization, which excludes the necessity of capital movements. It is interesting to see that by unequal exchange Emmanuel does not mean the exchange of unequal amounts of labor, but means the unfavorable terms of trade for countries where real wages are determined exogenously at a low level by social and historical factors.

6. Marginal revolution and after

As the precursors of the so-called marginal revolution against classical economics, we may name Johann Heinrich von Thünen (1783–1850), the author of *Der Isolierte Staat in Beziehung auf Landwirtschaft und Nationalökonomie* (1826–1863), who is the founder of the location theory and pioneered the use of the concept of marginal productivity, Antonie Augustin Cournot (1801–1877), the author of *Recherches sur les principes mathématiques de la théorie des richesses* (1838), who developed the theories of monopoly and oligopoly and clarified the implication of perfect competition, Arsene Jules Etienne Juvenal Dupuit (1804–1866), the pioneer of the consumers' surplus analysis, and Hermann Heinrich Gossen (1810–1858), the author of *Entwicklung der Gesetze des Menschlichen Verkehrs und der Daraus Fliessenden Regeln für Menschliches Handeln* (1854), who is famous for Gossen's first and second laws of marginal utility.[16]

Those who developed the marginalist theory of economics systematically are, however, William Stanley Jevons (1835–1882), the author of *The Theory of Political Economy* (1871), Carl Menger (1840–1921), who wrote *Grundsätze der Volkswirtschaftslehre* (1871), and Marie-Esprit Leon Walras (1834–1910), the author of *Éléments d'économie politique pure* (1874–1877). This is called marginal revolution, since these economists, independently – at Manchester in England, Vienna in Austria and Lausanne in Switzerland – and almost at the same time, developed similar theories which are radically different from the classical one, on the basis of such marginal relations as marginal utility and marginal productivity. Although their theories are similar in the sense that they emphasized the role of utility and demand by the theory of marginal utility against the classical labor or cost theory of value, however, these three economists are quite different from each other in their relations to classical economics, in their cultural and social background, and in their significance to the modern theory of economics.

For Walras, what is important is not to insist on replacing the theory of marginal utility with the classical cost theory of value. While classical economics aims to establish the laws of causal relations among economic variables, Walras tries to develop the general equilibrium theory which emphasizes the mutual interdependency of economic variables (see Chapter 7, section 2). In Lausanne, Walras was succeeded by Vilfredo Pareto (1848–1923), the author of *Manuale di economia politica con una introduzione alla scienza sociale* (1906), who is well known by the Pareto optimal criterion in welfare economics.[17] Walras, Pareto and some followers in Italy are called economists of the Lausanne school. Walras's significance is, however, not limited to being the founder of this small school. What is more important is the fact that the Walrasian tradition is wholly succeeded by the current mainstream economics, the neo-classical economics. As we shall see, this is because the Walrasian theory of general equilibrium has developed itself in to a more general theory by absorbing and synthesizing many important contributions of other schools freely and skilfully.

[16] See Chapter 7, section 1 and Chapter 9, section 1, respectively, for Cournot and Gossen.
[17] The English translation of *Manuale, Manual of Political Economy* (1971) is translated from the French edition (1909), which contains a mathematical appendix.

The significance of the utility theory of value is much greater, unlike in the case of Walras, for the Austrian school of Menger and his followers. They developed the concept of the opportunity cost – that cost is nothing but the utility lost – and considered that values of the factors of production are imputed from the utility values of consumers' goods. Unlike Walras, who considered perfect markets, Menger is interested in the workings of more realistic, imperfect markets. He emphasizes, therefore, the importance, not only of prices, i.e., the ratios of quantities of commodities exchanged, but also of the marketability or saleableness of commodities in unorganized, imperfect markets. He developed an interesting theory of money – that money is a commodity that has the greatest marketability – which is an unintended result of the independent behavior of many economizing individuals to exchange their commodities with more marketable ones (see section 7 of this Chapter and Chapter 8, section 1).

One of the most important followers of Menger is Eugen von Böhm-Bawerk (1851–1914). He criticized many different theories of interest, which include exploitation theory, in the first volume of his *Kapital und Kapitalzins, Geschichte und Kritik der Kapitalzins-Theorien* (1884). In the second volume, *Positive Theorie des Kapitals* (1889), he adduced three causes for the existence of interest and emphasized particularly the superiority of a more roundabout method of production (see Chapter 8, section 3). It was a Swedish economist, Knut Wicksell (1851–1926), who introduced the Austrian capital theory into the general equilibrium theory and emphasized the importance of the time element in the theory of production, which was not explicitly done in the Walrasian theory. Wicksell is also important as a pioneer of the monetary theory of macro dynamics.[18]

Another important follower of Menger is Friedrich von Wieser (1851–1926), the author of *Der natürliche Werth* (1889) and *Theorie der gesellschaftlichen Wirtschaft* (1914). He clarified the significance of imputed prices in welfare economics and pioneered in the economic theory of socialism (see Chapter 8, section 2). Joseph Alois Schumpeter (1883–1950) also came from the Austrian school and wrote, among others, *Theorie der wirtschaftlichen Entwicklung* (1912), in which he emphasized the role of entrepreneurs and the importance of technological innovation in economic development (see Chapter 8, section 4). His *Capitalism, Socialism and Democracy* (1942) envisages capitalism as moving towards socialism, though from a different reason from that of the Marxians.

The leading twentieth-century figures of the Austrian school are Ludwig

---

[18] Wicksell's representative work was translated from Swedish into English as *Lectures on Political Economy*, Volume one, General Theory (1934), Volume two, Money (1935).

Edler von Mises (1881–1973) and Friedrich A. von Hayek. Von Mises is the author of *Human Action* (1949) and regarded as the founding father of the neo-Austrian school. He contributed to the theory of business cycles, socialist calculation debate, and methodology. His methodology is known as praxeology, which emphasizes individual choices and purposive human action. Hayek is one of the best-known contemporary economists, who wrote extensively on business cycles, capital, socialism, methodology and liberalism.

Of the three great stars of the marginal revolution, it is Jevons who challenged classical economics most severely (Chapter 9, section 2). Unlike Walras and Menger, Jevons did not form a school. Francis Ysidro Edgeworth (1845–1926) succeeded, however, Jevon's attempt to explain how the arbitrage behavior of rational individuals can generate the unique market price for each commodity, i.e., the law of indifference, which Cournot and Walras simply presupposed. Edgeworth wrote *Mathematical Psychics* (1881) and pioneered, along with Cournot, the study of an important problem of modern mathematical economics, the problem of a large economy in which the number of individual participants is infinitely large (Chapter 9, sections 3 and 4).

In connection with the marginal revolution, the name of Alfred Marshall (1842–1924) should also be mentioned, though the publication of his representative work, *Principles of Economics* (1890), was slightly later than those of Jevons, Menger and Walras. Unlike Jevons, Marshall did not deny the significance of classical economics, but tried to generalize Ricardo's theory of value and distribution as expounded by J.S. Mill. He argued that utility and cost, or demand and supply, are both necessary to determine equilibrium prices, just as the upper blade and the lower blade of a pair of scissors are both necessary to cut a piece of paper (see Chapter 10, section 1). Marshall's vision of the time structure of demand and supply equilibria, i.e., temporary, short-run and long-run equilibria, is introduced into the general equilibrium theory by *Value and Capital* (1939) by John R. Hicks, along with that of dynamic economics developed by the Swedish school founded by Wicksell.

Originally, the name neo-classical economics was not given to the general equilibrium theory of the Walrasian tradition, as has often been done recently to designate the mainstream economic theory. It was the name given to the economics of the Cambridge school initiated by Marshall. Arthur Cecil Pigou (1877–1959), who wrote *The Economics of Welfare* (1920), was Marshall's successor at Cambridge. Sraffa's criticism of Marshall on increasing returns and the controversy between Pigou and Frank William Taussig (1859–1940) on railway rates gave birth to Joan Robinson's (1903–1983) *Economics of Imperfect Competition* (1933) and Edward Hastings Chamberlin's (1899–1967) *The Theory of Monopolistic Competition* (1933). R.

Triffin attempted to introduce imperfect and monopolistic competitions into the general equilibrium theory by his *Monopolistic Competition and General Equilibrium Theory* (1949).

The greatest topic in the Cambridge school after Marshall is, however, the appearance of a book of its self-criticism, John Maynard Keynes's (1883–1946) *The General Theory of Employment, Interest and Money* (1936), (see Chapter 10, section 4). Keynes admitted that mercantilists and Malthus were his predecessors in this respect. Although we have already discussed mercantilism in section 2, we should mention here that Malthus, although a classical economist, also denied Say's law and admitted the importance of the problem of the deficiency of effective demand (see Chapter 4, sections 5 and 6). Mercantilism was, however, criticized by David Hume (1711–1776) and classical economists, and Malthus could not persuade Ricardo in their controversy on the problem of effective demand. From the Keynesian point of view, it can be said that the so-called Keynesian revolution is necessary for the mercantilism–Malthus research program of effective demand to win against the classical and neo-classical research program of full-employment, which insists that there is no problem of effective demand, since investment is always equalized to saving through the automatic adjustment of the market mechanism. In other words, it is necessary for the research program of under-employment to have such Keynesian new protective belts as consumption function, investment function, multiplier and liquidity preference.

Keynesian economics was developed as a macroeconomics of effective demand. In his *Money, Interest and Prices* (1956), Don Patinkin tried to integrate the Keynesian macro theory and the microeconomics of the Walrasian general equilibrium theory. As Patinkin himself admitted, however, it is necessary to deny the first postulate of classical economics that the rate of real wage is equalized to the marginal productivity of labor. In other words, it requires the general equilibrium theory to get rid of the traditional Walrasian view of market equilibrium. The study of the so-called general disequilibrium theory is one of the most important problems in the frontier of contemporary economic theory.

Irving Fisher (1867–1947) is a pioneer of American economists of marginalism. He started with *Mathematical Investigations in the Theory of Value and Prices* (1892), which was written under the strong influence of Jevons, and wrote many important books. He made important contributions to the theory of capital and interest in his *The Nature of Capital and Income* (1906) and *The Theory of Interest (1930)*. In *The Purchasing Power of Money* (1911), he tried to formulate the quantity theory of money into the famous Fisher's equation of exchange. As for the quantity theory of money, we have to remember that the paradox of mercantilism was pointed out by Hume in his theory of specie-flow mechanism, which is nothing but an early application of the quantity theory (see Chapter 2, section 2). One of the most important aspects of the Keynesian revolution is, furthermore, the criticism of the quantity theory, which is based on the theory of liquidity preference. The quantity theory of money is, therefore, related deeply to the hard core of the classical and neo-classical paradigm or research program. The monetarism of Milton Friedman and his followers is the newest version of the quantity theory, which made possible the recent anti-Keynesian revolution. The reason for this success is that, unlike the quantity theory before Keynes, it now has a new, important protective belt, the theory of the short-run effects on output and employment of unexpected changes in the quantity of money supplied.

References

[1] Blaug, M., *Economic Theory in Retrospect*, Cambridge University Press, 1985.
[2] Bronfenbrenner, M., "The Structure of Revolution in Economic Thought", *History of Political Economy*, 3(1971), pp. 136–151.
[3] Caldwell, B., *Beyond Positivism*, George Allen and Unwin, 1982.
[4] Cesarano, F., "On the Role of the History of Economic Analysis", *History of Political Economy*, 15(1983), pp. 63–82.
[5] Easlea, B., *Liberation and the Aims of Science*, Sussex University Press, 1973.
[6] Ekelund, R.B., and R.D. Tollison, *Mercantilism as a Rent-Seeking Society*, Texas A & M University Press, 1981.
[7] Feyerabend, P., *Against Method*, NLB, 1975.
[8] Friedman, D.D., "In Defense of Thomas Aquinas and the Just Price", *History of Political Economy*, 12(1980), pp. 234–242.
[9] Heckscher, E.F., *Mercantilism*, E.F. Soderland, ed., George Allen and Unwin, 1955.
[10] Hutchison, T.W., *On Revolutions and Progress in Economic Knowledge*, Cambridge University Press, 1978.
[11] Itoh, M., *Value and Crisis, Essays on Marxian Economics in Japan*, Monthly Review Press, 1980.
[12] Keynes, J.M., *The General Theory of Employment, Interest and Money*, Macmillan, 1936.
[13] Kobayashi, N., *Keizaigakushi Chosakushu* (Collected works on the History of Economics), 1, Miraisha, 1976.
[14] Kuhn, T.S., *The Copernican Revolution*, Harvard University Press, 1957.
[15] Kuhn, T.S., *The Structure of Scientific Revolutions*, University of Chicago Press, 1970.
[16] Lachmann, L.M., *The Legacy of Max Weber, Three Essays*, Heinemann, 1970.
[17] Lakatos, I. and A. Musgrave, eds., *Criticism and the Growth of Knowledge*, Cambridge University Press, 1970.
[18] Leibenstein, H., "Bandwagon, Snob, and Veblen Effects in the Theory of Consumer Demand", *Quarterly Journal of Economics*, 62(1950), pp. 183–207.
[19] McCulloch, J.R., ed., *Early English Tracts on Commerce*, Cambridge University Press, 1954.
[20] Marx, K., *Capital*, I, Progress Publishers, 1954.
[21] Marx, K., *Theories of Surplus Value*, I, Foreign Language Publishing House, 1963.
[22] Marx, K., *Grundrisse, Foundations of the Critique of Political Economy* (rough draft), M. Nicolaus, tr., Allen Lane, 1973.

[23] Mawatari, S., "The Uno School; A Marxian Approach in Japan", *History of Political Economy*, 17(1985), pp. 403–418.

[24] Mehta, G., *The Structure of Keynesian Revolution*, Martin Robertson, 1977.

[25] Mitchell, W.C., *Types of Economic Theory*, 2, Kelley, 1969.

[26] Petty, W., *Economic Writings*, 1, C.H. Hull, ed., Cambridge University Press, 1899.

[27] Popper, K.R., *The Logic of Scientific Discovery*, Hutchinson, 1959.

[28] Rosdolsky, R., *The Making of Marx's 'Capital'*, P. Burgess, tr., Pluto Press, 1977.

[29] Schmitt, H.O., "Mercantilism: A Modern Argument", *The Manchester School*, 47(1979), pp. 93–111.

[30] Schumpeter, J.A., *Economic Doctrines and Method*, R. Aris, tr., George Allen and Unwin, 1954.

[31] Schumpeter, J.A., *History of Economic Analysis*, Oxford University Press, 1954.

[32] Smith, A., *An Inquiry into the Nature and Causes of the Wealth of Nations*, Oxford University Press, 1976.

[33] Stigler, G.J., *Essay in the History of Economics*, University of Chicago Press, 1965.

[34] Tawney, R.H., *Religion and the Rise of Capitalism*, John Murray, 1960.

[35] Veblen, T., *The Theory of the Leisure Class*, Huebsch, 1922.

[36] Viner, J., *Religious Thought and Economic Society*, Duke University Press, 1978.

[37] Walker, D.A., "Thorstein Veblen's Economic System", *Economic Inquiry*, 15(1977), pp. 213–237.

[38] Weber, M., *Roscher and Knies, The Logical Problems of Historical Economics*, G. Oakes, tr., Free Press, 1975.

CHAPTER 2

SOME PIONEERS IN ECONOMIC THEORY

1. Locke's microfoundation of quantity theory

John Locke (1632–1704) was a famous philosopher and political theorist who wrote *An Essay Concerning Human Understanding* (1869) and *Two Treatises of Government* (1689). He also made interesting contributions to economic theory. It is, therefore, not inappropriate to choose him as the first of the individual scholars whose economic theory we reconsider in the light of modern economic theory. Locke is to be followed by David Hume (in section 2) and François Quensay (sections 3 and 4). After a brief sketch of the life and works of John Locke, in this section we shall try to construct a simple economic model which can show that John Locke's original theory of value in terms of the ratio of vent and quantity of commodities does make sense, unlike its erroneous interpretation in terms of the ratio of demand and supply, so far as he used his theory of value to give a microeconomic foundation to his quantity theory of money, which is not necessarily identical to the classical quantity theory.

In 1632 John Locke was born in Somerset to a moderately well-off Puritan family of the minor gentry.[1] As a result of his father's service to Cromwell's army, he was able to be educated at Westminster School, one of the best public schools in England. In 1652 John entered Christ Church, Oxford where he remained for fifteen years. He took the position of lecturer in Greek in 1660 and was elected censor of moral philosophy for Christ Church in 1663. He decided, however, to study medicine, since he was enthusiastically interested in Bacon's experimental method which was becoming more and more accepted in the study of medicine. Locke was influenced by Robert Boyle, the leader of the Oxford empiricists, and interested in the study of experimental philosophy, which cumulated later in his famous *Essay Concerning Human Understanding*.

In 1666, Anthony Ashley Cooper, later the first Earl of Shaftesbury, visited Oxford and invited Locke to join his household in London as resident physician. Since Ashley was a politician interested in problems of trade, it is

---

[1] The following is largely dependent on Vaughn [40, pp. 1–16].

natural that Locke also became interested in economic problems, with the result that he wrote a paper "Some of the Consequences that are like to follow upon lessening of Interest to 4 Percent," responding to parliamentary agitation concerning a proposal to lower the rate of interest. In 1672, Ashley became Lord High Chancellor of England and the first Earl of Shaftesbury, and Locke became secretary of the Council of Trade and Plantations presided over by Shaftesbury and a member of a charter company organized by Shaftesbury. Shaftesbury was dismissed from all offices for plotting against the King in 1674, and Locke returned to Oxford, and then went to France for three years. While Shaftesbury was involved in the abortive Monmouth Rebellion in 1679 to 1683, Locke was quietly living at Oxford, where he wrote *Two Treatises of Government*, justifying the change of rulers who no longer protect the interests of their subjects. When Shaftesbury died in exile in Holland in 1683, Locke felt threatened enough to go to Holland, where he stayed for six years and completed his *Essay Concerning Human Understanding*.

Locke returned to England in 1689 after William of Orange deposed James II, and then quickly published *An Essay Concerning Human Understanding* and *Two Treatises of Government*. A bill was once again before Parliament to lower the rate of interest and Locke, revising his earlier paper on interest, published his *Some Considerations of the Consequences of the Lowering of Interest and Raising the Value of Money* in 1691. This was followed by his *Further Considerations Concerning Raising the Value of Money* in 1695. Although Locke did not much influence Parliament in the case of the former, he was more successful in the case of the latter. Locke retired to Oates in 1700 and died there in 1704.

John Locke's *Some Considerations* (1691) was subtitled as "In a Letter sent to a Member of Parliament" and was concerned with a current problem of economic policy which was being discussed in Parliament in the early 1680s. However, he started his discussions with a basic theory of value and founded his quantity theory of money on it. In his theory of value, Locke was concerned not with intrinsic but with marketable value. "The marketable value of any assigned quantities of two, or more commodities, are (pro hic et nunc) equal, when they will exchange one for another" (Locke [28, p. 43]).

Such a market value or price is determined not by the ratio of, but by the equality of demand and supply. This is made clear by J.S. Mill who declared that "the idea of a ratio, as between demand and supply, is out of place, and has no concern in the matter: the proper mathematical analogy is that of an equation" (Mill [31, p. 448]). This does not, of course, deny the idea that the ratio or the proportion between demand and supply determines the direction of changes of price. The extent of the required change in the price depends, however, not only on the ratio of the deficiency or excess of demand to supply, but also on elasticities of demand and supply with respect to price. After all, as Mill insisted, such a change in price is required that "the rise or the fall [of price induced by the difference in demand and supply] continues until the demand and supply are again equal to one another" (Mill [31, p. 448]).

Although his statement that "the price of any commodity rises or falls, by the proportion of the number of buyers and sellers" (Locke [28, p. 30]) may be interpreted as meaning that the price *changes* according to the ratio of demand and supply,[2] it is not easy to interpret Locke's theory of the *determination* of the marketable value or price in terms of the traditional equilibrium theory of demand and supply, since it is given in terms of quantity and vent.

That which regulates the price, i.e., the quantity given for money (which is called buying and selling) for another commodity, (which is called bartering) is nothing else but their quantity in proportion to their vent. (Locke [28, pp. 35–36].)

He that will justly estimate the value of any thing, must consider its quantity in proportion to its vent, for this alone regulates the price. The value of anything, compared with itself or with a standing measure, is greater, as its quantity is less in proportion to its vent: but, in comparing it, or exchanging it with any other thing, the quantity and vent of that thing too must be allowed for, in the computation of their value. (Locke [28, p. 40].)

4. The change of this marketable value of any commodity, in respect of another commodity, or in respect of a standing, common measure, is not the altering of any intrinsic value, or quality, in the commodity (for musty and smutty corn will sell dearer at one time than the clean and sweet at another) but the alteration of some proportion which that commodity bears to something else. 5. This proportion in all commodities, whereof money is one, is the proportion of their quantity to the vent. (Locke [28, p. 43].)

While the quantity can be taken simply as the given supply, the vent is not identical to the usual concept of demand, since it is the realized sale which is defined by Locke as follows.

The vent is nothing else but the passing of commodities from one owner to another in exchange; and is then called quicker, when a greater quantity of any species of commodity is taken off from the owners of it, in an equal space of time. 6. This vent is regulated, i.e., made quicker or slower, as greater or less quantities of any saleable commodity are removed out of the way and

[2] See Bowley [6], [7, p. 76], Kobayashi [24, p. 390], and Spiegel [38, p. 162].

course of trade; separated from public commerce; and no longer lie within the reach of exchange. (Locke [28, p. 43].)

As early as in 1705, however, John Law dared to interpret and reconstruct Locke's theory from the ordinary point of view of demand and supply in his *Money and Trade Considered*. "Mr. Locke sayes, *The Value of Goods is according to their Quantity in Proportion to their Vent*. The Vent of Goods cannot be greater than the Quantity, but the demand may be greater . . . So the Price of Goods are not according to the Quantity in Proportion to the Vent, but in Proportion to the Demand" (Law [26, p. 5]). This interpretation was followed by many eminent scholars.[3] If we follow John Law to substitute demand for vent and reconstruct Locke's theory of value that price is determined by the ratio of demand and supply, however, it is clear that it does not make sense at all, as was already pointed out by Mill.

More than two hundred and fifty years after John Law, Vaughn argued correctly that "Locke's price theory was not an early version of supply-and-demand analysis" and that "vent is not identical to the modern concept of demand" (Vaughn [40, pp. 25, 26]). She insisted that "the term *vent* was particularly appropriate for the kind of price theory Locke was developing" (Vaughn [40, pp. 20–21]), the purpose of which was to explain the determinants of the value of money. But the question which still remains is why the price is determined by the ratio of vent and quantity, or, in modern terminology, the realized sale and the available supply. To vindicate the original version of Locke's theory of value, in other words, we have to ask why the price of a commodity is higher when its rate of turnover is higher.

Let us construct a simple model of a stationary economy in which vent plays an essential role. Suppose two weeks are necessary for each individual supplier to sell out of the stock of newly acquired commodities, so that the vent in the current week is less than the quantity which can be offered, while demand and supply are equalized over two weeks.[4] The reason why vent is less than quantity is that the current market is imperfect in the sense that information is limited, search for buyers or sellers is necessary, and buying and selling costs exist, with the result that the current sale cannot be increased without reducing the price.

An individual supplier, having a stock S of a newly acquired commodity to sell, faces demand functions for the current and the next weeks, which are, respectively,

---

[3] See Bowley [6], [7, p. 77], Spiegel [38, p. 162], Colie [10], Leigh [27], and Hatori [20].
[4] The second week represents all future periods in the time horizon of the supplier and may be much longer than the current week.

$$p_1 = a - bx_1 \tag{1}$$

and

$$p_2 = q, \tag{2}$$

and the storage cost function

$$C = c_1 + c_2 x_2 + c_3 x_2^2, \tag{3}$$

where p_1 and p_2 are prices (in terms of *numéraire* or abstract unit of account[5]) in the current and the next weeks, x_1 and x_2 are the quantity of demand in the current and the next weeks, and a, b, q, c_1, c_2 and c_3 are positive constants. The supplier expects the perfect market with an infinitely elastic demand curve in the next week, i.e., in the long run, where the long-run normal price q prevails. Since demand and supply have to be equalized over two weeks,

$$x_1 + x_2 = S, \tag{4}$$

should be observed. In view of (1)–(2), the supplier will allocate his stock S to x_1 and x_2 so that his gain

$$(a - bx_1)x_1 + r[qx_2 - c_1 - c_2 x_2 - c_3 x_2^2], \tag{5}$$

is maximized, where r is a positive constant less than one, which signifies the time preference of the supplier.

Although Locke might know that the monopolist could drive up the price by restricting supply, he had no concept of an optimal price which would maximize the revenue (Vaughn [40, p. 59]). Obviously, therefore, Locke would not have been able to state his problem in the form of the maximization of the gain. The maximization of the gain (5) is, however, an assumption which is logically consistent with the conclusions he arrived at by experience and intuition, i.e., the positive association of the current price of a commodity and the ratio of its vent and quantity.

The condition for the maximization of the gain (5) is, of course, the zero marginal gain with respect to x_1, which is obtained through the elimination of x_2 in (5) by the use of (4) and the differentiation with respect to x_1 as

$$(a - rq + rc_2) - 2(b + rc_3)x_1 + 2rc_3 S = 0. \tag{6}$$

This can be solved for x_1 when S, q, a, b, c_2, c_3 and r are given. According to Locke, the current price p_1 should be higher if the proportion of vent to quantity x_1/S is higher.

Let us first consider whether Locke is right, when the proportion x_1/S is changed through a change in quantity S. By differentiating (6) with respect to

---

[5] For the abstract unit of account, see Patinkin [32, p. 18].

x_1 and S, we have

$$dx_1/dS = rc_3/(b + rc_3) > 0. \tag{7}$$

Expressed verbally, the vent is increased if the quantity is increased. In view of the demand function in the current week (1), this implies that the current price is reduced. On the other hand, in view of (6) and (7), we have

$$d(x_1/S)/dS = (rq - a - rc_2)/2S^2(b + rc_3), \tag{8}$$

which is negative, if a is not much smaller than q. In this case, therefore, there can be the positive association between the price and the proportion of vent and quantity.

Suppose next that vent x_1 is increased through an increase in demand in the current week while quantity S remains unchanged. In view of (1), the current demand is increased either by increasing a or by decreasing b. By the differentiation of (6) with respect to x_1 and a, we have

$$dx_1/da = 1/(2b + 2rc_3) > 0. \tag{9}$$

By the differentiation of (1), on the other hand,

$$dp_1/da = (b + 2rc_3)/(2b + 2rc_3) > 0. \tag{10}$$

Similarly, by the differentiation of (6) with respect to x_1 and b, we have

$$dx_1/db = -x_1/(b + rc_3) < 0. \tag{11}$$

By the differentiation of (1), furthermore,

$$dp_1/db = -rc_3 x_1/(b + rc_3) < 0. \tag{12}$$

In this case, therefore, p_1 changes in the same direction as x_1 and there always exists the positive relation between the price of the commodity and the proportion between vent and quantity.

The vent of a commodity can be increased through an increase in the current demand, at least temporarily, when the quantity of money or its velocity is increased.[6] This argument can be justified by slightly generalizing the following discussion of Locke's.

> The vent of any commodity comes to be increased, or decreased, as a greater part of the running cash of the nation is designed to be laid out, by several people at the same time, rather in that than another. (Locke [28, p. 31].)

Locke is right, in the cases considered so far, to say that the price of a commodity "compared with itself or with a standing measure" is higher if the

---

[6] In the long run other parameters than a and b may be changed. The effect on vent of a change in q is, however, smaller than that of the proportionally same change in a.

ratio of vent to quantity is larger, since p_1 is given in terms of *numéraire* or abstract unit of account and q is given and unchanged. This does not imply, however, that he is always right. Suppose there is a change in parameters like q, c_2, c_3 and r which have no relation to the current demand function (1). In view of (1), p_1 changes in the opposite direction to the change in x_1 induced by changes in such parameters. Since S is unchanged, there is a negative relation between the price and the ratio of vent and quantity.

We may vindicate Locke in that his theory of value is not constructed as a general theory of value which is always right but as a theory particularly designed to give microeconomic foundation to the quantity theory of money which explains the general price level. This is actually a view emphasized by Vaughn [40, pp 31–32]. If it is so, we have to be satisfied that Locke explained successfully the relation between the quantity of money and the general price level by applying his theory of the relation between the price and the ratio of vent to quantity. As we have already noted, an increase in the quantity of money or its velocity induces increases of vent of other commodities, which raises the general price level through the increased turnover of commodities, since we can take money as *numéraire*.[7] To consider the relation between the general price level and the quantity of money more directly, we also have to examine the relation between quantity and vent of money, since in the computation of the price of anything:

> in comparing it, or exchanging it with any other thing [money], the quantity and vent of that thing too must be allowed for.... Hence it is that other commodities have sometimes a quicker, sometimes a slower vent: for nobody lays out his money in them, but according to the use he has of them, and that has bounds. But every body being ready to receive money without bounds, and keep it by him, because it answers all things: therefore the vent of money is always sufficient, or more than enough. This being so, its quantity alone is enough to regulate and determine its value, without considering any proportion between its quantity and vent, as in other commodities. (Locke [28, pp. 40, 45].

Vaughn [40, p. 37] regards this passage as difficult to interpret, and, actually, many different scholars have interpreted it differently (Leigh [27]). From the point of view of our model given in the above, however, the implication of this passage is clear and simple. Since the money commodity

---

[7] To the extent that the quantity of money effects the rate of turnover of other commodities, Locke's quantity theory is different from the classical quantity theory. As was rightly pointed out by Hatori [20], money is not neutral if a change in its quantity has different effects on the ratio of vent and quantity of different commodities.

has an almost perfect market even in the current week, its vent is equalized with quantity.

Suppose in the above model that the commodity in question is money as a medium of exchange, S denotes the quantity of money to be spent, and p_1 is the marketable value or price of money commodity in terms of *numéraire* or abstract unit of account. Since the current market is almost perfect in the sense that b is very small in (1), the marginal gain obtained from (5), i.e.,

$$(a - rq + rc_2) - 2bx_1 + (2rc_3 S - 2rc_3 x_1), \tag{13}$$

is still positive when x_1 is equal to S. This is because the last term in (13) vanishes if $x_1 = S$, and the first term in (13) can be considered positive, as before. The maximization of the gain (5) is done at the corner, since by definition $x_1 \leqq S$. Expressed verbally, the rate of turnover is highest in the case of money commodity. Provided that the marginal gain (13) remains positive, therefore, any increase in S induces the same increase in x_1, and p_1 is reduced in view of (1).

Since its vent is always equal to its quantity, the value of money commodity in terms of *numéraire* or abstract unit of account is determined by its quantity alone. From the point of view of the general equilibrium theory, of course, the current demand for money (1) is not independent of the value (in terms of money) of vent of all the other commodities which are sold i.e., exchanged for money. Although this point is not explicitly taken care of in our partial equilibrium model, the demand for money (1) is not inconsistent with it, since x_1 is increased when S is increased and p_1 is reduced, i.e., the general price level is made higher, so that the value (in terms of money) of vent of all the other commodities are increased.[8] Furthermore, we might say that Locke recognized it when he said that "the natural value of money ... depends on the whole quantity of the then passing money of the kingdom, in proportion to the whole trade of the kingdom, *i.e.*, the general vent of all the commodities" (Locke [28, p. 46]). For the relative value of a commodity and money, on the other hand, we have to consider the ratio of vent to quantity of the commodity and quantity of money. "The natural value of money, in exchanging for any one commodity, is the quantity of the trading money of the kingdom designed for that commodity, in proportion to that single commodity and its vent" (Locke [28, p. 46]). This is right, so far as the price of the commodity in terms

---

[8] So far as S (quantity of money) effects the vent of other commodities, the elasticity of the total demand for money is larger than 1. In other words, at least temporarily, T is an increasing function of M and V in $PT = MV$, though V is assumed to be constant in the model. The elasticity of demand for the individual supplier of money commodity is, of course, larger than that of the total demand for money.

of *numéraire* or abstract unit of account changes in the same direction as the ratio of its vent and its quantity, since the price of money commodity in terms of *numéraire* or abstract unit of account is determined by its quantity.

Our interpretation that "the vent for money is always sufficient, or more than enough" so that it is always equalized to the quantity is, therefore, consistent with what Locke insisted in his *Some Considerations*, i.e., that it is not the rate of interest but the quantity of money which determines the value of money.

For example, half an ounce of silver in England will exchange sometimes for a whole bushel of wheat, sometimes for half, sometimes but a quarter, and this it does equally, whether by use it be apt to bring in to the owner six in the hundred of its own weight per annum, or nothing at all: it being only the change of the quantity of wheat to its vent, supposing we have still the same sum of money in the kingdom; or else the change of the quantity of our money in the kingdom, supposing the quantity of wheat, in respect to its vent, be the same too, that makes the change in the price of wheat. (Locke [28, p. 40].)

To make the argument in the passage just quoted, however, Locke based it on a seemingly different idea of the vent of money from the idea that it is equal to quantity. i.e., that it is constant.

Because the desire of money is constantly almost every where the same, its vent varies very little, but as its greater scarcity enhances its price, and increases the scramble: there being nothing else that does easily supply the want of it: the lessening its quantity, therefore, always increases its price, and makes an equal portion of it exchange for a greater of any other thing. (Locke [28, p. 40].)

Vaughn [40, pp. 37, 142–143] insisted that Locke's argument was that the demand for money is constant and rightly pointed out that then it is much the same way as Locke explained the price of the necessaries.

There is nothing more confirmed, by daily experience, than that men give any portion of money, for whatsoever is absolutely necessary, rather than go without it. And in such things, the scarcity of them alone makes their prices. (Locke [28,p. 31].)

When the current demand x_1 is constant, the condition for the maximum gain is

$$p_1 - rq + rc_2 + 2rc_3(S - x_1) = 0, \tag{14}$$

since marginal gains in weeks have to be equalized. From (14), it is easily seen that the current price is higher when quantity is smaller.

Both Locke and Vaughn were right, therefore, to say that when vent or current demand is constant, quantity alone can determine the price. In the case of money commodity, however, the assumption of the constant vent has an insurmountable difficulty, since from the point of view of the general equilibrium theory vent of money is related to the sum of value (in terms of money) of vent of all the other commodities so that a change in its price, i.e., the general price level, induced by a change in its quantity implies a change in its vent. The assumption of constant vent for money is, therefore, much less attractive than our interpretation that vent and quantity are equalized in the case of money.[9]

2. Hume and specie-flow mechanism

David Hume (1711–1776) was a philosopher who succeeded John Locke in the British tradition of empiricism. Intending his philosophy to serve as the center of all the moral sciences or of a general science of human experience, he wrote extensively on philosophy, political theory, economic problems, literature and history. After a brief description of the life and works of David Hume, this section is devoted to considering some recent interpretations of the classical price-specie-flow mechanism which was first discussed by Hume.

Hume was born in Edinburgh in 1711, to a family of well-established country gentry. His father died when he was an infant. He entered the Greek class at the University of Edinburgh in 1723 but did not graduate. Hume tried to be a lawyer and a merchant, without any success. In 1735, he went to France where he wrote his *Treatise of Human Nature*, of which Book I, *Of the Understanding* and Book II, *Of the Passions* appeared in 1739, and Book III, *Of Morals*, in 1740. To his great disappointment, however, the work was neither a financial nor a critical success. He fared better with his two volumes of *Essays Moral and Political*, which he published anonymously in 1741 and 1742. Back in Scotland, he made an unsuccessful bid for the chair of Ethics and Pneumatic Philosophy at the University of Edinburgh, which was followed by two appointments, tutor to the Marquess of Annandale and secretary to General St. Clair on missions abroad.

He returned to London in 1749, and was engaged in writing *The Dialogues on Natural Religion* (published after his death), *Inquiry concerning the*

---

[9] What is constant is, not the vent, but the ratio of vent and quantity, i.e., the velocity in the case of money. See Vaughn [40, pp. 40–42].

Principles of Morals (published in 1751) and the *Political Discourses* (published in 1752). Hume's economic writings consist of nine of the twelve essays in the last work. In 1752, the Faculty of Advocates in Edinburgh elected him their librarian, which gave him both the time and materials to write the *History of England*, a standard text which retained its authority until well into the nineteenth century. In 1763, Hume went to France as secretary to the ambassador, Lord Hertford, and returned to London in 1766 with Rousseau, with whom Hume had later one of the most famous quarrels and reconciliations ever known between men of letters. In 1767, Hume undertook the duties of an Under-Secretary of State, but retired in 1769 to Edinburgh and resumed his friendship with other leading Scottish thinkers, including Adam Smith. In 1775, learning that his disease was mortal, Hume wrote *My Own Life* and died in 1776, just after the publication of Smith's *Wealth of Nations*.

The classical economists did not doubt that the arguments of their predecessors, the mercantilists, in favor of a chronic export surplus were based on an intellectual confusion. Even Thomas Mun, who realized that an inflow of bullion through export surplus raises domestic prices and turns the balance of trade against the country did not hesitate to advocate the indefinite accumulation of hard money (McCulloch [29, pp. 115–209]). This is the so-called mercantilist dilemma. The classical refutation of the mercantilist principle is derived from the so-called Cantillon–Hume price-specie-flow mechanism.[10] By this mechanism an inflow of bullion raises domestic prices, and selling dear and buying cheap tends to turn the balance of trade against the country. Purely automatic forces tend, therefore, to establish a natural distribution of specie between the trading countries of the world and there is a level of domestic prices such that each country's value of exports equals that of imports.

The crux of the classical price-specie-flow mechanism is thus the change in prices caused by redistribution of specie due to the trade imbalance. The famous and concise statement in Hume's essay "Of the Balance of Trade" runs as follows:

> Suppose four-fifths of all the money in Great Britain to be annihilated in one night and the nation reduced to the same conclusion, with regard to specie, as in the reigns of the Harrys and Edwards, what would be the consequence? Must not the price of all labour and commodities sink in proportion, and everything be sold as cheap as they were in those ages? What nation could then dispute with us in any foreign market, or pretend to navigate or to sell

[10] For Cantillon's version of price-specie-flow mechanism, see Cantillon [8, pp. 167–169]. The life and work of Cantillon is sketched in section 3.1 of this Chapter.

manufactures at the same price, which to us would afford sufficient profit? In how little time, therefore, must this bring back the money which we had lost, and raise us to the level of all the neighbouring nations? ... Again, suppose that all the money of Great Britain were multiplied fivefold in a night, must not the contrary effect follow? Must not all labour and commodities rise to such an exorbitant height, that no neighbouring nations could afford to buy from us, while their commodities, on the other hand, became comparatively so cheap, that, inspite of all the laws which could be formed, they would be run in upon us, and our money flow out, till we fall to a level with foreigners, and lose that great superiority of riches, which had laid us under such disadvantages? (Hume [22, pp. 62–63].)

One might wonder why "the price of all the labour and commodities" rise in a country which gained money and sink in a country which lost money, since the same good has always the same gold price in different countries, if it is internationally traded in the absence of obstacles. Staley [39] rightly argued that what Hume had in mind is a model in which international trade takes place not continuously but discretely, so that the same good can have different prices in different countries unless the international distribution of gold has already settled in equilibrium. He based his interpretation on a letter of Hume to James Oswald.

You allow, that if all the money in England were increased fourfold in one night, there would be a sudden rise of prices; but then, say you, the importation of foreign commodities would soon lower the prices. Here, then, is the flowing out of the money already begun. But, say you, a small part of this stock of money would suffice to buy foreign commodities, and lower the prices. I grant it would for one year, till the imported commodities be consumed. But must not the same thing be renewed next year? (Hume [22, p. 197].)

In Hume's day, certainly arbitrage took much time to establish the law of indifference internationally. If international trade does not take place quickly and continuously, it is certain that prices rise temporarily not only for exportables and domestic goods but also for importables in the gold-gaining country. There is no reason to assume that the adjustment process in international trade to establish uniform prices is much quicker than the process of the specie-flow mechanism to achieve the balance of trade equilibrium. The traditional interpretation which follows Viner [41, pp. 313–317] considers, however, that uniform gold prices always prevail for identical commodities in different countries. Since it is insisted on as the interpretation of the classical specie-flow mechanism in general, to consider it is worthwhile, as Staley [39] admitted, independently of one's view about the nature of the price changes envisioned by Hume. As the same price change is now assumed to occur in all countries at the same time, the price variations responsible for adjustment in the balance of trade are changes in terms of trade, i.e., the relative price of exportables and importables for countries. The price of exportables must rise relative to that of importables in the gold-gaining country, and vice versa, if the classical price-specie-flow mechanism works successfully.

Modern literature on international transfer has made it clear, however, that the resultant changes in price can be in either direction, depending on the international difference in demand patterns, and are not necessarily in the direction suggested by the classical price-specie-flow theory; that is, the terms of trade rise in the surplus country and fall in the deficit country (Kemp [23, pp. 79–81]). If, for example, two countries are identical in taste which can be expressed by a homothetic social indifference map,[11] the equilibrium prices are independent of the distribution of income between the two countries, including the distribution of specie. In this case, as is pointed out by Dornbusch, Fischer and Samuelson [11], there is no price effect associated with a redistribution of the world money supply and therefore no effects on real variables in the adjustment process for monetary disequilibrium, contrary to the classical price-specie-flow mechanism.

Let us construct a simplified version of the model used by Dornbusch, Fischer and Samuelson. For the sake of simplicity, we consider the case of a two-good, two-country model, in which each country completely specializes in the production of exportables.[12] The production is of constant returns to scale with respect to the sole factor of production, called labor.[13] As for the demand side, let us assume that the level of aggregate expenditure of each country is proportional to the supply of money in the country[14] and that the ratio of expenditure on each good to the aggregate expenditure is a given constant.[15] The sum of supplies of money in the two countries is assumed to be constant.

The condition for the equilibrium of demand and supply of labor in the home country is then

$$wL = aV(M/G)G + a^* V^*(1 - (M/G))G, \tag{1}$$

[11] In other words, Engel curves are always straight lines through the origin.

[12] Dornbusch, Samuelson and Fischer [11] considered the case with infinitely many goods.

[13] For the more general neo-classical case, see Anderson and Takayama [1].

[14] See Dornbusch and Mussa [12], where such a behavior of expenditure is explained by intertemporal optimization.

[15] See Chipman [9], which explains this assumption as the generalization of numerical example considered by J.S. Mill.

where L is the given supply of labor, w is the money rate of wage, a is the given ratio of expenditure on the exportables of the home country, V is the constant velocity of the circulation, M is the domestic money supply, G is the given world money supply, variables and parameters with(out) asterisk are those of foreign (home) country, and rate of foreign exchange is assumed to be 1. Similarly, for the labor in the foreign country, we have

$$w^*L^* = (1-a)V(M/G)G + (1-a^*)V^*(1-(M/G))G. \tag{2}$$

If the distribution of specie, M, is given, we can solve (1) and (2) for w and w^*. If two countries have identical taste, such that $a = a^*$ and $V = V^*$, furthermore, it is easily seen that equilibrium w and w^* are independent of the distribution of specie.

The specie-flow mechanism is given as

$$dM/dt = wL - VM, \tag{3}$$

where t denotes time; the supply of money is increased as a result of a trade surplus that is equal to the difference of income and absorption. Since w remains unchanged when M changes, if two countries are identical in tastes, it can easily be seen that the solution of (3) is stable and a trade balance is eventually established. Since the price of each good is completely determined by wage cost in our model, there is no price effect of specie flow in this special case. Something must be done to explain the changes in prices in the direction suggested by the classical price-specie-flow theory.

Dornbusch, Fischer and Samuelson showed that even in this special case the introduction of non-traded domestic goods revitalizes the classical conclusion that in the adjustment process prices decline along with the money stock in the deficit country while both rise in the surplus country. Let us therefore introduce non-traded goods in our model and assume that the ratio of expenditure on non-traded goods in each country is constant; that is, $(1-k)$. Non-traded goods and exportables are produced in each country but there is still no import competing production. In view of identical taste, then, (1) and (2) are, respectively, modified into

$$wL = aVG + (1-k)(M/G)VG \tag{4}$$

and

$$w^*L^* = (k-a)VG + (1-(M/G))(1-k)VG, \tag{5}$$

from which equilibrium w and w^* are obtained if M is given.[16] Now

---

[16] Numerical values of a in (4) and (5) are different from those in (1) and (2).

equilibrium wages are no longer independent of the distribution of specie. An increase in M increases w and reduces w^*. The prices of goods produced in a country change in the same direction as the supply of money in the country. Since we have from (4)

$$dw/dM = (1 - k)V/L, \qquad (6)$$

the right-hand side of (3) is decreasing with respect to M and therefore the price-specie-flow mechanism is stable.

In view of the importance of non-traded goods, if not in the classical theory of international trade, but in the actual world of international trade, there is no doubt that the result obtained by Dornbusch, Fischer and Samuelson is interesting as a vindication of the classical price-specie-flow theory. In one respect, however their model of international trade is different from that of classical economics. This is the role of exporters and importers in international trade, which is an important role in classical theory but one completely neglected in the neo-classical theory on which the model of Dornbusch, Fischer and Samuelson is based. As will be shown, price changes in the direction suggested by the classical price-specie-flow theory even in the case of identical and homothetic tastes and no non-traded goods, if the role of exporters and importers is properly taken into consideration.

Classical economic theory's emphasis on the role of exporters and importers can be seen in Ricardo's chapter on foreign trade [34, pp. 128–149] as well as in the following arguments of Adam Smith on the different employment of capitals.

The capital of the wholesale merchant replaces, together with their profits, the capital of the farmers and manufacturers of whom he purchases the rude and manufactured produces which he deals in, and thereby enables them to continue their respective trades. It is by this service chiefly that he contributes indirectly to support the productive labour of the society, and to increase the value of its annual produce. His capital employs too the sailors and carriers who transport his goods from one place to another, and it augments the price of those goods by the value, not only of his profits, but of their wages. (Smith [37, pp. 362–363].)

The capital employed in purchasing foreign goods for home-consumption, when this purchase is made with the produce of domestick industry, replaces too, by every such operation, two distinct capital; but one of them only is employed in supporting domestick industry. The capital which sends British goods to Portugal, and brings back Portuguese goods to Great Britain, replaces by every such operation only one British capital. The other is a Portuguese one. Though the returns, therefore, of the foreign trade of consumption should be as quick as those of the hometrade, the capital employed in it will give but one-half the encouragement to the industry or productive labour of the country. (Smith [37, p. 368].)

Let us first note that a role exists for exporters and importers even if the cost of transport is ignored. This role is to replace the capital of the producers. The role is clearly related to the time structure of the classical theory of production; that is, production requires time and the wage cost must be advanced by capitalists until the product is sold to the final consumers. There is, therefore, no room for this role of exporters and importers in the neo-classical theory of international trade, which is based on either a theory of timeless or instantaneous production or the assumption that there is no need to advance wage cost (Eagly [14, pp. 3–9]).

In the neo-classical theory of international trade, it is assumed that domestic consumers can buy directly from foreign producers in the foreign market. This assumption may not be so unrealistic in international trade among countries, like European ones, located close to one another and socially and culturally very similar. However, in international trade between countries far away and dissimilar, the United States and Japan for example, the role of consumers is very limited and international trade is carried out almost exclusively in the hands of specialists called exporters and importers. Domestic consumers buy the importables in domestic markets from foreign exporters or domestic importers, because consumers have neither enough information nor suitable credit to buy directly from foreign producers, cannot finance transportation cost individually, and are not well accustomed to doing foreign exchange business.

Our model, which is supposed to be that of classical economics, therefore, remains that of neo-classical economics unless the role of exporters and importers is explicitly incorporated. In view of the fact that the role of exporters and importers in classical economics is derived from the time structure of the classical theory of production, to replace the capital of producers advanced, we have to consider that conditions (1) and (2) or (4) and (5) are, in classical economics, not so much the conditions for equilibrium of demand and supply of labor service in the neo-classical sense, as the conditions for equilibrium of demand and supply of advanced funds to support labor in the period of production. In other words, w and w^* represent the average prices of the final products resulting, after the period of production, from the input of a unit of labor, which include wages as well as profits.

Let us dismiss the non-traded goods, and instead take the role of exporters and importers into consideration. Suppose that domestic importers share

$100(1 - s)$ per cent of the cost to be advanced by foreign producers by replacing the latter's capital earlier than the products are sold to the final consumers, and similarly foreign importers share $100(1 - r)$ per cent of the cost to be advanced by domestic producers. In other words, producers sell their products to importers $100(1 - s)$ per cent or $100(1 - r)$ per cent cheaper than they do directly to final consumers, since their capital is replaced earlier. Conditions (1) and (2) are now modified, in the case of identical taste, into

$$wL = aMV + aM^*Vr + (1 - a)MV(1 - s) \tag{7}$$

and

$$w^*L^* = (1 - a)M^*V + (1 - a)MVs + aM^*V(1 - r), \tag{8}$$

where $M + M^* = G$ and r and s are positive constants less than 1. The last term of the right-hand side may be considered as the demand for the service of importers, while w and w^* represent the average prices of the products or services resulted from the input of a unit of labor. Alternatively, the last term of the right-hand side may be considered as part of a demand for the importables, i.e., the demand for the service of capital of importers, while w and w^* represent the average prices of the products of capital advanced to support a unit of labor.

The equilibrium values of w and w^* are obtained from (7) and (8) if M and M^* are given. An increase in M coupled with a decrease in M^* so as to keep G unchanged clearly increases w and decreases w^*. Since w and w^* are prices paid by consumers, the specie-flow changes prices in the direction suggested by classical theory even in the case of identical taste, if the role of exporters and importers is properly taken into consideration. The stability of (3) is also easy to show.

Now our interpretation of classical price-specie-flow mechanism is located in a sense between that of Staley's disequilibrium interpretation of Hume's theory and that of Viner's equilibrium interpretation. As in the Hume–Staley model, the consumers' price of the same commodity may be different in different countries. Consumers in a money-gaining country have to pay a higher price for their importables than the consumers of the country from which they are imported, and consumers in a money-losing country pay a lower price for their importables than the domestic consumers of the exporting country. As is insisted on by Viner, however, the uniform gold price of the same commodity prevails in different countries, in the sense that producers sell their products at the same price to foreign importers and domestic merchants at the same time. The terms of trade in terms of prices importers pay to the producers of an exporting country will change favorably for a money-gaining country and unfavorably for a money-losing country.

3. Quesnay's *Tableau Économique*

3.1

François Quesnay (1694–1774) was the founder of the physiocratic school, who greatly influenced Adam Smith and Karl Marx. The purpose of the present and the following sections is to consider his *Tableau Économique* from the point of view of modern economic theory. Before giving a sketch of Quesnay's life and works in this subsection, however, we describe briefly those of Richard Cantillon (1697–1734), since Quesnay was much influenced by Cantillon (Cantillon [8, pp. 353–355], Meek [30, pp. 266–269]). The rest of this section is devoted to discussing the nature of the economy described by the *Tableau Économique* by the use of linear economic models. In subsection 3.2, the state of the economy described by the so-called *Formule du Tableau Économique* is derived as an optimal solution of a linear programming model which is based on Marx's interpretation. The subsection 3.3 is devoted to reviewing Barna's [3] mathematical model of economic development which ends up at the economy described by the *Tableau*. Section 4 is a critical study of Eltis's [16], [17] analysis of the *Tableau Économique*, not only the *Formule* but also the original table, which follows Meek's interpretation.

Richard Cantillon was born in Ireland in 1697, was active as a banker in Paris until 1720, and was murdered in London in 1734. Based on his rich business experience, Cantillon wrote much, but his only remaining is the famous *Essai sur la nature du commerce en général* (1755). *Essai* was written first in English and translated into French. It was circulated in manuscript form before it was finally published in 1775. *Essai* is famous not only for Cantillon's theory, along with that of David Hume, on price-specie-flow mechanism, but also for its undeniable influence on the physiocrats, particularly Quesnay.

In the beginning paragraph, it insists that "The Land is the Source or Matter from whence all Wealth is produced. The Labour of man is the Form which produces it" and its Chapter 12, Part One is entitled "All Classes and Individuals in a State subsist or are enriched at the Expense of the Proprietors of Land." What is more important than these statements of physiocratic flavor is, however, the land theory of value, by which Cantillon reduced the pluralism of Petty ("Labour is the father of wealth, as lands are the mother") to the monism of land.

> The labour of an adult Slave of the lowest class is worth at least as much as the quantity of Land which the Proprietor is obliged to allot for his food and necessaries and also to double the Land which serves to breed a Child up till he is of age fit for labour, seeing half the children that are born die before the age of 17, according to the calculations and observations of the celebrated Dr. Halley. (Cantillon [8, p. 33].)

While wealth is produced from land and labor, labor is merely an intermediate product which is reproduced from the consumption of the products of land and labor. Land is the only one primary factor of production. The value of products can be expressed, therefore, by the quantities of land which are necessary, directly or indirectly (through labor) in their production. The significance of this land theory of value was emphasized by Schumpeter and was used by Samuelson in his criticism of Ricardo who, unlike Cantillon, eliminates land in his labor theory of value.[17]

The significance of Cantillon's *Essai* is not limited to its theory of specie-flow, its influence on the Physiocrats, and its land theory of value. For example, we can find an embryo form of the modern theory of rate of interest and risk premium. In view of the fact that James Steuart's *Principles of Political Oeconomy* was published in 1767, Cantillon's *Essai* is actually the first systematic treatise on economic science in our history.

François Quesnay was born in 1694 at Méré in the suburb of Paris. After receiving his surgical training in Paris, he began practicing in 1718 at Mantes. At that time a method of treatment called phlebotomy, or blood-letting, had come into vogue as a result of Harvey's discovery of the circulation of the blood. In 1730 Quesnay explored, by experiment using a hydro apparatus, the blood circulation theory of Jean Baptiste Silvia, one of the most famous physicians of the day, and was elected by the surgeons to lead their struggle for equality with the physicians. Because of failing eyesight and rheumatism in the hands, however, Quesnay was forced to become a physician. It was far from disappointing for him, for he was appointed physician to Madame de Pompadour and also to Louis XV. He died at Versailles in 1774.

Although his concern with social problems can already be seen in the second edition (1747) of *Essai physique sur l'économie animale*, Quesnay wrote nothing on economics until the age of sixty. In 1756 he contributed *Fermiers* to *Grande Encyclopédie* of Diderot and d'Alembert, in which he compared large-scale

---

[17] For a mathematical model of the land theory of value, see Chapter 4, section 2.1.

agriculture in England with traditional agriculture in France and insisted that the former should be introduced in France. Another contribution to *Encyclopédie* was *Granis* (1757) in which the term *produit net* first appeared. He also prepared, but never published, *Hommes*, which discussed population problems, and *Impôt*, which insisted that only the net revenue from land should be taxed. In 1758, the first edition of the *Tableau Économique* appeared and Mirabeau called it one of the three greatest inventions in human history, along with those of letters and money. Since the original *Tableau* is too complicated to be understood easily, however, Quesnay simplified it into *Formule du Tableau Économique* in 1766.[18]

Although the controversy between Silvia and Quesnay was a detour from the point of view of the development process from Harvey to modern medicine, and Quesnay had a false conception of the circulation of blood, it is interesting to see the relation between his concept of blood circulation and the *Tableau Économique*.[19] The *Tableau* portrays the circulation of money and goods during the course of a year. As the year begins, the money of the society is collected in the hands of landowners as the land rents for the previous year and they divide their funds into two portions, one being spent to buy manufactured goods in the city, and the other going to their tenants to finance the year's crops. These two recipient classes are represented by columns as the right- and left-hand sides of the *Tableau*, and subdivide the funds received from landowners, spending half within its own class and sending half to the class represented by the opposite column. Similarity between the *Tableau* and Quesnay's concept of blood circulation lies in the fact that they both begin with an initial division of the circulating medium into two separate and equal flows. The blood leaves the heart and goes equally to the upper and lower parts of the body (ignoring the pulmonary loop), and thence into the subdivisions and sub-subdivisions of the lesser arteries, just as currency goes from landowners in equal amounts to agriculture and manufacture, and is redivided in the same repeating pattern as each recipient of funds splits his income evenly between his own and opposite classes in the *Tableau*.

Like many other medical men of his time, furthermore, Quesnay believed that the arteries possessed the power of contraction and hence played an active role in forcing the blood through the system, while the veins carried the blood

---

[18] For the original *Tableau* (*Tableau Fondamental*), see Table 2.6 in section 4 and Kuczynski and Meek [25]. It describes, like Kahn's multiplier process in Keynesian economics, the dynamic process of the circulation of money and goods among three classes, i.e., landowners, agriculture and manufacture. As for the *Formule*, see Table 2.1 in section 3.2 and Meek [30, p. 158]. Like a static multiplier in Keynesian economics, it shows the aggregate transactions among three classes in the equilibrium.

[19] The following exposition depends largely on Foley [19].

in a merely passive fashion. We can see, therefore, another similarity between Quesnay's concept of blood circulation and the *Tableau*. Quesnay considered that the rural agriculture class is productive while the urban manufacture class is sterile. The sterile class does not add any value to the flows which pass through their hands and they serve merely as a passive conduit for money and goods, just as the veins make no changes in the impetus of the blood flows which traverse their interiors. Only in agriculture, owing to Nature's bounty, can *produit net* be added to the economy, just as only in the arterial columns of the vascular system does the contractive power of the tube walls actively augment the force and flow of the blood. Finally, just as the heart is the indispensable center of the entire network, far outweighing the arteries as a source of motion, so the landowners are the heart of the economy, because their division of funds between the sterile and the productive classes determines the health of the economy.

3.2

Quesnay's *Tableau Économique* is the first complete description of economic circulation, in which he considered a country where the agriculture is mostly developed, commercial competition prevails and the ownership of private capital in agriculture is guaranteed. The essence of the *Tableau Économique* can best be seen in its simplified or final version, i.e., *Formule du Tableau Économique*, reproduced here somewhat modified as Table 2.1.[20] This is a sort of resumé of Quesnay's various studies of economic problems, which is, however, so simplified that it is very difficult to interpret it and that there have been many different interpretations of it. It is well known that Karl Marx evaluated the significance of the *Formule* very highly. Actually, his reproduction scheme is a developed version of his own "*tableau économique*". Marx's interpretation of Quesnay's *Tableau Économique* can be seen in Engels's *Herrn Eugen Dührings Umwälzung der Wissenschaft* (1878).

According to Marx (Engels [18, p. 234]), as is seen in Table 2.1, the agricultural sector produces annually 50 units of output from the input of 20 agricultural products as annual advances (working capital) and 100 manufactured products as original advances (fixed capital), of which 10 units depreciate annually, and pays 20 to the landowners as rent.[21] Out of this 20 rent, the landowners spend 10 for agricultural products and 10 for

---

[20]See Meek [30, p. 158]. Table 2.1 is changed from the original *Formule*, in view of the suggestion given by Bauer [4].

[21]All the units are given in terms of money and money prices are considered as constant.

Table 2.1

Agriculture's annual advances	Landowners' revenue	Manufacture's annual advances
20	20	20
10		
		10
10		
		10
10		
20		
50		20

manufactured products. The manufacturing sector produces 20 units of output from the input of 20 agricultural products as annual advances.[22] In the Table, it is assumed that the agricultural sector has initially 20 units of money which are paid to the landowners as rent. The landowners spend them to buy 10 agricultural products and 10 manufactured products. With the 10 units of money received from the landowners, the manufacturing sector buys 10 agricultural products so as to replace the first half of the annual advances, while the agricultural sector buys 10 manufactured products with the money received from the landowners so as to replace the depreciated part of the original advances. Finally, the manufacturing sector buys 10 agricultural products so as to replace the second half of the annual advances by the money received from the agricultural sector. Twenty unsold agricultural products replace the annual advances of the agricultural sector. Since the agricultural sector regains 20 units of money and all the advances are properly replaced, the same process can be repeated in the next period.[23]

The *Tableau Économique* describes the stationary state of an economy where rent is explicitly introduced while wage is implicitly considered as part of the annual advances. There is, however, no place for profit. Some Marxian economists seem to explain this absence of profit by the fact that in the days of

---

[22] Following the suggestion of Eagly [13], we assume, unlike in the original *Formule*, that the length of the period of production for the agricultural and manufacturing sectors is equal. Eagly also suggests that we may either assume that there is no original advance in the manufacturing sector or that the output of that sector is net of depreciation.

[23] See also Blaug [5, p. 27], and Eagly [14, p. 23].

Quesnay, i.e., those of the *ancien régime*, capitalism was not far enough developed to allow for the existence of profit.[24] This might be true in view of the French social structure in the days of Quesnay, where feudalistic production relation and landownership prevailed, with small manufacturers based on primitive hired labor. It should be noted, however, that the *Tableau Économique* is not a positive model of the French economy as it was in the days of Quesnay, since Quesnay's intention was to describe an ideal state of the economy. Some non-Marxian economists seem, on the other hand, to explain the zero profit by the condition of a long-run competitive equilibrium in which price is just equal to the average total cost of production.[25]

The *Tableau Économique* can be converted into a closed Leontief table, as was done by Blaug and reproduced here as Table 2.2.[26] The landowners, as sector 2, are considered to produce a productive service of the land by consuming the agricultural products of sector 1 and the manufactured products of sector 3. Although we can mechanically compute input–output coefficients a_{ij}, i.e., the ith sector's product used as input to produce a unit of the jth sector's output, we have to be careful since different a_{ij} has different stability. Coefficients a_{11}, a_{12}, a_{32} and a_{13} may be stable as technological and consumption coefficients (or products of them). The coefficient a_{21} will, however, change as the rate of rent, i.e., the scarcity of land is changed. The coefficient a_{31} is, furthermore, meaningless, unless the fixed capital is properly accumulated. The mechanical application of the Leontief analysis is, therefore, of questionable significance.[27]

Table 2.2

| | Purchasing sector | | | |
Producing sector	1	2	3	Annual output
1 Agriculture	20	10	20	50
2 Landowners	20	0	0	20
3 Manufacture	10	10	0	20
Total purchases	50	20	20	90

[24] For an example of Marxian interpretation, see Yokoyama [43, pp. 151–152].

[25] For an example of such an explanation, see Ekelund and Hébert [15, p. 75].

[26] See Blaug [5, p. 28], which is based on Phillips [33].

[27] Hishiyama [21] developed a unique Leontief-like analysis and dynamization of the *Tableau Économique* on the basis not of the simplified Table 2.1 but of the original version of the *Tableau Économique*, i.e., *Tableau Fondamental*.

As an application of linear economic analysis on Quesnay's *Tableau Économique*, what is more interesting is to consider the following linear programming problem, which will explain why there is no profit. Still considering three sectors as in Table 2.2, let us consider the maximization of the level of surplus of the economy, defined as $t = \min(c_1, c_3)$, where c_i denotes the net output (*produit net*) of the economy in terms of the product of the sector i. Consider the maximization of t, being subject to following conditions.

$$X_1 \leq L \tag{1}$$

$$2X_1 \leq F \tag{2}$$

$$0.4X_1 \leq K_1 \tag{3}$$

$$c_1 + K_1 + K_3 \leq X_1 \tag{4}$$

$$X_3 \leq K_3 \tag{5}$$

$$c_3 + 0.1F \leq X_3 \tag{6}$$

where L denotes the total available amount of land, F denotes the fixed capital of the sector 1, i.e., the agriculture, X_i denotes the output of the sector i, and K_i denotes the working capital of the sector i available initially and to be reproduced. It is assumed in (1) that the input coefficient of land in the sector 1 is unity, while other coefficients are as shown in Table 1. Conditions (1) to (4) are concerned with agriculture, restrictions of land, fixed capital, and working capital, and the equilibrium condition of demand and supply of agricultural products. Similarly, conditions (5) and (6) are concerned with the manufacturing sector, the restriction of working capital and the equilibrium of the demand and supply of manufactured products.

Let us denote the Lagrangean multipliers corresponding to conditions (1) to (6), respectively, by r, p, w_1, p_1, w_3 and p_3. In view of (4) and (6), we can safely consider that $t = c_1 = c_3$ in the maximizing problem. If t is maximized with respect to X_i, K_i, F and t, then, we have

$$-r - 2p - 0.4w_1 + p_1 = 0 \tag{7}$$

$$p_1 = p_3 = w_1 = w_3 \tag{8}$$

$$p - 0.1p_3 = 0 \tag{9}$$

and

$$1 - p_1 - p_3 = 0, \tag{10}$$

from the conditions for the maximization, assuming non-zero values for the maximizing variables. It can easily be seen that *Tableau Économique* describes this maximized situation. From (7) to (10) and the dual theorem of linear programming, we have

$$t = rL = 0.4p_1 X_1 = p_1 c_1 + p_3 c_3 \tag{11}$$

which implies that the surplus or the rent to be paid to the landowners is two-fifths of the value of the output of the sector 1, i.e., the agriculture, since Lagrangean multipliers can be interpreted as the competitive prices which indicate the scarcity of the corresponding goods or factors of production.

Suppose F is fixed at the level lower than the optimal one. From (9) we have $p > 0.1p_3$, which implies that positive profit (net of depreciation) is to be imputed to fixed capital in a competitive situation, since p denotes the gross value imputed to a unit of fixed capital and $0.1p_3$ denotes the value of the depreciation of a unit of such capital. Similar considerations can also be made with respect to annual advances.[28] In other words, there is no profit in the *Tableau Économique* because the capital is fully accumulated to the optimal level so that there is no scarcity or net productivity of capital.[29] In this case, of course, it is to be understood that the normal profit necessary to keep the supply unchanged is included in the cost of production.

3.3

Quesnay's *Tableau Économique* is not a positive model of the French economy as it was in the 1750s, but a normative model of Utopia which describes the French economy as it could have been if proper economic policies had been adopted. The situation described by it is optimal, however, not only with respect to the level of capital accumulation, as considered in the above, but also with respect to the modernisation of the agricultural sector, as emphasized by Barna [3].[30] In the 1750s France was an underdeveloped country which lacked the advances in agriculture seen in large-scale agriculture in England except in the north-west, the region nearest to England. Quesnay believed that the solution to the French economic problem was to replace her traditional agriculture by agriculture *à l'Anglaise*, which requires capital accumulation. To create profit so as to accumulate capital, he suggested the promotion of free trade and tax reform.

[28] The supply of labor may be assumed to be perfectly elastic at the given real wage in terms of the agricultural products.

[29] Eagly [13] dynamized the *Tableau Économique* correctly by introducing profit as the source of capital accumulation. He did not, however, consider how profit is generated and merely assumed that it is proportional to the level of output.

[30] See also Meek [30, pp. 297–312, especially 306–307].

Barna [3] considered a mathematical model of economic development which ends up at the optimal situation described by the *Tableau Économique* when enough capital is accumulated and traditional agriculture is totally replaced by modern agriculture. Unlike Marx, Barna insisted that a significant feature of all Quesnaian models is that agriculture does not use manufactured products as original as well as annual advances.[31] The outstanding feature of Barna's model is that there are two distinct agricultural productive activities which are called the traditional and the modern. These two linear activities produce the same output from different inputs. Let a_1 and a_2 be input coefficients (the amount of input necessary to produce a unit of output) of land in traditional and modern agriculture and, similarly, let k_1 and k_2 be input coefficients of capital in the two agricultures. Capital consists of the stock of agricultural products and embraces both fixed and working capitals. It is assumed that $a_2 < a_1, k_2/a_2 > k_1/a_1$ and $s_2/a_2 > s_1/a_1$ where s_1 and s_2 are surplus coefficients (in terms of agricultural products) of traditional and modern agriculture.

Let A^* be the maximum area of land available for agriculture. Since $k_2/a_2 > k_1/a_1$, the maximum amount of the capital stock that the economic system can use is $K^* = A^* k_2/a_2$, which corresponds to the situation where all available land is in the modern sector. Since $a_2 < a_1$ and $s_2/a_2 > s_1/a_1$, the maximum agricultural output X^* and the maximum surplus S^* are reached in the same situation, which is to be described by the *Tableau Économique*.

Let, on the other hand, K_0 be the capital stock used when all land A^* is in the traditional sector, i.e., $K_0 = A^* k_1/a_1$. The corresponding agricultural output and surplus are, respectively, denoted by X_0 and S_0. If the available amount of capital stock K is between K_0 and K^*, i.e., $K_0 \leq K \leq K^*$, then Barna argues that K determines the proportion of land in the modern sector m as $(K - K_0)/(K^* - K_0)$. The corresponding agricultural output X and surplus S are then $m(X^* - X_0) + X_0$ and $m(S^* - S_0) + S_0$, respectively. As capital accumulates from K_0 to K^*, traditional agriculture is gradually replaced by modern agriculture and X and S increase from X_0 and S_0 to X^* and S^*.

Suppose $K = K_0$ initially and that favourable policies like free trade and/or tax reform are introduced. Being based on a part of Mirabeau's *Philosophie Rurale*, which is due to Quesnay,[32] Barna considered that land is leased to capitalist farmers at the rents fixed for the period of the lease. During that period, therefore, farmers can make profits which they reinvest, though at the

---

[31] Barna [2], [3] distinguished production accounts for agriculture from the household accounts of agricultural families and assumed that households consume manufactured products but there is no input of manufactured products into agricultural production.

[32] See Meek [30, pp. 138–149].

end of the period competition among farmers pushes up rents until the whole surplus is again absorbed in rent. Since $s_2/a_2 > s_1/a_1$ farmers can make a temporal profit which they reinvest, so that capital is further increased.

Let us note, firstly, that in this Quesnay–Barna process of development there is no profit except temporality, even if capital is scarce, i.e., its net productivity is positive. This implies that the land market is not competitive, even though capitalists are competitive, and that landowners are differentiating monopolists who absorb all the surplus as rent. In other words, a farmer cannot sublease land and he cannot change the quantity of land to be leased, let alone the rate of rent. Since there is no surplus in the manufacturing sector even if capital is scarce, he has no incentive to shift his capital out of agriculture. We might say that these points are reflecting some aspects of the feudalistic economy with its very primitive manufacturing.

Secondly, Barna's assumption that traditional agriculture always exists and all the land A^* is used for K smaller than K^* may imply inefficiency, not only from the point of view of total surplus but also from the point of view of individual farmers. Since $s_2/a_2 > s_1/a_1$, the surplus is maximized for any given K if all the land is transferred from the traditional sector to the modern sector and is used in the modern sector as far as capital permits, i.e., Ka_2/k_2 land is used in the modern sector and the rest of the land is left unused when $s_2/k_2 > s_1/k_1$.[33] In Figure 2.1, the output of the traditional sector is measured horizontally, while that of the modern sector is measured vertically. The line AB is the land constraint and the line CE is the capital constraint. If equi-surplus lines are as dotted lines, i.e., $s_2/k_2 > s_1/k_1$, it is clear that not the point D but the point C is optimal. In terms of mathematical programming, the disposal process of land rather than the traditional agriculture process should be used with the modern agriculture process.

From the individual farmer's point of view, furthermore, it is always profitable to transfer land and capital from the traditional sector to the modern sector, since a temporal profit is accrued to farmers. Even if the fixed capital is not transferred, the depreciation allowance obtained in the traditional sector with corresponding working capital should not be re-invested in the same sector but should be transferred to the modern sector. Then, the traditional sector eventually disappears, possibly before the accumulation of capital to K^*, even if there is no initial profit created by favourable policies. We have, therefore, to consider, as Barna seems to do, that it takes time for traditional farmers to know and to apply modern techniques,

---

[33] Barna [3] admitted that Quesnay assumed this.

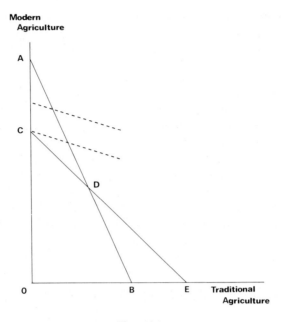

Figure 2.1

with the result that the traditional sector does not disappear in Barna's model.[34]

There is another possible explanation of this point, if we follow Marx as in the previous subsection and assume that fixed capital in agriculture is the stock of manufactured products which is used only in the modern sector but is not used in the traditional sector, while working capital is the stock of agricultural products. In Figure 2.1, the line CE now represents working capital constraint and there is an additional constraint of fixed capital which is a horizontal line passing point D. The economy remains at point D unless profit is created by policies. Even if there exists such profit to be invested, furthermore, the rate of expansion of the modern sector is limited by the capacity of the manufacturing sector, the expansion of which is limited in turn by the existing amount of fixed capital stock of manufactured products invested in the manufacturing sector. The traditional sector does not disappear suddenly or before the capital is fully accumulated, though there appear some unused lands, the existence of which, as emphasized by Eltis [16],

----

[34] We are grateful to Professor T. Barna, who kindly replied to our questions and gave us useful comments, but he is not responsible for our possible misinterpretations.

Quesnay was well aware of. When agriculture is completely modernized, we arrive at the situation which corresponds to the one described by the *Tableau Économique*, as interpreted by Marx, with agriculture using a fixed capital stock of manufactured products.

Barna [2] is right to argue that there is not a very large amount of input of manufactured products into agriculture, if they are considered as implements originating outside agriculture. Apart from the problem of what Quesnay really meant, however, Marx's interpretation that the fixed capital of agriculture consists entirely of the manufactured products may be defended purely logically, since in the *Tableau Économique* agriculture is to be defined not as agriculture in general but as the only sector which can yield surplus in the form of rent, i.e., the most productive sector, represented by grain farming with the most efficient horse-drawn-plough technique, and all the other unproductive activities, which may include cattle breeding, are to be called manufacturing.

4. Expenditure patterns in the *Tableau Économique*

Marx's interpretation of the simplified form or the final version of Quesnay's *Tableau Économique* was, as we saw in the previous section, based on the supposition that landowners spend half their rent income on agricultural and half on manufactured products, while laborers, both in agriculture and in manufacturing, spend their whole wage income on food, i.e., agricultural products, and that the fixed capital, i.e., the original advances, of agriculture, i.e., the productive sector, consists entirely of the products of manufacturing, i.e., the unproductive sector. This interpretation suffers from the weakness that the supposition of different expenditure patterns between landowners and laborers is not consistent with Quesnay's assumption of the identical expenditure pattern of all the classes in his original *Tableau* with zigzags, i.e., *Tableau Fondamental*.

The modern interpretation, which was developed by Meek [30] and followed with Barna [2], [3], and Eltis [16], [17], insists, on the other hand, that all the problems and apparent inconsistencies in the interpretations of Quesnay's *Tableau Économique* are solved when Quesnay's published works, including some parts of Mirabeau's *L'Ami des hommes* and *Philosophie rurale*, are read as a whole. According to this new interpretation, the fixed capital of agriculture consists entirely of agricultural products, mainly horses and other animals, and international trade, i.e., export of food and import of manufactured products, is emphasized so as to make an identical expenditure pattern between landowners and laborers possible.

Table 2.3 is essentially identical to Table 2.1, though the numerical scale is changed so that it is convenient for the purpose of discussions in this section. Each year agriculture advances 1000 million livres, i.e., 500 of agricultural products and 500 of manufactured products for the laborers and produces 2500 million livres of agricultural products, while manufacturing advances 1000 million livres, i.e., 500 of agricultural products for raw materials, 250 of agricultural products and 250 of manufactured products for the laborers and produces 1000 million livres of manufactured products. In additon to the annual advances, agriculture advances also original advances consist entirely of agricultural products, the annual depreciation of which is 500 million livres. The surplus of agriculture, 1000 million livres, is paid to the landowners as rent. Note that the expenditure pattern of the laborers in both agriculture and manufacturing is assumed to be identical to that of the landowners who spend half their income on agricultural and half on manufactured products.

Since the landowners spend their rent income of 1000 million livres half on agricultural products and half on manufactured products, the first 500 of agricultural products and the first 500 of manufactured products are sold out to them. Manufacturing buys the second 500 of agricultural products with the 500 million livres received from the landowners, and agriculture buys the second 500 of manufactured products in return. Finally, manufacturing buys the third 500 of agricultural products with the 500 million livres received from agriculture for the second 500 of manufactured products.

Now 1000 million livres of money, 500 of manufactured products, and 1000

Table 2.3

Agriculture	Landowners	Manufacturing
	1000 million livres	
500		500
500		
		500
500		
1000		

of agricultural products, are in the hands of agriculture. Agriculture pays 1000 million livres rent to the landowners, replaces annual advances of 500 agricultural products and 500 manufactured products, and covers the depreciation of the fixed capital, the so-called 'interest' cost of agriculture, i.e., to replace horses, etc., with the remaining 500 of agricultural products. Manufacturing, having 1000 of agricultural products, exports 250 of agricultural products and imports 250 of manufactured products, so that annual advances of 750 agricultural products and 250 of manufactured products are replaced. The economy can continue, therefore, to produce 2500 agricultural products and 1000 manufactured products.

Thus, the introduction of international trade certainly makes it possible to interpret Quesnay's *Tableau Économique* consistently, under the assumption of identical patterns of expenditure for all the classes of a nation. Quesnay insisted, however, on not only assuming an identical expenditure pattern for all classes but also on changing it properly, so as to make the economy grow rather than decay. The introduction of international trade, unfortunately, makes the following argument of Quesnay's entirely untenable, in spite of Eltis's [17] argument to the contrary.

> It can be seen from the distribution delineated in the Tableau that if the nation's expenditure went more to the sterile expenditure side than to the productive expenditure side, the revenue would fall proportionally, and that this fall would increase in the same progression from year to year successively. It follows that a high level of expenditure on luxury in the way of ornamentation and conspicuous consumption is ruinous. If on the other hand the nation's expenditure goes to the productive expenditure side the revenue will rise, and this rise will in the same way increase successively from year to year. Thus it is not true that the type of expenditure is a matter of indifference.[35]

As was emphasized by Eltis [17], this argument, if it is correct, is really remarkable for those who are familiar with modern growth theory, since it insists that the rate of growth of an economy is a function of what is consumed rather than the ratio of investment to consumption. From the point of view of the philosophy of physiocracy, this statement may follow quite naturally, since it is assumed that only the land is productive and any increase in expenditure on agricultural products gives rise to an increase in rent, while no other form of expenditure has similar favorable effects. It is, however, one thing to insist on this physiocratic policy on the basis of its philosophy, and it is quite another to

---

[35] See Kuczynski and Meek [25, p. 12] and Eltis [17].

demonstrate it by the use of the *Tableau Économique*. The type of expenditure in the *Tableau Économique* is a matter of indifference, if any change in it can always be adjusted by a corresponding change in international trade so that there are no changes in the production and the revenue (rent) of the nation.[36] We shall demonstrate this first by using the final version of the *Tableau* (*Formule*), i.e., by comparing Tables 2.3, 2.4 and 2.5.

Suppose the propensity to consume agricultural products changes from 0.5 to 0.6 not only for the landowners but also for the laborers in agriculture and manufacturing. The *Tableau* shifts from Table 2.3 to Table 2.4, though identical outputs, i.e., 2500 agricultural products and 1000 manufactured products, are already produced from the annual advances made before the propensity to consume changed. Now the landowners spend 600 million livres on agricultural products and 400 million livres on manufactured products, so that the first 600 of agricultural products and the first 400 of manufactured products are sold out to the landowners. Manufacturing then buys 400 of the agricultural products with the 400 million livres received from the landowners, and agriculture in return buys the second 400 of manufactured products. Finally, manufacturing buys a further 400 of agricultural products with the 400 million livres received from agriculture.

Now, 1000 million livres of money, 400 of manufactured products and 1100 of agricultural products are in the hands of agriculture, so that it can pay 1000 million livres to the landowners as rent, advance 600 of agricultural products and 400 of manufactured products to the laborers, and cover the interest cost with the remaining 500 of agricultural products. Having now 800 of agricultural products and 200 of unsold manufactured products, manufacturing can replace advances for raw materials, i.e., 500 of agricultural products, and an advance of 300 of agricultural products and 200 of manufactured products for the laborers. Changes in the propensity to consume are entirely absorbed by changes in international trade, and the economy can continue to produce the unchanged outputs, i.e., 2500 of agricultural products and 1000 of manufactured products, under the changed patterns of expenditure.

Similarly, Table 2.5 shows the case where the propensity to consume agricultural products changes from 0.5 to 0.4. The landowners spend 400 million livres on agricultural products and 600 million livres on manufactured products, so that the first 400 of agricultural products and the first 600 of manufactured products are sold out to the landowners. Manufacturing then buys 600 of agricultural products with the 600 million livres received from the

---

[36] Samuelson [35] is also against Quesnay in this respect, but argued that expenditure patterns effect the level of output of different sectors, without paying attention to international trade.

Table 2.4

Agriculture	Landowners	Manufacturing
	1000 million livres	

Agriculture	Landowners	Manufacturing
600		400
400		
400		400
		200
1100		

Table 2.5

Agriculture	Landowners	Manufacturing
	1000 million livres	

Agriculture	Landowners	Manufacturing
400		600
600		400
600		(200)
900		(300)

landowners, and agriculture buys 400 of manufactured products with the 400 million livres received from the landowners. The next step for manufacturing is to export 500 of agricultural products so as to import 500 of manufactured products, which implies that manufacturing can supply 1500 of manufactured products in all, i.e., 1000 produced and already sold and 500 imported and circled in Table 2.5. Agriculture then buys 200 of imported manufactured products from manufacturing with 200 million livres, i.e., part of the money already received from manufacturing when 600 of agricultural products were sold. Finally, manufacturing uses this 200 million livres and 400 million livres, already received when 400 of manufactured products were sold to agriculture, to buy a further 600 of agricultural products.

Since 400 million livres are left unused out of 600 million livres received from manufacturing when the first 600 of agricultural products were sold, agriculture now has 1000 million livres to pay in rent. Also 600 of manufactured products and 900 of agricultural products are in the hands of agriculture, so as to advance 400 of agricultural products and 600 of manufactured products for the laborers, and to cover interest with the remaining 500 of agricultural products. Having bought 1200 of agricultural products and exported 500, manufacturing has 700 of agricultural products and 300 of unsold manufactured products, just enough to replace the advanced raw materials, i.e., 500 of agricultural products and to advance 200 of agricultural products and 300 of manufactured products for the laborers. The economy can continue, therefore, to produce 2500 of agricultural products and 1000 of manufactured products under new patterns of expenditure.

Thus, changing expenditure patterns makes neither growth nor decline in output possible, if the possibility of international trade is introduced in the *Tableau Économique*. There is, of course, an implicit assumption of a small country in the given terms of trade. Otherwise, a country exporting agricultural products and importing manufactured products can certainly grow by changing its domestic expenditure pattern so that it is favorable to agriculture, which makes the terms of trade favorable. The reason for this possibility, however, of an economic growth through changing expenditure patterns is not that agriculture alone is productive, as Quesnay and the Physiocrats supposed, but that the country happens to be an exporter of agricultural products. For a country which exports manufactured products, it is necessary to change the domestic expenditure pattern so that it favors manufacturing, to make economic growth possible through a favorable change in terms of trade. This possibility, therefore, cannot be a vindication of Quesnay's physiocratic view of economic growth.[37]

Eltis [17] insisted that the effect of the propensity to consume agricultural products on the rate of growth can best be analyzed by using, not the final version of the *Tableau* as we did, but the original Tableau with zigzags and by focusing attention on the financial receipts of agricultural producers. The original *Tableau Économique* with zigzags is given in a generalized form as Table 2.6 when the propensity to consume agricultural products is q and rent or revenue is R.[38] The landowners spend qR on agricultural products and $(1-q)R$ on manufactured products. Agriculture then spends $(1-q)qR$ on

---

[37]We are grateful to Professor W.A. Eltis for our highly useful discussions, though he is not responsible for our possible misunderstandings.

[38]Table 2.6 is originally due to Hishiyama [21] and reproduced in Eltis [16].

Table 2.6

Agriculture	Landowners	Manufacturing
	R	
Rq		$R(1-q)$
$Rq(1-q)$		$Rq(1-q)$
$Rq^2(1-q)$		$Rq(1-q)^2$
$Rq^2(1-q)^2$		$Rq^2(1-q)^2$
$Rq^3(1-q)^2$		$Rq^2(1-q)^3$
Total		Total
$R(2q-q^2)/(1-q+q^2)$		$R(1-q^2)/(1-q+q^2)$

manufactured products out of qR received from the landowners, while manufacturing spends $q(1-q)R$ on agricultural products out of $(1-q)R$ received from the landowners. Agriculture further spends $(1-q)q(1-q)R$ on manufactured products out of $q(1-q)R$ just received from manufacturing, while manufacturing spends $q(1-q)qR$ on agricultural products out of $(1-q)qR$ just received from agriculture. In this way, agriculture ends up with the total receipt of money $R(2q-q^2)/(1-q+q^2)$ while manufacturing ends up with the total receipt of $R(1-q^2)/(1-q+q^2)$.

As is well known, it is not easy to interpret rationally how the reproduction of an economy is carried out in this *Tableau*. Eltis's [16] interpretation is as follows. Suppose agriculture advances annually 1000 million livres and pays a rent of 1000 million livres, and the propensity to consume agricultural products is 0.5. In the *Tableau*'s zigzags, both agriculture and manufacturing receive 1000 million livres and spend 500 million livres on the products of the other sector, while manufacturing is assumed to use the other 500 million livres as advances for raw materials which are bought from agriculture at the end of the year, i.e., after the process of zigzags is over. Thus, the economy's whole stock of money, 1000 million livres, will reach agriculture by the end of the year. Since agriculture is assumed to produce 2000 million livres of products from 1000 million livres of annual advance, it is left with 1000 million livres of money, 500 million livres of manufactured products and 500 million livres of agricultural products, so that it can pay again 1000 million livres of rent and advance again 1000 million livres of agricultural and manufactured products for the laborers. Manufacturing is left with 500 million livres of raw materials and 500 million livres of other agricultural products, half of which is assumed to be exported to import manufactured products. It can, then, advance 250 million livres of agricultural products and 250 million livres of manufactured products to the laborers. The economy can continue, therefore, to produce 2000 million livres of agricultural products and 1000 million livres of manufactured products.[39]

Although we agree with Eltis [16] that the original *Tableau* with zigzags can be interpreted rationally when q is 0.5, it does not imply that there is no difficulty in similarly interpreting accounts of the effect of changes in q on the rate of growth, which are found in *Philosophy rurale* and *L'Ami des hommes*, actually written by Quesnay and Mirabeau. Suppose that q is 0.4. The *Tableau*'s zigzags bring 842 million livres (obtained by substituting $q = 0.4$ into $1000(2q - q^2)/(1 - q + q^2)$) instead of 1000 million livres to agriculture, and 1105 million livres (obtained from $1000(1 - q^2)/(1 - q + q^2)$) instead of 1000 million livres to manufacturing. Eltis [17] considers that agriculture receives a further 552.5 million livres from manufacturing for sales of raw materials at the end of the year, since half of the 1105 million livres manufacturing receives is assumed to be put aside by manufacturing for its advance. However, agriculture spends six-tenths of the 842 million livres it receives from the zigzags or 505 million livres on manufactured products and has to pay 1000 million livres in rent. Agriculture therefore has a financial deficit of 110.5 million livres (i.e., $842 + 552.5 - 505 - 1000$). Following Quesnay and Mirabeau, Eltis assumes that half the deficiency is met by landowners who accept lower rents than those previously agreed. Then half of the 110.5 million livres has to be met by a fall in the annual advance of agriculture from 1000 to 945 million livres, since Eltis considers that agriculture must sell its advance for the next year to get enough money to pay the rent. The economy has to start the next year with 945 million livres of agricultural advance and the same amount of rent, which implies that agricultural products are only 1890 million livres. It can be shown that in this way the economy declines eventually at a rate of 5.5 per cent per annum.

Naturally questions may arise about the above arguments put forward by Eltis to explain Quesnay's theory of economic growth and decline. When $q = 0.4$, the *Tableau*'s zigzags bring 1105 million livres to manufacturing, and manufacturing spends four-tenths of it or 442 million livres on agricultural

---

[39] The existence of original advances is dismissed.

products in zigzags, so that at the end of the year manufacturing has 663 million livres of money. Why does manufacturing not spend the whole 663 million livres, instead of only 552.5 million livres, on agricultural products at the end of the year? Since manufacturing need not pay rent to the landowners, there is no reason for it to keep money unutilized. Eltis insisted that a part of the annual advance of agriculture has to be sold, i.e., capital must be decumulated in agriculture, when agriculture has a financial deficit. Since a financial deficit means that agriculture has unsold products which were originally intended to be sold, however, it implies the accumulation of an unintended stock of products and not necessarily the decumulation of capital to be advanced. To get enough money to pay the rent, therefore, it is enough to sell these products originally intended to be sold, and it is not necessary to sell products which are intended to be advanced.

If manufacturing spends all the money it does not spend in zigzags, i.e., 663 million livres, at the end of the year on agricultural products, agriculture can pay 1000 million livres rent after it spends in zigzags 505 million livres on manufactured products, since $842 + 663 - 505 = 1000$. The propensity to consume agricultural products lower than 0.5 does not cause any financial deficit for agriculture and the economy can continue to produce an unchanged amount of agricultural and manufactured products. Incidentally, manufacturing has to sell 1105 million livres of the manufactured products in the zigzags while it produces only 1000 million livres of manufactured products, if $R = 1000$ million livres and $q = 0.4$. In the course of the zigzags, therefore, manufacturing has to export some of the agricultural products it bought so as to import the additional manufactured products necessary to carry on the zigzags. This point was already pointed out in our consideration of Table 2.5.

Similarly, we cannot accept Eltis's [17] argument that agriculture has a financial surplus and the economy grows eventually at 4.2 per cent when $q = 0.6$. Eltis considered that agriculture receives 1105 million livres in the *Tableau*'s zigzags, spends 442 million livres there on manufactured products and receives 421 million livres from manufacturing at the end of the year. Since manufacturing receives merely 842 million livres in the zigzags and spends 505 million livres there, however, how can manufacturing spend 421 million livres at the end of the year? If manufacturing spends all the money it has, i.e., 337 million livres (obtained by 842×0.4), on agricultural products at the end of the year, agriculture has neither surplus nor deficit, since $1105 + 337 - 442 = 1000$. Manufacturing need not buy more than 337 million livres from agriculture at the end of the year, since it has already bought enough agricultural products in the course of the zigzags, so as to advance the raw materials (500) and feed the laborers (300), since $500 + 300 < 505 + 337$.[40]

In spite of Eltis's efforts, therefore, we have to conclude that Quesnay's doctrine of economic growth and expenditure patterns cannot be rationally explained by the use of the original *Tableau* with zigzags.[41] As Eltis pointed out, many developing countries today face precisely the same conditions in which Quesnay analyzed the problems involved in achieving economic growth. We cannot, however, blame these countries for adopting policies of favoring manufacturing at the expense of agriculture, at least from the point of view of Quesnay's physiocratic doctrine of economic growth.

References

[1] Anderson, R.K., and A. Takayama, "Devaluation, the Specie Flow Mechanism and the Steady State", *Review of Economic Studies*, 44(1977), pp. 347–361.
[2] Barna, T., "Quesnay's *Tableau* in Modern Guise", *Economic Journal*, 85(1975), pp. 485–496.
[3] Barna, T., "Quesnay's Model of Economic Development", *European Economic Review*, 8(1976), pp. 315–338.
[4] Bauer, S., "Quesnay's *Tableau Économique*", *Economic Journal*, 5(1895), pp. 1–21.
[5] Blaug, M., *Economic Theory in Retrospect*, Cambridge University Press, 1978.
[6] Bowley, M., "Some Seventeenth Century Contributions to the Theory of Value", *Economica*, 30(1963), pp. 122–139.
[7] Bowley, M., *Studies in the History of Economic Theory before 1870*, Macmillan, 1973.
[8] Cantillon, R., *Essai sur la nature du commerce en general*, H. Higgs, ed., and tr., Macmillan, 1931.
[9] Chipman, J.S., "A Survey of the Theory of International Trade, 1", *Econometrica*, 33(1965), pp. 477–519.
[10] Colie, R.L., "Locke, John", *International Encyclopedia of Social Sciences*, 9, pp. 464–471, D.L. Sills, ed., Macmillan, 1968.
[11] Dornbusch, R.S., S. Fischer and P.A. Samuelson, "Comparative Advantage, Trade and Payments in a Ricardian Model with a Continuum of Goods", *American Economic Review*, 67(1976), pp. 823–839.
[12] Dornbusch, R.S., and M. Mussa, "Consumption, Real Balances and the Hoarding Function", *International Economic Review*, 16(1975), pp. 415–421.
[13] Eagly, R.V., "A Physiocratic Model of Dynamic Equilibrium", *Journal of Political Economy*, 77(1969), pp. 66–84.
[14] Eagly, R.V. *The Structure of Classical Economic Theory*, Oxford University Press, 1974.

---

[40] Actually, we have to understand that manufacturing sold back 42 million livres of agricultural products to buy back 42 million livres of manufactured products in the course of the *Tableau*'s zigzags. Similarly, agriculture has to sell 42 million livres of manufactured products to buy back 42 million livres of agricultural products in zigzags, since otherwise it sold 1442 (i.e., $1105 + 337$) million livres of agricultural products and the remaining 558 (i.e., $2000 - 1442$) million livres of agricultural products are not enough to advance 600 million livres of agricultural products to the laborers. We have to say that the original *Tableau* with zigzags is very clumsy and inconvenient in this respect.

[41] See Shibata [36] and Watanabe [42, pp. 341–398].

[15] Ekelund, R.B., and R.F. Hébert, *A History of Economic Theory and Method*, McGraw-Hill, 1983.

[16] Eltis, W.A., "François Quesnay: A Reinterpretation 1. The *Tableau Économique*", *Oxford Economic Papers*, 27(1975), pp. 167–200.

[17] Eltis, W.A., "François Quesnay: A Reinterpretation 2. The Theory of Economic Growth", *Oxford Economic Papers*, 27(1975), pp. 327–351.

[18] Engels, F., "Herrn Eugen Dühring Unwälzung der Wissenschaft", (1878), *Karl Marx Friedrich Engels Werke*, 20, pp. 1–303, Berlin, Dietz Verlag, 1962.

[19] Foley, V., "An Origin of the Tableau Economique", *History of Political Economy*, 5(1973), pp. 121–150.

[20] Hatori, T., "John Locke no Seijitetsugaku to Keizairiron (John Locke's System of Political and Economic Thoughts), II", *Shogaku-Ronshu* (Fukushima University Journal of Commerce, Economics and Economic History), 22–3(1953), pp. 82–125.

[21] Hishiyama, I., "The Tableau Economique of Quesnay", *Kyoto University Economic Review*, 30–1(1960), pp. 1–45.

[22] Hume, D., *Writings on Economics*, E. Rotwein, ed., Nelson, 1955.

[23] Kemp, M.C., *The Pure Theory of International Trade*, Prentice-Hall, 1964.

[24] Kobayashi, N., *Keizaigakushi Chosakushu* (Collected works on the History of Economics), 3, Miraisha, 1976.

[25] Kuczynski, M., and R.L. Meek, eds., *Quesnay's Tableau Économique*, Macmillan, 1972.

[26] Law, J., *Money and Trade Considered*, Kelley, 1966.

[27] Leigh, A.H., "John Locke and the Quantity Theory of Money", *History of Political Economy*, 6(1974), pp. 200–219.

[28] Locke, J., *Works*, 5, Scientia Verlag Aalen, 1963.

[29] McCulloch, J.R., ed., *Early English Tracts on Commerce*, Cambridge University Press, 1954.

[30] Meek, R.L., *The Economics of Physiocracy*, Allen and Unwin, 1962.

[31] Mill, J.S., *Principles of Political Economy*, Longmans, Green and Co., 1909.

[32] Patinkin, D., *Money, Interest and Prices*, Row, Peterson and Co., 1956.

[33] Phillips, A., "The *Tableau Economique* as a simple Leontief Model", *Quarterly Journal of Economics*, 69(1955), pp. 137–144.

[34] Ricardo, D., *On the Principles of Political Economy and Taxation*, Cambridge University Press, 1951.

[35] Samuelson, P.A., "Quesnay's Tableau Economique as a Theorist would Formulate it Today", *Classical and Marxian Political Economy*, pp. 45–78, I. Brandley and M. Howard, eds., Macmillan, 1982.

[36] Shibata, K., "Quesnay no Keizaihyo no Nazo nitsuite (On the Mystery of Quesnay's Tableau Economique)", *Yamaguchi Journal of Economics*, 7–5(1956), pp. 1–10.

[37] Smith, A., *An Inquiry into the Nature and Causes of the Wealth of Nations*, Oxford Economic University Press, 1983.

[38] Spiegel, H.W., *The Growth of Economic Thought*, Duke University Press, 1983.

[39] Staley, C.E., "Hume and Viner on the International Adjustment Mechanism", *History of Political Economy*, 8(1976), pp. 252–265.

[40] Vaughn, K.I., *John Locke*, University of Chicago Press, 1980.

[41] Viner, J., *Studies in the Theory of International Trade*, Harper, 1937.

[42] Watanabe, T., *Sosetsusha no Keizaigaku* (Economics of Founders), Miraisha, 1961.

[43] Yokoyama, M., *Junoshugi Bunseki* (Analysis of Physiocracy), Iwanami, 1955.

CHAPTER 3

ADAM SMITH AND THE FORMATION OF CLASSICAL ECONOMICS

1. *The Wealth of Nations*

Adam Smith (1723–1790) was the founder of the classical school of economics. Although classical economics was later developed by Ricardo and Marx insisted that he was the sole successor to it, Smith's economic theory was not strictly succeeded by the labor theory of value of Ricardo and Marx and it is much more similar to modern neo-classical economics. There remain, however, some important ideas presented by Smith but not yet fully developed by neo-classical economic theory. This is why we should study the economics of Adam Smith carefully.

After a brief description of the life and early writings of Adam Smith, we shall explain the content of *The Wealth of Nations* in this section. Section 2 is devoted to a critical review of Samuelson's mathematical model of Smith's economic theory, which will show what aspects of Smith's theory remain to be discussed from the point of view of modern economic theory. In section 3, Smith's theory of value and that of natural price, particularly his theory of the natural rate of wage, will be considered from the point of view of modern theories of economic growth and human capital, from which it will be concluded that Smith's theory is not properly developed by the Ricardo–Marx theory of embodied labor value. The last two sections are devoted to discussing Smith's two theorems on the division of labor, firstly that the division of labor is limited by the extent of the market, and secondly that capital accumulation is necessary for the division of labor.

Adam Smith was born in Kircaldy, Scotland, in 1723 and studied at Glasgow University (1737–1740) and Balliol College, Oxford (1740–1746). He began to deliver lectures on literature at Edinburgh in 1748, became Professor of Logic at Glasgow in 1751 and was transferred to the chair of Moral Philosophy in 1752. *The Theory of Moral Sentiments* was published in 1759, and his *Lectures on Jurisprudence* at Glasgow are available, having been compiled from the notes of his students. He resigned his chair in 1763 and visited France (1763–1766) as traveling tutor to the young Duke of Buccleuch. *The Wealth of Nations* was begun in France, where he met with and was influenced by the French physiocrats, and was published in 1776. He died in 1790.

The early writings of Adam Smith include "Principles which lead and direct philosophical Enquiries, illustrated by the History of Astronomy" (Smith [31, pp. 30–108]), which shows Smith's wide knowledge of Newton's astronomy and mechanics. Indeed, astronomy occupies a very important place in Smith's system of sciences. As Jaffé [10] pointed out, Smith drew an analogy between natural philosophy or natural science which explains "the great phenomena of nature, the revolutions of the heavenly bodies, eclipses, comets, thunder, lightning and other extraordinary meteors" on the one hand, and moral philosophy, which we would rather call social or behavioral science, on the other. Smith argued that after natural philosophy showed the example of "a systematical arrangement of different observations connected by a few common principles, . . . something of the same kind was attempted in morals."[1]

The Theory of Moral Sentiments is a book on ethics, but it is the foundation of Smith's system of moral sciences, including political economy. Smith's ethical theory was greatly influenced by the theories of the Stoics and David Hume, and he critically developed the theory of non-intellectualistic moral sentiments of his teacher at Glasgow, F. Hutcheson. Morality is explained by the existence of sympathy to others of self-interested men and the impartial spectator within one's breast. Smith conceived a man who stoically controls self-interest to be approved by the impartial spectator. One can draw an analogy between the principle of gravity which governs the mutual relationship among things in Newtonian mechanics and that of moral sentiments which regulates the social relationship among self-interested men. As in the case of gravity, the effects of the sentiments depend on the distance.

> The sentiments weaken progressively as one moves from one's immediate family to one's intimate friends, to one's neighbors in a small community, to fellow-citizens in a great city, to the members in general of one's own country, to foreigners, to mankind taken in the large, to the inhabitants, if any, of distant planets. (Viner [38, p. 80].)

Smith's theory of political economy is already developed in his *Lectures on Jurisprudence*. He insisted that division of labor is necessary to increase national wealth and that exchanges and the system of prices are necessary as the division of labor develops. There is, however, no reference to the existence

---

[1]Smith [33, pp. 767, 768]. See also Thomson [37].

of profits in his analysis of the system of prices. It was not until the publication of *The Wealth of Nations*, after his return from France, that Smith gave a place to profits in his system of political economy.

The Wealth of Nations, or, more precisely, *An Inquiry into the Nature and Causes of the Wealth of Nations*, starts with the declaration that wealth consists not of gold and silver but of labor products, i.e., the famous opening sentence in the Introduction and Plan of the Work, "The annual labour of every nation is the fund which originally supplies it with all the necessaries and conveniences of life which it annually consumes, and which consist always, either in the immediate produce of that labour, or in what is purchased with that produce from other nations" (Smith [32, p. 10]). The supply per head of these necessaries and conveniences of life, therefore, "must in every nation be regulated by two different circumstances; first by the skill, dexterity, and judgement with which its labour is generally applied; and, secondly, by the proportion between the number of those who are employed in useful labour, and that of those who are not so employed" (Smith [33, p. 10]). The concept of the division of labor, one of the greatest contributions made by *The Wealth of Nations* to economic science, is concerned with this first 'circumstance', i.e., the productivity of labor. As we discuss later, the second circumstance has much to do with the accumulation of capital, through the distinction of useful labor and productive labor.

The Wealth of Nations consists of five Books, i.e.,

Book I: Of the Causes of Improvement in the productive Powers of Labour, and of the Order according to which its Produce is naturally distributed among the different Ranks of the People.
Book II: Of the Nature, Accumulation, and Employment of Stock.
Book III: Of the different Progress of Opulence in different Nations.
Book IV: Of Systems of political Oeconomy.
Book V: Of the Revenue of the Sovereign or Commonwealth.

An outline of each Book now follows.

Since "the greatest improvement in the productive powers of labour, and the greater part of the skill, dexterity, and judgement with which it is any where directed, or applied, seem to have been the effects of the division of labour" (Smith [33, p. 13]), Book I starts with the famous exposition of the division of labor in the production of pins and that of nails in Chapter I. It is insisted "that the Division of Labour is limited by the Extent of the Market" in Chapter III, and Chapter IV discusses "the origin and use of money," since people have to exchange their products as the division of labor established and a commodity is chosen as money to avoid the inconvenience of barter trades.

If exchanges of commodities are necessary to develop the division of labor, it is important to see what determines the ratio of exchange, i.e., the price of commodities. Chapter VI "Of the component Parts of the Price of Commodities" insists on the relevance of the embodied labor theory of value "in that early and rude state of society which precedes both the accumulation of stock and the appropriation of land" (Smith [33, p. 65]), by using the famous example of beaver and deer. It is, however, only in such a special situation that Smith insists on the embodied labor theory of value to which Ricardo and Marx later attached so much importance. Smith has also the commanding labor theory of value that "it was not by gold or by silver, but by labour, that all the wealth of the world was originally purchased; and its value, to those who possess it and who want to exchange it for some new productions, is precisely equal to the quantity of labour which it can enable them to purchase or command" (Smith [33, p. 48]). Although it may be interesting as a measure of economic welfare,[2] this is concerned not with the determinant of price, but rather with the measure of value.

If we leave the "early and rude state of society" and consider a modern society where all land is private property and stocks are used in production, profits should be left to those employers who use their own stocks after wages are paid to employees and rents are paid to landowners. The price of a commodity consists of three parts: wages, rents and profits. "Wages, profits, and rent, are the three original sources of all revenues as well as of all exchangeable value" (Smith [33, p. 69]). It should be noted that a place is given to profits alongside those of rents and wages in the distribution of products. The existence of profit implies that the commanding labor is not identical to the embodied labor and the latter is no longer the determinant of price. Unlike the former, furthermore, it is not the measure of value.

Chapter VII "Of the natural and market Price of Commodities" discusses the determination of the price of commodities, which consists of the three parts, wages, rents and profits. There is an ordinary or average rate of wages, rents and profits which is regulated by the general circumstances of society. Smith calls these rates the natural rates.

> When the price of any commodity is neither more nor less than what is sufficient to pay the rent of the land, the wages of the labour, and the profits of the stock employed in raising, preparing, and bringing it to market, according to their natural rates, the commodity is then sold for what may be called its natural price. (Smith [33, p. 72].)

---

[2] Blaug [3, pp. 51–54], Bowley [5, pp. 113, 116], Kimura [11], and Okada [21, pp. 116–120].

The effectual demand is then defined as the demand from those who are willing to pay the natural price.

The natural price is the central price to which actual market prices are attracted. When the quantity of a commodity which is brought to market falls short of the effectual demand, the market price will rise more or less above the natural price, each component part of the price must rise above its natural rate, and more land, labor and stock are used in raising, preparing and bringing to market the commodity so that the quantity brought to market is sufficient to supply the effectual demand. This implies, then, that the market price falls to the natural price and each component part to its natural rate, respectively. Similarly, when the quantity brought to market exceeds the effectual demand, the market price sinks below the natural price and each component part falls below its respective natural rate, with the result that the quantities of labor, land and stock used are diminished, the quantity of the commodity is equalized to the effectual demand, and the natural price is regained with the natural rates of its component parts.

This equilibrium theory of Chapter VII was evaluated very highly by Schumpeter [30, p. 189] as the one which "points toward Say and, through the latter's work, to Walras." Smith's equilibrium theory is, however, "rudimentary" and falls, of course, short of Walras's general equilibrium. The natural rates of wages, rents and profits are rightly considered to reflect respectively the demand and supply conditions of labor, land and stock, since they are defined as high in a progressive society and low in a declining one. Smith emphasized, however, only the one-way causal relationship from the natural rates of wages, rents and profits to the natural price of commodities, and the mutually dependent relationships between them are not sufficiently pursued by the use of the general equilibrium theory. For example, Smith argued that "the increase in the wages of labour necessarily increases the price of many commodities, by increasing that part of it which resolves itself into wages" (Smith [33, p. 104]). It was Ricardo [23, p. 46] who criticized Smith from the point of view of the general equilibrium theory, arguing that an increase in wages necessarily implies a fall in the rate of profit and that only the price of labor intensive goods would rise while the price of capital intensive goods would fall.

While Book I of *The Wealth of Nations* is a theory of prices and distribution, Book II is a theory of capital and development. In the Introduction of Book II, it is emphasized that the accumulation of stock is necessary for the development of the division of labor.

The first problematic chapter in Book II is Chapter III "On the Accumulation of Capital, or of productive and unproductive Labour". Productive labor is, firstly, defined as labor "which adds to the value of the subject upon which it is bestowed" (Smith [33, p. 330]), i.e., labor which brings forth profits. Secondly, it is described as labor which "fixes and realizes itself in some particular subject or vendible commodity, which lasts for some time at least after that labour is past" (Smith [33, p. 330]), i.e., storable labor. In other words, it is labor which is maintained by capital (i.e., the stock which is used to obtain a profit) and takes time to realize its result. The concept of productive labor implies that capital is productive.

On the other hand, unproductive labor is labor which, like the service of servants, is maintained by revenue, i.e., rents and profits, which does not bring forth profits, and which perishes instantaneously. Unproductive labor is also useful labor, and constitutes a part of the annual labor of a nation which originally supplies it with all the necessities and conveniences of life it annually consumes. As the proportion of the products used to maintain productive labor is larger, however, the larger can be the next year's quantity of products, since productive labor alone can replace capital and increase it.

The second problematic chapter in Book II is Chapter V "Of the different Employment of Capitals" where Smith insists on the natural order of investment. It is the order of agriculture, manufacture, domestic trade and foreign trade, which constitute the theoretical foundation of Smith's arguments on economic history and economic policy in Book III and Book IV of *The Wealth of Nations*. Smith's explanation of this important theory is, however, much confused, as we shall see in section 5. According to Kobayashi [12, chapter 7], "it is almost entirely bankrupt." In view of the important role assigned to this theory in the system of *The Wealth of Nations*, we shall try to reconstruct it on the basis of Smith's second theorem of division of labor that capital accumulation is the prerequisite to the development of the division of labor.

Following static and dynamic economic theories in Book I and Book II, Book III explains the economic history of various nations. Its basic point of view is, of course, the natural order of things, agriculture, manufacture and foreign commerce, and it is concluded as follows. "Though this natural order of things must have taken place in some degree in every such society, it has, in all the modern states of Europe, been, in many respects, entirely inverted" (Smith [32, p. 380]).

Book IV is Smith's theory of economic policies. On the basis of the arguments in Books I to III, Smith insists on *laissez-faire*, and criticizes mercantilism (the commercial System) and physiocracy (the agricultural System). The criticism against the former is particularly thorough and is concluded as follows.

It cannot be very difficult to determine who have been the contrivers of this whole mercantile system; not the consumers, we may believe, whose interest has been entirely neglected; but the producers whose interest has been so carefully attended to; and among this latter class our merchants and manufacturers have been by far the principal architects. (Smith [33, p. 661].)

Incidentally, the famous "invisible hand" is discussed in Chapter II, Book IV.

Every individual necessarily labours to render the annual revenue of the society as great as he can. He generally, indeed, neither intends to promote the publick interest, nor knows how much he is promoting it. By preferring the support of domestic to that of foreign industry, he intends only his own security; and by directing that industry in such a manner as its produce may be of the greatest value, he intends only his own gain, and he is in this, as in many other cases, led by an invisible hand to promote an end which was no part of his intention. (Smith [33, p. 456].)

In the beginning of Book IV, Smith argued that the object of political economy is, firstly, to provide a plentiful revenue for the people, and secondly, to supply the state with sufficient revenue. Book V is concerned with this second object of political economy, i.e., public finance. The expenses of the state, the revenue of the state, and public debts are discussed. Cheap government is insisted on and the role of the state is limited to defence, justice, public works such as road construction, and education.

2. Samuelson's mathematical model

Samuelson, who was very critical in his mathematical reformulation of economics of Ricardo and Marx [27, pp. 341–422], vindicated Adam Smith strongly in a similar reformulation [28] of the economics of *The Wealth of Nations*. He concluded that: (1) Smith's value-added accounting which was attacked by Marx as involving vicious circle reasoning[3] is shown to be correct by Leontief–Sraffa modeling; (2) Smith's pluralistic supply and demand analysis in terms of all three components of wages, rents, and profits is a valid and valuable anticipation of general equilibrium modeling; (3) though Smith's vision of growth is isomorphic with the models of Ricardo, Malthus, and Marx, Smith is less guilty than these three of believing in a rigid subsistence wage supply of labor in the short and intermediate run.

[3] Marx [15, pp. 366–393]. See also Hollander [9, pp. 144–147].

Samuelson starts with Smith's "early rude state" where land is redundant and free and output and input are simultaneous so that there is no need to advance capital. Assuming a linear production process for each good i, $i=1,\ldots,n$, we have equilibrium conditions

$$L-\sum_j a_{0j}q_j=0 \tag{1}$$

$$-m_iL+q_i-\sum_j a_{ij}q_j=0, \quad i=1,\ldots,n, \tag{2}$$

where L is the sustainable amount of labor population, a_{0j} is the input coefficient of labor in the production of good j, q_j is the level of output of good j, m_i is the input coefficient of good i to reproduce labor power, and a_{ij} is the input coefficient of good i to produce good j. Demand and supply are equalized in labor markets by (1) and in n good markets by (2). The system of equations (1) and (2) can be solved for $L, q_1, \ldots, q_n$, when its Jacobian is zero.[4]

Competition assures the price–cost relation that

$$p_j=wa_{0j}+\sum_i p_i a_{ij}, \quad j=1,\ldots,n, \tag{3}$$

where p_j is the price of good j and w is the market rate of wage, or

$$p=wa_0(I-a)^{-1}, \tag{4}$$

where p is an n vector of p_i, a_0 is an n vector of a_{0j}, a is an n by n matrix of a_{ij}, i, $j=1,\ldots,n$, and I is the n by n identity matrix. From (2) we have

$$(I-a)q=mL, \tag{5}$$

where q is an n vector of q_j and m is an n vector of m_i, $i=1,\ldots,n$. Pre-multiply p to (5) and post-multiply q $(I-a)$ to (4). Then, from (1), we have

$$(pm)(a_0q)=wa_0q, \quad pm=w. \tag{6}$$

The market wage is at the subsistence level. In view of (4), furthermore, we have

$$a_0(I-a)^{-1}m=1. \tag{7}$$

Suppose that, from a technical progress, some set of elements of a_0, a, m decrease. In view of the fact that the Leontief inverse can be expressed as a convergent series,

$$(I-a)^{-1}=I+a+a^2+\cdots, \tag{8}$$

[4]Alternatively, when the Jacobian of (2), with (1) being substituted for L, is zero.

we have

$$a_0(I-a)^{-1}m<1. \tag{9}$$

From (4), this implies that $pm<w$, the market wage is higher than the subsistence level.

With the market wage w higher than the subsistence level pm, the labor population grows according to the Malthusian relation, which Samuelson writes as

$$(L_{t+1}-L_t)/L_t=f\left[1-\sum_j(p_j/w)m_j\right], \quad f[0]=0,$$
$$f'[\cdot]>0, \quad f[\cdot]\geq-1, \tag{10}$$

where t denotes time and L_t is the labor population at t. Eventually, land becomes scarce. Samuelson then proceeds to the case where land is not free and there is a positive rent of land. However, we shall discuss this case by a linear programming model, which is slightly different from, but easier than Samuelson's non-linear programming model.

Still assuming that inputs and outputs are simultaneous, let us suppose that there are only two goods, the first good being consumed by both laborers and landowners, while the second good is consumed by landowners alone. Let us consider the maximization of the net output of the first good, being subject to any given net output of the second good and constraints for land and labor supplies. Instead of the neo-classical production function with a continuous substitution of labor and land which Samuelson considered, we analyze a linear programming model of production where each good has different alternative linear production processes.

The problem is to maximize D_1 being subject to

$$D_1+\sum_j a_{12j}Y_j\leq\sum_i X_i, \tag{11}$$

$$\bar{D}_2+\sum_i a_{21i}X_i\leq\sum_j Y_j, \tag{12}$$

$$\sum_i a_{01i}X_i+\sum_j a_{02j}Y_j\leq L, \tag{13}$$

and

$$\sum_i b_{01i}X_i+\sum_j b_{02j}Y_j\leq T, \tag{14}$$

where D_1 is the net output of good 1, $\bar{D}_2$ is the given net output of good 2, a_{12j} is the input coefficient of good 1 in the production of good 2 by its jth process, Y_j

is the amount of the second good produced by its jth process, L is the total amount of available labor, X_i is the output of good 1 by its ith process, a_{01i} is the labor input coefficient in the production of good 1 by its ith process, b_{02j} is the land input coefficient in the production of good 2 by its jth process, T is the total amount of available land, and so on. Conditions (11) to (14) imply, of course, that demand does not exceed supply in the market of good 1, good 2, labor and land, respectively.

If we denote the Lagrangean multipliers corresponding to (11), (12), (13) and (14), as p, q, w and r, respectively, we have as part of the conditions for the maximization,

$$p - a_{21i}q - a_{01i}w - b_{01i}r = 0, \tag{15}$$

for any i such that $X_i > 0$, and

$$q - q_{12j}p - a_{02j}w - b_{02j}r = 0, \tag{16}$$

for any j such that $Y_j > 0$. From the dual theorem of linear programming, furthermore, we have

$$pD_1 = wL + rT - q\bar{D}_2, \tag{17}$$

since $p = 1$ in view of another condition for the maximization.

From the well-known property of Lagrangean multipliers, we can consider p, q, w and r as the price of the first good, that of the second good, wage and rent to be established in a competitive market (Lange [13]). This is the linear programming version of Smith's invisible hand doctrine, as interpreted by Samuelson to the effect that self interest, under perfect conditions of competition, can organize a society's production efficiently. From (15) and (16) we can solve p and q respectively as the summation of direct and indirect wage and rent components. This can also be seen from (17). Smith's resolution of each price and national income into wage and rent components was thus essentially correct, despite doubts expressed by Marx [15].

Samuelson finally discusses the case of realistic time phasing of production, where inputs and outputs are not simultaneous so that capital has to be advanced. He merely considered, however, the case of a long run equilibrium where the real wage is at the subsistence level and the rate of profit is exogenously given at such a low rate that there is no accumulation of capital, with the result that the rate of profit is not explained endogenously. We have to, therefore, discuss using our own model, this time not to simplify Samuelson's argument but to supplement it. To make the story as simple as possible, let us ignore inter-industry relations and assume that each good is produced directly from the use of labor and land. Instead, a new additional condition is added that wages must be paid before the completion of the production. This implies that the wages fund which consists of the stock of the only wage good in the model, i.e., the good 1, must be advanced as capital to which profit is paid after the completion of production.[5]

Conditions (11) and (12) are now simplified into

$$D_1 \leqq \sum_i X_i \tag{18}$$

and

$$\bar{D}_2 \leqq \sum_j Y_j. \tag{19}$$

The output D_1 is to be maximized being subject to (13), (14), (18) and (19), while (13) is assumed to be satisfied with the quality. The market rate of wage is given by $\bar{X}/L$, where $\bar{X}$ is the wages fund available at the beginning of the production period. Again, let the Lagrangean multipliers corresponding to (13), (14), (18) and (19) be w, r, p and q. We still have (17) where, however, wL is no longer the wage income but the labor's contribution to production realized at the end of the production period. Since $\bar{X}$ is already paid as wage, $wL - \bar{X}$ accrues as profit to the capitalists who advanced the wage cost. Now (17) can be written as

$$pD_1 + q\bar{D}_2 = p\bar{X} + (wL - p\bar{X}) + rT, \tag{20}$$

which implies that "of the produce of land one part replaces the capital of the farmer, the other pays his profit and the rent of the landlord, and thus constitutes a revenue both to the owner of this capital, as the profits of his stock, and to some other person, as the rent of his land" (Smith [33, p. 332]). On the other hand, (15) is now rewritten as

$$p - a_{01i}v(1 + i) - b_{01i}r = 0, \tag{21}$$

where $v = \bar{X}/L$ is the market rate of wage and $i = (wL - \bar{X})/\bar{X}$ is the rate of profit. This implies that the price p resolves itself into three component parts, wage, profit and rent.

If the market wage exceeds the subsistence level, the labor population L grows. On the other hand, capital accumulates i.e., $\bar{X}$ increases if the rate of profit i is higher than a certain minimum rate at which capitalists and landowners will spend all their incomes on current consumption. An increase in the labor population L reduces the market wage v when $\bar{X}$ is given, while an increase in capital $\bar{X}$ reduces the rate of profit i, though increases v, when L is given. Eventually, both population and capital cease to grow and we shall arrive at the long-run equilibrium which Samuelson considered.

Although some important aspects of *The Wealth of Nations*, i.e., Smith's

---

[5] For the wages fund doctrine of Smith, see Blaug [3, p. 45] and Schumpeter [30, pp. 269, 667].

correct value added accounting, his pluralistic supply and demand analysis, his invisible hand doctrine, etc., are rigorously formulated by Samuelson's non-linear programming model, of which our linear programming model is merely a simplified version, certainly there are some others, equally important, which escaped from and are not covered by Samuelson's mathematical model. In this respect, two remarks are in order.

According to Samuelson, Smith is to be vindicated as less guilty than Ricardo and Marx of believing in a rigid subsistence wage in the short-run and Smith's transient rise in wage rates is a credit to his model's realism. In Samuelson's mathematical model, this is considered as Smith's Malthusian relation (10) in which the market wage w deviates from the subsistence level. As for the market wage, however, even Ricardo did acknowledge it clearly. "Notwithstanding the tendency of wages to conform to their natural rate, their market rate may, in an improving society, for an indefinite period, be constantly above it; ... if the increase of capital be gradual and constant, the demand for labor may give a continued stimulus to an increase of people" (Ricardo [23, pp. 94–95]). What distinguishes Smith from Ricardo and Marx is that Smith considers not the market rate but the natural rate of wage as well as natural rate of profit higher in a growing economy than in the stationary economy, irrespective of their absolute levels of output. Unfortunately, Samuelson did not discuss the behavior of wages and profit in a growing economy using his rigorous mathematical model. Neither can our supplementary model help us in this respect, since the wages fund merely explains a market wage in the short-run. We shall consider this problem fully in the next section.

There is another important aspect of Smith's economics which is missing in Samuelson's mathematical model, in which constant returns to scale are assumed. It is the possibility of increasing returns to scale due to the division of labor which is limited by the extent of the market. From what Smith discussed, as a matter of fact, Samuelson considered only what the modern mathematical programming technique can do better with the basic assumption of convexity. While Samuelson considered a neo-classical production function in which output is a linear homogeneous function of input of factors of production, Barkai [2] graphically analyzed a Smithian macro model of growth on the basis of a non-homogeneous production function

$$Y = Y(K, N, T(t, m)),\qquad(22)$$

where Y, K, N and T are respectively the aggregate output, capital, labor and the state of technology. The state of technology is considered to be a function of the extent of the market $m = m(Y)$, such that $m'(Y) > 0$, and of the technical efficiency of equipment $t = t(K/N)$, such that $t'(K/N) > 0$. There remains, however, the question of how increasing returns and competition are compatible in Smith's microeconomics. Section 4 will be devoted to discussing this problem.

3. Wages and profit in a growing economy

The traditional interpretation of Adam Smith's theory of value is that commodities exchange in proportion to embodied labor, which equals commandable labor in pre-capitalist society while they do not exchange in proportion to the former labor which is now smaller than the latter in modern capitalistic society.[6] It is well known that the Ricardo–Marx embodied labor theory of value was developed from critical evaluations of Smith's theory of value.[7]

If we read *The Wealth of Nation* with a growth economy in mind, however, it seems that Smith has a model of growth, or at least suggests, a growth model, according to which the relation between embodied and commandable labors can be seen from a different point of view. Embodied and commandable labors are identical in a stationary state, irrespective of whether it is a pre-capitalist society where labor is the only factor of production or an economy with capital where, however, the rate of profit is zero. Commandable labor is, on the other hand, larger than embodied labor in a growing economy where the rate of profit is positive. Smith argues that the surplus appears in such an economy not only as profit in a sector where a commodity is produced from the input of labor but also in the higher natural rate of wage in a sector where labor (power) is produced from the input of commodities. This latter surplus, which is also due to the difference between embodied and commandable labors, cannot be explained by the Ricardo–Marx theory of embodied labor value in which the natural price of labor or the value of labor power is defined so as to just reproduce labor (power) expended in production. In other words, the embodied labor theory of value can be applied only in a stationary state where the rate of profit is zero.

Smith begins his arguments in Chapter VI, Book I of *The Wealth of Nations* with a consideration of pre-capitalist society.

In that early and rude state of society which precedes both the accumulation of stock and the appropriation of land, the proportion between the

[6] Hollander [9, p. 117] and Meek [19, p. 81].
[7] Ricardo [23, pp. 11, 13–14] and Marx [17, pp. 71–72].

quantities of labor necessary for acquiring different objects seems to be the only circumstance which can afford any rule for exchanging them for one another. If among a nation of hunters, for example, it usually costs twice the labor to kill a beaver which it does to kill a deer, one beaver should naturally exchange for or be worth two deer. ... In this state of things, the whole produce of labour belongs to the labourer; and the quantity of labour commonly employed in acquiring or producing any commodity, is the only circumstance which can regulate the quantity of labour which it ought commonly to purchase, command, or exchange for. (Smith [33, p. 65].)

Let us consider an aggregate product–labor model of an economy corresponding to such an "early and rude state". Suppose one unit of aggregate labor product is produced from the input of a units of labor so that its embodied labor value is a. Similarly, if one unit of labor (power) is reproduced by the consumption of b units of labor products, its embodied labor value is b times the value of the labor product. Namely,

$$v_1 = a \tag{1}$$
$$v_2 = bv_1 = ba, \tag{2}$$

where v_1 and v_2 denote respectively the embodied labor value of the labor product and the labor (power). Since all the products belong to the laborers and no surplus value exists in the production of labor products, $v_1 = av_2$, from which it is derived that $ab = 1$ by the substitution of (1) and (2). In other words, the embodied labor value of the product a is equal to its commandable labor value $1/b$. Similarly, the embodied labor value of the labor (power) ba is equal to the commandable labor value which is by definition equal to one (Schumpeter [30, p. 188]). Namely, the system of the commandable labor values p_1, p_2 respectively of the labor product and labor (power) is

$$p_1 = ap_2 = a \tag{3}$$
$$p_2 = 1 = bp_1 = ba. \tag{4}$$

In the case of the early and rude state, the production of the labor product from the input of labor and that of the labor power from the consumption of the product should be instantaneous, since it precedes the accumulation of stock which is necessary to carry out a time consuming production (section 2 above and Samuelson [28]). Our models (1) to (4) where profit does not exist can, however, also be applied to the case of a stationary economy where production does take time. Suppose that the period of production is a unit period for both sectors so that a units of labor must be expended one period to produce one unit of product, and b units of the product must be consumed one period to produce one unit of labor (power). Let us denote the stock of the product at time t by $X(t)$ and the labor population at time t by $L(t)$. Then, from our assumptions of production coefficients a and b,

$$X(t) = bL(t+1) \tag{5}$$
$$L(t) = aX(t+1). \tag{6}$$

It is easily seen that a stationary solution $X(t) = X(t+1)$ and $L(t) = L(t+1)$ exists in (5) and (6) if and only if $ab = 1$. Of course, in a stationary state, inputs and outputs are unchanged through time, so that we can ignore the delay between them and consider them as synchronized and the production as instantaneous.

What Smith had in mind is not inconsistent with our stationary state with capital but the zero rate of profit.

> In a country which had acquired that full complement of riches which the nature of its soil and climate, and its situation with respect to other countries allowed it to acquire; which could, therefore, advance no further, and which was not going backwards, both the wages of labour and the profits of stock would probably be very low. . . . In a country fully stocked in proportion to all the business it had to transact, as great a quantity of stock would be employed in every particular branch as the nature and extent of the trade would admit. The competition, therefore, would everywhere be as great, and consequently the ordinary profit as low as possible. (Smith [33, p. 111].)[8]

Consideration of the early and rude state or the stationary state is not very interesting, since there is no possibility of economic growth (Smith [33, pp. 82—83]). Economic growth is possible if, and only if, the net capital accumulation is caused by the existence of the positive rate of profit. If the rate of profit is positive, however, Smith argues that the embodied labor no longer equals the commandable labor.

> In this state of things, the whole produce of labour does not always belong to the labourer. He must in most cases share it with the owner of the stock which employs him. Neither is the quantity of labour commonly employed in acquiring or producing any commodity, the only circumstance which can regulate the quantity which it ought commonly to purchase, command, or exchange for. An additional quantity, it is evident, must be due for the profits of the stock which advanced the wages and furnished the materials of that labour. (Smith [33, p. 67].)

[8] Of course, rent exists in such a state. We may consider, however, that our models (1) to (6) apply to the marginal land where there is no rent paid, in view of Smith's argument on the relation between price and rent (Smith [33, p. 162]).

If we ignore land and rent, therefore, Smith's natural price of a commodity is defined as the sum of wages and profit, both at the natural rate, which is defined as follows.

There is in every society or neighbourhood an ordinary or average rate both of wages and profit in every different employment of labour and stock. This rate is naturally regulated ... partly by the general circumstances of the society, their riches or poverty, their advancing, stationary, or declining condition; and partly by the particular nature of each employment. ... These ordinary or average rates may be called the natural rate of wages, profit, ... (Smith [33, p. 72].)

If a units of labor are necessary at t to produce one unit of the product at $t+1$ as in (6), the natural price of the product at $t+1$ is

$$p(t+1)=(1+r)aw(t), \tag{7}$$

where r is the natural rate of profit and $w(t)$ is the natural rate of wage at t. Similarly, the natural rate of wage at $t+1$ is

$$w(t+1)=(1+r')bp(t), \tag{8}$$

if b units of the product have to be consumed at t to produce one unit of labor (power) at $t+1$ as in (5), where r' is positive if r is positive. In other words, the natural rate of wage is higher than the subsistence level in a growing economy.

"The liberal reward of labour, therefore, as it is the necessary effect, so it is the natural symptom of increasing national wealth. The scanty maintenance of the labouring poor, on the other hand, is the natural symptom that things are at a stand, and their starving condition that they are going fast backwards" (Smith [33, p. 91]). This argument of Smith's should not be interpreted as meaning that the market rate of wage, which deviates from the natural rate, is higher in a growing economy.[9] The natural rate of wage is an average of wages for many different types of labor, which include what Smith considered as profits to be paid to human capital (Spengler [34]).

A man educated at the expence of much labour and time to any of those employments which require extraordinary dexterity and skill, may be compared to one of those expensive machines. The work which he learns to perform, it must be expected, over and above the usual wages of common

---

[9] When Smith defined the natural rate of wages and profit in Chapter VII, Book I of *The Wealth of Nations* (Smith [33, p. 72]), he footnoted that the natural rate of wage is shown in Chapter VIII, Book I [33, pp. 82–104], to be different according to whether the economy is "advancing, stationary or declining."

labour, will replace to him the whole expence of his education, with at least the ordinary profits of an equally valuable capital. (Smith [33, p. 118].)

[Fixed capital includes] the acquired and useful abilities of all the inhabitants or members of the society. The acquisition of such talents, by the maintenance of the acquirer during his education, study, or apprenticeship, always costs a real expence, which is a capital fixed and realized, as it were, in his person. .... The improved dexterity of a workman may be considered in the same light as a machine or instrument of trade which facilitates and abridges labour, and which, though it costs a certain expence, repays that expence with a profit. (Smith [33, p. 282].)

All types of labor are, however, like fixed capital, since time and costs are necessary to produce them. Profit to be paid to human capital r' cannot be lower than profit earned in the production of the labor product r, if self-employment is easily substituted for wage labor, which Smith admitted in the case of new colonies (Smith [33, p. 565], Perelman [22, p. 140]). On the other hand, r' cannot be much higher than r, if the natural rate of wage is not as high as to make the labor of slaves cheaper to masters than that of free laborers (Smith [33, p. 99]).

Suppose that profits are all invested so that all the stock of product is advanced as wages fund, i.e., $p(t)X(t)=w(t)L(t)$. Let us consider a balanced growth solution of our models (5) and (6) in which stock of product $X(t)$ and labor population $L(t)$ grow at the common rate of g. By substituting $X(t+1)=(1+g)X(t)$ and $L(t+1)=(1+g)L(t)$ into (5) and (6), we have $ab(1+g)^2=1$.

Since relative prices $p(t)/w(t)$ remain unchanged in such a steady growth path, and $w(t)$ is defined as being equal to one in order to consider the commandable labor value, (7) and (8) are reduced to a modified version of (3) and (4),

$$p=(1+r)aw=(1+r)a \tag{9}$$

$$w=1=(1+r')bp=(1+r)(1+r')ab, \tag{10}$$

where w is the natural rate of wage and p is the commandable labor value of the product, which is from (9) clearly larger than a, i.e., the embodied labor value, if r is positive. Similarly, the commandable labor value of labor (power) which is by definition equal to 1 is larger than its embodied labor value ab from (10), if r is positive. By substitution, we have from (9) and (10) $ab(1+r)(1+r')=1$. Since $ab(1+g)^2=1$, r and r' which are defined as being of the same sign are positive, if g is positive. In a steadily growing economy, the rate of profit is positive and the natural rate of wage is higher than the substitution level.[10]

Furthermore, it can be shown that $r = r'$ in such a growing economy. Since all the profits are invested, $pX(t) = wL(t)$. In view of (5), therefore, $w = pb(1 + g)$. Since $w = (1 + r')pb$ in (10), however, this implies that $r' = g$. From $(1 + g)^2 ab = 1$ and $(1 + r)(1 + r')ab = 1$, then, we arrive at $r = r' = g$.

In other words, our Smithian growth model is a von-Neumann growth model of the production of commodities by means of commodities where commodities include the labor power commodity. In the von-Neumann model, all the commodity stock expands at the constant common growth rate, relative prices remain constant, and the rate of interest equals the rate of growth. In Smithian terminology, this implies that the natural price of commodities and the natural rate of wages and profit prevail and the natural rate of wages exceeds the subsistence level by the natural rate of profit. As Smith admitted for the case of new colonies that "in our North American and West Indian colonies, not only the wages of labour, but the interest of money, and consequently the profits of stock, are higher than in England" (Smith [33, p. 109]), a high natural rate of wages and a high natural rate of profit coexist in an economy with a high rate of growth. Surpluses appear both in the production of labor products and in the production of labor power, as simultaneous causes and effects of economic growth.

In his critical evaluation of Adam Smith, Marx referred to what he thought to be Smith's definition of the "natural price of wages" (Marx [17, p. 68]; Smith [32, p. 85]). This definition, which is based on Cantillon's calculation, is unfortunately that of the natural rate of wage in a stationary economy, since it is just to maintain labor population constant. It cannot be applicable to a growing economy. With his interpretation, however, Marx argues that surplus appears only in the production of labor product as exploited from laborers," Adam Smith ... reduced profit to the appropriation of the unpaid labour of others" (Marx [17, p. 79]), since wages are at the subsistence level, i.e., $r' = 0$ in our model. Unfortunately, the rate of profit r is zero in a stationary economy where this interpretation of the natural rate of wage is applicable, if all the profit is to be invested.[11] If wages are at subsistence level, only the labor

---

[10] We may consider that this solution corresponds to an economy with which land is still redundant (Samuelson [28]). Alternatively, we may argue that the marginal labor productivity a remains unchanged in economic growth even if land is scarce, since diminishing marginal productivity is counterbalanced with increasing productivity due to the division of labor which is conditioned by the enlarging extent of the market (see section 4). In this case, our model applies to the marginal land where there is no rent paid. While all the profits are invested, all the rents paid to intra-marginal lands are consumed, i.e., expended on the labor products.

[11] If the profit is invested, the stationary economy cannot be maintained. If all the profits are consumed, it can be maintained. If capitalists are rational and not myopic, however, it is difficult to suppose that profits are all consumed in a stationary state. See Chapter 6, section 3 below.

power expended in past production is reproduced and the labor population cannot grow. An increase in the labor population, therefore, is not explained in a growing economy by the natural rate of wage as interpreted by Marx.

If the production of labor (power) is instantaneous, i.e., (5) is replaced by

$$bL(t) = X(t), \tag{11}$$

then there will be no problem. The economy grows at such a rate of g as $ab(1+g) = 1$, as contrasted to the case of (5) and (6), $ab(1+g)^2 = 1$ and it is possible that $r = g > 0$ and $r' = 0$, since $(1+r)(1+r')ab = 1$. It is clearly seen, however, that the production of labor (power) is not instantaneous, not only from Smith's arguments just referred to, but also from Marx's own (Marx [14, p. 168]). This is simply because children cannot grow instantaneously.

If production is not instantaneous, we cannot ignore it, since, unlike in the case of a stationary state, inputs and outputs cannot be regarded as synchronized in a growth economy.

Nor can we argue that the rate of wage as a market price in the sense of Marx is higher than the value of labor power (subsistence wage) in a growing economy. In Marxian economics, market price may deviate from value if, and only if, demand and supply are not equalized (Marx [16, p. 189]). On our von-Neumann equilibrium growth path, demand and supply are certainly equalized in the labor market as well as in the product market, so that market prices are equalized to values. Otherwise, the Marxian value theory can only be applied to a stationary state. On the other hand, the value of the labor power must be higher than the subsistence level if the Marxian value theory can be applicable to a growing economy.

We have to conclude that the Marxian interpretation of Smith and the Marxian theory of value do not make sense unless in a stationary economy and that Smith's natural price and natural wage are more interesting than Marxian values, according to which wages are at subsistence level, from the point of view of economic growth.

4. Division of labor and market

A.A. Young [39] evaluated Adam Smith's theorem that the division of labor which causes increasing returns depends upon the extent of the market as one of the most illuminating and fruitful generalizations in the whole literature of economics. Unfortunately, however, modern economic theory has not yet been able to utilize this wonderful theorem exhaustively.

Smith considers that the wealth of every nation is regulated by two circumstances, first, by "the skill, dexterity, and judgement with which its labour is generally applied," i.e., the labor productivity, and, secondly, by "the number of those who are employed in useful labour" (Smith [33, p. 10]). Then he emphasizes that the greatest improvement in labor productivity seems to have been the effects of the division of labor (Smith [32, p. 13]). Smith gives two different kinds of illustrations of the division of labor; one is concerned with an inter-firm division of labor or the specialisation of firms in the same industry, the extent of which is limited by the demand for the industry, while the other is concerned with the subdivision of different operations to produce a given product, the extent of which is limited by the demand for the output of the firm or the plant.

The illustration of the former division of labor is drawn from nail making in *The Wealth of Nations*.

> A smith who has been accustomed to make nails, but whose sole or principal business has not been that of a nailer, can seldom with his utmost diligence make more than eight hundred or a thousand nails in a day. I have seen several boys under twenty years of age who had never exercised any other trade but that of making nails, and who, when they exerted themselves, could make, each of them, upwards of two thousand three hundred nails in a day. The making of a nail, however, is by no means one of the simplest operations. The same person blows the bellows, stirs or mends the fire as there is occasion, heats the iron, and forges every part of the nail: In forging the head too he is obliged to change his tools. The different operations into which the making of a pin, or of a metal button, is subdivided, are all of them much more simple, and the dexterity of the person, of whose life it has been the sole business to perform them, is usually much greater. (Smith [33, p. 18].)

The difference between nail making and pin and button making, which is Smith's illustration of the latter kind of division of labor, can be explained by the theorem that the division of labor is limited by the extent of the market. Demand for the output of the plant was sufficiently large in the case of pins and buttons to justify a labor force adequate for subdivision (Hollander [9, pp. 208, 239]). Smith describes the effect of this latter kind of division of labor in the following extract.

> The trade of the pin-maker; a workman not educated to this business, nor acquainted with the use of the machinery employed in it, could scarce, perhaps, with his utmost industry, make one pin in a day, and certainly could not make twenty. But in the way in which this business is now carried on, not only the whole work is a peculiar trade, but it is divided into a number of branches, of which the greater part are likewise peculiar trades.

One man draws out the wire, another straights it, a third cuts it, a fourth points it, a fifth grinds it at the top for receiving the head; to make the head requires two or three distinct operations, to put it on, is a peculiar business, to whiten the pins is another; it is even a trade by itself to put them into the paper; and the important business of making a pin is, in this manner, divided into about eighteen distinct operations, which , in some manufactories, are all performed by distinct hands, though in others the same man will sometimes perform two or three of them. I have seen a small manufactory of this kind where ten men only were employed, ... Those ten persons could make among them upwards of forty-eight thousand pins in a day. Each person, therefore, ... might be considered as making four thousand eight hundred pins in a day. (Smith [33, pp. 14–15].)

Although Smith argues that the latter type of division of labor, i.e., the case of pin and button making, is in a more advanced stage than the former type of division of labor, i.e., the case of nail making, however, later scholars such as Young [39] and Richardson [24], who emphasized the importance of Smithian increasing returns based on the division of labor, put more emphasis on the former type of division of labor, i.e., the specialisation of industries and firms rather than on the latter type of division of labor, i.e., the subdivision of labor within a firm or a plant. One of the reasons for this seems to be the historically celebrated inconsistency between competition and increasing returns due to the internal economy of scale of a firm. Richardson, for example, argues that competition must produce concentration and, in the end, monopoly if any of the firms making identical products experiences increasing returns, and that increasing returns should be considered as the characteristic which leads to the specialization of firms in an industry in order to go along with Adam Smith, who was not troubled by the inconsistency of competition and increasing returns.[12]

Increasing returns due to the internal economy of a firm or the diminishing cost with respect to the level of output of a firm is certainly inconsistent with the assumption of the perfect competition that a firm faces an infinitely elastic demand curve for its product, even if the demand curve for the industry is downward, so that it can sell whatever amount of its product at the given market price. Such a neo-classical concept of the perfect competition may be justified in two different ways. As Cournot [7] showed, firstly, it can be considered as the limiting case of an oligopolistic industry in which firms act

---

[12] Robinson [26, pp. 336–339] argued, however, that there is no reason why such a specialisation of firms is impossible from the beginning, when the scale of industry is small, unless there are internal economies in individual firms.

non-cooperatively, when the number of the firms is infinitely large. On the other hand, it is not rational for an individual firm to act non-cooperatively as a price taker in a well-organized market with a Walrasian auctioneer who "cries" market prices and adjusts them to equalize demand and supply, unless the number of firms is infinite (Roberts and Postlewaite [25]). Alternatively, we can consider firms as price takers, if the cost of information gathering and the cost of organizing coalitions are negligible in an industry composed of a finite number of firms which act cooperatively with an infinite number of consumers (Farrell [8] and Schitovitz [29]).

In view of these justifications of the neo-classical concept of perfect competition, we have to admit that Smith's concept of competition is different. For Adam Smith, as well as for other classical economists, competition is characterized by free entry, as was emphasized by Sylos-Labini [36]. This can be seen, for example, in the following arguments of Smith's.

> The whole of the advantages and disadvantages of the different employments of labour and stock must, in the same neighbourhood, be either perfectly equal or continually tending to equality. If in the same neighbourhood, there was any employment evidently either more or less advantageous than the rest, so many people would crowd into it in the one case, and so many would desert it in the other, that its advantages would soon return to the level of other employments. This at least would be the case in a society where things were left to follow their natural course, where there was perfect liberty, and where every man was perfectly free both to chose what occupation he thought proper, and to change it as often as he thought proper. (Smith [33, p. 116].)

If entry is not free, there exists a monopoly on which Smith says that "the monopolists, by keeping the market constantly understocked, by never fully supplying the effectual demand, sell their commodities much above the natural price" (Smith [33, p. 78]). Free entry makes such monopolistic behavior impossible and an individual firm perceives a demand curve infinitely elastic at the natural price for quantities less than the effectual demand for the firm. For quantities larger than the effectual demand, however, it is possible to sell, if firms so wish, at a price lower than the natural one, since "the competition of the different dealers obliges them all to accept of this price, but does not oblige them to accept of less" (Smith [33, p. 74]).

Under an increasing return to scale due to the division of labor, firms are facing deficiency of demand, in the sense that they can achieve a rate of profit higher than the natural rate if they can increase their supplies with the current price unchanged. Unless the size of the firm is infinitely small relative to that of the industry or the number of firms actually supplying is infinitely large, however, the price must be reduced so as to increase its supply. Taking the possible reactions of other firms and customers into consideration, each firm perceives a relation between the necessary reduction in price and the quantity of supply to be increased. Unless the number of actual firms is infinitely large, it is impossible to expect that an infinitely large increase in supply is made possible by a slight reduction in price. The perceived demand curve is, therefore, downwardly sloping for quantities larger than the effectual demand for the firm.

A Smithian equilibrium for a firm at the natural price and effectual demand is shown as the point E in Figure 3.1, where the price or cost is measured vertically and the quantity, horizontally. A downwardly sloping curve CC' is the average cost curve for a firm, which includes the profit at the natural rate. The natural price is OA and the corresponding effectual demand is OB, for the firm. The firm perceives a demand curve AED, which has a kink at E. There is no incentive for the firm to increase its supply at E, since it cannot expect the rate of profit to be higher than the natural one by increasing its supply, in view of the perceived demand curve ED being more inelastic than the diminishing cost curve EC', which is due to the possibility of the division of labor within the firm.

This is an equilibrium under demand deficiency, since the firm wishes to sell more if the current price is unchanged by the increase in supply. What prevents supply from increasing is not an increase in the cost of production but the deficiency of demand in the sense of "the difficulty of selling the larger quantity of goods without reducing the price" (Sraffa [35]).[13] The reason why the division of labor in the firm is limited is that the extent of the market is small. If demand increases, however, the cost is reduced by a further division of labor and the natural price is diminished along the downward curve CC' in Figure 3.1.

> The increase of demand, though in the beginning it may sometimes raise the price of goods, never fails to lower it in the long run. It encourages production, and thereby increases the competition of the producers, who in order to undersell one another, have recourse to new divisions of labour and new improvements of art which might never otherwise have been thought of. (Smith [33, p. 748].)

Smith's theory of international trade has been interpreted as the vent for surplus argument, "without such exportation, a part of the productive labour

---

[13] Smith's model of a firm is, therefore, isomorphic to a model recently considered for a microeconomic foundation of Keynesian macroeconomics. See Negishi [20, pp. 35–36, 87–90].

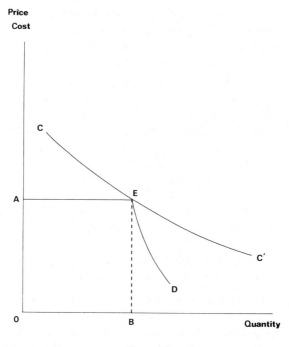

Figure 3.1

of the country must cease, and the value of its annual produce diminish"
(Smith [33, p. 372]). A host of questions arises from the point of view of the
neo-classical theory of production. Why do surpluses tend to be produced in
the first place? And why, if foreign markets for them are not available, are the
resources involved not transferred to the production of other goods at home
for which there is a demand, and especially goods of a kind imported from
abroad? "Smith speaks often of the internal mobility of factors" points out
Bloomfield [4], and he observes that the problem does not, "at least in the case
of Great Britain, seem to arise from any serious lack of employment
opportunities." Assuming factor mobility and full employment, Smith's theory
of international trade should, therefore, be interpreted rather as a theory based
on increasing returns due to large markets caused by international division of
labor.

By means of [foreign trade], the narrowness of the home market does not
hinder the division of labour in any particular branch of art or manufacture
from being carried to the highest perfection. By opening a more extensive

market for whatever part of the produce of their labour may exceed the home consumption, it encourages them to improve its productive powers, and to augment its annual produce to the utmost, and thereby to increase the real revenue and wealth of the society. (Smith [32, p. 446–447].)

The neo-classical theory of trade follows Ricardo [23, Chapter 7] and excludes the possibility of increasing returns. It explains the comparative advantage by presupposing the existence of international differences in climate, resources, technology and factor endowments. Trade between similar countries, or trade in manufacturing, therefore, cannot be explained by the neo-classical theory, while almost two-thirds of world trade is between large industrial areas that are very similar. Smithian theory, on the other hand, can explain extensive trade between similar industrial areas, since it considers comparative advantages to be created by division of labor induced in export industries by the large world market. Comparative advantage is, therefore, not the cause, but the result of international trade.

It seems to be basic to Smith's philosophy to explain, rather than assume, the existing difference by the division of labor (Arrow [1]).

The difference of natural talent in different men is, in reality, much less than we are aware of; and the very different genius which appears to distinguish men of different professions, when grown up to maturity, is not upon many occasions so much the cause, as the effect of the division of labour. The difference between the most dissimilar characters, between a philosopher and a common street porter, for example, seems to arise not so much from nature, as from habit, custom, and education. (Smith [33, p. 28–29].)

5. Division of labor and capital accumulation

Smith's arguments on the theory of the natural order of investment in Chapter V, Book II of *The Wealth of Nations*, "Of the different Employment of Capitals", are surprisingly confused, though the theory is very important as the theoretical foundation to his argument in Book III and Book IV. It is natural that Smith's arguments supporting the hierarchy of productivity of industries, headed by agriculture, followed by manufacturing, inland trade, and foreign trade have been subject to severe criticism from many eminent scholars, including Ricardo [23] and J.S. Mill [18]. They are, as a matter of fact, not systematic or persuasive; rather, they are ambiguous, confusing, and mutually inconsistent (Kobayashi [12, Chapter 7]). It is, furthermore, strange that they are given independently of Smith's second theorem of the division of labor which Smith emphasized so much in the Introduction of Book II.

When the capital of any country is not sufficient for all ... purposes, in proportion as a greater share of it is employed in agriculture, the greater will be the quantity of productive labour which it puts into motion within the country; as will likewise be the value which its employment adds to the annual produce of the land and labour of the society. After agriculture, the capital employed in manufacture puts into motion the greatest quantity of productive labour, and adds the greatest value to the annual produce. That which is employed in the trade of exportation, has the least effect of any of the three. (Smith [33, p. 366].)

The order of investment should be decided according to the value of the annual produce added by the employment of the capital. Let us note, however, that such a value is not determined exclusively by the quantity of the productive labor put into motion, unless the productivity of labor is given. It is really surprising that the concept of labor productivity disappears here, although it was emphasized so much in the theory of the division of labor in Book I. For Smith, however, the concept of productive labor is sometimes flexible enough so that cattle and even nature herself are productive. It may be argued, therefore, that the quantity of productive labor implies not only the number of laborers but also their productivity.

No equal capital puts into motion a greater quantity of productive labour than that of the farmer. Not only his labouring servants, but his labouring cattle, are productive labours. In agriculture too nature labours along with man; and though her labour costs no expence, its produce has its value, as well as that of the most expensive workmen ... The labourers and labouring cattle, therefore, employed in agriculture, not only occasion, like the workmen in maufactures, the reproduction of a value equal to their own consumption, or to the capital which employs them, together with its owners profits; but of a much greater value. Over and above the capital of the farmer and all his profits, they regularly occasion the reproduction of the rent of landlord. This rent may be considered as the product of those powers of nature, the use of which the landlord lends to the farmer ... The capital employed in agriculture, therefore, not only puts into motion a greater quantity of productive labour than any equal capital employed in manufactures, but in proportion too to the quantity of productive labour which it employs, it adds a much greater value to the annual produce of the land and labour of the country, to the real wealth and revenue of its inhabitants. Of all the ways in which a capital can be employed, it is by far the most advantageous to the society. (Smith [33, p. 363–364].)

Smith's argument that agriculture is more productive than manufacturing because there is land rent only in agriculture in this somewhat physiocratic statement was criticized by Ricardo [23, p. 76] and Mill [18, pp. 28–29] to the effect that the reason the use of land bears a price is simply the limitation of its quantity. The existence of rent is, certainly, not a necessary condition for agriculture being more productive than manufacturing. It is, however, a sufficient condition for the investment already made in agriculture to be more productive than that made in manufacturing. It is equally true that investment in intra-marginal land is more productive than that in marginal land. The argument just quoted is quite confusing and, furthermore, Smith insisted that investment should be, and actually was, made first in agriculture when rent is low, while investment should be, and actually was, shifted into manufacturing as rent increased (Smith [33, pp. 366–367, 378–379]). According to Hollander [9, p. 287], Smith's emphasis on agricultural investment as the most advantageous to society, on the grounds that rents are thereby generated, is a serious error in logic, but Smith's emphasis on agricultural investment itself is correct from the neo-classical point of view of relative factor prices.

The capital employed in home trade purchases "in one part of the country in order to sell in another the produce of the industry of that country, generally replaces by every such operation two distinct capitals that had both been employed in the agriculture or manufactures of that country, and thereby enables them to continue that employment" (Smith [33, p. 368]). Such capital may, therefore, be as productive as capital employed in domestic manufacturing, but by no means more productive than the latter. The foreign trade of consumption purchases, on the other hand, foreign goods for home consumption with the product of home industry, and "replaces too, by every such operation, two distinct capitals; but one of them only is employed in supporting domestick industry." It will, therefore, "give but one-half of the encouragement to the industry or productive labour of the country." This is certainly true as far as immediate effects on employment are concerned. If foreign industries are more profitable than domestic ones, however, foreign trade will yield more and may eventually be more favorable to the labor of the country than the home trade.

Smith argues further that "the returns of the foreign trade of consumption are very seldom so quick as those of the home-trade" and therefore the capital employed in home trade will give "more encouragement and support to the industry of the country than" the capital employed in foreign trade. In a note to this passage in his edition of *The Wealth of Nations*, Cannan points out that "if this doctrine as to the advantage of quick returns had been applied earlier in the chapter, it would have made havoc of the argument as to the superiority of agriculture" (Smith [32, p. 349], [33, p. 369]).

In view of these quotations from *The Wealth of Nations* and considerations on them, we can hardly say that Smith's expositions of the doctrine of the natural order of investment are systematic, consistent, and persuasive, although the conclusion of the doctrine that "according to the natural course of things, therefore, the greater part of the capital of every growing society is, first, directed to agriculture, afterwards to manufactures, and last of all to foreign commerce" (Smith [33, p. 380]) appeals in part to our intuition. Why its exposition does not appeal to us is that so many *ad hoc* reasons, such as the quantity of productive labor, land rents, speed of returns, are unsystematically introduced and there is no single principle used throughout to order the different employment of capitals. Since the conclusion itself sounds reasonable, however, it seems that such a principle has been presented to us by Smith somewhere in *The Wealth of Nations*. This reminds us of the theorem that the division of labor advances with the accumulation of capital, which was emphasized in the Introduction as the basic theorem in Book II, but strangely does not appear in Chapter V.

> In that rude state of society in which there is no division of labour, in which exchanges are seldom made, and in which every man provides everything for himself, it is not necessary that any stock should be accumulated or stored up beforehand in order to carry on the business of the society.... But when the division of labour has once been throughly introduced, the produce of a man's own labour can supply but a very small part of his occasional wants. The far greater part of them are supplied by the produce of other men's labour, which he purchases with the produce, or, what is the same thing, with the price of the produce of his own. But this purchase cannot be made till such time as the produce of his own labour has not only been completed, but sold. A stock of goods of different kinds, therefore, must be stored up somewhere sufficient to maintain him, and to supply him with the materials and tools of his work till such time, at least, as both these events can be brought about. (Smith [33, p. 276].)

> As the accumulation of stock must, in the nature of things, be previous to the division of labour, so labour can be more and more subdivided in proportion only as stock is previously more and more accumulated. The quantity of materials which the same number of people can work up, increases in a great proportion as labour comes to be more and more subdivided; and as the operations of each workman are gradually reduced to a greater degree of simplicity, a variety of new machines come to be invented for facilitating and abridging those operations. As the division of labour advances, therefore, in order to give constant employment to an

equal number of workmen, an equal stock of provisions, and a greater stock of materials and tools than what would have been necessary in a ruder state of things, must be accumulated beforehand. (Smith [33, p. 277].)

In view of these arguments of Smith's, we may construct a simple model to consider the relation between the division of labor and capital accumulation. Consider a stationary economy with a given supply of labor, producing two goods by using two goods and labor. Let us compare the required capital accumulaton for two different situations. Consider first the situation with no division of labor, where each production unit produces two goods, so that firms are not specialized and there is one single industry. In the second situation there is division of labor, where each production unit produces only one good, so that firms are specialized and there are two industries. In the latter situation, of course, the productivity of labor is increased by the division of labor. For the sake of later discussions, it is convenient to distinguish three cases.

Suppose first the turnover of capital in the production of the second good is $n (> 1)$ times as quick as in the production of the first good. In other words, the period of production of the first good is identical to the given unit period, whereas that of the second good is only one nth of it. Even in the situation with no division of labor, a stock of both goods are necessary at the beginning of the period in the hands of each producer, but the stock of the second good is relatively smaller, since the new output of the first good is not available until the period is over, while that of the second good is available after only one nth of the period is passed. In the situation with the division of labor, however, the necessary stock of the second good in the hands of the producers of the first good is relatively larger, since the first industry producing the first good cannot purchase the new output of the second good until its own new output is available. If input coefficients and the allocation of labor between two goods are not changed very much between the two situations, therefore, division of labor requires a larger stock of the second good, in the production of which turnover of capital is quicker, to be accumulated at the very beginning of the period in the hands of the producers of the first good, in the production of which turnover of capital is slower.

Even if there is no difference in the period of production between two goods ($n = 1$), furthermore, the required capital to be accumulated at the beginning of the period may be larger in the situation with division of labor than in the situation with no division of labor. This is because the use of materials is increased through the increased speed of operation due to the division of labor, a case Smith emphasized. There is, however, a counteracting tendency to save the waste of materials through more careful operations made possible by the division of labor.

Finally, even if there is no difference in the period of production between two goods and the use of materials remain unchanged in spite of the division of labor, one may argue that turnover of capital is slower in the situation with division of labor than in the situation with no division of labor. This is because not only the period of production but also the period of circulation must pass before a producer can purchase products of others in the former situation. If the turnover of capital in the latter situation is k (> 1) times as quick as in the former situation, so that the period of production is only one kth of the given unit period, while the sum of the period of production and the period of circulation is identical to the given unit period in the former situation, the division of labor requires k times as large capital accumulation for any given allocation of labor.

The "accumulation of stock is previously necessary for carrying on this great improvement in the productive powers of labor (due to the division of labor], so that accumulation naturally leads to this improvement" (Smith [33, p. 277]). Since the natural order of investment is concerned with exactly how the capital accumulation leads to improvement in productivity due to the division of labor, it is clear that the optimal path of investment must start in a highly unspecialized, self-sufficient industry and gradually proceed so that industries are more and more subdivided and specialized as more and more capitals are accumulated.[14]

Agriculture can be regarded as such a highly inclusive and unspecialized industry if we include household and coarser manufacturing into agriculture. This is not so foreign to Smith's view of agriculture.

It has been the principal cause of the progress of our American colonies towards wealth and greatness, that almost their whole capitals have hitherto been employed in agriculture. They have no manufactures, those household and coarser manufactures excepted which necessarily accompany the progress of agriculture, and which are the work of the women and children in every private family. (Smith [33, p. 366].)

Without the assistance of some artificers, indeed, the cultivation of land cannot be carried on .... When an artificer has acquired a little more stock

[14] The progressive division of industries and specialization of firms in industries is an essential part of the process by which increasing returns are realized. There is a strong resemblance between this concept of process of capital accumulation and the later development of the theory of capitalist process of production by Böhm-Bawerk (Young [39]; Bowley [6]). The division of labor and the number of specialized subindustries of the former corresponds to the roundabout production and the length of the period of production of the latter.

than is necessary for carrying on his own business in supplying the neighbouring country, he does not, in North America, attempt to establish with it a manufacture for more distant sale, but employs it in the purchase and improvement of uncultivated land. (Smith [33, pp. 378–379].)

We can explain this priority of agriculture by the fact that the capital accumulation is not large enough to support "a manufacture for more distant sale," which is profitable only if operated on a large scale, so that the division of labor is not advanced. All three cases considered above support the argument that an all-inclusive agriculture cannot be divided into independent manufacturing and agriculture unless a certain stock of capital is accumulated.

When enough capital is accumulated to support manufacturing as an independent, specialized industry, however, investment should be and actually is made so as to develop the occasional jobs in the neighborhood of artificers into a regular manufacturing for more distant sale. As Smith explained: "... every artificer who has acquired more stock than he can employ in the occasional jobs of the neighbourhood, endeavours to prepare work for more distant sale. The smith erects some sort of iron, the weaver some sort of linen or woollen manufactory" (Smith [33, p. 379]).

As capital accumulates, the division of labor advances to inter-district specialization of local manufacturing industry. Inter-district specialization requires still larger capital accumulation, since, first, returns from such specialized manufacturing for distance sale are very slow, so that the consideration given in the final case in the above applies. Since the specialization here is due, second, not so much to such local differences such as climate and factor endowments, as to the increasing returns caused by the division of labor between manufacturing industries considerations on the required accumulation of capital in the first two cases in the above are also relevant. Investment in home trade should be made, therefore, only when the accumulation of capital has already reached the stage when inter-district specialization is possible.[15]

The highest stage of the division of labor is that of international trade based on the international division of labor. Only in this last stage is investment in foreign trade relevant. Since "the returns of foreign trade of consumption are very seldom so quick as those of the home-trade" (Smith [33, p. 368]), the consideration given in the final case in the above applies and the required domestic capital accumulation is larger than in the case of home trade. The process of the division of labor described is the process of the subdivision of

---

[15] Since capital of traders replaces the capital of producers, required capital may be accumulated in the hands of traders.

industries and of the specialization of each of such subdivisions. Smith's theory of international trade based on this process is, therefore, a theory of intra-industrial specialization rather than a neo-classical theory of inter-industrial specialization. It can be applied to international trade between identical, homogeneous countries. The neo-classical theory, on the other hand, explains trade between different, heterogeneous countries. The case of Britain's trade with its colony, America, to which Smith often referred, is the trade that should be explained in the neo-classical way as was done by Hollander on the basis of the difference in factor endowments. It is no wonder, then, that the natural order of investment was not followed in colony and foreign trade preceded the development of manufacturing (Kobayashi [12, p. 227]).

References

[1] Arrow, K.J., "The Division of Labor in the Economy, the Polity and Society", *Adam Smith and Modern Political Economy*, pp. 153–164. G.P. O'Driscoll, ed., Iowa State University Press, 1979.
[2] Barkai, H., "A Formal Outline of a Smithian Growth Model", *Quarterly Journal of Economics*, 83(1969), pp. 396–414.
[3] Blaug, M., *Economic Theory in Retrospect*, Cambridge University Press, 1978.
[4] Bloomfield, A.I., "Adam Smith and the Theory of International Trade", *Essays on Adam Smith*, pp. 153–164, A.S. Skinner and T. Wilson, eds., Oxford University Press, 1975.
[5] Bowley, M., *Studies in the History of Economic Theory before 1870*, Macmillan, 1973.
[6] Bowley, M., "Some Aspects of the Treatment of Capital in The Wealth of Nations", *Essays on Adam Smith*, pp. 361–376. A.S. Skinner and T. Wilson, eds., Oxford University Press, 1975.
[7] Cournot, A.A., *Researches into the Mathematical Principles of the Theory of Wealth*, N.T. Bacon, tr., Macmillan, 1927.
[8] Farrell, M.J., "Edgeworth Bounds for Oligopoly Prices", *Economica*, 37(1970), pp. 342–361.
[9] Hollander, S., *The Economics of Adam Smith*, University of Toronto Press, 1973.
[10] Jaffé, W., "A Centenarian on a Bicentenarian, Leon Walras's Elements on Adam Smith's Wealth of Nations", *Canadian Journal of Economics*, 10(1977), pp. 19–33.
[11] Kimura, K., "Cambridge Gakuha niokeru Adam Smith no Dento (The Tradition of Adam Smith in the Cambridge School)", *Rironkeizaigaku no Shomondai* (Problems in Economic Theory), pp. 21–106, T. Yanaihara, ed., Yuhikaku, 1949.
[12] Kobayashi, N., *Kokufurontaikei no Seiritsu* (Formation of the System of Wealth of Nations), Miraisha, 1977.
[13] Lange, O., "The Foundation of Welfare Economics", *Econometrica*, 10(1942), pp. 215–228.
[14] Marx, K., *Capital*, I, Progress Publishers, 1954.
[15] Marx, K., *Capital*, II, Progress Publishers, 1956.
[16] Marx, K., *Capital*, III, Progress Publishers, 1959.
[17] Marx, K., *Theories of Surplus Value*, I, Foreign Language Publishing House, 1963.
[18] Mill, J.S., *Principles of Political Economy*, University of Toronto Press, 1965.
[19] Meek, R.L., *Studies in the Labor Theory of Value*, Monthly Review Press, 1956.
[20] Negishi, T., *Microeconomic Foundations of Keynesian Macroeconomics*, North-Holland, 1979.
[21] Okada, J., *Adam Smith*, Nihonkeizaishinbunsha, 1977.
[22] Perelman, M., *Classical Political Economy*, Rowman and Allanheld, 1984.

[23] Ricardo, D., *On the Principles of Political Economy and Taxation*, Cambridge University Press, 1951.

[24] Richardson, G.B., "Adam Smith on Competition and Increasing Returns", *Essays on Adam Smith*, pp. 350–360, A.S. Skinner and T. Wilson, eds., Oxford University Press, 1975.

[25] Roberts, D.J., and A. Postlewaite, "The Incentives for Price-Taking Behavior in Large Exchange Economies", *Econometrica*, 44(1976), pp. 115–127.

[26] Robinson, J., *The Economics of Imperfect Competition*, Macmillan, 1933.

[27] Samuelson, P.A., *Collected Scientific Papers*, I, MIT Press, 1966.

[28] Samuelson, P.A., "A Modern Theorist's Vindication of Adam Smith", *American Economic Review*, 67(1977), pp. 42–49.

[29] Schitovitz, B., "Oligopoly in Markets with a Continuum of Traders", *Econometrica*, 41(1973), pp. 467–501.

[30] Schumpeter, J.A., *History of Economic Analysis*, Oxford University Press, 1954.

[31] Smith, A., *The Early Writings of Adam Smith*, J.R. Lindgren, ed., Kelley, 1967.

[32] Smith, A., *An Inquiry into the Nature and Causes of the Wealth of Nations*, edited with an introduction, notes, marginal summary and an enlarged index by E. Cannan, Modern Library, 1973.

[33] Smith, A., *An Inquiry into the Nature and Causes of the Wealth of Nations*, Oxford University Press, 1976.

[34] Spengler, J.J., "Adam Smith on Human Capital", *American Economic Review*, 67(1977), pp. 32–36.

[35] Sraffa, P., "The Law of Returns under Competitive Conditions", *Economic Journal*, 36(1925), pp. 535–550.

[36] Sylos-Labini, P., "Competition: The Product Markets", *The Market and the State*, pp. 200–232, T. Wilson and A.S. Skiner, eds., Oxford University Press, 1976.

[37] Thomson, H.F., "Adam Smith's Philosophy of Science", *Quarterly Journal of Economics*, 79(1965), pp. 213–233.

[38] Viner, J., *The Role of Providence in the Social Order*, Princeton University Press, 1972.

[39] Young, A.A., "Increasing Returns and Economic Progress", *Economic Journal*, 38(1928), pp. 527–542.

CHAPTER 4

RICARDO, MALTHUS AND THE DEVELOPMENT OF CLASSICAL ECONOMICS

1. Ricardo and the moderns

David Ricardo (1772–1823), the representative theorist of the classical school of economics, was born in London as the third child of a Jewish family that had emigrated from Holland. At the age of fourteen he began to work for his father, who was a successful member of the stock exchange. David himself was also successful as a stockjobber and loan contractor. In 1799, he read Adam Smith's *The Wealth of Nations* and became interested in economics. At the age of forty-two he retired from business and purchased an estate in Gloucestershire. In the so-called bullionist controversy, he insisted that the current inflation was due to the Bank of England's failure to restrict the issue of currency. His *Essay on the Influence of a Low Price of Corn on the Profits of Stock* was published in 1814 and he argued against Malthus in the corn law controversy that a low price of corn due to free trade leads to the accumulation of capital through the high rate of profit. The first edition of *On the Principles of Political Economy and Taxation* appeared in 1817 and the third edition in 1821, with some important changes and a new chapter entitled "On Machinery." In 1819 Ricardo obtained a seat in the House of Commons and took an active part in parliamentary discussions for the next few years. He died in 1823, with his "Absolute Value and Exchangeable Value" unfinished.

The strong influence of Adam Smith can clearly be seen in the thirty-two chapters of Ricardo's *Principles* (1821), which can be grouped into three parts, i.e., "Principles of Political Economy" (Chapters I to VII), "Principles of Taxation" (Chapters VIII to XIX) and "Comments on Adam Smith and Others" (Chapters XX to XXXII).

As Sraffa noted (Ricardo [41, pp. xxiv–xxv]), the first part covers the same topics discussed in Chapters V to XI, Book I of Adam Smith's *The Wealth of Nations*, i.e., value (price), rent, wages and profits. The differences are, firstly, that Ricardo, unlike Smith, deals with rent immediately after value and before wages and profits, and secondly, that Ricardo devotes a separate chapter to discussing foreign trade. These are not accidental, since the theory of rent and the theory of comparative cost are the most important contributions of Ricardo. It should be remembered that in Chapter I, On Value, an important role is played by a criticism against Smith.

> Adam Smith, and all the writers who have followed him, have, without one exception that I know of, maintained that a rise in the price of labour would be uniformly followed by a rise in the price of all commodities. I hope I have succeeded in showing, that there are no grounds for such an opinion, and that only those commodities would rise which had less fixed capital employed upon them than the medium in which price was estimated, and that all those which had more, would positively fall in price when wages rose. (Ricardo [41, p. 46].)

While the law of economic distribution among rent, wages and profits is determined as the principal problem of political economy in the first part of *Principles*, the ultimate incidence of a tax is shown to be governed by such a law of distribution in the second part of *Principles*. The parallel with Smith applies equally here. Topics discussed in Book V, Chapter II, Part II of *The Wealth of Nations* are covered by Chapters VIII to XVII in *Principles*. Chapter XVIII deals with poor rates and Chapter XIX is devoted to considering a problem raised in Chapter XVIII.

The last part of *Principles* consists of the chapters commenting upon various doctrines of other writers, forming the appendix or a series of critical excursuses, with little connection with each other (Ricardo [41, pp. xxiii–xxiv]). Again, however, criticism against Smith is most important here. It is insisted, for example, in Chapter XXI, "Effects of Accumulation on Profits and Interest," that

> ... no accumulation of capital will permanently lower profit, unless there be some permanent cause for the rise of wages. If the funds for the maintenance of labour were doubled, trebled, or quadrupled, there would not long be any difficulty in procuring the requisite number of hands, to be employed by those funds; but owing to the increasing difficulty of making constant additions to the food of the country, funds of the same value would probably not maintain the same quantity of labour. If the necessaries of the workman could be constantly increased with the same facility, there could be no permanent alteration in the rate of profits or wages, to whatever amount capital might be accumulated. Adam Smith, however, uniformly ascribes the fall of profits to accumulation of capital, and to the competition which will result from it, without ever adverting to the increasing difficulty of

providing food for the additional number of labourers which the additional capital will employ. (Ricardo [41, p. 289].)

The plan of the first half of this chapter is as follows. After a critical review of some of the mathematical models of Ricardo's economics constructed by modern theorists in section 2, we shall discuss in section 3 some difficulties with Ricardo's theory of value and distribution. In section 4, on the other hand, we shall vindicate Ricardo by showing that his theory of foreign trade is much more profound than is interpreted by J.S. Mill and neo-classical economists. The rest of the present section is devoted to showing the significance of Ricardo in the history of economics as well as for the current theories of economics.

Ricardo is immortal.

It is easy to understand the following statement of Schumpeter to the effect that Marx is possessed by Ricardo.

Ricardo is the only economist whom Marx treated as a master. I suspect that he learned his theory from Ricardo. But much more important is the objective fact that Marx used the Ricardian apparatus: he adopted Ricardo's conceptual layout and his problems presented themselves to him in the forms that Ricardo had given to them. No doubt, he transformed these forms and he arrived in the end at widely different conclusions. But he always did so by way of starting from and criticizing, Ricardo ... *criticism of Ricardo was his method in his purely theoretical work* (Schumpeter [48, p. 390].)

It is, however, slightly surprising to hear that, in spite of marginal revolution,

... the analytical backbone of Marshall's *Principles* is nothing more or less than a completion and generalization, by means of a mathematical apparatus, of Ricardo's theory of value and distribution as expounded by J.S. Mill. It is not, as many have supposed, a conflation of Ricardian notions with those of the marginal utility school. Nor is it an attempt to substitute for Ricardian doctrine a new system of ideas arrived at by a different line of approach. True, the process of completion and generalization involved a transformation more thoroughgoing than Marshall himself was disposed to admit. Nevertheless, so far as its strictly analytical content is concerned, the *Principles* is in the direct line of descent through Mill from Ricardo. (Shove [49].)

Keynes was, of course, critical of Ricardo. "The almost total obliteration of

Malthus's line of approach and the complete domination of Ricardo's for a period of a hundred years has been a disaster to the progress of economics" (Keynes [19, p. 98]).

> The completeness of the Ricardian victory is something of a curiosity and a mystery. It must have been due to a complex of suitabilities in the doctrine to the environment into which it was projected. That it reached conclusions quite different from what the ordinary uninstructed person would expect, added, I suppose, to its intellectual prestige.... But although the doctrine itself has remained unquestioned by orthodox economists up to a late date, its signal failure for purposes of scientific prediction has greatly impaired, in the course of time, the prestige of its practitioners. (Keynes [18, pp. 32–33].)

The so-called Cambridge (England) post-Keynesians insist, however, on the synthesis of classical and Keynesian economics rather than that of neo-classical and Keynesian economics.

> To historians of economic theory the triumph of the neo-classical synthesis should appear as most inappropriate, for the basis of Keynes's formal training in the economics of Ricardo and Marshall left a strong imprint on his own contributions to economic theory. It would seem more appropriate to link Keynes's own theory with the long-period theory of the classical political economists. The possibility of such a relation has become obvious with the post-Keynesian construction of a long-period theory based on Keynes's short-period theory which closely resembles, in both content and concern, the classical theory of Ricardo and Marx. (Kregel [23, p. xv].)

Finally, Leijonhufvud considered that "Friedman has Ricardo in his intellectual ancestry." According to Ricardo, "[the interest of money] is not regulated by the rate at which the Bank will lend ... but by the rate of profit which can be made by the employment of capital, and which is totally independent of the quantity or of the value of money" (Ricardo [41, p. 363]). Then, continues Leijonhufvud,

> Keynes criticized the above Ricardo passage for its classical full employment presumption ... Ricardo derived the proposition that the rate of profit uniquely determined the interest rate by assuming the system to be at full employment. My impression of Friedman's thought over the years is that he starts by assuming Ricardo's conclusion and from it deduces Ricardo's assumption, i.e., he assumes that the market real rate will equal the natural real rate and proceeds logically to the natural rate of unemployment doctrine. (Leijonhufvud [25, p. 188].)

Indeed, like the case of post-Keynesians, there are many different post-Ricardians.

Under the circumstances, it is no wonder that Ricardo has a long history of many different mathematical models, the beginning of which perhaps dates back to 1833, i.e., the model of Whewell.[1] In the next section, however, only four recent attempts to construct a mathematical model of Ricardo's economics are reviewed critically. Firstly, we shall consider (1) the land theory of value which was suggested by Cantillon[2] under the assumption of homogeneous land (2) the roll of landowners' demand in the theory of value when land is heterogeneous, and (3) the labor and land theories of value when the production requires times, on the basis of Ricardo's liner models developed by Samuelson [47, pp. 373–422]. While Samuelson considered Ricardo-like models to check the general validity of Ricardian propositions in a wider setting than assumed by Ricardo, Pasinetti [39] tried to show the validity of what Ricardo really meant by making the necessary assumptions for Ricardian conclusions explicit, as we shall see subsequently. Casarosa's [8] attempt to modify the Pasinetti model will also be considered as an example of the new interpretation of Ricardo with respect to the role of the market wages.[3] Finally, we shall review the Brems [6] model which, unlike others, introduces fixed capital explicitly and considers the Ricardian problem of machinery.

2. Some mathematical models

2.1.

Samuelson [47, pp. 373–422] seems to consider that the Ricardian theory of value is the labor theory of value which insists that relative prices are proportional to quantities of labor embodied and independent of the pattern of demand from landowners and capitalists. His aim in constructing Ricardo-like models is, therefore, to criticize this theory of value under fairly general conditions.

Samuelson starts with the case where labor is the only limiting factor of production, there is no capital, and land is not scarce. In the case of two goods, the production frontier is a straight line AB in Figure 4.1 when two goods have

---

[1]See Whewell [54], and also Cochrane [10] and Brems [6].
[2]For the life and work of Cantillon [7], see also Chapter 2, section 3.1.
[3]See also Hicks and Hollander [6], Hollander [17, pp. 375–404], Levy [26], and Watarai [53].

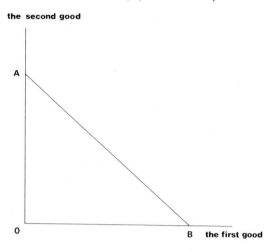

Figure 4.1

a constant input coefficient of labor. This is the world of the labor theory of value where goods are exchanged in proportion to the amount of labor embodied, i.e., at the ratio given by the slope of *AB*, which is independent of demand for two goods. When the homogeneous land is added as a scarce factor of production, however, the production frontier is like *AED* in Figure 4.2, where *AB* corresponds, as in Figure 4.1, to the labor constraint and *CD* corresponds to the new land constraint, input coefficients of land also being assumed to be constant. Depending on the pattern of demand, relative prices can be at anywhere between the slope of *AB* and that of *CD*. They are not necessarily proportional to the quantities of embodied labor.

In a Ricardian world, however, labor is not a limiting factor of production, since it can be produced from the input of goods corresponding to the subsistence wage. Samuelson showed that goods are then exchanged in proportion to their embodied land content, which is independent of demand pattern, when input coefficients to produce labor are constant. In the two-good case, let us denote the price of the ith good by p_i, the input coefficient of good i to produce labor by c_i, the labor input coefficient to produce the ith good by a_i, the land input coefficient to produce the ith good by b_i, the wage by w and the rent by r. Competition requires

$$p_1 = wa_1 + rb_1, \tag{1}$$

$$p_2 = wa_2 + rb_2, \tag{2}$$

$$w = c_1 p_1 + c_2 p_2. \tag{3}$$

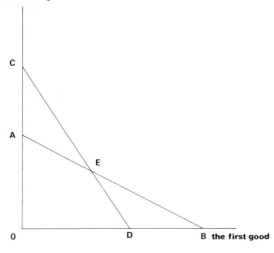

Figure 4.2

Multiply (1) by c_1 and (2) by c_2 and add them to get

$$w/r = (c_1 b_1 + c_2 b_2)(1 - c_1 a_1 - c_2 a_2)^{-1}. \tag{4}$$

Having w/r as in (4), we can solve for p_1/r and p_2/r by substituting (4) into (1) and (2) as

$$p_1/r = (c_1 b_1 + c_2 b_2)(1 - c_1 a_1 - c_2 a_2)^{-1} a_1 + b_1, \tag{5}$$

$$p_2/r = (c_1 b_1 + c_2 b_2)(1 - c_1 a_1 - c_2 a_2)^{-1} a_2 + b_2. \tag{6}$$

Working with ratios to r is equivalent to using the land as *numéraire*, expressing all other prices in terms of land embodied directly and indirectly.

While prices are determined by technology and labor's requirements for subsistence and are independent of any shift in the composition of the landowners' demand, the net output of goods (gross output minus labor's requirements) are determined by the pattern of the landowners' demand which satisfies

$$(p_1/r)Y_1 + (p_2/r)Y_2 = L, \tag{7}$$

where L is the total amount of land and Y_i is the demand for the ith good. Condition (7) is not only the budget constraint for the landowners but also the linear production frontier when Y_i is the net output of the ith good, i.e., AB in

Figure 4.3 where $OB(OA)$ is the process to produce the first (second) good from labor, i.e., from two goods.

The history of the land theory of value is very long. "Labour is the father of wealth, as lands are the mother."[4] To express the cost of goods in terms of one factor only, Ricardo tried to eliminate land by considering the case of marginal land with no rent. It is Cantillon, on the other hand, who eliminates labor by reducing it to land, on the basis of the consideration that the labor *du plus vil esclave adulte vaut au moins la quantité de terre* that must be employed to provide for his needs.[5] Labor is merely an intermediate product and the cost and price of all the goods are expressed by the amount embodied of the sole primary factor of production, land. Since they can also be expressed in terms of labor embodied in this case, however, what is important is not so much the problem of whether land or labor, as the independence of prices from shifts in the composition of the landowners' demand.

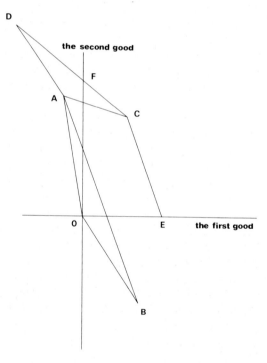

Figure 4.3

[4]Petty [40, p. 68]. See also Schumpeter [48, p. 213] and Blaug [5, p. 5].
[5]Cantillon [7, pp. 32–33]. See also Schumpeter [48, p. 219].

This property will be lost when the heterogeneity of land is introduced. Samuelson considers the case of heterogeneous land and differential rent, firstly by a Thunen-like concentric circle model with smooth differences in land quality, the most fertile land being at the center. The output is maximized, being subject to the given amount of labor. Then he considers a linear programming model in which there are a finite number of different grades of land and the labor input is minimized, being subject to the given amount of outputs. The conclusion is that we can no longer end up with the straight line production frontier (see Figure 4.1 and (7)), even if we adhere to Ricardo's long-run assumption of the constant reproduction cost of labor, which can easily be shown in Figure 4.3 for the two-good two-grade land case. The line AB is the linear production frontier (7) of the first grade land with the origin O, with OB (OA) being the process to produce the first (second) good from labor, i.e., from two goods, while DC is the linear production frontier (7) of the second grade land with the origin displaced to A, with AC (AD) being the process to produce the first (second) good from labor i.e., two goods. Different lands suit, at least relatively speaking, different goods (sandy land good for cucumber is terrible for rice), so that the slope of AB is different from that of DC. The aggregate production frontier FCE is obtained by sliding DCA along AB.[6] The relative prices are certainly not independent of the landowners' demand pattern.

Ricardo tried to get rid of land by considering marginal land where there is no rent. This does not work if there is no such land, as in the case of Figure 4.3. If, for example, AD and AC are of the same slope with DC in Figure 4.3, the second grade land is such a marginal land and the price ratio coincides with the slope of DC, only when the landowners' demand is on FC. When it is on EC, however, there is still rent in the second grade land and the price ratio is given by the slope of EC. It is impossible to determine price ratios in the marginal land, independently of the pattern of demand from the landowners.

This is also the case with the so-called internal margin, i.e., not the land with no rent but the marginal unit of labor (and capital) which does not pay rent. In terms of linear programming, it can be shown as follows. A production process, say process a, actually producing output from inputs of labor and land can be fictitiously decomposed into the combination of another similar process, say process b, and a production process producing output from input of labor alone, say process c, in the sense that, given the input of process a, the efficient output from the combination of b and c is the output of a. It is true that we can express the price of output in terms of the labor embodied in process c,

---

[6]The similarity with the international trade of intermediate products can be seen, for example, from Figure 1.2 in Chipman [9].

and the rent of land from the comparison of processes b and c (Roncaglia [46, p. 17]). If a change in demand causes an increase in output, given land input, process a must be changed into a' which is more labor intensive and with lower labor productivity. The corresponding c' shows, then, the higher embodied labor of the unit output.[7] Prices are, again, not independent of demand.[8]

Having finished with the failure of the labor theory of value due to the existence of land, Samuelson turned to the problem of the time required in the production. The simplest model to show that relative exchange values cannot be predicted from the labor theory of value alone is the following, i.e.,

$$p_1 = wa_1(1+i)^t, \quad p_2 = wa_2(1+i)^s, \tag{8}$$

where land is assumed free, p_i is the price of the ith good, w is the rate of wage, a_i is the required labor input per unit of the ith good, i is the rate of interest, and t (s) is the period of production of the first (second) good. Unless $t = s$ or $i = 0$, we cannot predict unchanging relative prices from the embodied labor coefficients a_i alone. As for the determination of i, the extreme Torrens–Ricardo model is,

$$p_1 = wa_1(1+i), \quad w = c_1 p_1, \quad \text{or} \quad (1+i) = 1/c_1 a_1, \tag{9}$$

where the first good is the wage good, $t = 1$, and c_1 is the amount of wage good necessary to reproduce labor. For Ricardo, however, a dynamic model which neglects scarcity of land is like a whodunit without a corpse. When land is heterogeneous, we can write down the formulas for intra-marginal and marginal lands respectively

$$p_1 = (wa_1' + rb_1')(1+i)^{t'}, \quad p_1 = wa_1''(1+i)^{t''}, \tag{10}$$

where r is the rent, b_1 is the land input required per unit to produce the first good, and i is not determinable even if we knew $w/p_1 = c_1$, since there is a suitable a_1'' to satisfy (10) for any i. In other words, margins vary in response to changes in the rate of interest.

Finally, Samuelson restates the land theory of value for the case where the land is homogeneous, the circulating as well as the fixed capital are so

---

[7]The reason is that, in a linear programming model of production, an increase in the limited quantities of the factors of production reduces the imputed prices of the relevant factors in terms of the output.

[8]Even a neo-Ricardian has to admit that "the determination of prices is then subordinate to the determination of the levels of production" (Roncaglia [46, p. 16]).

sufficiently accumulated that the rate of interest is at the constant minimum possible level d, the first good is the wage good whose period of production is 1, the period of production of the second good is 2, the good zero is the machine whose period of production is 1 and the period of duration is 2, the third good requires machine (new or old) as well as labor and land to be produced. The cost of production relations are

$$w = p_1 c_1, \tag{11}$$

$$p_1 = (w a_1 + r b_1)(1 + d), \tag{12}$$

$$p_2 = (w a_2 + r b_2)(1 + d)^2, \tag{13}$$

$$p_0 = (w a_0 + r b_0)(1 + d), \tag{14}$$

$$p_3 + e_3 p_0' = (w a_3 + r b_3 + p_0 f_3)(1 + d) \tag{15}$$

and

$$p_3 = (w a_3' + r b_3' + p_0' g_3')(1 + d), \tag{16}$$

where p_i, a_i, b_i are respectively the price, labor and land input coefficient of the ith good, p_0' is the price of the old machine, (15) implies that the production of the third good requires f_3 new machine but leaves us, as a by-product, e_3 old machine,[9] and (16) implies that the third good can also be produced from a_3' labor, b_3' land and g_3' old machine. The determination of $w/r, p_1/r, p_2/r, p_0/r, p_0'/r$ and p_3/r is independent of the pattern of consumption demand.

How relevant to Ricardo are conclusions derived from Samuelson's models? It is certainly true that the labor theory of value makes no more sense than the land theory of value. Ricardo's theory of value is, however, not the naive labor theory of value to the effect that relative prices are proportional to quantities of embodied labor. Perhaps what is important is the lesson that the independence of relative prices from the pattern of demand is impossible unless we make somewhat restrictive assumptions. While Samuelson [47, 373–432] tried to show the invalidity of what he considered as the Ricardian theory of value in general situations, Pasinetti [39] attempted to construct a mathematical model in which Ricardian propositions are valid by explicitly making the necessary assumptions. By studying both Samuelson's and Pasinetti's models, therefore, we can see the significance and limit of Ricardian propositions clearly.

[9]For the joint-output of the old machine, see Morishima [31, pp. 195–196] and Roncaglia [46, p. 36].

2.2.

Pasinetti's arguments can be summarized by considering a model in which there is only one wage good (corn) and two luxury goods. Given the quality and quantity of land, the production function of the first, i.e., wage good is

$$X_1 = f(N_1), \quad f'(N_1) > 0, \quad f''(N_1) < 0 \tag{17}$$

where X_1 is the output and N_1 is the labor input. The luxury goods do not use land and their production functions are much simpler,

$$X_2 = aN_2 \tag{18}$$
$$X_3 = bN_3 \tag{19}$$

where X_i and N_i denote the output and labor input in the production of the ith goods and a and b are positive constants. Let us define the total number of laborers as

$$N = N_1 + N_2 + N_3 \tag{20}$$

which must be supported by the given wages fund W,

$$W = Nx \tag{21}$$

where x is the given natural real wage necessary to reproduce the labor population.

Since the revenue of capitalists from the labor input at the margin of the production of the first good is $f'(N_1)$ and the excess of revenue from intra-marginal units of labor input must be paid as differential rent, the total rent is

$$R = f(N_1) - N_1 f'(N_1). \tag{22}$$

If we denote the prices in terms of such units of luxury goods that the input of one unit of labor produces, prices are determined so as to satisfy

$$p_1 X_1 - p_1 R = N_1 \tag{23}$$
$$p_2 X_2 = N_2 \tag{24}$$
$$p_3 X_3 = N_3 \tag{25}$$

where p_i is the price of the ith goods, since capitalists allocate labor inputs so as to maximize the total revenue, i.e., equalize the marginal revenues. Finally, we have demand functions for luxury goods of the landowners,

$$X_2 = D_2(p_1, p_2, p_3, R) \tag{26}$$

and

$$X_3 = D_3(p_1, p_2, p_3, R).\tag{27}$$

Now we can determine 11 variables, i.e., $N, R, p_1, p_2, p_3, X_1, X_2, X_3, N_1, N_2$ and N_3 from 11 equations in (17) to (27). The most typical characteristic of the Ricardian model is, however, that the solutions for all the variables of the system, except X_2, X_3, N_2 and N_3, are independent of (26) and (27), i.e., the pattern of demand from the landowners. This can be seen as follows. Behind (26) and (27), we have the budget constraint of the landowners,

$$p_2 X_2 + p_3 X_3 = p_1 R\tag{28}$$

which, in view of (20), (24) and (25), can be rewritten as

$$N = N_1 + p_1 R.\tag{29}$$

We can determine N, R, p_1, X_1 and N_1 from (17), (21), (22), (23) and (29). On the other hand, p_2 and p_3 are determined from (18), (19), (24) and (25). Therefore, all the macroeconomic variables such as total employment, total rent, all the prices, and all the variables referring to the wage good, are independent of the demand equations for luxury goods.

Furthermore, only the output of, employment in, and price of luxury goods depend on the production functions of luxury goods, i.e., on a and b. Particularly, if we define total profit as

$$p = p_1 X_1 + p_2 X_2 + p_3 X_3 - p_1 R - p_1 W\tag{30}$$

and the rate of profit as

$$r = p/p_1 W,\tag{31}$$

the latter can be shown as

$$r = (f'(N_1)/x) - 1\tag{32}$$

in view of (17) and (20) to (25). The rate of profit is independent from the conditions of production of luxury goods. This is, as emphasized by Pasinetti, due to the peculiarity that luxury goods are not necessary to produce any goods, while the wage good is. In other words, luxury goods are non-basic commodities while the wage good is a basic commodity in Sraffa's terminology [51, pp. 7–8].

Provided that the rate of profit is above a certain positive minimum rate, a part of the profit is not consumed but saved, so that the wages fund W is increased. Therefore, total employment N is increased from (21). "If the funds for the maintenance of labour were doubled, trebled, or quadrupled, there would not long be any difficulty in procuring the requisite number of hands, to be employed by those funds" (Ricardo [41, p. 289]). By substituting (22) into (29) and considering (17), (22) and (23), we obtain

$$N = f(N_1)/f'(N_1).$$ (33)

Since $f(N_1)$ is an increasing function of N_1 and $f'(N_1)$ is a decreasing function of N_1 in the right hand side of (33), N and N_1 can be changed only in the same direction. Accumulation of capital increases, therefore, N and N_1 with the result that the rate of profit r falls in (32). If we differentiate (22) with respect to N_1, we have

$$dR/dN_1 = f'(N_1) - f'(N_1) - N_1 f''(N_1) > 0$$ (34)

so that total rent will increase with N_1 as capital is accumulated. Though the real wage x is constant, the monetary wage rate will rise as N_1 is increased, since p_1 increases with N_1 in view of (17), (22) and (23) while p_2 and p_3 remain unchanged, and the gold is one of the luxury goods.

Two remarks are now in order on Pasinetti's model of the Ricardian system.

As was pointed out, firstly, the demand and production of luxury goods play very minor roles in Pasinetti's model. The secret lies in the fact that luxury goods are assumed to be produced without using land. This is clear from the consideration of Ricardo-like models by Samuelson [47, pp. 373–422], which we have already reviewed. If land is used in the production of luxury goods, changes in the demand and production of luxury goods induce changes in the allocation of land between the wage good and luxury goods and can affect all the variables, including the relative prices and the rate of profit. Incidentally, Pasinetti's criticism of Samuelson seems to miss the mark. Pasinetti argued that the classification of lands in order of fertility, i.e., the function $f(N_1)$, is perfectly determined even though there are many wage goods, if the proportion of the different wage goods is fixed, so that Samuelson's argument of the different classification of land fertility due to the type of goods considered is irrelevant. The problem here is, however, not the substitutability of wage goods, but that of luxury goods. The proportion of wage goods may be considered fixed, perhaps from physiological reasons. There seem to be no reasons, however, to consider the non-substitutability of luxury goods.

In the price–cost system of Sraffa's [51] Ricardo-like model, there is a distinction between basic and non-basic commodities and the rate of profit is independent of the non-basic commodities. We must remember, however, that Sraffa's price–cost relations are based on the assumption of the given level of outputs. If basic and non-basic goods are competing for the given land, input coefficients of basic goods and therefore the rate of profit are not independent of the non-basic goods through the changes in the level of production.

Secondly, although it is used superficially in (23), (24) and (25), the labor theory of value does not play an essential role in Pasinetti's model, while Ricardo attached much importance to it in *Principles* [41]. It is partly because the rate of profit is determined exclusively in the production of the first good, i.e., in (32), in Pasinetti's model. In other words, the profits in the first industry regulate the profits of all other industries. This is, as a matter of fact, the principle in Ricardo's *Essay*, where the profits of the farmer regulate the profits of all other trades. The rational foundation of this principle is that in agriculture the same commodity, corn, forms both the capital (wages fund) and the product, so that the rate of profit can be determined without any theory of value. In *Principles*, however, Ricardo treated wages, unlike Pasinetti, as being composed of a variety of products including manufactured products, so that the principle used in his *Essay* can no longer be applied. Instead of corn, then, labor is considered by Ricardo to appear both as input and output, so that the rate of profit is no longer determined by the ratio of corn produced to the corn used up in agriculture, but by the ratio of the total labor of the country to the labor required to produce the necessities for that labor. This is why Ricardo has to be concerned with the labor theory of value in *Principles*.

Pasinetti [39] considered that most of Ricardo's analysis is carried out as if the demographic adjustment has already been fully worked through, while the capital accumulation process has not yet been completed. In other words, Ricardo put more emphasis, according to Pasinetti, on the so-called natural equilibrium where the rate of the real wage is at the exogenously given natural level than on the so-called market equilibrium. Casarosa [8], on the other hand, emphasized the role of the market real wage rate in Ricardo's system. "Notwithstanding the tendency of wages to conform to their natural rate, their market rate may, in an improving society, for an indefinite period, be constantly above it" (Ricardo [41, pp. 94–95]). To describe such a behavior of a Ricardian economy out of the natural equilibrium, he modified Pasinetti's model and considered a dynamic equilibrium where the rate of growth of the capital (wages fund) is instantaneously equal to the rate of growth of the labor population.

Pasinetti's (21) is now replaced by

$$W = Nw \tag{21}'$$

where w is the market real wage rate in terms of the wage good. Correspondingly, Pasinetti's (32) is also replaced by

$$r = (f'(N_1)/w) - 1 \tag{32}'$$

from which we can derive the inverse relationship between the monetary wage rate $p_1 w$ and the rate of profit, in view of (17), (22) and (23). A dynamic equilibrium is defined by

$$(1/N)(dN/dt) = (1/W)(dW/dt) \tag{35}$$

where t denotes the time. Let us assume that

$$(1/N)(dN/dt) = c(w - x)/x \tag{36}$$

where c is a given constant and that

$$(1/W)(dW/dt) = s(p_2, p_3)r \tag{37}$$

where s denotes the share of profits which is invested. Finally, (26) and (27) are modified to

$$X_2 = D_2(p_1, p_2, p_3, R, p) \tag{26}'$$

$$X_3 = D_3(p_1, p_2, p_3, R, p) \tag{27}'$$

so that luxury goods are consumed not only by landowners but also by capitalists.

   We now have fourteen equations, (17) to (20), (21)', (22) to (25), (26)', (27)', (35) to (37) which can be solved for fourteen variables, $p_1, p_2, p_3, N_1, N_2, N_3, X_1, X_2, X_3, R, w, (1/N)(dN/dt), (1/W)(dW/dt)$ and (N/W). In other words, a dynamic equilibrium is determinate if a value of W is specified. As Casarosa himself admitted, this dynamic equilibrium is not a steady growth equilibrium, since the decreasing returns in the production of the wage good make the latter impossible. He argues, however, that the economy is continuously attracted towards the dynamic equilibrium position, in view of the fact that the rate of growth of population is an increasing function of w, the rate of growth of capital is an increasing function of r, and w and r are inversely related. Since capitalists are assumed to consume luxury goods in (37), furthermore, it is no longer true that the rate of profit is independent of the conditions for the production of the luxury goods.

   In view of (18), (19), (24) and (25), p_2 and p_3 remain unchanged if a and b are constants. From (32)', and (35) to (37), w and N_1 are inversely related, since

$$sf'(N_1) = sw + cw((w/x) - 1) \tag{38}$$

where s is constant and $w > x$. In view of (33), therefore, Ricardo's conclusion that "in the natural advance of society, the wages of labour will have a tendency to fall, as far as they are regulated by supply and demand," (Ricardo [41, p. 101]), i.e., as far as the market rate of wage is higher than the natural rate, is nicely explained by Casarosa's model.

2.3

In his mathematical model of Ricardo's long run equilibrium, Brems [6] carefully incorporated fixed capital in the form of durable producers' goods and concluded that much of Ricardo's pessimism in "On Machinery" (Chapter XXXI, *Principles*) was unfounded.

Let us consider two industries, a producers' goods industry and a consumers' goods industry, called industries 1 and 2 respectively. The production function of industry 1 is

$$L_1 = a_1 I \tag{39}$$

where L_1 is the labor employed, I is the level of output and a_1 is a positive constant. Industry 2 is agriculture and its production function is given by

$$L_2 = a_2 S \tag{40}$$

and

$$X = S^a M \tag{41}$$

where L_2 is the labor employed, S is the physical capital stock of producers' goods, X is the level of output, a_2, a and M are positive constants, and $0 < a < 1$.

Let u be the given useful life of new producers' goods. The present worth of the sum total of revenue minus the operating labor cost over the entire useful life of a unit of new producers' goods is

$$\int_0^u ((PX/S) - a_2 w) e^{-it} \, dt = ((PX/S) - a_2 w)(1 - e^{-iu})/i = K \tag{42}$$

where P is the price of consumers' goods, w is the wage, i is the rate of interest, and t is the time. The present net worth of acquiring a capital stock of S physical units of producers' goods is

$$(K - a_1 w)S \tag{43}$$

where K is a function of S, in view of (41) and (42). The maximization of (43) with respect to S gives us

$$S = (cw/aMP)^{1/(a-1)} \tag{44}$$

where $c = a_1 i/(1 - e^{-iu}) + a_2$.

In a stationary economy, each year $1/u$ of the stock of producers' goods is retired and must be replaced, so that

$$I = S/u. \tag{45}$$

In view of (39), (40), (44) and (45), the total employment is

$$L = L_1 + L_2 = ((a_1/u) + a_2)(cw/aMP)^{1/(a-1)} \qquad (46)$$

where w/P and i are given constants in a Ricardian stationary state. Then, L is a function of M, a_1 and a_2, given u and a.

Brems considered the effect of technological progress, i.e., an increase in M and decreases in a_1 and a_2, on the total employment L. An increase in M is a disembodied technological progress, i.e., technological progress not embodied in S. This corresponds to the following example raised by Ricardo. "If, by the introduction of a course of turnips, I can feed my sheep besides raising my corn, the land on which the sheep were before fed becomes unnecessary, and the same quantity of raw produce is raised by the employment of a less quantity of land" (Ricardo [41, p. 80]). It can easily be seen from (46) that the higher M implies the higher L. Decreases in a_1 and a_2 are embodied technological progress, i.e., embodied in S, which corresponds to the following examples mentioned by Ricardo. "Such improvements ... are rather directed to the formation of the capital applied to the land, than to the cultivation of the land itself. Improvements in agricultural implements, such as the plough and the thrashing machine, ... are of this nature" (Ricardo [41, p. 82]). We can see from (44) that such improvements increase the optimal level of S, since c is decreased there by decreases in a_1 and a_2. Brems also confirmed from (46) that L is increased by a decrease in a_1. As for the effect of a decrease in a_2, furthermore, Brems argued that from (46) L is very likely to be increased, given the empirically plausible values for i, u and a.

On the basis of the above results, Brems concluded that the following pessimism of Ricardo is unfounded. "There will necessarily be a diminution in the demand for labour, population will become redundant, and the situation of the labouring classes will be that of distress and poverty" (Ricardo [41, p. 390]). "The opinion entertained by the labouring class, that the employment of machinery is frequently detrimental to their interests, is not founded on prejudice and error, but is conformable to the correct principles of political economy" (Ricardo [41, p. 392]).

As a criticism of Ricardo, however, Brems's argument is irrelevant. The pessimistic conclusion of Ricardo referred to by Brems was derived from the study of an example of short run disequilibrium which has nothing to do with the long run equilibrium considered by Brems. Let us consider the example given by Ricardo in detail (Ricardo [41, pp. 388–390]). A capitalist, a farmer who produces food and at the same time is a manufacturer of necessities, employs a capital of £20,000, of which £7,000 is invested in fixed capital and the remaining £13,000 is the wages fund. The rate of profit is 10 per cent and therefore the capital yields a net profit of £2,000. Each year, the gross produce is £15,000, of which £13,000 is to replace the wages fund and the net produce of £2,000 is consumed by the capitalist. Suppose, now, that the capitalist decided to employ half his men in constructing a machine for a year, and the other half in producing food and necessities as usual. In the following year, while the machine of £7,500 is available, only one half of the usual quantity of food and necessities, i.e., of £7,500 would be available, of which only £5,500 can be used as wages fund, after the capitalist consumed £2,000. The capitalist's means to employ labor would be reduced in the proportion of 13,000 to 5,500, and the labor which was before employed by £7,500 would become redundant. This happens even though the reduced quantity of labor can produce, with the assistance of the machine, £7,500, so that the net profit is stll £2,000.

Now the difference between Ricardo and Brems is evident. While Ricardo's problem is that of short run, i.e., employment in the year following the construction of a new machine, Brems is concerned with sustainable employment in the long run equilibrium. For Ricardo the problem is the short-run availability of the wages fund to be advanced, which becomes less important in a stationary state considered by Brems where input and output can be synchronized. In modern terminology, Ricardo's example may be considered as that of a forced saving imposed on the laborers by the capitalists's over-investment. The capitalist made an investment, i.e., the construction of a new machine, without making any saving himself. This can be realized, then, only if the laborers consume less, so that resources are transferred from the consumers' goods industry to producers' goods industry. A forced saving may be created by raising prices through the reduction of the real wage. In a Ricardian economy, however, the real wage is fixed at subsistence level. The only possible way to make laborers consume less is, therefore, to reduce the level of employment.

Although Ricardo was pessimistic for the short run effect of the introduction of machines, he is, like Brems, rather optimistic for the long run effect on employment.

As, however, the power of saving from revenue to add to capital, must depend on the efficiency of the net revenue, to satisfy the wants of the capitalist, it could not fail to follow from the reduction in the price of commodities consequent on the introduction of machinery, that with the same wants he would have increased means of saving, – increased facility of transferring revenue into capital. But with every increase of capital he would employ more labourers; and, therefore, a portion of the people thrown out of work in the first instance, would be subsequently employed; and if the increased production, in consequence of the employment of the machine, was so great as to afford, in the shape of net produce, as great a quantity of food and necessaries as existed before in the form of gross produce, there would be the same ability to employ the whole population, and, therefore, there would not necessarily be any redundancy of people. (Ricardo [41, p. 390].)

3. Value and distribution

The principal problem in political economy is, according to Ricardo, to determine the laws which regulate distribution among three classes of the community; namely, the proprietor of the land, the owner of the stock or capital, and the laborers, under the names of rent, profit, and wages (Ricardo [41, p. 5]). We have seen in section 2.2 that, in a growing economy, the wage rate would remain at subsistence level, the rate of profit would fall, and the total rent would rise by using Pasinetti's model of the Ricardian economy. Particularly, Ricardo [41, p. 77] emphasized that "the rise of rent is always the effect of the increasing wealth of the country, and of the difficulty of providing food for its augmented population." He seems to be more interested, however, in the share of, or "the proportion of the whole produce," to be distributed to the landowners than the size of the total rent, since

> ... it is not by the absolute quantity of produce obtained by either class, that we can correctly judge of the rate of profit, rent, and wages ... . By improvements in machinery and agriculture, the whole produce may be doubled.... But if wages partook not of the whole of this increase; if they, instead of being doubled, were only increased one-half; if rent, instead of being doubled, were only increased three-fourths, and the remaining increase went to profit, it would, I apprehend, be correct for me to say, that rent and wages had fallen while profits had risen. ([41, pp. 5, 49].)

Again using Pasinetti's model, therefore, let us consider how the share of rent will behave in a growing economy. As in (22) in section 2.2, the total rent is defined in terms of the first good, corn, as

$$R = f(N_1) - N_1 f'(N_1) \tag{1}$$

where the production function of corn

$$X_1 = f(N_1) \tag{2}$$

has the diminishing marginal productivity of labor input N_1, given the quality and quantity of the available land. The total produce of the economy is defined as

$$Y = p_1 X_1 + p_2 X_2 + p_3 X_3 \tag{3}$$

where X_i denotes the level of output of the ith good and p_i denotes the price of the ith good. The second and third goods are manufactured luxury goods, whose production functions show constant returns to scale ((18) and (19) in section 2.2). Since capitalists allocate labor inputs N_i's in order to maximize the total revenue, i.e., equalize the marginal revenues,

$$p_1 f'(N_1) = 1 \tag{4}$$

$$p_2 X_2/N_2 = 1 \tag{5}$$

$$p_3 X_3/N_3 = 1, \tag{6}$$

where prices are given in terms of such units of goods that the marginal inputs of labor can produce.

By substituting (4) to (6) into (3),

$$Y = (f(N_1)/f'(N_1)) + (N - N_1) \tag{7}$$

where N is defined as the sum of all N_i's. As in (33) in section 2.2, furthermore, N_1 and N are related as

$$N = f(N_1)/f'(N_1) \tag{8}$$

in Pasinetti's model. By substituting (8) into (7), we have

$$Yf'(N_1) = 2f(N_1) - N_1 f'(N_1). \tag{9}$$

In view of (4) and (9), then, the share of rent is

$$p_1 R/Y = (f(N_1) - N_1 f'(N_1))/(2f(N_1) - N_1 f'(N_1)) \tag{10}$$

the behavior of which under economic growth is what Ricardo should have studied as the principal problem in political economy.

Quite ironically for Ricardo, however, the share of rent (10) may not rise but fall in a growing economy, as N and therefore N_1 increase, since

$$d(p_1 R/Y)dN_1 = (-f(N_1)f''(N_1)N_1 - f'(N_1)R)/(2f(N_1) - N_1 f'(N_1))^2 \leqq 0. \tag{11}$$

Even if the share of rent, not in the total produce of the economy as in (10) but only in the agricultural produce, is considered, furthermore, the share does not necessarily rise in a growing economy, as was pointed out by Barkai [2]. Barkai considered the share of rent

$$R/f(N_1) = 1 - (f'(N_1)N_1/f(N_1)) \tag{12}$$

and argued that whether it rises in economic growth is indeterminate since

$$d(R/f(N_1))/dN_1 = -(N_1 f''(N_1)-f'(N_1)(e-1))/f(N_1), \qquad (13)$$

where

$$e = N_1 f'(N_1)/f(N_1) < 1. \qquad (14)$$

Barkai further showed that the share of rent (12) rises in Ricardo's numerical example [2, p. 83], which is obtained by assuming a special quadratic production function. Ricardo there is concerned, however, not with the share of rent (12), but with the share of rent in a particular farm. "In speaking of the rent of the landlord, we have rather considered it as the proportion of the produce, obtained with a given capital on any given farm." "It is according to the division of the whole produce of the land of any particular farm, between the three classes of landlord, capitalist, and labourer, that we are to judge of the rise or fall of rent, profit, and wages."[10]

Let us consider an intra-marginal farm which employs $\bar{N}_1$th laborer $(\bar{N}_1 \leq N_1)$. Rent in such a particular firm $\bar{R}$ is

$$\bar{R} = f'(\bar{N}_1) - f'(N_1) \qquad (15)$$

when the marginal farm employs the N_1th laborer. The share of rent in such a particular farm is

$$\bar{R}/f'(\bar{N}_1) = 1 - f'(N_1)/f'(\bar{N}_1) \qquad (16)$$

which certainly increases as N_1 increases. Ricardo himself admitted clearly, however, that this does not necessarily imply that the share of rent in the produce of the total corn industry increases, since the produce of the industry increases by the output of the new marginal farm which does not pay rent.[11]

As the corn industry expands, the share of rent increases in any particular existing farm, i.e., except for the newly entering farm, but the share of rent in the whole corn industry may not increase. Is there any role to be played by this rather clumsy conclusion derived from Ricardo's analysis? One possibility is the application to a short run problem where the total labor population is given, so that other industries have to be shrunk as the corn industry expands. For example, suppose an import restriction is imposed on corn as a result of the corn laws, so that the domestic corn price and the level of output of corn are raised. The share of rent rises in any particular farm except for the newly entering ones which do not pay rents. The produce of the domestic corn

---

[10]Ricardo [41, pp. 83, 49]. It is interesting to note that the phrases "on any given farm" and " of any particular farm" are added only in the third edition of *Principles*. See Ricardo [41, p. lvi].
[11]Ricardo [42, p. 193]. See also Barkai [3].

industry is increased by the output of such new farms, but the produce of other industries is decreased by the shift of labor to the corn industry. Even if the share of rent is not increased in the produce of the domestic corn industry, therefore, it can be increased in the total produce of the domestic industries.

This can be confirmed by the use of Pasinetti's model. In view of (4), (5), and (6), the total produce of the domestic economy measured "by the quantity of labour required to obtain that produce" (Ricardo [41, p. 49]) at the margin of the production is given by (7). The share of rent in it is, then, given by

$$p_1 R/Y = (f(N_1) - N_1 f'(N_1))/(f(N_1) + (N - N_1)f'(N_1)) \qquad (10)'$$

where the total labor population N is considered as a given constant. It clearly rises if labor is shifted to the corn industry from other industries since

$$\mathrm{d}(p_1 R/Y)/\mathrm{d}N_1 = -Nf(N_1)f''(N_1)/(Yf'(N_1))^2 > 0. \qquad (11)'$$

In the above, the total produce of the domestic economy is measured by the quantity of labor required to obtain that produce at the margin of production. This is because Ricardo made a clear distinction between riches and value and studied the problem of distribution in terms of value.

> Value, then, essentially differs from riches, for value depends not on abundance, but on the difficulty or facility of production. The labour of a million of men in manufactures, will always produce the same value, but will not always produce the same riches. ... for every thing rises or falls in value, in proportion to the facility or difficulty of producing it, or, in other words, in proportion to the quantity of labor employed on its production. (Ricardo [41, p. 273])
>
> It is not by the absolute quantity of produce obtained by either class, that we can correctly judge of the rate of profit, rent, and wages, but by the quantity of labour required to obtain that produce. (Ricardo [41, p. 49].)

Value is, therefore, firstly defined as the difficulty of production and then considered as the quantity of embodied labor. "The value of a commodity, or the quantity of any other commodity for which it will exchange, depends on the relative quantity of labour which is necessary for its production, and not on the greater or less compensation which is paid for that labour" (Ricardo [41, p. 11]). If commodities are produced by the simultaneous input of labor alone, the difficulty of production is certainly expressed by the quantity of embodied labor, and the rate of wage, or the rate of profit, has nothing to do with it. However, "not only the labour applied immediately to commodities affect their value, but the labour also which is bestowed on the implements, tools, and buildings, with which such labour is assisted" (Ricardo [41, p. 22]). In other words, we have to consider not only the labor directly consumed to produce commodities, but also past labors consumed indirectly through the use of fixed capitals. If the time patterns of such a series of dated labors necessary to produce commodities are identical, of course, the value or the difficulty of the production of a commodity can still be given by "the aggregate sum of these various kinds of labour" (Ricardo [41, p. 25]). If the time patterns are different, however, it is "the principle that the quantity of labour bestowed on the production of commodities regulates their relative value, considerably modified by the employment of machinery and other fixed and durable capital" (Ricardo [41, p. 30]). The value is no longer given by the simple aggregate sum of dated labors embodied and "the principle that value does not vary with the rise or fall of wages, modified also by the unequal durability of capital, and by the unequal rapidity with which it is returned to its employers" (Ricardo [41, p. 38]).

With the rise of wages, the value rises for those commodities which relatively embody more current labors than past labors, and vice versa. In spite of Ong [38], however, this should not be interpreted as meaning value differs from the difficulty of production. We should rather think that the difficulty of production also varies as the rate of wage, or the rate of profit which is inversely related to it, changes, even though the series of dated labors remains unchanged. To obtain the difficulty of production, differently dated labors have to be weighed according to their scarcity. When the rate of profit is high, for the economy it is more difficult to produce such a commodity which embodies relatively more past labors than the current labor, since past labors are relatively more scarce in the economy. Productions of commodities are interrelated, since they are competing for the given limited resources of the economy. It is no wonder, then, that the difficulty of the production of a commodity depends, through the rate of profit, on the conditions of the production of other commodities, including the labor power.

Consider a three-good economy, where a unit of the ith good is produced by the labor input a_i, $i = 1, 2, 3$, but the period of production for the first two goods is 1, while that of the third good is 2. The natural rate of the real wage is assumed to be equivalent to the consumption of w_1 of the first good and w_2 of the second good. From the efficiency of a competitive economy, we may consider that the total labor input in the period $(t-2)$, $L(t-2)$ is being minimized, with respect to the level of output of three goods in the period t, those of the first two goods in the period $(t-1)$, and the total labor inputs in the periods $(t-1)$ and $(t-2)$, under the following conditions of no excess demands for goods and labor.

Firstly, in the period t,

$$x_1(t) - z_1 \geqq 0 \tag{17}$$

$$x_2(t) - z_2 \geqq 0 \tag{18}$$

$$x_3(t) - z_3 \geqq 0 \tag{19}$$

where $x_i(t)$ denotes the level of output of the ith good and z_i denotes the given demand for the ith good. Secondly, in the period $(t-1)$,

$$x_1(t-1) - w_1 L(t-1) - c_1(t-1) \geqq 0 \tag{20}$$

$$x_2(t-1) - w_2 L(t-1) - c_2(t-1) \geqq 0 \tag{21}$$

where $x_i(t-1)$, $L(t-1)$ and $c_i(t-1)$ denote, respectively, the level of output of the ith good, the total labor input, and given level of consumption of capitalists of the ith good. Of course, $w_i L(t-1)$ signifies the consumption of laborers of the ith good. Finally, for labor markets in the periods of $(t-1)$ and $(t-2)$,

$$L(t-1) - a_1 x_1(t) - a_2 x_2(t) - a_3 x_3(t+1) \geqq 0 \tag{22}$$

$$L(t-2) - a_1 x_1(t-1) - a_2 x_2(t-1) - a_3 x_3(t) \geqq 0 \tag{23}$$

where the differences in the period of production is to be noted and the level of output of the third good in the period $(t+1)$, $x_3(t+1)$ is assumed to be given.

To minimize $L(t-2)$, with respect to $x_1(t)$, $x_2(t)$, $x_3(t)$, $x_1(t-1)$, $x_2(t-1)$, $L(t-1)$ and $L(t-2)$, being subject to (17) to (23), let us consider the Lagrangean multipliers, $p_1, p_2, p_3, q_1, q_2, v_1$ and v_2, respectively to the left-hand side of (17) to (23) and by adding them to $(-L(t-2))$. Conditions for the minimization are obtained by the differentiation of the Lagrangean with respect to $x_1(t)$, $x_2(t)$, $x_3(t)$, $x_1(t-1)$, $x_2(t-1)$, $L(t-1)$ and $L(t-2)$,

$$p_1 - v_1 a_1 = 0 \tag{24}$$

$$p_2 - v_1 a_2 = 0 \tag{25}$$

$$p_3 - v_2 a_3 = 0 \tag{26}$$

$$q_1 - v_2 a_1 = 0 \tag{27}$$

$$q_2 - v_2 a_2 = 0 \tag{28}$$

$$v_1 - q_1 w_1 - q_2 w_2 = 0 \tag{29}$$

$$-1 + v_2 = 0. \tag{30}$$

The value or the difficulty of production of the ith good can be indicated by p_i, since as a Lagrangean multiplier it represents the necessary increase in the minimized $L(t-2)$ caused by a unit increase in z_i. The relative value between the first two goods is simply the ratio of embodied labors a_1/a_2 as is easily seen from (24) and (25). The relative value between, say, the second and the third goods is, on the other hand,

$$p_3/p_2 = a_3/a_2 v_1 \tag{31}$$

in view of (30). Substituting (27) and (28) into (29), we have

$$v_1 = a_1 w_1 + a_2 w_2. \tag{32}$$

From the right-hand side of (32), the implication of v_1 can be seen as follows. Consider the cost–price relations of the first two goods,

$$p_1 = (1+r)a_1(w_1 p_1 + w_2 p_2) \tag{33}$$

$$p_2 = (1+r)a_2(w_1 p_1 + w_2 p_2) \tag{34}$$

where p_i denotes the price of the ith good and r denotes the rate of profit. By solving (33) and (34) for $(1+r)$ and (p_1/p_2), we have

$$v_1 = 1/(1+r) \tag{35}$$

in view of (32).

The relative value between the second and the third goods, having different periods of production, is, therefore, not simply the ratio of embodied labors, but the ratio of discounted embodied labors. This is the final position of Ricardo to the labor theory of value as is seen from his "Absolute Value and Exchangeable Value".

Tho' it is not strictly right to say that these two commodities are valuable in proportion to the quantity of labour actually bestowed on them, would it be not correct to say that the value of the wine after two years was in proportion to the labour actually employed on it the first year, and to the labour which might have been employed on wine or on some other commodity if it had been brought to market after the first year of its production. An oak which is the growth of 100 years in like manner has perhaps from first to last only one day's labour bestowed upon it, but its value depends on the accumulations of capital by the compound profits on the one day's labour and the quantity of labour which such accumulated capital would from year to year have employed. (Ricardo [43, pp. 387–388].)

4. Dichotomy in the theory of international trade

In his criticism of mercantilism, Adam Smith declared that "wealth does not consist in money, or in gold and silver; but in what money purchases" (Smith [50, p. 438]). A contribution of the classical school of economics is, therefore, to recognize and analyze the working of the real economic system behind the curtain of money. This reminds us of the so-called "classical dichotomy" between the real theory which determines relative prices and the monetary theory which determines the absolute price level (Negishi [34, pp. 247–263]). As Akhtar [1] rightly suggested, however, the dichotomy in Ricardian economics is different from the so-called "classical dichotomy", which should rather be called the neo-classical dichotomy, since gold plays the dual roles of a luxury good and money in the former while the latter assumes a fiat paper money which has no use as a consumers' good.

The idea of a dichotomy in Ricardian economics can be seen most clearly in his theory of international trade.

> Gold and silver having been chosen for the general medium of circulation, they are, by the competition of commerce, distributed in such proportions amongst the different countries of the world, as to accommodate themselves to the natural traffic which would take place if no such metals existed, and the trade between countries were purely a trade of barter. (Ricardo [41, p. 137].)

In other words, the pattern of international specialization and terms of trade between countries remain unchanged, irrespective of whether the gold is a mere luxury good or whether it also plays the role of money. Such a dichotomy clearly exists in Pasinetti's model of a closed Ricardian economy discussed in subsection 2.2, since relative prices in a moneyless real model are independent of the demand equations for luxury goods and they remain unchanged if the role of money is newly assigned to the gold which has been a mere luxury good.

Our aim in the following is to consider, by using Pasinetti's model, whether the dichotomy is also possible for the two-country model of the Ricardian theory of international trade where the produce of the labor of 100 Englishmen is exchanged for the produce of 80 Portuguese (Ricardo [41, p. 135]).[12] It will be shown that it is possible only if the Ricardian theory is interpreted as in Negishi [36], so that the capital is imperfectly mobile between countries, an international difference exists, not in the natural wage, but in the rate of profit, and terms of trade can be determined without introducing Mill's reciprocal demands.

Suppose the first country is specialized in the production of the first and the third goods (corn and gold) while the second country is specialized in the production of the second good (a manufactured luxury good). Since, unlike in the case of Smith, the possibility of increasing returns is excluded, the specialization is due to the comparative advantage (different production functions) which existed before the international trade.

The production functions of the first and third goods in the first country are like (17) and (19) in section 2.2

$$X_1 = f(N_{11}) \tag{1}$$

$$X_3 = bN_{13} \tag{2}$$

where X_j denotes the output of the jth good and N_{1j} signifies the labor input allocated in the production of the jth good. Real wage w_1 and the total rent R_1 in the first country are defined as

$$K_1 = N_1 w_1 \tag{3}$$

where N_1 is the total labor population and K_1 is the wages fund of the first country and

$$R_1 = f(N_{11}) - N_{11} f'(N_{11}) \tag{4}$$

as in the case of (21) and (22) in section 2.2. Capitalists in the first country allocate labor N_1 into N_{11} and N_{13}

$$N_1 = N_{11} + N_{13} \tag{5}$$

so as to maximise the total revenue, i.e., to equalize the marginal revenues from

[12]Ricardo's numerical example of the comparative cost principle is as follows. Suppose one unit of cloth made in England is being exchanged against one unit of wine made in Portugal. "England may be so circumstanced that to produce the cloth may require the labour of 100 men for one year, and if she attempted to make wine, it might require the labour of 120 men for the same time. England would therefore find it her interest to import wine, and to purchase it by the exportation of cloth. To produce the wine in Portugal might require only the labour of 80 men for one year, and to produce the cloth in the same country might require the labour of 90 men for the same time. It would therefore be advantageous for her to export wine in exchange for cloth" (Ricardo [41, p. 135]).

the labor input in the production of the first and the third goods, so that

$$p_1 f'(N_{11}) = X_3/N_{13} \tag{6}$$

where p_1 is the price of the first good and the third good is taken as the *numéraire*. The rate of profit in the first country is given by

$$r_1 = (p_1 X_1 + X_3 - p_1 R_1)/p_1 K_1 - 1 = f'(N_{11})/w_1 - 1 \tag{7}$$

in view of (1) and (3) to (6).

The production function of the second good in the second country is like (19) in section 2.2

$$X_2 = aN_2 \tag{8}$$

where X_2 is the output of the second good and N_2 is the total labor population of the second country, and the real wage in the second country w_2 is given by

$$K_2 = N_2 w_2 \tag{9}$$

where K_2 is the wages fund of the second country. The rate of profit in the second country is defined as

$$r_2 = p_2 X_2/p_1 K_2 - 1 \tag{10}$$

where p_2 is the price of the second good.

Finally, the demand functions of the second and the third goods are like (26) and (27) in section 2.2

$$X_2 = D_2(p_1, p_2, R_1, G) \tag{11}$$

$$X_3 = D_3(p_1, p_2, R_1, G) \tag{12}$$

where the second good is assumed to be perishable and the third good is assumed to be gold, the existing stock of which is denoted by G, so that D_3 is the net demand for the gold.

Ricardo admitted that "the same rule which regulates the relative value of commodities in one country, does not regulate the relative value of the commodities exchanged between two or more countries" (Ricardo [41, p. 133]).

England would give the produce of the labour of 100 [Englishmen], for the produce of the labour of 80 [Portuguese]. Such an exchange could not take place between the individuals of the same country. The labour of 100 Englishmen cannot be given for that of 80 Englishmen, but the produce of the labour of 100 Englishmen may be given for the produce of the labour of 80 Portuguese, 60 Russians, or 120 East Indians. (Ricardo [41, p. 135].)

Consider the exchange between the first good and the third good in the same country, i.e., the first country. From (2) and (6),

$$p_1 = b/f'(N_{11}).$$ (13)

Since one unit of the first good embodies $1/f'(N_{11})$ unit of labor at the margin of its production and one unit of the third good embodies $1/b$ units of labor, two goods are exchanged according to the embodied labor value. In other words, the produce of one laborer in the production of the first good is exchanged for the produce of one laborer in the production of the third good.

This is, however, not the case with exchanges between two countries. Consider the exchange between the second and the third goods. From (2), (6), (7), (8), (9) and (10),

$$p_2 = (b/a)(w_2/w_1)(1 + r_2)/(1 + r_1).$$ (14)

Since one unit of the second good embodies $1/a$ units of labor of the second country and one unit of the third good embodies $1/b$ units of labor of the first country, the produce of one laborer of the first country is not exchanged for the produce of one laborer of the second country, if the rate of profit is different or the rate of wages is different between countries.

Ricardo explained this difference between domestic exchange and international exchange, not by the international difference of wages, but by the difference in the rate of profit which is due to the difficulty of capital mobility.

> The difference in this respect, between a single country and many, is easily accounted for, by considering the difficulty with which capital moves from one country to another, to seek a more profitable employment, and the activity with which it invariably passes from one province to another in the same country.... Experience ... shews, that the fancied or real insecurity of capital, when not under the immediate control of its owner, together with the natural disinclination which every man has to quit the country of his birth and connections, and intrust himself with all his habits fixed, to a strange government and new laws, check the emigration of capital. These feelings ... induce most men of property to be satisfied with a low rate of profits in their own country, rather than seek a more advantageous employment for their wealth in foreign nations. (Ricardo [41, pp. 135–137].)

The difficulty with which capital is moved does not, however, imply the impossibility of capital movements. In the classical economic theories of Smith and Ricardo, the role of capital is mainly that of advancing wage costs until the product is sold to the consumers. We have to, therefore, take into consideration the role of the capital of foreign trade merchants in replacing the capital of foreign as well as domestic producers.

The capital employed in purchasing foreign goods for home-consumption, when this purchase is made with the produce of domestick industry, replaces too, by every such operation, two distinct capitals; but one of them only is employed in supporting domestick industry. The capital which sends British goods to Portugal, and brings back Portuguese goods to Great Britain, replaces by every such operation only one British capital. The other is a Portuguese one. Though the returns, therefore, of the foreign trade of consumption should be as quick as those of the home-trade, the capital employed in it will give but one-half the encouragement to the industry or productive labour of the country. (Smith [50, p. 368].)

There must, then, be at least some capital movement, depending on the changing ratio of the capital of two countries engaging in foreign trade. When there is a profit rate differential between countries, capital moves from the domestic production of the lower rate country to the import–export business, in order to share the higher profit rate of the latter, which replaces the capital of producers in higher rate as well as lower rate countries. The result is a narrowing down of the profit rate differential, since the wages fund for the labor of the lower rate country is decreased while that of the higher rate country is increased by the shift of its capital from the import–export business to domestic production.[13]

In view of the factors which, as Ricardo emphasized, induce most men of property to be satisfied with a low rate of profits in their own country rather than to seek a higher rate in foreign countries, however, capital mobility is by no means so perfect as to equalize r_1 and r_2. As in Negishi [36], therefore, let us consider an equilibrium relation between r_1 and r_2,

$$r_1 = cr_2 \tag{15}$$

where c is a given constant determined by psychological and social factors.[14]

As for the real wages, w_1 and w_2, they are exogenously given at the level of the natural wage.

The natural price of labour is that price which is necessary to enable the labourers, one with another, to subsist and to perpetuate their race, without

---

[13]In our model the rate of profit is changed in the first country through changes in N_1 and N_{11} or in w_1.

[14]The value of c is larger or smaller than 1, depending on which country is the lower rate country and exporting capital. In Ricardo's numerical example of comparative costs, it is England where capital is more heavily accumulated and the rate of profit is lower. "If in consequence of the diminished rate of production in the lands of England, from the increase of capital and population, wages should rise, and profits fall, it would not follow that capital and population would necessarily move from England to Holland, or Spain, or Russia, where profits might be higher" (Ricardo [41, p. 134]).

either increase or diminution. The power of the labourer to support himself, and the family which may be necessary to keep up the number of labourers, does not depend on the quantity of money which he may receive for wages, but on the quantity of food, necessaries, and conveniences become essential to him from habit, which that money will purchase. The natural price of labour, therefore, depends on the price of the food, necessaries, and conveniences required for the support of the labourer and his family.... However much the market price of labour may deviate from its natural price, it has, like commodities, a tendency to conform to it. (Ricardo [41, pp. 93–94]).[15]

If we consider the so-called natural equilibrium with imperfect capital mobility, fourteen variables $X_1, X_2, X_3, R_1, N_1, N_2, p_1, p_2, N_{11}, N_{13}, r_1, r_2, K_1$ and K_2 have to be determined by fourteen equations, (1) to (12), (15) and

$$K_1 + K_2 = K, \tag{16}$$

where K is the given total wages fund in the world.

So far we have been assuming that all exchanges are barter exchanges. If all exchanges are carried out by the use of money and the role of money is assigned to the gold, the third good, equations (11) and (12) have to be changed into

$$X_2 = D_2(p_1, p_2, R_1, G', G) \tag{17}$$

$$X_3 = D_3(p_1, p_2, R_1, G', G) \tag{18}$$

where G' is the stock of gold as a luxury good which is obtained by subtracting demand for money L from the total stock of gold G,

$$G' = G - L(p_1, p_2, N_1, N_2, X_1, X_2, X_3, R_1). \tag{19}$$

In general, this changes the natural equilibrium value of all the variables.

Suppose, however, that the marginal productivity of labor in the production of the first good $f'(N_{11})$ changes stepwise as is shown in Figure 4.4 (see also Casarosa [8]) and remains unchanged by the changes in N_{11} caused by

---

[15]"It is not to be understood that the natural price of labour, estimated even in food and necessaries, is absolutely fixed and constant. It varies at different times in the same country, and very materially differs in different countries.... An English labourer would consider his wages under their natural rate ... if they enabled him to purchase no other food than potatoes, and to live in no better habitation than a mud cabin; yet these moderate demands of nature are often deemed sufficient in countries where man's life is cheap, and his wants easily satisfied" (Ricardo [41, pp. 96–97]). In Ricardo's numerical example of comparative costs, therefore, the real wage in England should not be considered lower than that in Portugal, and the reason why the produce of the labor of 100 Englishmen is exchanged for the produce of 80 Portuguese is, not the lower wage, but the lower rate of profit in England.

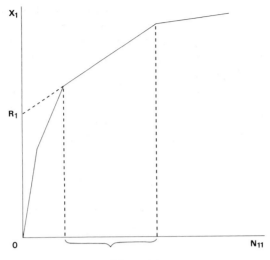

Figure 4.4

changes of (11) and (12) into (17) and (18). Then, we see that p_1 remains unchanged from (13). On the other hand, (15) can be rewritten as

$$r_1 = f'(N_{11})/w_1 - 1 = cr_2 = c(ap_2/p_1w_2 - 1) \tag{20}$$

in view of (7), (8) and (9). Since w_1 and w_2 are given as the natural price of labor, p_2 remains unchanged if $f'(N_{11})$ and p_1 do not change. As far as the rate of profit r_1, r_2 and the terms of trade p_1, p_2 are concerned, therefore, they are independent of the substitution of (11) and (12) by (17) and (18) and we have a dichotomy in the sense of Ricardo.[16]

In the standard neo-classical theory of international trade, it is generally assumed that factors of production, labor and capital, do not move internationally. Capital is conceived, not as the advancement of wage costs, but as physical capital instruments in neo-classical Walrasian economics.[17] Since "it is rare ... that capital instruments wander about" (Ohlin [37, p. 404]), the assumption of capital immobility is rather plausible. Furthermore, imperfect specialization is assumed to prove the Heckscher–Ohlin theorem, the Samuelson–Stolper theorem, and the international factor price equaliza-

[16]Since prices, wages, and the rate of profit are unchanged, there is no change in the pattern of international specialization. If we consider the so-called market equilibrium where N_1 and N_2 are constants but w_1 and w_2 are variables, however, a Ricardian dichotomy is impossible, since p_2 cannot be determined in (20) and is not independent of changes of (11) and (12) to (17) and (18).

[17]See Eagly [12, pp. 3–9] for the difference in the concept of capital between classical and neo-classical theories.

tion theorem. Neo-classical theory tends, therefore, to regard Ricardian theory as a special case where complete specialization is assumed.

From the point of view of such a neo-classical interpretation of Ricardo's theory of international trade, we have twelve equations (1) to (12) to determine twelve variables, $X_1, X_2, X_3, R_1, N_1, N_2, p_1, p_2, N_{11}, N_{13}, r_1$ and r_2, since both K_1 and K_2 are given constants. As before, the domestic price ratio p_1 is obtained independently of demands from (13), if $f'(N_{11})$ is constant. The terms of trade p_2, however, cannot be independent from demands. We have to determine $R_1, p_2,$ and N_{11} from

$$aK_2/w_2 = D_2(b/f'(N_{11}), p_2, R_1, G) \tag{21}$$

which is obtained from (8), (9), (11) and (13),

$$b(K_1/w_1 - N_{11}) = D_3(b/f'(N_{11}), p_2, R_1, G) \tag{22}$$

which is obtained from (2), (3), (5), (12), (13), and

$$R_1 = f(N_{11}) - N_{11} f'(N_{11}). \tag{4}$$

Even if $f'(N_{11})$ is constant, it is clear that Ricardian dichotomy is impossible, since p_2 is not independent of the substitution of (11) and (12) by (17) and (18).[18]

It is no wonder that the neo-classical trade theory's interpretation of Ricardo is inconsistent with Ricardian dichotomy, since it insists, following J.S. Mill, that the terms of trade cannot be determined by comparative costs alone and it is necessary to take reciprocal demands into consideration. If the dichotomy is important to the Ricardian theory of international trade, therefore, a Mill-neo-classical interpretation of Ricardo cannot be accepted and we have to consider that the terms of trade can be determined without introducing reciprocal demands.[19] This is possible if capital is, at least imperfectly, mobile and wages are at the natural price of labor.[20]

5. Malthus as a precursor of Keynes

Thomas Robert Malthus (1766–1834), another representative thinker of the classical school of economics, was born in 1766, near Dorking, Surrey, in

---

[18]Neo-classical interpretation may insist that N_1 and N_2 are constants while w_1 and w_2 are variables. Even then, we can show the impossibility of a Ricardian dichotomy in a similar way.
[19]Kojima [22, p. 77] and Morita [33] also insist that the terms of trade are determined in Ricardian theory without taking reciprocal demands into consideration.
[20]From the point of view of Ricardian theory, therefore, Emmanuel's [14] criticism of the traditional theory of international trade is very interesting, since he insisted on the assumption of capital mobility and of exogenously given wages.

England. He entered Jesus College, Cambridge where he was elected to a fellowship at the age of twenty-seven, took holy orders in 1797 and held a curacy for a short period. In 1798 he published a long pamphlet entitled *An Essay on the Principle of Population, as It Affects the Future Improvement of Society; With Remarks on the Speculations of Mr. Godwin, M. Condorcet, and Other Writers*, and criticized the optimistic belief of Godwin and Condorcet that nothing stood in the way of a regime of ideal equality. According to Malthus, every effort to realize such a perfect human society would always founder on the tendency of population to outgrow the food supply. Population, when unchecked, increases in a geometric ratio, while the food supply at best increases in an arithmetical ratio, hence, population tends to increase up to the limits of the means of subsistence. We have already seen that the concept of the so-called natural equilibrium of the Ricardian system is founded on this Malthusian principle of population. In 1805, Malthus was appointed Professor of Modern History and Political Economy at the East India Company's college at Haileybury, the first appointment of this kind in England. In the so-called corn laws controversy, he insisted on protecting agriculture and emphasized the importance of land rent as the source of effectual demand, by publishing three pamphlets. Ricardo acknowledged one of them, "Inquiry into the Nature and Progress of Rent" (1815), in the Preface of his *Principles*, saying that, together with Edward West's "Essay on the Application of Capital to Land," it presented to the world the true doctrine of rent. Malthus's *Principles of Political Economy* was published in 1820, and Ricardo wrote *Notes on Malthus* (1828) to it. After the publication of *Definitions in Political Economy* in 1827, Malthus died at Haileybury in 1834.

Although Malthus is popular for his principle of population and made an important contribution to the classical theory of rent, he should also be remembered for his prescient opposition to the Ricardian doctrine of the impossibility of general gluts. It was Keynes who emphasized the "brilliant intuitions" of Malthus's principle of effective demand which he considered more "far-reaching" than the principle of population. "If only Malthus, instead of Ricardo, had been the parent stem from which nineteenth-century economics proceeded, what a much wiser and richer place the world would be today. We have laboriously to re-discover and force through the obscuring envelopes of our misguided education what should never have ceased to be obvious" (Keynes [19, 100–101]). The plan of the last part of this chapter is, therefore, firstly to devote this section to the review of some modern mathematical models of Malthus's economics and to the considerations on how far Malthus had anticipated Keynes. In the final section we shall give our own view of Malthus, Malthus as rather a supply-side economist who emphasized the motives to produce as functions of the rate of profit.

Let us start with a Malthusian aggregative model constructed by Eagly [12, pp. 93–102]. The total work force is divided into two main categories. i.e., (1) productive labor N_1 which produces material objects that can be transferred and (2) unproductive labor N_2 which produces non-transferable service. With the size of the total work force $\bar{N}$ assumed to be historically given, an equilibrium prevails in the labor market if

$$\bar{N} = N_1 + N_2. \tag{1}$$

The production of material objects requires that the given total capital stock $\bar{K}$, which Eagly seems to regard as malleable, be allocated to the variable capital to support laborers and to the fixed capital. In other words, both laborers and machines are required in the production of commodities and productive laborers are demanded by capitalists. The demand for productive labor is

$$N_1 = \bar{K}/(w + p/\alpha) \tag{2}$$

where w is the wage per laborer, p is the given price of the unit of machinery (fixed capital) and α is the labor–machine ratio.

Since there is no time lag between the realization of output and input, unproductive labor does not require capital to be advanced. The net commodity output in the economy is denoted by Z and can be described as a function of the number of productive laborers employed, i.e.,

$$Z = aN_1. \tag{3}$$

This net disposable commodity income can be spent in two ways, i.e., (1) for increments to capital stock, i.e., net investment I and (2) for the services of unproductive labor, i.e., consumption C. That portion of commodities which is not invested is exchanged for personal services produced by unproductive labor. The supply of commodities placed on the inter-sectoral market between the productive labor sector and the unproductive labor sector may be defined as some proportion of the net commodity output,

$$C = cZ. \tag{4}$$

The quantity of commodities offered in exchange for personal services constitutes the wage bill for the unproductive laborers. The demand for the unproductive labor is then

$$N_2 = caN_1/w \tag{5}$$

in view of (3) and (4).

The total demand for commodities is equal to consumption demand plus investment demand, so that an equilibrium of the commodity market requires

$$aN_1 = I + wN_2, \tag{6}$$

in view of (3), (4) and (5), where investment demand I would appear to be determined as a function of the rate of profit, or we may consider it simply as given.

If investment I is given, we have four equations, (1), (2), (5) and (6), to determine only three unknowns, N_1, N_2 and w. Therefore, the system is overdetermined.[21] In other words, the full employment equilibrium requires the proper level of investment expenditure by capitalists. Here, Eagly emphasized, lies the core of Malthus's critique of Say's law, i.e., a theory of automatic adjustment process by which deviations from full employment tend to be self-correcting. Eagly concluded that Malthus's critique of Say's law made the point that the classical theory had not conceptualized a mechanism designed to perform the task of dividing net income between consumption expenditure and investment expenditure. The theoretical mechanism designed to meet this criticism is, according to Eagly, the loanable funds theory. It introduces the rate of interest i as a new unknown and to make I and/or c depend on i. Since the equilibrium of the market for loanable funds can be derived from other equilibria by the use of Walras's law, we still have four independent equations. The number of unknown is, however, four, and there is no overdeterminancy. The impact of the loanable funds theory is, therefore, to remove the very basis of Malthus's critique against Say's law.[22]

Eltis also constructed a mathematical model to explain Malthus's theory of effective demand and growth [13, pp. 140–181]. He started with a consideration of the potential output. Aggregate production function is assumed to be

$$Y = Ae^{at}L^Z \quad (1 > Z > 0) \tag{7}$$

where Y is the output, L is labor employed, A is a positive constant, t is time, and Z is a constant which indicates the share of wages and profits while $(1 - Z)$ indicates that of rent in total output. Then, the rate of growth of commodity output is

$$g = a + Zn \tag{8}$$

where n is the rate of growth of the labor force.

---

[21]This reminds us of unsuccessful Keynesian attempts to show the overdeterminancy of the full-employment equilibrium. See Hahn [15], Klein [21, pp. 84–86], Modigliani [30], Morishima [32, Chapter 7], and Negishi [35].

[22]Eltis [13, pp. 177–178], insisted, however, that it is anachronistic to expect Malthus to write as if a sophisticated modern capital market was already in existence.

As for the rate of technical progress a, let us consider that it is influenced by the profitability

$$a = a_0 + a_1(r - r_s) \qquad (9)$$

where a_0 and a_1 are positive constants, r is the rate of profit, and r_s is the rate of profit at which the capital stock is constant. Equation (9) can be used to substitute for a in (8) to obtain

$$g = a_0 + a_1(r - r_s) + Zn. \qquad (10)$$

The rate of growth of capital stock k is assumed also to be influenced by the profitability

$$k = \beta(r - r_s) \qquad (11)$$

where β is a positive constant. By the use of (11), (10) can be rewritten as

$$g = a_0 + a_1(k/\beta) + Zn \qquad (12)$$

and in equilibrium growth where output, capital and labor all grow at the same rate,

$$g = k = n = a_0/(1 - Z - a_1/\beta). \qquad (13)$$

To consider the rate of growth of investment, Eltis simplifies (11) by assuming that $r_s = 0$, so that the investment function can be written as

$$I_t = \beta P_{t-1} \qquad (14)$$

where I_t denotes the investment in the period t and P_{t-1} denotes the total profits in the period $t - 1$. If s_c is written for the fraction of their incomes which capitalists save, and s_r for the fraction of rents that landlords save, while R_t is written for the total rents in the period t,

$$s_c P_t + s_r R_t - \beta P_{t-1} = 0 \qquad (15)$$

in view of (14), so that

$$(\beta/s_c)(P_{t-1}/P_t) = 1 + (s_r R_t)/(s_c P_t). \qquad (16)$$

Therefore, from (14) and (16),

$$I_{t+1}/I_t = P_t/P_{t-1} = (\beta/s_c) \text{ (saving from profits/total saving)}_t. \qquad (17)$$

To realize an economy's full growth potential, investment, profits, and demand must grow at a rate at least equal to the economy's long-term growth potential,

$$(\beta/s_c) \text{ (saving from profits/total saving)} - 1$$
$$= a_0/(1 - Z - a_1/\beta) \qquad (18)$$

in view of (13) and (17). An economy will not be prevented from achieving its maximum growth potential in the long-run if the demand-side factors on the left-hand side of this final equation are larger than the supply-side factors on the right, though, of course, on average, it can grow no more rapidly than potential supply. If, however, the right-hand side of this equation exceeds the left-hand side, effective demand will grow persistently more slowly than the potential rate of growth of supply. Eltis concluded that equation (18) gives the solution to Malthus's problem of the optimal saving ratio.

> No considerable and continued increase of wealth could possibly take place without that degree of frugality which occasions, annually, the conversion of some revenue into capital, and creates a balance of produce over consumption; but it is quite obvious . . . that the principle of saving, pushed to excess, would destroy the motive to production . . . If consumption exceeds production, the capital of the country must be diminished, and its wealth must be gradually destroyed from its want of power to produce; if production be in a great excess above consumption, the motive to accumulate and produce must cease from the want of an effectual demand in those who have the principal means of purchasing. The two extremes are obvious; and it follows that there must be some intermediate point, though the resources of political economy may not be able to ascertain it, where, taking into consideration both the power to produce and the will to consume, the encouragement to the increase of wealth is the greatest. (Malthus [28, pp. 6–7].)

Keynes argued that the whole problem of the balance between saving and investment had been posed here [19, p. 102] and Lange [24] solved the problem by using a simple Keynesian model,

$$Y = C + I \tag{19}$$

$$I = F(i, C) \tag{20}$$

$$M = L(i, Y), \tag{21}$$

where Y, C, I, i and M denote respectively the national income, the total expenditure on consumption, the investment, the rate of interest and the given amount of money to be held by individuals. The problem of the optimal propensity to consume is solved by choosing a level of C which maximizes I to be determined jointly with Y and i from (19) to (21).

The condition that investment be at a maximum is given by the differentiation of (20), i.e.,

$$dI = F_i \, di + F_c \, dC = 0, \tag{22}$$

where F_i denotes the partial differentiation of F with respect to i and the like.

The differentiation of (19) and (21) also gives

$$dY = dC + dI \tag{23}$$

and

$$L_i \, di + L_Y \, dY = 0, \tag{24}$$

since M is constant. By substituting (23) and (24) into (22) we arrive at

$$L_Y/L_i = F_c/F_i. \tag{25}$$

The equation (25), together with the equations (19) to (21), determines Y, C, I and i, and therefore the optimum propensity to consume C/Y which maximizes I. The increase in investment caused by the higher level of consumption is more than offset by the decrease in investment caused by the higher rate of interest induced by the higher level of consumption through (23) and (24). Similarly, the reduction of investment caused by lower consumption outweighs the increase in investment caused by the lower rate of interest induced by the lower consumption through (23) and (24).

Lange's solution is, of course, based on the Keynesian interpretation of Malthus to the effect that Malthus was one of the most important precursors of the Keynesian way of thinking (Keynes [18, pp. 362–364], [19, pp. 71–108]). It is an important fact that such an interpretation has had some influences on the development of Keynesian theory, a fact no one can deny. Whether the Keynesian interpretation of Malthus is consistent with what Malthus really meant is, however, quite another problem. Although there is rarely agreement between any two modern commentators on the fundamental nature of Malthus's contribution, and Eagly and Eltis still support the Keynesian interpretation, Meek, Stigler, Corry, Blaug, Hollander and many others do not consider Malthus as a forerunner of Keynes.[23]

To argue that Malthus is a precursor of Keynes, one has to show that Malthus considered the aggregate level of production variable, i.e., not fixed at the so-called full employment level, and that Malthus does not insist on the identity of investment and saving. As for the former, Keynes rightly argued that "Ricardo is investigating the theory of the distribution of the product in conditions of equilibrium and Malthus is concerned with what determines the volume of output day by day in the real world. Malthus is dealing with the monetary economy in which we happen to live, Ricardo with the abstraction of a neutral money economy" [19, p. 97]. This comparison of Ricardo and

---

[23]Meek [29], Stigler [52, p. 319], Corry [11], Blaug [4, pp. 85–86], [5, p. 171], and Hollander [17, pp. 523–524, 533–534].

Malthus should be read together with the following sentences in Keynes's "Monetary Theory of Production". "The main reason why the problem of crisis is unsolved, or at any rate why this theory is so unsatisfactory, is to be found in the lack of what might be termed a monetary theory of production. . . . I am saying that booms and depressions are phenomena peculiar to an economy in which money is not neutral" [20, pp. 408–411].

As for the latter, one may argue that Malthus had a clear idea of the distinction between demand and supply of saving, and refer to a letter from Say to Malthus, "Mr. Ricardo claims . . . that all savings are always employed because the capitalists do not wish to lose the interest. On the contrary, there are considerable savings that are not invested when it is difficult to find a use for them," and to the fact that Malthus claimed that this was "all that I contend for" in his letter to Ricardo (Ricardo [44, p. 260]). Even if saving and investment are not identical, they may be equated by changes in the rate of interest at the level of full employment. Malthus's theory thus interpreted was, therefore, not complete from the point of view of Keynes. As Eagly admitted, Malthus's criticism against Say's law can be removed by the loanable funds theory of interest. This is well recognized by Keynes. "Malthus perceived, as often, what was true, but it is essential to a complete comprehension of why it is true, to explain how an excess of frugality does not bring with it a decline to zero in the rate of interest" [19, p. 102]. In other words, unemployment is not explained by over-saving unless the non-zero rate of interest is shown to be prevented from falling by the liquidity preference, as in (21) of Lange's Keynesian model.

If savings are not invested, in other words, they must be hoarded. It is quite unfortunate for the Keynesian interpretation of Malthus that Malthus explicitly denied the existence of hoarding. In *Principles of Political Economy*, he declared that "No political economist of the present day can by saving mean mere hoarding" [27, p. 38]. He also stated in *Definitions in Political Economy* that "saving, in modern times, implies the accumulation of capital, as few people now lock up their money in a box" [28, p. 238]. We have to admit, therefore, the possibility of the interpretation that Malthus, as a classical economist, assumed the saving–investment identity and that his problem was not the lack of effective demand caused by oversaving relative to investment.

6. The motives to produce

If saving and investment are identical and there is no Keynesian problem of effective demand, then, how can Malthus be "concerned with what determines the volume of output day by day"? Let us see Malthus's explanation of glut in his *Principles*. Suppose the propensity to save is increased excessively.

> There would evidently be an unusual quantity of commodities of all kinds in the market, owing to those who had been before engaged in personal services having been converted, by the accumulation of capital, into productive labourers; while the number of labourers altogether being the same, and power and will to purchase for consumption among landlords and capitalists being by supposition diminished, commodities would necessarily fall in value compared with labour, so as very generally to lower profits, and to check for a time further production. But this is precisely what is meant by the term glut, which, in this case, is evidently general not partial. (Malthus [28, p. 316].)[24]

Saving is invested and capital accumulates, but wages do not rise at this stage, since the supply of productive labor, to be demanded by increased capital, is also increased by a shift of unproductive labor to productive labor caused by increased saving. The real wage rises, however, eventually. Since capitalists and landlords who are assumed to have increased savings cannot purchase much of the commodities whose supplies are increased by the capital accumulation, an increased amount of commodities must be exchanged with labor whose total supply takes time to be increased, and the relative price of commodities against labor must fall.

Ricardo commented that "they would fall in labour value, but not in money value." But Malthus considered that the real wage rises with the money wage relatively unchanged, i.e., the price of commodities falls in money value. "Commodities in general, and corn most particularly, are continually rising or falling in money-price, from the state of the supply as compared with the demand, while the money-price of labour remains much more nearly the same." A rise in the real wage implies a fall in the rate of profit. Ricardo further argued as follows.

> I agree too that the capitalists being in such a case without a sufficient motive for saving from revenue, to add to capital, will cease doing so . . . will, if you please, even expend a part of their capital; but I ask what evil will result from this? . . . enough would remain to employ all the labour that could be obtained, and to pay it liberally, so that in fact there would be little diminution in the quantity of commodities produced.[25]

[24]See also Malthus [27, pp. 247, 242].
[25]Ricardo [42, p. 309], Malthus [27, p. 61], Ricardo [45, pp. 24–25].

For Malthus, however, the diminished rate of profit due to excess accumulation implies the reduction of employment and production.

If the conversion of revenue into capital pushed beyond a certain point must, by diminishing the effectual demand for produce, throw the labouring classes out of employment, it is obvious that the adoption of parsimonious habits beyond a certain point, may be accompanied by the most distressing effects at first, and by a marked depression of wealth and population afterwards. (Malthus [28, p. 326].)

Diminishing effectual demand implies here the reduced rate of profit, since, like Adam Smith, Malthus defined effectual demand as the demand which makes the supply continue at the natural price, i.e., with sufficient profits.

The commodity will not be produced, unless the estimation in which it is held by the society or its intrinsic value in exchange be such, as not only to replace all the advances of labour and other articles which have been made for its attainment, but likewise to pay the usual profits upon those advances; or in other words, to command an additional quantity of labour, equal to those profits. (Malthus [28, p. 302].)

But why are employment and production reduced when the rate of profit is diminished? The reason is the destruction of the capitalists' motives to produce.

The deficiency in the value of what they produced would necessarily make them either consume more, or produce less; and when the mere pleasure of present expenditure, without the accompaniments of an improved local situation and an advance in rank, is put in opposition to the continued labour of attending to business during the greatest part of the day, the probability is that a considerable body of them will be induced to prefer the latter alternative, and produce less. (Malthus [28, pp. 400–401].).

By employing ten families he might perhaps, owing to the richness of the soil, obtain food for fifty; but he would find no proportionate market for this additional food, and would be soon sensible that he had wasted his time and attention in superintending the labour of so many persons. He would be disposed therefore to employ a smaller number. (Malthus [28, p. 332].)[26]

Indeed, the emphasis on motivation distinguishes Malthus from Ricardo.

[26]In spite of Corry [11], therefore, the investment is reduced by the fall in the rate of profit through the reduction of the level of production.

When the first edition of *Principles* was published, Malthus wrote to Ricardo:

> You constantly say that it is not a question about the motives to produce. Now I have certainly intended to make it almost entirely a question about motives. We see in almost every part of the world vast powers of production which are not put into action, and I explain this phenomenon by saying that from the want of proper distribution of the actual produce adequate motives are not furnished to continued production. (Ricardo [45, p. 10].)

Although Malthus considered money wages to be sticky, the unemployment resulting from the diminished motive to produce cannot be cleared, even if money wages are reduced.

> Though labour is cheap, there is neither the power nor the will to employ it all; because not only has the capital of the country diminished, compared with the number of labourers, but, owing to the diminished revenues of the country, the commodities which those labourers would produce are not such request as to ensure tolerable profits to the reduced capital.[27]

Bearing in mind our readings of Malthus in the above, let us reconsider Malthus's problem of the optimum propensity to consume, the problem considered by Lange and Eltis on the basis of Keynesian interpretation (section 5), by constructing a very simple classical, non-Keynesian, model of an aggregated economy.

Suppose firstly that the level of unproductive consumption C is very high, with the result that the rate of profit r is at such a high level that employers are willing to employ all the available labor supply $\bar{N}$, which is a given constant. The real wage w and the rate of profit R can be determined as functions of unproductive consumption C by solving

$$wN = F(N) - C \tag{1}$$

and

$$w(1 + r) = F'(N) \tag{2}$$

where $N = \bar{N}$, $F(N)$ is the aggregate production function with N being labor input and $F' > 0$, $F'' < 0$. Condition (1) signifies the equality of demand and supply of the aggregated commodity, i.e., the sum of the productive consumption $w\bar{N}$ and the unproductive consumption C is equal to the production F. Condition (2) gives the definition of the rate of profit r at the margin of the production.[28]

[27]Malthus [28, p. 417], Hollander [17, p. 533]. See also Blaug [4, p. 86].
[28]If not the limiting principle, but only the regulating principle applies on profits (Malthus [28, p. 271]), we should have $F'' = 0$. I owe this footnote to Mr. T. Dome of Kyoto University.

By differentiating (1) and (2) with respect to w, r, and C, we can derive

$$dr/dC = (1+t)/\bar{N}w > 0 \tag{3}$$

and

$$dw/dC = -w/\bar{N}w > 0. \tag{4}$$

The curve AB in Figure 4.5 shows the relation between r and C, which is positively sloped in view of (3). If C is drastically reduced, however, r falls to such a low level that employers have no motive to employ all the available labor force. "The conversion of revenue into capital pushed beyond a certain point must, by diminishing the effectual demand for produce, throw the labouring classes out of employment." It must be remembered that the diminishing effectual demand implies the falling rate of profit which destroys the motive to produce. Let us denote the level of employment employers are willing to keep at the level of the rate of profit r as

$$N = N(r), \quad N'(r) > 0. \tag{5}$$

By substituting (5) into (1) and (2), we can solve them for r and w as functions of C. The differentiation of them with respect to w, r and C gives

$$dr/dC = (1+r)/A > 0 \tag{6}$$

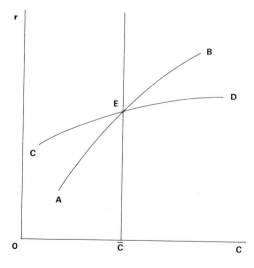

Figure 4.5

and

$$dw/dC = (F''N' - w)/A < 0, \tag{7}$$

where

$$A = Nw - NF''N' + (1+r)(F'N' - wN') > 0 \tag{8}$$

in view of the fact that $F' > w$ when $r > 0$ and $F'' < 0$. It is clear that dr/dC in (6) is smaller than dr/dC in (3) at such a level of unproductive consumption $\bar{C}$ that $\bar{N} = N(r)$. The curve CD in Figure 4.5 shows the relation between r and C when (5) is assumed.

Since $N(r) > \bar{N}$ is physically impossible and $\bar{N}$ cannot be employed if $\bar{N} > N(r)$, the relation between r and C is shown in Figure 4.5 by a kinked curve CEB. When $\bar{N} > N(r)$, there exists involuntary unemployment which cannot be cleared even if money wages fall. Employment cannot be increased unless the real wage w falls and the rate of profit r rises. With a given level of employment, a falling money wage implies diminishing productive consumption which causes excess supply of the aggregate commodity. Since the money price of the aggregate commodity also falls, the fall of the money wage fails to reduce the real wage and fails to increase employment.

The problem with the optimum propensity to consume is the maximization of wealth or capital W, which in our case is a non-durable wages fund created by annual investment identical to saving from the revenue, i.e.,

$$W = wN = F(N) - C. \tag{9}$$

Suppose (5) $N = N(r)$, then the condition for the maximization is

$$dW/dC = F'N'(1+r)/A - 1 = 0 \tag{10}$$

in view of (6). If the level of unproductive consumption C^* which satisfies (10) is lower than $\bar{C}$ which corresponds to $\bar{N} = N(r)$, as is shown in Figure 4.6, the optimum propensity to consume is given as $C^*/F(N(r^*))$ where r^* corresponds to C^* when r is solved as a function of C from (1), (2) and (5). The curve CD shows the relation between W and C when (5) is assumed, while the line AB shows the relation when $N = \bar{N}$. An increase in W caused by the reduction of consumption is more than offset by the decrease in W caused by the lower rate of profit induced by the lower rate of consumption through (6). Similarly, a reduction of W caused by a larger consumption outweighs the increase in W caused by the higher rate of profit induced by the larger consumption through (6). Unemployment remains in this case, which is likely to occur if N' is smaller at r corresponding to $\bar{C}$ so that the slope of CD at E, i.e., dW/dC is negative at $\bar{C}$.

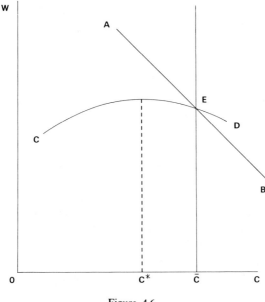

Figure 4.6

If there is no $C^* < \bar{C}$ as in the case of Figure 4.7, W attains the maximum at $\bar{C}$ since the relation between W and C is shown by the kinked curve CEB. The optimum propensity to consume is simply $\bar{C}/F(\bar{N})$. This case will be obtained if N' is large at r corresponding to $\bar{C}$ so that the slope of CD, i.e., dW/dC under the assumption (5) is positive at $\bar{C}$. Unfortunately, the current "resources of political economy may not be able to ascertain" which case, i.e., whether that of Figure 4.6 or that of Figure 4.7, is more likely.

Both Malthus and Keynes emphasized the importance of unproductive consumption, but for different reasons. Keynes considered a modern economy where production is run by salaried managers and capital is mainly fixed capital whose cost is already sunk. Even if wages are high and the rate of profit is low (or negative), production is continued (provided only the variable costs are covered by revenue) if there is the effective demand. When investment demand is low due to low rate of profit, unproductive consumption is important to compensate low investment demand so as to keep the level of the effective demand high.

Malthus considered a classical economy where production is run by individual capitalists and capital is mostly circulating capital represented by advanced wage costs. Production is not continued, unless individual capital-

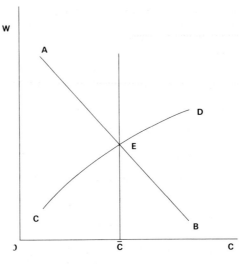

Figure 4.7

ists are motivated to produce by a high rate of profit. Unproductive consumption is important to reduce the investment so as to generate the effectual demand, i.e., the demand which assures a sufficiently high rate of profit.

> If I recommend a certain proportion of unproductive consumption, it is obviously and expressly with the sole view of furnishing the necessary motive to the greater continued production.... Now among the motives to produce, one of the most essential certainly is that an adequate share of what is produced should belong to those who set all industry in motion. (Ricardo [45, pp. 19–20].)

Malthus is concerned, not with Keynesian effective demand, but with Smithian effectual demand, which assures the individual capitalists motives to produce. Malthus is not so much as an underconsumptionist as a supply sider.[29]

References

[1] Akhtar, M.A., "The Classical Dichotomy in Ricardian Economics", *History of Political Economy*, 7(1975), pp. 299–311.

[29]Since the conversion of unproductive to productive laborers (Malthus [28, p. 316]) is a prolongation of the period of production, Malthus is rather a Hayekian.

[2] Barkai, H., "Ricardo on Factor Prices and Income Distribution in a Growing Economy", *Economica*, 26(1959), pp. 240–250.

[3] Barkai, H., "Ricardo's Second Thoughts on Rent as a Relative Share", *Southern Economic Journal*, 32(1966), pp. 285–293.

[4] Blaug, M., *Ricardian Economics*, Yale University Press, 1958.

[5] Blaug, M., *Economic Theory in Retrospect*, Cambridge University Press, 1978.

[6] Brems, H., "Ricardo's Long Run Equilibrium", *History of Political Economy*, 2(1970), pp. 225–245.

[7] Cantillon, R., *Essai sur la nature du commerce en général*, H. Higgs, ed. and tr., Macmillan, 1931.

[8] Casarosa, C., "A New Formulation of the Ricardian System", *Oxford Economic Papers*, 30(1978), pp. 38–63.

[9] Chipman, J.S., "A Survey of the Theory of International Trade, 1", *Econometrica*, 33(1965), pp. 477–519.

[10] Cochrane, J., "The First Mathematical Ricardian Model", *History of Political Economy*, 2(170), pp. 419–431.

[11] Corry, B.A., "Malthus and Keynes, A Reconsideration", *Economic Journal*, 69(1959), pp. 717–724.

[12] Eagly, R.V. *The Structure of Classical Economic Theory*, Oxford Economic University Press, 1974.

[13] Eltis, W., *The Classical Theory of Economic Growth*, Macmillan, 1984.

[14] Emmanuel, A., *Unequal Exchange*, B. Pearce, tr., Monthly Review Press, 1972.

[15] Hahn, F.H., "The Rate of Interest and General Equilibrium Analysis", *Economic Journal*, 65(1955), pp. 52–66.

[16] Hicks, J.R., and S. Hollander, "Mr. Ricardo and the Moderns", *Quarterly Journal of Economics*, 91(1977), pp. 351–369.

[17] Hollander, S., *The Economics of David Ricardo*, University of Toronto Press, 1979.

[18] Keynes, J.M., *The General Theory of Employment, Interest and Money*, Macmillan, 1936.

[19] Keynes, J.M., *Collected Writings*, X, Macmillan, 1972.

[20] Keynes J.M., *Collected Writings*, XIII, 1973.

[21] Klein, L.R., *The Keynesian Revolution*, Macmillan, 1947.

[22] Kojima, K., *Kokusaikeizairiron no Kenkyu* (Studies in the Theory of International Economics), Toyokeizai, 1952.

[23] Kregel, J.A., *The Reconstruction of Political Economy*, Macmillan, 1973.

[24] Lange, O., "The Rate of Interest and the Optimum Propensity to Consume", *Economica*, 5(1938), pp. 12–32.

[25] Leijonhufvud, A., *Information and Coordination*, Oxford University Press, 1981.

[26] Levy, D., "Ricardo and the Iron Law: A Correction of the Record", *History of Political Economy*, 8(1976), pp. 235–251.

[27] Malthus, T.R., *Definitions in Political Economy*, John Murray, 1826.

[28] Malthus, T.R., *Principles of Political Economy*, Pickering, 1836.

[29] Meek, R.L., "Physiocracy and the Early Theories of Under-Consumption", *Economica*, 18(1951), pp. 229–269.

[30] Modigliani, F., "Liquidity Preference and the Theory of Interest and Money", *Econometrica*, 12(1944), pp. 45–88.

[31] Morishima, M., *Marx's Economics*, Cambridge University Press, 1973.

[32] Morishima, M., *Walras' Economics*, Cambridge University Press, 1977.

[33] Morita, K., "Kotenha Kokusaibungyoron Saiko (The Classical Theory of International Division of Labor: A Reappraisal)", *Keizaigakuronshu* (University of Tokyo Journal of Economics), 43–3(1977), pp. 2–20.

[34] Negishi, T., *General Equilibrium Theory and International Trade*, North-Holland, 1972.

[35] Negishi, T., Book Review of [32], *The Economic Review* (Hitotsubashi University), 31(1980), pp. 89–91.

[36] Negishi, T., "The Labor Theory of Value in the Ricardian Theory of International Trade", *History of Political Economy*, 14(1982), pp. 199–210.

[37] Ohlin, B., *Interregional and International Trade*, Harvard University Press, 1933.

[38] Ong, N.P., "Ricardo's Invariable Measure of Value and Sraffa's Standard Commodity", *History of Political Economy*, 15(1983), pp. 207–227.

[39] Pasinetti, L., "A Mathematical Formulation of the Ricardian System", *Review of Economic Studies*, 27(1960), pp. 78–98.

[40] Petty, W., *Economic Writings*, 1, C.H. Hull, ed., Cambridge University Press, 1899.

[41] Ricardo, D., *On the Principles of Political Economy and Taxation*, Cambridge University Press, 1951.

[42] Ricardo, D., *Works and Correspondence*, II, Cambridge University Press, 1951.

[43] Ricardo, D., *Works and Correspondence*, IV, Cambridge University Press, 1951.

[44] Ricardo, D., *Works and Correspondence*, VIII, Cambridge University Press, 1952.

[45] Ricardo, D., *Works and Correspondence*, IX, Cambridge University Press, 1952.

[46] Roncaglia, A., *Sraffa and the Theory of Prices*, John Wiley, 1978.

[47] Samuelson, P.A., *Collected Scientific Papers*, 1, MIT. Press, 1966.

[48] Schumpeter, J.A., *History of Economic Analysis*, Oxford University Press, 1954.

[49] Shove, G.F., "The Place of Marshall's Principles in the Development of Economic Theory," *Economic Journal*, 52(1942), pp. 294–329.

[50] Smith, A., *An Inquiry into the Nature and Causes of the Wealth of Nations*, Oxford University Press, 1976.

[51] Sraffa, P., *Production of Commodities by Means of Commodities*, Cambridge University Press, 1960.

[52] Stigler, G.J., *Essays in the History of Economics*, University of Chicago Press, 1965.

[53] Watarai, K., "Ricardo Kihon Model nitsuite (On the Basic Model of Ricardo)", Meijigakuindaigaku Keizaikenkyu (Meijigaduin University Journal of Economics), 67(1983), pp. 1–69.

[54] Whewell, W., "Mathematical Exposition of Some of the Leading Doctrines in Mr. Ricardo's Principles of Political Economy and Taxation", *Transactions of the Cambridge Philosophical Society*, 4(1833), pp. 155–198.

CHAPTER 5

J.S. MILL AND THE CLOSE OF CLASSICAL ECONOMICS

1. Equilibrium of demand and supply

John Stuart Mill (1806–1873) published *Essays on some Unsettled Questions of Political Economy* in 1844. In the same year "On the Measurement of the Utility of Public Works" by Jules Dupuit appeared. Dupuit was an important pioneer of the marginal revolution. Similarly, 1848 was the year of Mill's *Principles of Political Economy* and also that of *The Communist Manifesto* of Marx and Engels. New paradigms began to be developed to replace that of classical economics. Mill played the role of rear guard in the retreat of classical economics. As the history of armies shows, to bring up the rear is the most difficult task. Whether Mill played the role successfully or not depends on how one interprets the essence of classical economics. Currently there are two different interpretations, both emphasizing the significance of classical economics to contemporary economics, i.e., those of the neo-Ricardians and the new classical economics.

Neo-Ricardians and post-Keynesians insist on linking Keynesian economics with classical economics rather than synthesizing it with neo-classical economics. "To historians of economic theory the triumph of the neoclassical synthesis should appear as most inappropriate.... It would seem more appropriate to link Keynes's own theory with the long-period theory of the classical political economists" (Kregel [19, p. xv]). They, like Marxian economists, regard the labor theory of value as the essence of classical economics. "For the Classicists value was something related to the physical concept of costs, related to the application of real resources (primarily labour) to the growth of output" (Kregel [19, p. 30]). From the point of view of the neo-Ricardians, therefore, Mill is considered to have played the role of the rear guard of classical economics very badly, since Mill admitted that the cost theory of value including labor theory sometimes fails and that in such a case "we must revert to a law of value anterior to cost of production, and more fundamental, the law of demand and supply" (Mill [24, p. 570]). If we follow their interpretation, then, the title of this chapter should be changed to "J.S. Mill and the Decline and Fall of Classical Economics."

The essence of classical economics is, however, interpreted quite differently in the new classical macroeconomics. "The model that we construct is in a fundamental sense a direct descendant of the textbook classical model, being an equilibrium model [of demand and supply]" (Sargent [30, p. 367]). While Keynesian economics insist on the existence of disequilibrium in the labor market (involuntary unemployment) and rejects the classical dichotomy and the neutrality of money, the classical doctrine is interpreted here in such a way that "employers and employees are continuously operating on their supply and demand schedules" (Sargent [30, p. 366]) and that "the money supply plays no role in determining the levels of employment and output, although, ..., under some circumstances it may affect their rates of growth over time" (Sargent [30, p. 45]). In this chapter we are going to follow this interpretation of classical economics, i.e., as the economics of the equilibrium of demand and supply. Our conclusion will be that Mill played the role of the rear guard of classical economics extremely well, by reorganizing it on the basis of the fundamental law of value, i.e., the law of demand and supply, and paved the way to the development of neo-classical economics.

After a brief description of the life of J.S. Mill, the rest of this section will be devoted to explaining the content of his *Principles of Political Economy*.[1] In section 2 we shall start with a review of Ekelund's model of Mill's wages fund doctrine and argue that Mill's recantation of the doctrine can be explained by an equilibrium model of the labor market where multiple equilibria exist. Then, in section 3, we shall consider how Mill can reconcile his assertions of the impossibility of overproduction, i.e., Say's law, and the fact that consumption influences production. We can see in Mill's arguments an embryo form of the equilibrium theory of business cycles. Mill is perhaps best known to contemporary economic theorists by his theory of reciprocal demand in international trade. Section 4 will be devoted to reviewing a recent controversy on how to evaluate Mill's contribution to equilibrium theory in his "Great Chapter" of international values. Finally, we shall return to the problem of the wages fund doctrine. In section 5 we shall see how Mill defended the equilibrium theory in general from Thornton's criticism in the recantation of the doctrine.

John Stuart Mill was born in 1806 as the eldest son of James Mill, an economist, a disciple and promoter of Jeremy Bentham, and the author of *Elements of Political Economy* (1821). He received an unusual and exacting education from his father to become an ardent Benthamite utilitarian, as was described in his *Autobiography* (1873). At the age of twenty, however he

---

[1] For Mill's economic theory in general, see an encyclopaedic exposition of Hollander [16]. See also Mawatari [21] for Mill's methodology.

suffered a prolonged period of mental crisis and his views were seriously modified. Then he was influenced by Coleridge, Wordsworth, Saint-Simon, Comte, as well as by his future wife, Harriet Taylor.[2] In 1823, J.S. Mill, like his father, joined the East India Company and remained there until 1858. He was also the Member of Parliament for Westminster from 1865 to 1868, and died in 1873. As well as *Essays* and *Principles*, his publications included, *A System of Logic* (1843), *On Liberty* (1859), *Considerations on Representative Government* (1861), *Utilitarianism* (1863) and *The Subjection of Women* (1869).

J.S. Mill's *Principles of Political Economy* consists of "Preliminary Remarks" and five Books, i.e.,

Book I: Production,
Book II: Distribution,
Book III: Exchange,
Book IV: Influence of the Progress of Society on Production and Distribution,
Book V: On the Influence of Government.

In "Preliminary Remarks," Mill starts with the declaration that the subject of political economy is wealth and defines it as "all useful or agreeable things which possess exchangeable value; or, in other words, all useful or agreeable things except those which can be obtained, in the quantity desired, without labour or sacrifice" (Mill [24, p. 9]). Mercantilism, which insists "that wealth consisted solely of money" (Mill [24, p. 2]), is rejected, since "the uses of money are in no respect promoted by increasing the quantity which exists and circulates in a country; the service which it performs being as well rendered by a small as by a large aggregate amount" (Mill [24, p. 6]). After a sketch of economic development in the past, which shows the extraordinary differences between different nations and between different ages with regard to the production and distribution of wealth, the distinction between the laws of production and those of distribution is noted.

Book I is concerned with the laws of production. It starts with the consideration of two primary factors of production, i.e., labor and land, in Chapter I, which is followed by two chapters on labour. Chapters IV, V, and VI deal with capital, i.e., the accumulated stock of the produce of labor. The productivity of land, labor and capital is discussed in Chapters VII, VIII (Co-operation), and IX (Large Scale Production). The final four chapters are devoted to considering the law of the increase of production which depends on increases in labor, capital and land. It is concluded that

the laws and conditions of the Production of wealth partake of the character

[2] For Harriet Taylor, see Hayek [14] and Kamm [17].

of physical truths. There is nothing optional or arbitrary in them ... a double quantity of labour will not raise, on the same land, a double quantity of food, ... the unproductive expenditure [consumption] of individuals will *pro tanto* tend to impoverish the community, and only their productive expenditure [investment] will enrich it. (Mill [24, p. 199].)

Of the 13 chapters of Book I, perhaps the most important to us would be Chapter V, "Fundamental Propositions respecting Capital." The first proposition is "That industry is limited by capital" (Mill [24, p. 63]). This implies that the employment of labor cannot be increased without a further capital formation. In other words, it is considered that capital consists essentially of advances to laborers. "Self-evident as the thing is, it is often forgotten that the people of a country are maintained and have their wants supplied, not by the produce of present labour, but of past. They consume what has been produced, not what is about to be produced" (Mill [24, p. 64]). The second proposition is that capital is the result of saving and the third is that it is nevertheless consumed so that it is kept up, not by preservation, but by perpetual reproduction. The fourth proposition is the most controversial one, but it is a natural result of the implicit assumption of Say's law and Mill's concept of capital and forms the basis of the wages fund doctrine, which we shall discuss in detail in the following section.

Demand for commodities is not demand for labour. The demand for commodities determines in what particular branch of production the labour and capital shall be employed; it determines the *direction* of the labour; but not the more or less of the labour itself, or of the maintenance or payment of the labour. These depend on the amount of the capital, or other funds directly devoted to the sustenance and remuneration of labour. (Mill [24, p. 79].)

The laws of distribution, which are to be discussed in Book II, are different from those of production, since distribution "is a matter of human institution solely. The things once there, mankind, individually or collectively, can do with them as they like. They can place them at the disposal of whomsoever they please, and on whatever terms" (Mill [24, p. 200]). The first two chapters of Book II deal with private property and its absolute or partial negation, socialism. Chapter III discusses the classes among whom the produce is distributed i.e., the owners of the three factors of production, labor, capital and land. It is noted that sometimes the same person owns either two of the three factors, or all three. In Chapter IV, it is argued that "under the rule of individual property, the division of the produce is the result of two determining agencies: Competition and Custom" and that "political economists generally, and English political economists above others, have been accustomed to lay almost exclusive stress upon the first of these agencies; to exaggerate the effect of competition, and to take into little account the other and conflicting principle" (Mill [24, p. 242]). Chapters V to VIII, then, are devoted to dealing with the states of economical relation "in which competition has no part, the arbiter of transactions being either brute force or established usage" (Mill [24, p. 248]), i.e., slavery, peasant proprietors, and metayers, while the cottier tenure, i.e., cases "in which the conditions of the contract, especially the amount of rent, are determined not by custom but by competition" (Mill [24, p. 318]), is discussed in the two subsequent chapters. Wages, which "depend mainly upon the demand and supply of labour; or, as it is often expressed, on proportion between population and capital" (Mill [24, p. 343]) are discussed in Chapters XI and XII, while the differences of wages is dealt with in Chapter XIV. The final two chapters are devoted to discussing profits and rent, respectively.

Discussions on exchange, value, price and money are postponed until Book III, which implies that Mill's concept of political economy is much wider than Catallactics (the science of exchanges) or the science of value.

It is true that in the preceding Books we have not escaped the necessity of anticipating some small portion of the theory of Value, especially as to the value of labour and land. It is nevertheless evident, that of the two great departments of Political Economy, the production of wealth and its distribution, the consideration of Value has to do with the latter alone; and with that, only so far as competition, and not usage or custom, is the distributing agency. (Mill [24, p. 435].)

The first six chapters of Book III discuss value, and demand and supply, cost of production and rent, respectively, in their relation to value.

The temporary or Market Value of a thing depends on the demand and supply.... Besides their temporary value, things have also a permanent, or, as it may be called, a Natural Value, to which the market value, after every variation, always tends to return.... The natural value of some things is a scarcity value; but most things naturally exchange for one another in the ratio of their cost of production, or at what may be termed their Cost Value. (Mill [24, p. 478].)

While value is considered in real terms, i.e., in terms of the command which the possession of a thing gives over purchasable commodities in general, price is defined as the value in relation to money. After the laws of value are discussed without introducing money, Chapters VII to XIII are devoted to considerations on money and credit as a substitute for money. Chapter XIV deals with excess of supply, which is based on Essay II, "On the Influence of Consumption upon Production", of Mill's *Essays on Some Unsettled Questions of Political Economy*. It is to be noted that the problem of glut is considered in Book III after money is taken into consideration. We shall discuss this problem in section 3. After a measure of value and a joint cost of production are discussed respectively in Chapters XV and XVI, two chapters follow which consider the problem of international trade. The principles of comparative advantage and of reciprocal demand are explained in Chapters XVII and XVIII respectively. We shall review a recent controversy on the latter chapter in section 4. The four subsequent chapters are devoted to the problems of the monetary aspect of international trade. The rate of interest, the regulation of currency (currency and banking schools) and underselling are discussed in Chapters XXIII, XXIV and XXV respectively. Book III concludes with Chapter XXVI, stating that exchange and money make no difference to the law of wages, rent and profits.

Book IV, "Influence of the Progress of Society on Production and Distribution," starts with the distinction between statics and dynamics in Chapter I. The three preceding Books are concerned with statics, i.e., the economical laws of a stationary and unchanging society.

> We have still to consider the economical condition of mankind as liable to change, and indeed as at all times undergoing progressive changes. We have to consider what these changes are, what are their laws, and what their ultimate tendencies; thereby adding a theory of motion to our theory of equilibrium – the Dynamics of political economy to the Statics (Mill [24, p. 695].)

Chapter II deals with the influence of the progress of industry and population on values and prices, while Chapter III discusses those influences on rents, profits and wages. The tendency of profits to a minimum is the subject of the two subsequent chapters.

Mill's view of the stationary state as the ultimate goal of industrial progress, expressed in Chapter VI, is different from those of other classical economists.

> It is scarcely necessary to remark that a stationary condition of capital and population implies no stationary state of human improvement. There would be as much scope as ever for all kinds of mental culture, and moral and social progress; as much room for improving the Art of Living, and much more likelihood of its being improved, when minds ceased to be

engrossed by the art of getting on. Even the industrial arts might be as earnestly and as successfully cultivated, with this sole difference, that instead of serving no purpose but the increase of wealth, industrial improvements would produce their legitimate effect, that of abridging labour. (Mill [24, p. 751].)

I cannot, therefore, regard the stationary state of capital and wealth with the unaffected aversion so generally manifested towards it by political economists of the old school. I am inclined to believe that it would be, on the whole, a very considerable improvement on our present condition. I confess I am not charmed with the ideal life held out by those who think that the normal state of human beings is that of struggling to get on; that the trampling, crushing, elbowing, and treading on each other's heels, which form the existing type of social life, are the most desirable lot of human kind, or anything but the disagreeable symptoms of one of the phases of industrial progress. (Mill [24, p. 748].)

Finally, Book IV ends with Chapter VII, "On the Probable Futurity of the Labouring Classes".

The final Book of Mill's *Principles* is entitled "On the Influence of Government". The subject is divided, in Chapter I, into (1) the economical effects of the necessary and acknowledged functions of government, (2) governmental interferences of the optional kind which take place under the influence of false theories, and (3) the optional class of governmental interference which is really advisable. Chapters II to VI are devoted to the theory of taxation, as one of the means adopted by governments to raise the revenue so as to perform their functions. National debt is then discussed in Chapter VII. Chapters VIII and IX deal with the economical effects of the ordinary functions of government, the security of person and property, and the system of the laws and the administration of justice. Influences of government grounded on erroneous theories are considered in Chapter X. The doctrine of protection to native industry is considered as one of these erroneous theories, though Mill permits one exception.

The only case in which, on mere principles of political economy, protecting duties can be defensible, is when they are imposed temporarily (especially in a young and rising nation) in hopes of naturalizing a foreign industry, in itself perfectly suitable to the circumstances of the country. The superiority of one country over another in a branch of production often arises only from having begun it sooner.... But it is essential that the protection should be confined to cases in which there is good ground of assurance that the industry which it fosters will after a time be able to dispence with it. (Mill [24, p. 922].)

This is the so-called Mill's condition for the protection of the infant industries, which is necessary but by no means sufficient (Negishi [27, pp. 90–99]). Book V concludes with Chapter XI, "Of the Grounds and Limits of the Laissez-Faire or Non-Interference Principle".

2. Recantation of the wages fund doctrine

While the long-run wage theory of classical economics is that of the natural wage, i.e., the subsistence wage necessary to reproduce labor (power), its short-run wage theory is the wages fund doctrine. As we have seen in the previous section, it can clearly be seen in the capital and wage theories in Mill's *Principles*, i.e., "Demand for commodities is not demand for labor," and "[wages] depend mainly upon the demand and supply of labor; or, as it is often expressed, on proportion between population and capital." Mill [25], however, recanted this corner stone of classical economics in 1869. It is generally believed that it shook the foundations of the classical theoretical system and is an important factor in explaining the decline and fall of classical economics (Ekelund and Hébert [10, pp. 164, 171]). If so, we have to say that Mill played the role of the rear guard of classical economics very badly. Our view is, of course, different. Even in his recantation of the wages fund doctrine, Mill defended the equilibrium theory in the labor market very skilfully. Although he sacrificed the wages fund doctrine, a protective belt of the classical research programme, he firmly retained the equilibrium theory of demand and supply, the hard core of the programme.

Recanting the wages fund doctrine in the equilibrium theory implies denying some conditions for the wages fund doctrine in an equilibrium model. It is convenient, therefore, to see what kind of assumptions are being made in a recent short-run equilibrium model of the classical wages fund doctrine constructed by Ekelund [9]. They are: (1) an aggregate point–input–point–output production function for all produced goods; (2) an economy's real output composed solely of machinery (fixed capital), wage goods, and the capitalist (non-wage-earner) consumables; (3) a constant ratio of fixed to circulating capital in the economy; (4) perfect competition (at constant cost) in all markets; (5) a fixed money stock; and (6) constant population and productivity over the period or periods under discussion. Of these conditions for the wages fund doctrine, assumptions (1) and (2) which we may call respectively the annual harvest assumption and the wage good assumption, are the most important.

If we neglect, as Ekelund did following Mill in the recantation, investment in fixed capital and consider a naive version where the demand for labor has a unitary elasticity, the annual harvest assumption may be described in Figure 5.1 as follows. At time t_1, a given stock of wage goods K exists, which is invested in the circulating capital to sustain labor over the period of production $t_1 t_2$, which is a technologically given constant as in the case of traditional agriculture. Then, a stock of ripened (wage) goods K' is available at time t_2, which (or a part of which) is again invested to tide labor over $t_2 t_3$ ($= t_1 t_2$). The annual harvest assumption implies not only that the period of production, i.e., the time interval $t_1 t_2$ between an input and the resulted output is given, but also the period of production is identical to the time interval between successive inputs and also to the time interval between successive outputs i.e., the market interval, since to make input means to purchase labor with wage goods and output has to be sold in markets.

The wage good assumption implies that laborers consume only wage goods, while capitalists consume only non-wage goods. A textual support for differential consumption patterns for labor and capitalist classes may be as follows:

> It may be said, perhaps, that wines, equipages, and furnitures, are not subsistence, tools, and materials, and could not in any case have been applied to the support of labour; that they are adapted for no other than unproductive consumption, and that the detriment to the wealth of the community was when they were produced, not when they were consumed. (Mill [24, p. 72].)

Since the stock of wage goods available at t_1 is given as K, and laborers cannot be supported by non-wage goods, the aggregate real capital to be used to employ labor at t_1 is determined by this predetermined wages fund K, and the demand for labor has the unitary elasticity with respect to real wage, i.e., wage in terms of wage goods. A higher real wage is possible only at the sacrifice of employment, or only if the population given in the assumption (6) is small. Allocation of labor for the production of different goods in the period of production $t_1 t_2$ is determined by the demand for different goods expected at

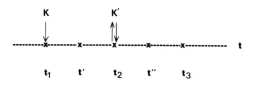

Figure 5.1

t_2. The demand for labor is determined, however, by the predetermined wages fund K existing at t_1.

> What supports and employs productive labour, is the capital expended in setting it to work, and not the demand of purchasers for the produce of the labour when completed. Demand for commodities is not demand for labour. (Mill [24, p. 79].)

Mill [25] recanted the wages fund doctrine, accepting the criticism made by Thornton [32]. Mill had in mind a case of the wage indeterminancy due to demand for labor inelastic with respect to wage. Supply being a given constant, this is the case where schedules of supply and demand are coincidental, at least within certain limits.

> When the equation of demand and supply leaves the price in part indeterminate, because there is more than one price which would fulfil the law .... The price, in this case, becomes simply a question whether sellers or buyers hold out longest; and depends on their comparative patience, or on the degree of inconvenience they are respectively put to by delay.

> If it should turn out that the price of labour falls within one of the excepted cases – the case which the law of equality between demand and supply does not provide for, because several prices all agree in satisfying that law; we are already able to see that the question between one of those prices and another will be determined by causes which operate strongly against the labourer, and in favour of the employer.

Schwartz [31, pp. 95, 275] argued that the rejection of the yearly period of production, i.e., the annual harvest assumption, lies at the origin of Mill's recantation, since Mill [25] insisted that the capitalist's "profit is made as his transactions go on, and not at Christmas or Midsummer, when he balances his book." As Ekelund [9] noted, however, the rejection of the annual harvest assumption should not be taken to make the period of production $t_1 t_2$ shorter. It should be taken to make the market interval $t_1 t'$ shorter than the period of production $t_1 t_2$ in Figure 5.1. While the period of production itself is not necessarily made shorter as manufacturing predominates over agriculture and agriculture itself is highly artificialized, the market period can certainly be made shorter since, unlike in the case of traditional agriculture, production can now be started at any time.

Suppose the period of production is still $t_1 t_2$ (and $t_2 t_3$) but it is twice as long as the market interval and markets are open not only at t_1, t_2, t_3 but also at t' (the mid-point of t_1 and t_2) and t'' (that of t_2 and t_3). Let the rate of the real wage in terms of wage goods at t_1 be w_1 and the normal rate of the real wage expected by a capitalist in the wage good industry to prevail at time t' be w.

Having a stock of wage goods at hand, the capitalist has two alternatives at t_1, either to exchange his wages fund with labor at t_1 and start production immediately so that output is available at t_2, or to wait until t' and then to exchange his wages fund with labor to start production with the result that output is not available until t''. The internal rate of return for the unit market interval from the first alternative, r, is calculated by

$$y/(1+r)^2 +(-w_1)=0 \tag{1}$$

and that from the second alternative r' is obtained from

$$y/(1+r')^3 +(-w)=0 \tag{2}$$

where y denotes per head output of wage goods. Note that capital is left idle for the first market interval, $t_1 t'$, in the case of the second alternative.

Suppose that expectation w is inelastic with respect to current w_1. If w_1 is higher than a certain critical level which corresponds to the condition that $r=r'$, the capitalist will not expend his stock of wage goods to employ labor at t_1 and will choose the second alternative. Since different capitalists have different expectations, we can say that more and more capitalists will choose the second alternative as the current rate of wage gets higher. The aggregate wages fund actually offered to be exchanged against labor is not pre-determined but is a decreasing function of the current real wage, given the distribution of the expected wage. Since the demand for labor is of unitary elasticity with respect to the real wage when the real wages fund to be offered is predetermined, the elasticity of the demand for labor is now larger than one. This is the result of the abandonment of the annual harvest assumption. Although it is to deny the naive version of the wages fund doctrine that the elasticity of demand for labor is one, the rejection of the annual harvest assumption is not an essential aspect of the recantation, since in the recantation Mill admitted not only that the elasticity is no longer equal to one but also that it is less than one so that "trade combination can raise wages" and "the power of Trade's Unions may therefore be so exercised as to obtain for the labouring classes collectively, both a larger share and a larger positive amount of the produce of labour."

What is essential for Mill's recantation of the wages fund doctrine is, then, the rejection of not the annual harvest assumption but the wages good assumption. While Ekelund [9], in his model of a wages fund doctrine explained above, emphasized that the pre-determined wages fund is real, not monetary, Mill [25] argued in terms of monetary funds in his recantation, as the following quotation can be interpreted to show.

The capitalist's pecuniary means consist of two parts – his capital, and his profits or income.... If he has to pay more for labour, the additional payment comes out of his own income; perhaps from the part which he would have saved and added to capital; ... perhaps from what he would have expended on his private wants or pleasures. There is no law of nature making it inherently impossible for wages to rise to the point of absorbing not only the fund which he had intended to devote to carrying on his business, but the whole of what he allows for his private expenses, beyond the necessaries of life.

It was easy, therefore, for Ekelund to show, by using his model of a wages fund, that Mill was wrong in the recantation. Since stocks of both wage goods and non-wage goods are pre-determined, and money stock is also fixed by Ekelund's assumption (5), capitalists' larger expenditure on labor in terms of money due to a higher nominal wage simply results in a proportionally higher money price of wage goods and a lower money price of non-wage goods. Even though the level of the nominal wage is indeterminate, changeable by capitalists' decisions on the allocation between the monetary wages fund and their private expenses, the real wage is determined by the wages fund and the population. The real wages fund remains unchanged under the wage good assumption, since the stock of wage goods is pre-determined. Without the wage good assumption, however, changes in the allocation of the monetary fund may cause changes in the real wages fund, since money is merely a veil in the classical dichotomy of real and monetary economics and capitalists' decisions in terms of monetary funds merely reflect their decisions in terms of real funds.

To make the demand for labor completely inelastic as Mill [25] had in mind in his recantation, the wages good assumption has to be discarded, since otherwise the elasticity of demand for labor is unitary or may be larger than one. Taking the existence of fixed capital into consideration, furthermore, Hollander [15] argued rightly that the fixed technical coefficients in production are required, so that the demand for labor does not change through the substitution effect between fixed capital and labor caused by changes in wage. Without the wage good assumption, however, a boomerang effect is instantaneous, since investment in and disinvestment out of circulating capital can be effected instantaneously.[3] The wages fund may not be changed propor-

---

[3] In other words, there is no pre-determined wages fund. Since changes in wages fund are absorbed in changes in capitalists' consumption, there is no problem of partial and aggregate equilibrium analyses due to capital released and invested elsewhere in the economy. See, however, Hollander [16, pp. 414, 416]. For the so-called boomerang effect, i.e., the negative effect of high wage and low profit on capital accumulation, see Schwartz [31, p. 79].

tionally to the rate of wage and the demand for labor may be changed through this boomerang effect caused by changes in the rate of wage. For example, a higher wage and a lower rate of profit makes capitalists consume more and invest less in (or disinvest from) the circulating capital so that the wages fund gets smaller relative to the rate of wage. In other words, the abandonment of the wage good assumption is, though necessary, by no means sufficient for the zero elasticity of demand for labor. To avoid this difficulty, it seems to us that the fixed intertemporal coefficients in consumption are required, in addition to the fixed technical coefficients in production, to make the elasticity of demand for labor completely inelastic with respect to wage.

Let us construct a simple model of a capitalist, in which the demand for labor is completely inelastic with respect to the rate of wage, keeping all the assumptions made in Ekelund's [9] short-run model of a wages fund, except the wage good assumption. The economy's real output is assumed to be composed solely of machinery (fixed capital) and the consumables which can be consumed by both laborers and capitalists. Following Mill in the recantation, however, we disregard the existence of the fixed capital.

Suppose the capitalist has been in a stationary condition up to time t_1. A given stock of the consumables Y is in the hands of the capitalist at t_1, which can either be consumed by the capitalist himself or advanced to employ laborers, i.e.,

$$Y = wL + c_1 \tag{3}$$

where w, L and c_1 signify respectively the real rate of wage, the current level of employment, i.e., the demand for labor, and the current level of consumption, all at time t_1. Let us denote the average product of labor by a, which is considered as technically given, as in the case of Hollander's [15] assumption of the fixed technical coefficients in production. Then, after the technologically given period of production $t_1 t_2$, a stock of the consumables aL is available, which can again be either consumed or advanced as wages fund at t_2, i.e.,

$$aL = wL' + c_2 \tag{4}$$

where L' and c_2 denote respectively the demand for labor and the level of the capitalist's consumption, all at t_2, and the rate of wage is expected to be still at w in t_2.

As for the demand for labor at t_2, i.e., L', let us suppose that the capitalist expects the economy to return to the stationary condition in which it has been up to t_1, after a short-run variation in the rate of wage at t_1 and t_2, and plans to employ such a number of laborers at t_2 as is sufficient to rebuild his stock of the consumables Y at t_3. With unchanged productivity of labor, this requires that

L' should be Y/a. If L' can be given in this way, equations (3) and (4) are combined into the budget equation of the capitalist for $t_1 t_2$, i.e.,

$$c_1 + c_2/(1+r) = Y - Y/(1+r)^2 \tag{5}$$

where the rate of profit r corresponding to w is implicitly defined by

$$a = (1+r)w. \tag{6}$$

As the result of the maximization of the utility, which is a function of c_1 and c_2, under the condition of (5), then, we have the following familiar condition:

$$U_1 = (1+r)U_2 \tag{7}$$

where U_1 is the marginal utility of current consumption c_1 at t_1 and U_2 is the marginal utility of the next period consumption c_2 at t_2. Since Y and a are constants, we now have four conditions, i.e., (3) and (5) to (7), to determine four unknowns c_1, c_2, L and r as functions of w. As is easily seen, however, the demand for labor L is, in general, not completely inelastic with respect to the rate of wage w. We have, therefore, to impose restrictions on the form of the utility function to make the demand for labor inelastic with respect to wage.

Let us first generalize (7) into

$$U_1^{(-)} \geqq (1+r)U_2^{(+)} \tag{8}$$

and

$$U_1^{(+)} \leqq (1+r)U_2^{(-)} \tag{9}$$

where $U_1^{(-)}$ and $U_1^{(+)}$ are respectively the left-hand side derivative of the utility function with respect to current consumption and the right-hand side derivative of the utility function with respect to the next period's consumption and so forth. Condition (8) implies that the marginal utility to be lost by the unit reduction of current consumption is not smaller than the marginal utility to be gained by the increased consumption in the next period made possible by the unit reduction of current consumption. Similarly, condition (9) means that the marginal utility to be gained by the unit increase in current consumption is not larger than the marginal utility to be lost by the reduction in the next period's consumption which is the inevitable sacrifice due to the unit increase in current consumption. Obviously these two conditions have to be satisfied if the consumption stream is optimal through time under the intertemporal budget restriction (5).

If, incidentally, the utility function is differentiable and the right- and left-hand derivatives are identical, (8) and (9) are combined into the single condition (7). In the case of the fixed intertemporal coefficients in consumption, however, the utility function is, though continuous, not differentiable, since the right-hand side marginal utility of (utility gain of an increase in) the consumption of any period at the optimal consumption stream is zero, while the left-hand side marginal utility of (utility loss of a decrease in) the consumption of any period at the optimal consumption stream is positive. Indifference curves of this case are shown in Figure 5.2, where the current consumption c_1 is measured horizontally, and the next period's consumption c_2 is measured vertically. The $(c_1 = c_2)$ line OA indicates the fixed intertemporal coefficients in consumption, and indifference curves are L shaped with a kink on the line OA. The dotted line corresponds to the budget equation (5). With any intertemporal price ratio, i.e., $(1 + r)$, the optimal consumption is always at the kink, i.e., on the line OA.

In the case of fixed intertemporal coefficients in consumption, the conditions (8) and (9) require merely that $c_1 = c_2$ as is seen in Figure 5.2. Since the right-hand side marginal utilities are zero while the left-hand side marginal utilities are positive, any point on the line OA satisfies conditions (8) and (9). On the other hand, all other points violate either (8) or (9), since the marginal utility in both directions of either c_1 or c_2 are positive and those of the other are zero. From (3) and (4) with $c_1 = c_2$, then, we have

$$(w + a)(Y - aL) = 0 \qquad (10)$$

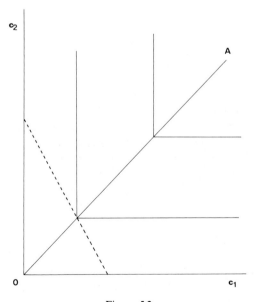

Figure 5.2

in view of our supposition that $L' = Y/a$. The demand for labor L is Y/a from (10), and independent of w.

A rise in wage merely reduces the capitalist's consumption and the wages fund increases proportionally to the rate of wage, so that demand for labor is completely inelastic with respect to wage. This non-existence of the boomerang effect is a strictly short-run story, however, since the capitalist is assumed to expect that changes in the wage rate are merely temporary. Thus, the shape of the demand cure which Mill had in mind in his recantation can be explained by the endogenous decision process of the capitalist.

3. Say's law and business cycles

In his *General Theory*, Keynes quoted the following, as an example of the doctrine that supply creates its own demand, from Mill's *Principles*.

> What constitutes the means of payment for commodities is simply commodities. Each person's means of paying for the production of other people consist of those which he himself possesses. All sellers are inevitably, and by the meaning of the word, buyers. Could we suddenly double the productive powers of the country, we should double the supply of commodities in every market; but we should, by the same stroke, double the purchasing power. Everybody would bring a double demand as well as supply; everybody would be able to buy twice as much, because every one would have twice as much to offer in exchange. (Keynes [18, p. 18]. See also Mill [24, pp. 557–558].)

As was pointed out by Balassa [3] and Leijonhufvud [20, p. 101], however, it is impossible to consider that Mill held Say's law in the form of the identity. This is because, firstly, in his quotation Mill had rather Walras' law in mind, as he concluded the quoted paragraph with: "money is a commodity; and if all commodities are supposed to be doubled in quantity, we must suppose money to be doubled too, and then prices would no more fall than values would." Secondly, in the same chapter, i.e., Chapter XIV, Book III, Mill admitted the possibility of a temporal excess of all commodities.

> At such times there is really an excess of all commodities above the money demand: in other words, there is an under-supply of money ... so that there may really be ... an extreme depression of general prices, from what may be indiscriminately called a glut of commodities or a dearth of money. (Mill [24, p. 561].)

Suppose there are $n-1$ non-monetary commodities and money. Following Balassa [3], we may say that Mill insisted on Walras' identity when he considered a commodity money, i.e.,

$$\sum_i p_i E_i(p_1,\ldots,p_{n-1}) + E_m(p_1,\ldots,p_{n-1}) \equiv 0 \tag{1}$$

where E_i and p_i denote respectively the excess demand and the price in terms of money of the ith commodity $(i=1,\ldots,n-1)$ and E_m denotes the excess demand of money. In other words, he did not insist on Say's identity

$$\sum_i p_i E_i(p_1,\ldots,p_{n-1}) \equiv 0 \tag{2}$$

which implies, in view of (1),

$$E_m(p_1,\ldots,p_{n-1}) \equiv 0. \tag{3}$$

Similarly, we may say that Mill insisted on Say's equality when he considered the case of credit money, i.e.,

$$\sum_i p_i E_i(p_1,\ldots,p_{n-1}) = 0 \tag{4}$$

which is satisfied only by an equilibrium set of prices. In other words, in view of (1), (3) is not valid, and should be replaced by

$$E_m(p_1,\ldots,p_{n-1}) = 0 \tag{5}$$

in the equilibrium. The implication of Say's equality is that temporary disequilibria in markets are possible but the economic system will automatically and quickly return to the general equilibrium where

$$E_i(p_1,\ldots,p_{n-1}) = 0, \quad i=1,\ldots,n-1,n, \tag{6}$$

through the smooth adjustments of prices $p_1,\ldots,p_{n-1}$, so that we may safely regard the system as always in the general equilibrium.[4]

This does not, however, exclude the possibility of the influence of consumption upon production, since Mill's concept of markets is, unlike the case of well-organized exchanges, such that a large proportion of capital remains idle in the form of inventories of finished goods waiting for customers. We can see it more clearly in *Essays* (Mill [23]) than in *Principles* (Mill [24]).[5]

> When we have thus seen accurately what really constitutes capital, it becomes obvious, that of the capital of a country, there is at all times a very large proportion lying idle. The annual produce of a country is never

---

[4]See Becker and Baumol [4] and Patinkin [29, Chap. VIII and note L].
[5]We owe greatly to Fukagai [11] for a highly thought-provoking exposition of Mill's theory in [23].

anything approaching in magnitude to what it might be if all the resources devoted to reproduction, if all the capital, in short, of the country, were in full employment. (Mill [23, p. 55].)

Every dealer keeps a stock in trade, to be ready for a possible sudden demand, though he probably may not be able to dispose of it for an indefinite period. This perpetual non-employment of a large proportion of capital, is the price we pay for the division of labour. The purchase is worth what it costs; but the price is considerable. (Mill [23, p. 56].)

An additional customer, to most dealers, is equivalent to an increase of their productive capital. He enables them to convert a portion of their capital which was lying idle (and which could never have become productive in their hands until a customer was found) into wages and instruments of production; … . The aggregate produce of the country for the succeeding year is, therefore, increased; not by the mere exchange, but by calling into activity a portion of the national capital, which, had it not been for the exchange, would have remained for some time longer unemployed. (Mill [23, pp. 57–58].)

In such a not well-organized market, the law of indifference is not established easily, as was recognized by Mill. The law "that there cannot be for the same article, of the same quality, two prices in the same market" applies to the case of "such prices as are quoted in price-currents; prices in the wholesale markets, in which buying as well as selling is a matter of business; in which the buyers take pains to know, and generally do know, the lowest price at which an article of a given quality can be obtained." It does not apply in the case of "retail prices; the prices paid in shops for articles of personal consumption. For such things there often are not merely two, but many prices, in different shops, or even in the same shop" (Mill, [24, p. 440]).

Either from indolence, or carelessness, or because people think it fine to pay and ask no questions, three-fourths of those who can afford it give much higher prices than necessary for the things they consume; while the poor often do the same from ignorance and defect of judgement, want of time for searching and making inquiry, and not unfrequently from coercion, open or disguised. For these reasons, retail prices do not follow with all the regularity which might be expected the action of the causes which determine wholesale prices. (Mill [24, p. 441].)

Perhaps we may consider the market Mill had in mind by using the following model. Consider a distribution of different prices expected as normal by individual suppliers. The ith supplier expects the price p_i^* as normal, depending on his own condition of production costs and his past experiences in the market, and is willing to sell the commodity for the offer of a price higher than or equal to p_i^*. Let us denote by p^* the average value of such different p_i^*'s in the market. Similarly, let us consider a distribution of different prices expected as normal by individual demanders. The jth demander expects the price p_j^{**} as normal, depending on his taste, income, and past experiences in the market, and is willing to buy the commodity for the offer of a price lower than or equal to p_j^{**}. Let us denote by p^{**} the average value of such different p_j^{**}'s in the market.

Suppose that suppliers with different expected normal supply prices meet randomly with demanders with different expected normal demand prices. The purchase and sale of the commodity is realized if a demander's normal price is not lower than that of the supplier whom the former happens to meet. Then we may suppose a distribution of different realized prices, the average of which is denoted by p. Since suppliers are willing to sell for prices not lower than their normal prices and an increase in sale results in an increase in production by converting capital lying idle into wages and instruments, we can assume that the total supply S of the commodity is an increasing function of p/p^*. Similarly, demanders are willing to buy for prices not higher than their normal prices, and we may assume that the total demand D for the commodity is a decreasing function of p/p^{**}.

If we consider that the market will automatically and quickly return to the equilibrium of demand and supply, the following condition must be satisfied continuously.

$$D(p/p^{**}, M/p^{**}) = S(p/p^*) \tag{7}$$

where M denotes a parameter denoting the supply of (credit) money to buy goods. At least in the short run, we may assume that the normal prices expected by suppliers and demanders are inelastic with respect to realized prices and the parameter M of the demand function. Then, we can solve (7) for p, since p^*, p^{**} and M are constants. Suppose that an increase in M increases D. Since D is decreasing with respect to p/p^{**} and S is increasing with respect to p/p^*, it is easily seen that an increase in M increases p. If the commodity we are considering is the representative commodity which reflects the condition of the whole economy, we can say that an increase in the aggregate consumption caused by an increased supply of money increases the aggregate production, since S is increasing with respect to p/p^*.

There is a brisk demand and a rapid circulation, when goods, generally speaking, are sold as fast as they can be produced. There is slackness, on the contrary, and stagnation, when goods, which have been produced, remain for a long time unsold. In the former case, the capital which has been locked up in production is disengaged as soon as the production is completed; and can be immediately employed in further production. In the latter case, a large portion of the productive capital of the country is lying in temporary inactivity. (Mill [23, p. 67].)

In Figure 5.3, p is measured vertically and D and S are measured horizontally. If p^*, p^{**} and M are given, the curve D corresponds to the left-hand side of (7), while the curve S corresponds to the right-hand side. The equilibrium level of p is OB while the corresponding level of production is OA. If M is increased while p^* and p^{**} are unchanged, the curve D is shifted to D'. The equilibrium level of p is now higher than OB and the equilibrium volume of production is now larger than OA. Such an increase in production is only possible temporarily, however, since eventually p^* and p^{**} are reconsidered in the face of changed p. If they are changed proportionally to M, it is easily seen from (7) that p is also changed proportionally, so that there is no change in S. In Figure 5.3, the curves D and S are shifted upwardly in such a way that the abscissa of their intersection remains unchanged at OA.

For, the calculations of producers and traders being of necessity imperfect,

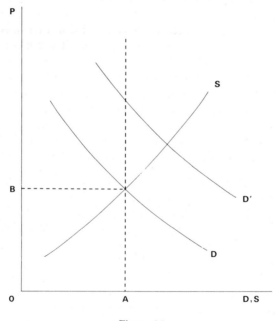

Figure 5.3

there are always some commodities which are more or less in excess, ... there would always be some classes of producers contracting, not extending their operations. If *all* are endeavouring to extend them, it is a certain proof that some general delusion is afloat. The commonest cause of such delusion is some general, or very extensive, rise of prices (whether caused by speculation or by the currency) which persuades all dealers that they are growing rich. And hence, an increase of production really takes place during the progress of depreciation, as long as the existence of depreciation is not suspected; .... But when the delusion vanishes and the truth is disclosed, those whose commodities are relatively in excess must diminish their production. (Mill [23, pp. 67–68].)

In other words, expected normal prices remain unchanged in inflation caused by a larger supply of money if there exists money illusion, and the aggregate output is increased. Similarly, our model can also be applied to Mill's explanation of a commercial crisis.

It is a great error to suppose, with Sismondi, that a commercial crisis is the effect of a general excess of production. It is simply the consequence of an excess of speculative purchases. It is not a gradual advent of low prices, but a sudden recoil from prices extravagantly high: its immediate cause is a contraction of credit, and the remedy is, not a diminution of supply, but the restoration of confidence. It is also evident that this temporary derangement of markets is an evil only because it is temporary. The fall being solely of money prices, if prices did not rise again no dealer would lose, since the smaller price would be worth as much to him as the larger price was before. In no manner does this phenomenon answer to the description which these celebrated economists have given of the evil of over-production. The permanent decline in the circumstances of producers, for want of markets, which those writers contemplate, is a conception to which the nature of a commercial crisis gives no support. (Mill [24, p. 561].)

Conversely, in the face of the fall of money prices in a commercial crisis caused by a contraction of credit, expected normal prices remain unchanged if there exists money illusion, and the aggregate output is diminished. In Figure 5.3, the demand curve D shifts downwards when M is diminished but p^* and p^{**} remain unchanged in (7). The economic system will automatically return to its equilibrium position with smaller aggregate output via price changes.

Thus we can see an embryo form of the recent new classical macroeconomics in Mill's explanation of how "it is not desirable that the whole capital of the country should be in full employment" (Mill [23, p. 67]), i.e., the natural rate of unemployment hypothesis, how an increase of the currency promotes industry when delusion (money illusion) exists and how, in a commercial crisis, one evil is the temporary fall of prices which does not change the expected normal prices. The basic model of the new classical macroeconomics (the equilibrium theory of business cycles) embodies the natural rate hypothesis.

> Within the confines of such a hypothesis, if one is to explain why high inflation and high nominal aggregate demand seem to induce high aggregate output, it is necessary to construct an operational model of money illusion. (Sargent [30, p. 325].)

4. The existence of a trade equilibrium

The standard interpretation in the neo-classical theory of international trade is that, while the limits of the terms of trade are given by the Ricardian principle of comparative costs, it is Mill's theory of reciprocal demands that determines the exact value of the terms of trade between countries.

> When two countries trade together in two commodities, the exchange value of these commodities relatively to each other will adjust itself to the inclinations and circumstances of the consumers on both sides, in such manner that the quantities required by each country, of the articles which it imports from its neighbour, shall be exactly sufficient to pay for one another. As the inclinations and circumstances of consumers cannot be reduced to any rule, so neither can the proportions in which the two commodities will be interchanged. We know that the limits, within which the variation is confined, are the ratio between their costs of production in the one country, and the ratio between their costs of production in the other. (Mill [24, p. 587].)

> As 17 yards of linen are to 10 yards of cloth, so are 1000 times 17 yards to 1000 times 10 yards. At the existing exchange value, the linen which England requires [17,000 yards] will exactly pay for the quantity of cloth which, on the same terms of interchange, Germany requires [10,000 yards]. The demand on each side is precisely sufficient to carry off the supply on the other. The conditions required by the principle of demand and supply are fulfilled, and the two commodities will continue to be interchanged, as we supposed them to be, in the ratio of 17 yards of linen for 10 yards of cloth. (Mill [24, p. 586].)

> The law which we have now illustrated, may be appropriately named, the Equation of International Demand. ... This law of International Values is but an extension of the more general law of Value, which we called the

Equation of Supply and Demand. ... the supply brought by the one constitutes his demand for what is brought by the other. So that supply and demand are but another expression for reciprocal demand: and to say that value will adjust itself so as to equalize demand with supply, is in fact to say that it will adjust itself so as to equalize the demand on one side with the demand on the other. (Mill [24, pp. 592–593].)

The above quotations are from the chapter on international values of Mill's *Principles*, which was originally composed of five sections. In the third edition (1852), however, Mill added three sections since, according to him, "the doctrine stated in the preceding pages, though correct as far as it goes, is not yet the complete theory of the subject matter" (Mill [24, p. 596]). The reason is, Mill argues, "that several different rates of international value may all equally fulfil the conditions of this law" (Mill [24, pp. 596–597]). These added sections were, unfortunately, criticized by many great scholars including Edgeworth [8], who called the chapter great and stupendous but the added sections laborious and confusing. It was Chipman [6], however, who defended Mill by insisting that these sections contain "a convincing proof (admittedly for a special case) of the existence of equilibrium." Interpreting Mill as assuming identical demand functions for two countries, Chipman showed that Mill's arguments in these sections can be reformulated to a non-linear programming problem of maximizing an aggregate world utility function. "In its astonishing simplicity, it must stand as one of the great achievements of the human intellect; and yet it has passed practically unnoticed for over a hundred years, if only because it was so advanced for its time."

As for the demand functions of two countries, Germany and England, Mill assumed that "in both countries any given increase of cheapness produces an exactly proportional increase of consumption; or, in other words, that the value expended in the commodity, the cost incurred for the sake of obtaining it, is always the same, whether that cost affords a greater or smaller quantity of the commodity" (Mill [24, p. 598]). Such demand functions with unitary elasticities can be derived by assuming that the German and English aggregate utility functions are, respectively, $U' = x'^{a'} y'^{b'}$ and $U'' = x''^{a''} y''^{b''}$, where x' and y' denote the consumption of cloth and linen respectively in Germany and x'' and y'' the same in England, and a', b', a'' and b'' are the positive constants such that $a' + b' = 1$ and $a'' + b'' = 1$. It can easily be seen that a' and b' are the constant proportions in which expenditure is devoted to cloth and linen respectively in Germany and a'' and b'' are the corresponding constant proportions in England. Chipman [6] assumed further that $a' = b' = a'' = b'' = \frac{1}{2}$. The aggregate world utility function is then $U = (x' + x'')^{1/2}(y' + y'')^{1/2}$.

Criticizing Chipman [6], however, Appleyard and Ingram [1] insisted that

Mill made no reference to the specific magnitudes of these four parameters, a', b', a'', and b''.[6] Chipman [7] agreed to accept this criticism, since Mill's arguments in no way depend on this interpretation, and revised his analysis in [6] of the contents of section 7 of Mill's chapter as follows, without using the non-linear programming of the world utility.

Let X' and Y' denote the outputs of cloth and linen respectively in Germany, and X'' and Y'' the same in England. Production possibilities in the two countries are given by

$$X'/A' + Y'/B' \leq 1, \quad X''/A'' + Y''/B'' \leq 1 \tag{1}$$

where the parameters A', B', A'', and B'' are positive constants. Although Mill did not refer to the specific magnitudes of these four parameters, he assumed that Germany has a comparative advantage in linen and England in cloth, so that

$$p = B'/A' > q = B''/A''. \tag{2}$$

If we denote by t the price of cloth in terms of linen, and by M' and M'' Germany's and England's respective incomes, both expressed in terms of linen, M' and M'' are given as

$$M' = \max(tA', B'), \quad M'' = \max(tA'', B'') \tag{3}$$

since they are obtained by the maximization of the value of outputs, $tX' + Y'$ and $tX'' + Y''$, subject to respective constraints (1).

Demand functions are derived from the maximization of utilities U' and U'' subject to the respective budget constraints,

$$tx' + y' = M', \quad tx'' + y'' = M'', \tag{4}$$

i.e.,

$$x' = a' M'/t, \quad y' = b' M', \quad x'' = a'' M''/t, \quad y'' = b'' M''. \tag{5}$$

Since it is easily seen that $q \leq t \leq p$, the incomes of the two countries are from (20)

$$M' = B', \quad M'' = tA'' \tag{6}$$

and therefore demand functions are from (5) and (6)

$$x' = a' B'/t, \quad y' = b' B', \quad x'' = a'' A'', \quad y'' = b'' A'' t. \tag{7}$$

If Germany specializes in linen, it will import the unknown amount $x' = a' B'/t$ of cloth. Likewise, if it specializes in cloth, England will import the unknown amount $y'' = b'' A'' t$ of linen. To "equalize the demand on one side with the

---

[6] See also Harwitz [13] and Melvin [22].

demand on the other" in terms of linen, we must have

$$tx' = y'', \tag{8}$$

i.e.,

$$t = a' B'/b'' A'' \tag{9}$$

is the unique world price of cloth in terms of linen.

Unlike Chipman, Mill himself did not consider parameters a', b', a'', b'', A', B', A'', and B''. Apart from the domestic price ratio before trade, i.e., p and q defined in (2), he considered, instead, two parameters m and n, respectively, "the cloth previously required by Germany (at the German cost of production)" and "the quantity of cloth which England can make with the labour and capital withdrawn from the production of linen" (Mill [24, p. 600]). Since Germany's income in terms of cloth is A' and the proportion of expenditure devoted to cloth is a',

$$m = a' A'. \tag{10}$$

Similarly, the linen previously required and produced in England is $b'' B''$ and the domestic rate of transformation in England is B''/A''. Therefore,

$$n = b'' B''/(B''/A'') = b'' A''. \tag{11}$$

By substituting (10) and (11) into (9) and considering (2), we have

$$t = pm/n \tag{12}$$

as the equilibrium terms of trade between two countries expressed by the ratio and quantities already given before trade. Unfortunately, Mill made a slip by saying that "then will n, after the opening of the trade, exchange for $(p/q)m$" (Mill [24, p. 601]), which implies that $t = pm/qn$. Chipman concludes, however, that even with this small blemish, Mill made an enormous stride forward.

Appleyard and Ingram [1] argued that no new results were obtained in the newly added sections, since Mill had already concluded in the original sections that a unique exchange ratio would exist when demand elasticities were equal to 1. Chipman objected to this judgement by insisting on the importance of distinguishing between a statement of a proposition and its proof. Mill's original sections contained the statements concerning the nature of the trade equilibrium, but the existence of such an equilibrium is assumed there and not yet proved. It is proved only in the new sections.

In a theory of international trade, endogenous variables to be explained are terms of trade and quantities of commodities traded between countries. If a writer describes, as in Mill's original sections, a trade equilibrium that at the exchange ratio of 17 yards of linen to 10 yards of cloth the 17,000 yards of linen

England requires will pay for the 10,000 yards of cloth Germany requires, he is merely assuming the existence of such an equilibrium, since he is making assumptions on the value of endogenous variables. In the newly added sections, on the other hand, Mill explained the equilibrium values of such endogenous variables as t (terms of trade), pm (Germany's exports of linen), and tn (the value of its imports of cloth) by the given values of p, m and n. From the point of view of a theoretical model in the theory of international trade, parameters like p, m and n are exogenous variables observable before the opening of trade, i.e., the domestic price ratio in the autarky, the quantity of a commodity consumed in the autarky, and the product of such variables. In the new sections, Mill proved the existence of a trade equilibrium, by determining the unknown value of endogenous variables from the given value of exogenous variables.

Although we agree with Chipman [7] that Mill made an important contribution to the proof of the existence of an equilibrium, however, we cannot deny the argument of Appleyard and Ingram [1] that Mill's arguments are somewhat confusing in the newly added sections. Mill starts with the statement that the theory of international trade developed in the original five sections is not yet the complete theory, since several different rates of international value may all equally fulfil the condition of an equilibrium. A numerical example of multiple equilibria is given.

> There is still therefore a portion of indeterminateness in the rate at which the international values would adjust themselves; showing that the whole of the influencing circumstances cannot yet have been taken into account. ... to supply this deficiency, we must take into consideration not only, as we have already done, the quantities demanded in each country of the imported commodities; but also the extent of the means of supplying that demand which are set at liberty in each country by the change in the direction of its industry. (Mill [24, p. 597].)

> When the trade was opened, England would supply cloth to Germany, Germany linen to England, at an exchange value which would depend partly on the element already discussed, viz. the comparative degree in which, in the two countries, increased cheapness operates in increasing the demand; and partly on some other element not yet taken into account. In order to isolate this unknown element, it will be necessary to make some definite and invariable supposition in regard to the known element. Let us therefore assume, that the influence of cheapness on demand conforms to some simple law. (Mill [24, p. 598].)

Thus, the assumption of demand with unitary elasticities is introduced so as to simplify the known element which is already taken into account in the original five sections. Mill should have known, however, that the indeterminateness is caused by demand with elasticities less than one, since his numerical example of multiple equilibria assumes that at the rate of 10 cloth for 18 linen "England would want more linen than at the rate of 10 for 17, but not in the ratio of the cheapness; that she would not want the 18,000 which she could now buy with 10,000 yards of cloth, but would be content with 17,500, for which she would pay (at the new rate of 10 for 18) 9722 yards of cloth" (Mill [24, p. 597]). It is not, therefore, the introduction of the new element, but the simplifying assumption of the known element which makes the equilibrium determinate in Mill's newly added sections. Furthermore, as Mill himself admitted, the new element introduced – the capital which a country has to spare from the production of domestic commodities for its own consumption, to exchange its produce with foreign countries – is not independent of the other element already considered.

> These two influencing circumstances are in reality reducible to one: for the capital which a country has to spare from the production of domestic commodities for its own use is in proportion to its own demand for foreign commodities: whatever proportion of its collective income it expends in purchasing from abroad, that same proportion of its capital is left without a home market for its productions. The new element, therefore, which for the sake of scientific correctness we have introduced into the theory of international values, does not seem to make any very material difference in the practical result. (Mill [24, pp. 603–604].)

If a factor is dependent on another, the effect of the former is dependent on the assumptions of the latter. Nevertheless, the confusion of the argument is one thing; it is quite another if there is something new. Perhaps Mill was not aware of his achievement, nor did he intend it, but it cannot be denied that he has made a great contribution to the equilibrium theory in his added sections in the chapter on international value.

5. Equilibrium and disequilibrium

In this chapter we have considered the role played by Mill in the history of economics as that of a theorist of the demand and supply equilibrium. This implies that Mill had to be confronted with the criticism given by the economics of the demand and supply disequilibrium. As we saw in section 3, Mill rejected the macroscopic disequilibrium theories of Malthus and Sismondi, on the basis of Say's equality.

The fall of profits and interest which naturally takes place with the progress of population and production ... is obviously a totally different thing from a want of market for commodities .... Low profits ... are a different thing from deficiency of demand; and the production and accumulation which merely reduce profits, cannot be called excess of supply or of production. (Mill [24, pp. 561–562].)[7]

Mill's reaction to Thornton's [32] microscopic criticism of the equilibrium theory was the recantation of the wages fund theory (Mill [25]) which we discussed in section 2.[8] Mill misunderstood, however, the true nature of the examples Thornton constructed to show the irrelevancy of the equilibrium theory. Although Mill's model of the labor market to recant the wages fund doctrine is itself, as we saw, interesting from the point of view of equilibrium theory, it is more important to realize that Thornton's attempt was one of the pioneering ones to develop a disequilibrium model of markets, which has recently been extensively studied, for example, to give microeconomic foundations to macroeconomics.

Thornton presented several counter examples to the "equation theory" that the equation of supply and demand determines price. The first example given concerns what are called "Dutch" and "English" auctions for fish.

When a herring or mackerel boat has discharged on the beach, at Hastings or Dover, last night's take of fish, the boatmen, in order to dispose of their cargo, commonly resort to a process called Dutch auction. The fish are divided into lots, each of which is set up at a higher price than the salesman expects to get for it, and he then gradually lowers his terms, until he comes to a price which some bystander is willing to pay rather than not have the lot, and to which he accordingly agrees. Suppose on one occasion the lot to have been a hundredweight, and the price agreed to twenty shillings. If, on the same occasion, instead of the Dutch form of auction, the ordinary English mode had been adopted, the result might have been different. The operation would then have commenced by some bystander making a bid, which others might have successively exceeded, until a price was arrived at beyond which no one but the actual bidder could afford or was disposed to go. That sum would not necessarily be twenty shillings; very possibly it might be only eighteen shillings. The person who was prepared to pay the former price might very possibly be the only person present prepared to pay even so much as the latter price; and if so, he might get by English auction for

---

[7] As we saw in Chapter 4, section 6, however, for Malthus it is exactly this fall of profits that destroys the motive to produce and generates the unemployment of resources.

[8] As a matter of fact, it was also to reply to criticism of Thornton that Mill added three new sections to the chapter on international values which we discussed in section 4. See Chipman [7].

eighteen shillings the fish for which at Dutch auction he would have paid twenty shillings. In the same market, with the same quantity of fish for sale, and with customers in number and every other respect the same, the same lot of fish might fetch two very different prices. (Thornton [32, pp. 47–48].)

Mill [25] interpreted this example wrongly as meaning that "the demand and supply are equal at twenty shillings, and equal also at eighteen shillings," and argued that the equilibrium theory is incomplete but not incorrect and that the case may be conceived but in practice is hardly ever realized, since it is an exception to the rule that demand increases with cheapness. Recognizing the possibility of multiple equilibria from this example, however, Mill recanted the wages fund doctrine. As we saw in section 2, he considered a case of the wage indeterminacy due to a demand for labor inelastic with respect to wage.

Figure 5.4 shows both Mill's interpretation of Thornton's example of fish as well as Mill's model of the labor market in his recantation of the wages fund doctrine. In the former, the price of fish is measured vertically and the quantity of fish is measured horizontally. The given supply is indicated by OS, and the demand curve is $DCC'D'$, which violates the rule that demand increases with cheapness between C and C'. The equilibrium price is not uniquely determined, since any price between AO and BO equates demand and supply. The price

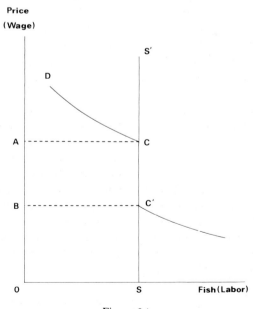

Figure 5.4

established by Dutch auction is OA and that arrived at by English auction is OB. Similarly, wage is measured vertically and number of laborers is measured horizontally, in the latter model. There is no predetermined wages fund, since clearly the aggregate wages paid is larger at C than at C'. Although the wages fund doctrine is recanted by Mill, however, the equilibrium theory is confirmed, since demand and supply are equalized at any point between C and C'.

Thornton's rejoinder to Mill's [25] interpretation of his example of auctions for fish is in Thornton [33], which is the revised second edition of Thornton [32]. After reproducing the same example, with the prices changed from 20 and 18 shillings to 8 and 6 shillings [33, pp. 56–57], he argued as follows:

> In this particular case it would not be possible for supply and demand to be equal at two different prices. For the case is one in which demand would increase with cheapness. A hawker who was ready to pay 8s. for a hundred herrings, would want more than a hundred if he could get a hundred for 6s. There being then but a given quantity in the market, if that quantity were just sufficient to satisfy all the customers ready to buy at 8s., it follows that it would not have sufficed to satisfy them if the price had been 6. If supply and demand were equal at the former price, they would be unequal at the latter. ([33, pp. 57–58].)

In Figure 5.5, the price of fish is measured vertically, and the quantity of fish is measured horizontally. The given supply of fish, a hundred herrings, is indicated by OS, and DD' is the demand curve which satisfies the rule that demand increases with cheapness. It may be considered that the person who wants fish most strongly demands OT, the one who wants next strongly demands TR, and so on. The price established by Dutch auction is AO and that arrived at by English auction is BO.

In Thornton's example of fish correctly interpreted, therefore, there is only an equilibrium price which equalizes demand and supply, i.e., the price AO established by Dutch auction. If English auction is adopted, however, trade takes place at the lower price BO with demand larger than supply and unsatisfied demand ST remains after trade is over. The reason why this is possible is, firstly, that there is no competition to put up the price by bidding, since no one except the actual purchaser, the one who most strongly wants fish, is willing to buy any at that price. Secondly, the actual purchaser himself would not put up the price by bidding, even though he wants to buy more than the quantity supplied, since he knows that the supply will not be increased.[9]

---

[9] In other words, as Professor Morishima pointed out to us, the excess demand here is merely subjective and not explicit in the market.

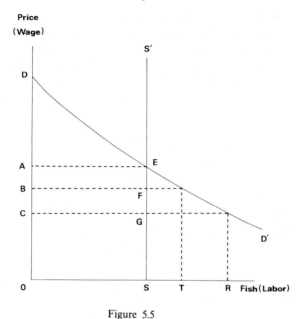

Figure 5.5

The price *BO* is not determined by the equality of demand and supply, but, according to Thornton, by the competition.

> It is competition, wherever competition exists, that determines price. Competition remaining the same, price cannot possibly vary. For, it is competition that determines the lowest price at which goods are offered for sale..... In a free and open market, and among dealers and customers actuated by the self-interest which political economy always takes for granted, competition is the only thing which determines price; the only thing indeed that directly influences it. (Thornton [33, p. 77].)

In Figure 5.5, competition with the person who next strongly wants the fish makes the price not lower than *BO*. Figure 5.5 can also be used to describe a model of a labor market without a predetermined wages fund, which is different from and much more general than the one considered by Mill. Measuring wage vertically, and the number of laborers horizontally, let us assume that the group of employers who need laborers most strongly demand *OT*, the group of employers who need laborers next strongly demand *TR*, and so on. Suppose wage is determined at *BO*, with excess demand of labor *ST*. Why is wage not increased by bidding because of excess demand? According to Thornton [33, p. 100], the reason is that "in practice it is not mutual competition, but the mutual combination of customers, which, in general, really determines the price of isolated labour."

But even though that should not be the case [employers cannot get as much labour as they are disposed to pay for at the current rate], every employer would probably make shift as well as he could with the labour which he could procure at the current rate, and anyone who should endeavour to tempt away another's servants by offers of increased pay, would be treated by his fellow-masters as a traitor to the common case. Such is the habitual policy of customers for labour. Instead of suffering the rate of wages to be settled naturally by competition, they endeavour by combination to settle it arbitrarily. (Thornton [33, pp. 103–104].)

Wage *BO* is, therefore, determined not by the equality of demand and supply, but by the combination of actual employers and competition with potential employers. Wage may be determined, however, not at *BO* but at *CO*, and is similarly not bid up by the excess demand *SR*. Thus, rate of wage is largely indeterminate, depending on the size of the group of actual employers who are in mutual combination. Even if there is a predetermined wages fund, it is not necessarily expended fully and aggregate wages paid at *F* is larger than that at *G*. It should be emphasized, however, that Thornton denied not only the wages fund doctrine, but also the equilibrium theory of demand and supply.

One may argue that Thornton's example of fish and the corresponding model of a labor market is not a case of perfect competition but is a case of imperfect competition with free entry in the sense that the actual purchaser is a single person or the actual employers are in combination.[10] Thornton emphasized, however, not so much the imperfectness of competition as the possibility of trade carried out at disequilibrium prices, since he produced two additional examples of the failure of supply and demand as the law of prices, which are the examples of horses and of gloves.

Suppose two persons at different times, or in different places, to have each a horse to sell, valued by the owner at £50; and that in the one case there are two, and in the other three persons, of whom every one is ready to pay £50 for the horse, though no one of them can afford to pay more. In both cases supply is the same, viz., one horse at £50; but demand is different, being in one case two, and in the other three, horses at £50. Yet the price at which the horses will be sold will be the same in both cases, viz., £50 (Thornton [32, p. 49], [33, p. 59].)

[10] Breit [5] argued that demand and supply are not equalized in the case of monopoly. For the relation between disequilibrium and imperfectness of the competition, see Hart [12] and Negishi [28, pp. 35–37, 87–98].

When a tradesman has placed upon his goods the highest price which any one will pay for them, the price cannot, of course, rise higher, yet the supply may be below the demand. A glover in a country town, on the eve of an assize ball, having only a dozen pair of white gloves in store, might possibly be able to get ten shillings a pair for them. He would be able to get this if twelve persons were willing to pay that price rather than not go to the ball, or than go ungloved. But he could not get more than this, even though, while he was still higgling with his first batch of customers, a second batch, equally numerous and neither more nor less eager, should enter his shop, and offer to pay the same but not a higher price. The demand for gloves, which at first had been just equal to the supply, would now be exactly doubled, yet the price would not rise above ten shillings a pair. Such abundance of proof is surely decisive against the supposition that price must rise when demand exceeds supply. (Thornton [32, pp. 51–52], [33, pp. 61–62].)

Figure 5.6 shows examples of horses and of gloves. The price of horses or of gloves is measured vertically, and quantities horizontally. The given supply is *OS*, a horse or twelve pairs of gloves, and *BO* indicates £50 or ten shillings.[11]

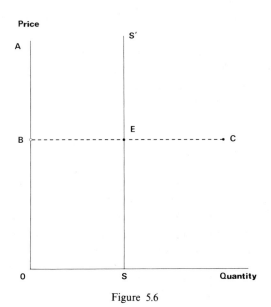

Figure 5.6

[11] Strictly speaking, the supply curve is discontinuous and consists of *OB* (but not including *B*) and *ES′* in the example of horses.

The demand curve consists of a half-line AB (but point B is not included) and a point C. As Mill [25] correctly recognized and Thornton [33] agreed, there exists no equilibrium of demand and supply in this case, and trade has to be carried out at the disequilibrium price BO. There is no problem of imperfectness of competition involved since, for example, actual purchasers are twelve persons who are not in mutual combination in the example of gloves.

One might object, like Mill, that these examples are too specific. "At £50 there is a demand for twice or three times the supply; at £50. 0s. $\frac{1}{4}d$. there is no demand at all. When the scale of demand for a commodity is broken by so extraordinary a jump, the law fails of its application; not, I venture to say, from any fault in the law, but because the conditions on which its applicability depends do not exist" (Mill [25, p. 638]). Though he recognized that the examples of horses and gloves show the non-existence of equilibrium due to a discontinuous demand curve, Thornton's original aim was not so much to show the non-existence of equilibrium as to deny the equilibrium theory that prices are determined by the equality of supply and demand by showing the cases where goods are traded at disequilibrium prices (Thornton [33, p. 68]).

Even though demand curves are continuous and an equilibrium exists toward which prices are adjusted by excess demand or supply, goods are traded at disequilibrium prices, unless adjustments are instantaneous.

> Even if it were true that the price ultimately resulting from competition is always one at which supply and demand are equalized, still only a small proportion of the goods offered for sale would actually be sold at any such price, since a dealer will dispose of as much of his stock as he can at a higher price, before he will lower the price in order to get rid of the remainder. (Thornton [32, p. 53], [33, p. 65].)

In other words, Thornton had in mind, not Walrasian *tâtonnement*, in which trade does not take place and contracts can be cancelled unless demand and supply are equalized, but the so-called non-Walrasian, non-*tâtonnement* process without recontract, in which goods are exchanged at prices which do not equate demand and supply.[12] The significance of such disequilibrium trades is much greater than admitted by Mill and by Breit [5], since the position of equilibrium eventually established is itself shifted by the conditions and volumes of such trades. In the case of a labor market, even if there is a given stock of wage goods, i.e., a predetermined wages fund, and the labor population is constant, the final equilibrium level of wage would be different, depending on how many laborers are employed at each different level of wages while demand and supply are not equal and wages are changing.

---

[12] See Arrow and Hahn [2, pp. 324–326] and Negishi [27, pp. 207–227].

In the Preface to the seventh edition of his *Principles of Political Economy* (1871), Mill stated that "there has been some instructive discussion on the theory of Demand and Supply, and on the influence of Strikes and Trades Unions on wages, by which additional light has been thrown on these subjects; but results, in the author's opinion, are not yet ripe for incorporation in a general treatise on Political Economy" (Mill [24, p. xciv]), and he footnoted that "the present state of the discussion may be learnt from a review (by the author) of Mr. Thornton's work "On Labour" [Thornton [32]], in the "Fortnightly Review" of May and June, 1869 [Mill [25]], and from Mr. Thornton's reply to that review in the second edition of his very instructive book [Thornton [33]]."

It is significant that not Thornton [32] but Thornton [33] is referred to, and that both the theory of demand and supply and the wages fund doctrine (i.e., the influence of strikes and trade unions on ages) are mentioned here equally.[13] This is a clear contrast with Mill's position in 1869 that "My object in the Fortnightly was to shew that the cases supposed by Thornton do not contradict and invalidate, as he thinks they do, the equation of supply and demand". "But in its application to labour, it does not merely add to our speculative knowledge; it destroys a prevailing and somewhat mischievous error [i.e., wages fund doctrine]."[14]

In other words, in view of Thornton [33], Mill recognized in 1871 that his interpretation of Thornton's example of fish auctions on which his recantation of the wages fund doctrine was based was clearly wrong, and that all of Thornton's examples consistently insist on the possibility of trades carried out in disequilibria. While Mill was ready to deny the validity of the wages fund doctrine in equilibrium theory, Thornton insisted on denying it from the point of view of disequilibrium theory. To accept Thornton's suggestion is, however, impossible for Mill, for whom the law of equality of supply and demand is the basic law which is antecedent even to the law of cost of production and the labor theory of value. Mill could not help but argue that "results are not yet ripe."

References

[1] Appleyard, D.R., and J.C. Ingram, "A Reconsideration of the Additions to Mill's Great Chapter", *History of Political Economy*, 11(1979), pp. 459–476.

[13] This point is not noticed by Breit [5].
[14] See Mill's letter to John Elliot Cairnes, on June 23, 1869, Mill [26, p. 1616] and Mill [25, p. 646].

[2]   Arrow, K.J., and F.H. Hahn, *General Competitive Analysis*, Holden-Day, 1971.
[3]   Balassa, B.A., "John Stuart Mill and the Law of Market", *Quarterly Journal of Economics*, 73(1959), pp. 263–274.
[4]   Becker, G.S., and J.W. Baumol, "The Classical Monetary Theory: The Outcome of the Discussion", *Economica*, 19(1952), pp. 355–376.
[5]   Breit, W., "The Wages Fund Controversy Revisited", *Canadian Journal of Economics and Political Science*, 33(1967), pp. 523–528.
[6]   Chipman, J.S., "A Survey of the Theory of International Trade: Part I, The Classical Theory", *Econometrica*, 33(1965), pp. 477–519.
[7]   Chipman, J.S., "Mill's 'Superstructure': How Well does It stand up?", *History of Political Economy*, 11(1979), pp. 477–500.
[8]   Edgeworth, F.Y., "Theory of International Values", *Economic Journal*, 4(1894), pp. 606–638.
[9]   Ekelund, R.B., "A Short-Run Classical Model of Capital and Wages: Mill's Recantation of the Wages Fund", *Oxford Economic Papers*, 28(1976), pp. 66–85.
[10] Ekelund, R.B., and R.F. Hébert, *A History of Economic Theory and Method*, McGraw-Hill, 1983.
[11] Fukagai, Y., "J.S. Mill no iwayuru Hanrosetsu to Kyokokan (J.S. Mill's View on the so-called Law of Market and Crisis)," *Kotenha Keizaigakukenkyu* (Studies in Classical Economics), I, pp. 333–369, T. Hayasaka, ed., Yushodo, 1984.
[12] Hart, O.D., "A Model of Imperfect Competiton with Keynesian Features", *Quarterly Journal of Economics*, 97(1982), pp. 109–138.
[13] Harwitz, M., "A Note on Professor Chipman's Version of Mill's Law of International Value", *Journal of International Economics*, 2(1972), pp. 181–188.
[14] Hayek, F.A., *John Stuart Mill and Harriet Taylor*, University of Chicago Press, 1951.
[15] Hollander, S., "The Role of Fixed Technical Coefficients in the Evolution of the Wages Fund Controversy", *Oxford Economic Papers*, 20(1968), pp. 320–341.
[16] Hollander, S., *The Economics of John Stuart Mill*, Blackwell, 1985.
[17] Kamm, J., *John Stuart Mill in Love*, Gordon and Cremonesi, 1977.
[18] Keynes, J.M., *The General Theory of Employment, Interest and Money*, Macmillan, 1936.
[19] Kregel, J.A., *The Reconstruction of Political Economy*, Macmillan, 1973.
[20] Leijonhufvud, A., *On Keynesian Economics and the Economics of Keynes*, Oxford University Press, 1966.
[21] Mawatari, S., "J.S. Mill's Methodology of Political Economy", *Keizai Gaku*, Annual Report of the Economic Society, Tohoku University, 44(1982), pp. 125–143, 249–269, 45(1983), pp. 33–54, 165–183.
[22] Melvin, J.R., "Mill's Law of International Value", *Southern Economic Journal*, 36(1969), pp. 107–116.
[23] Mill, J.S., *Essays on Some Unsettled Questions of Political Economy*, Longmans, Green, Reader and Dyer, 1874.
[24] Mill, J.S., *Principles of Political Economy*, Longmans, Green and Co., 1909.
[25] Mill, J.S., "Thornton on Labour and Its Claim", *Essays on Economics and Society*, pp. 631–668, Toronto University Press, 1967.
[26] Mill, J.S., *The Later Letters of John Stuart Mill, 1849–1873*, Toronto University Press, 1972.
[27] Negishi, T., *General Equilibrium Theory and International Trade*, North-Holland, 1972.
[28] Negishi, T., *Microeconomic Foundations of Keynesian Macroeconomics*, North-Holland, 1979.
[29] Patinkin, D., *Money, Interest and Prices*, Row, Peterson and Co., 1956.
[30] Sargent, T.J., *Macroeconomic Theory*, Academic Press, 1979.
[31] Schwartz, P., *The New Political Economy of J.S. Mill*, Duke University Press, 1972.
[32] Thornton, W.H., *On Labour*, Macmillan, 1869.
[33] Thornton, W.H., *On Labour*, Macmillan, 1870.

CHAPTER 6

MARX'S ECONOMICS

1. *Das Kapital*

As a part of the recent Renaissance of Marxism, Marx's economics have been intensively analyzed by the use of linear economic models, with the result that it now attracts the interest of many mathematical-minded, non-Marxian economists. Certainly it cannot be denied that the application of linear models has clarified some important aspects of Marx's economics, for example, the relation between surplus value and profit in the form of the so-called Fundamental Marxian Theorem, which demonstrated the significance of the value theory. This is partly because, as we shall see, some parts of the formal structure of *Das Kapital* requires linear input–output relations. There are, however, many other important problems raised by Marx, which, by their very nature, cannot be analyzed by linear models. In particular, dynamic rival relations among capitalists cannot be dealt with by the static linear equilibrium models of neo-classical or Walrasian economics.

After a brief description of the life and the writings of Karl Marx, we shall explain the content of *Das Kapital* in this section. Section 2 reviews some linear models of Marx's economics to explain the Fundamental Marxian Theorem and the transformation problem of values into prices of production. In section 3, we examine the key concept of Marx's economics, exploitation, from the point of view of its necessary prerequisite, the existence of the abstract human labor. While we are critical of the theory of exploitation of labor by capital in the time consuming production, a vindication is given to the theory of international exploitation due to unequal labor exchange. Section 4 is devoted to considering the structure of *Das Kapital* as the dichotomy between the exploitation of labor by the representative industrial capitalist and the redistribution of the exploited values among many different industrial capitalists, landowners and money-capitalists. It is shown that the assumption of linear input–output relations cannot always be relied on for the success of Marx's dichotomy. Marx's theory of the falling rate of profit is vindicated, in section 5, by the use of a non-linear dynamic model of rivalry among capitalists. The chapter ends with section 6, where we consider Marx's theory of market values, a dynamic equilibrium theory of industrial structure similar to Marshall's theory of the representative firm.

Karl Marx is the founder of international communism, philosopher of dialectical materialism, and one of the greatest economists in history. Born at Trier, Prussia, in 1818 as the son of middle-class Jewish parents, Marx studied at the University of Bonn as a law student, then at the University of Berlin, where he was influenced by Hegel and Feuerbach, and finished his dissertation at the University of Jena in 1841. In 1942, he assumed the editorship of the *Rheinishe Zeitung*, a radical German newspaper, but strict censorship made him resign. After his marriage to Jenny von Westphalen in 1843, he moved to Paris and founded a new journal, the *Deutsch-Französische Jarbücher*. The young Marx's economics can be seen in *Ökonomish-philosophische Manuscripte* (1844), where the key concept is alienation.[1] Profit is explained not by exploitation based on the labor theory of value, but simply as what he later called profit upon alienation, made possible by selling dearer than buying.

In 1845, France expelled Marx, under instigation from Prussia, and Marx went to Brussels, where he wrote *Die deutsche Ideologie* (with F. Engels, 1845–1846) and *Die heilige Familie oder Kritik der Kritischen Kritik* (1845) and *Misère de la philosophie: Réponse à la philosophie de la misère de M. Proudhon* (1847) were published. Marx's economics changed between *Ökonomish-philosophische Manuscripte* and *Misère de la philosophie*, since in the latter Marx emphatically asserted the validity of the labor theory of value he had learned from Ricardo.[2] In 1848, the famous *Manifest der Kommunistischen Partei* (with F. Engels) appeared. Marx and his family went to London in 1849, and he spent the rest of his life there, writing and studying in the library of the British Museum. Marx wrote *Grundrisse der Kritik der politischen Ökonomie* (Rohentwurf, 1857–1858) and published *Zur Kritik der politischen Ökonomie* in 1859. The first volume of *Das Kapital* was published in 1867, but Marx died in 1883, with the manuscripts of the second and third volumes of *Das Kapital* and of *Theorien über den Mehrwert* left unpublished.[3]

Although Marx was a successor of classical economics, he was critical of his predecessors for their basically ahistorical view of economic laws. Marx tried

[1] The concept of alienation, however, continues to play essential roles in Marx's system up to *Das Kapital*, as emphasized by Elliott [10].

[2] See Morishima and Catephores [28, pp. 1–21], for the young Marx and how Marx's economics changed.

[3] The second and third volume of *Das Kapital* were edited and published by Marx's friend and collaborator, F. Engels, in 1885 and in 1894 respectively. *Theorien über den Mehrwert*, Marx's history of economics, was first published by K. Kautsky, in 1905–1910. See Ekelund and Hébert [9, pp. 227–228], for Marx's life and works.

to relate the process of production to a stage of social development in human history. There are, however, two alternative interpretations of Marx's aim in *Das Kapital*. In the preface to the first German edition, Marx said

> The physicist either observes physical phenomena where they occur in their most typical form and most free from disturbing influences, or, whenever possible, he makes experiments under conditions that assure the occurrence of the phenomenon in its normality. In this work I have to examine the capitalist mode of production, and the conditions of production and exchange corresponding to that mode. Up to the present time, their classic ground is England. That is the reason why England is used as the chief illustration in the development of my theoretical ideas. (Marx [19, p. 19].)

As far as *Das Kapital* is concerned, therefore, Marx's aim can be considered as the pure economic analysis of the stable and unchanging structure of the idealized capitalist economy, although Marx insisted that capitalist economy is a mere single stage in the development of human society which necessarily shifts to a higher stage.[4]

An alternative, more fundamentalist interpretation takes note of the fact that Marx approvingly quoted the following review of *Das Kapital* in the afterword to the second German edition.

> With the varying degree of development of productive power, social conditions and the law governing them vary too. Whilst Marx sets himself the task of following and explaining from this point of view the economic system established by the sway of capital, he is only formulating, in a strictly scientific manner, the aim that every accurate investigation into economic life must have. The scientific value of such an inquiry lies in the disclosing of the special laws that regulate the origin, existence, development, death of a given social organism and its replacement by another and higher one. (Marx [19, p. 28].)[5]

The three volumes of *Das Kapital* are entitled, respectively, *The Process of Production of Capital, The Process of Circulation of Capital*, and *The Process of Capitalist Production as a Whole*. After a discussion of commodity circulation and the labor theory of value, the first volume concentrates on the theory of production to explain how surplus values are exploited by capital from labor. Volume 2 is concerned with the realization of surplus values, including the costs of circulation and the social balance of demand and supply.

---

[4] This is the view of the Uno school, which distinguishes pure theory or principles from stages theory. See Uno [53, pp. xxii–xxiii], Itoh [16, pp. 37–45], and Mawatari [26].

[5] This is the view of Engels, V.I. Lenin and J. Stalin. See Marx [18, I, pp. 27*–63*].

The third volume discusses the rate of profit, prices of production, market values, the rate of interest and land rents. In other words, it is concerned with how surplus values are distributed among different industrial capitalists, commercial capitalists, money capitalists and landlords.

Volume 1 of *Das Kapital* consists of eight parts. The most important chapter of Part 1, "Commodities and Money", is the first chapter, "Commodities". It starts with the statement that "the wealth of those societies in which the capitalist mode of production prevails, presents itself as an immense accumulation of commodities, its unit being a single commodity. Our investigation must therefore begin with the analysis of a commodity" (Marx [19, p. 43]). This implies that not the ahistorical concept of wealth but the historical concept of commodity plays the most important role in *Das Kapital*. Marx distinguishes the use value and the value (exchange value) of a commodity and, correspondingly, concrete labors and the abstract human labor. The labor theory of value is explained by the fact that "the exchange-values of commodities must be capable of being expressed in terms of something common to them all, of which thing they represent a greater or less quantity" (Marx [19, p. 45]). Since commodities "have only one common property left, that of being products of labour," the value of a commodity is determined by the quantity of the abstract human labor spent on it.

Marx defines the socially necessary labor to produce a commodity, not at the margin of the production, but under "the normal conditions of production, and with the average degree of skill and intensity prevent at the time" (Marx [19, p. 47]). Nor is the effect of demand taken into consideration. As Blaug [1, pp. 279–281] noted, this may suggest the implicit assumption of constant returns to scale and the possibility of the application of linear economic models. Marx then developed his theory of the form of value to show the necessity of money. While Marxian economists emphasize the importance of this theory, which is Marx's original contribution and not the residue of the classical value theory,[6] Blaug considered that "the reader will miss little by skipping the pedantic 'arguments' on which the hands of Hegel lie all too heavily." The first chapter ends with the famous discussion of the fetishism of commodities.

Since the producers do not come into social contact with each other until they exchange their products, the specific social character of each producer's labour does not show itself except in the act of exchange. In other words, the labour of the individual asserts itself as a part of the labour of society, only by means of the relations which the act of exchange establishes directly

[6]See Blaug [1, p. 281], Itoh [16, pp. 52–58], and Mawatari [26].

between the products, and indirectly, through them, between the producers. To the letter, therefore, the relations connecting the labour of one individual with that of the rest appear, not as direct social relations between individuals at work, but as what they really are, material relations between persons and social relations between things. (Marx [19, p. 77–78].)

Part 2 of Volume 1, "The Transformation of Money into Capital", suggests the solution of the riddle of surplus value, how it is created in the process of the general formula of capital (Chapter 4), $M-C-M'$, the transformation of money into commodities, and the change of commodities back again into money, throughout which all exchanges are made at value.

The conversion of money into capital has to be explained on the basis of the law that regulate the exchange of commodities, in such a way that the starting-point is the exchange of equivalents. Our friend, Moneybags, who as yet is only an embryo capitalist, must buy his commodities at their value, must sell them at their value, and yet at the end of the process must withdraw more value from circulation than he threw into it at starting. His development into a full-grown capitalist must take place, both within the sphere of circulation and without it. These are the conditions of the problem. Hic Rhodus, hic salta! (Marx [19, p. 163].)

The solution suggested is the buying and selling of labor-power (Chapter 6).

In order to be able to extract value from the consumption of a commodity, our friend, Moneybags, must be so lucky as to find, within the sphere of circulation, in the market, a commodity, whose use-value possesses the peculiar property of being a source of value, whose actual consumption, therefore, is itself an embodiment of labour, and, consequently, a creation of value. The possessor of money does find on the market such a special commodity in capacity for labour or labour-power. (Marx [19, p. 164].)

The value of labour-power is determined, as in the case of every other commodity, by the labour-time necessary for the production, and consequently also the reproduction, of this special article. (Marx [19, p. 167].)

After giving the definition of constant capital ("represented by the means of production, by the raw material, auxiliary material and the instruments of labor, does not, in the process of production, undergo any quantitative alternation of value" Marx [19, p. 202]) and variable capital ("represented by labour-power, does, in the process of production, undergo an alternation of value" Marx [19, p. 202]), in Chapter 8, Marx stated in Chapter 9 of Part 3, "Production of Absolute Surplus-Value", that the degree of exploitation of labour-power by capital, or of the laborer by the capitalist, is expressed by the rate of surplus-value, surplus-labor/necessary labor, where necessary labor is defined by the labor-time necessary to reproduce labor-power.

> Since, on the one hand, the values of the variable capital and of the labour-power purchased by that capital are equal, and the value of this labour-power determines the necessary portion of the working-day; and since, on the other hand, the surplus-value is determined by the surplus portion of the working-day, it follows that surplus-value bears the same ratio to variable capital, that surplus-labour does to necessary labour. (Marx [19, p. 209].)

Absolute surplus value is produced by the prolongation of the working-day. The long Chapter 10 discusses the history of the struggle for the normal working day and the English Factory Acts.

Part 4 of Volume 1 is entitled "Production of Relative Surplus-Value" and discusses co-operation, division of labor, and machinery, since the relative surplus value is defined as "arising from the curtailment of the necessary labour-time" (Marx [19, p. 299]) made possible by the rising productivity of labor. It is interesting for us to see that Marx considered dynamics of rivalry among capitalists as aiming extra surplus-value (Chapter 12) and the economy of the scale due to the simultaneous employment of a large number of laborers (Chapter 13).[7] The longest chapter, Chapter 15, discusses the history of machinery and modern industry. Part 5, "The Production of Absolute and of Relative Surplus-Value", is devoted to considering the effect of changes in absolute and relative surplus value, the combined effect of a change in working hours and a change in the productivity of labor.

Part 6, "Wages", deals with the transformation of the value, and respectively, the price, of labor-power into wages (Chapter 19) and emphasizes the importance of the distinction between labor which creates value and labor power, which is necessary since "on the surface of bourgeois society the wage of the labourer appears as the price of labour, a certain quantity of money that is paid for a certain quantity of labour" (Marx [19, p. 501]). This part also contains an important chapter, Chapter 22, "National Differences of Wages", which is the starting point of the Marxian theory of international economics (see section 3 below).

Marx starts Part 7, "The Accumulation of Capital", with a discussion on simple reproduction (Chapter 23). The general law of capitalist accumulation is considered in Chapter 25, where Marx introduces many important concepts and arguments, the organic composition of capital ("the value composition of

---

[7] See also Marx's *Das Kapital*, Volume 3, Chapter 5. This suggests the limit of the application of linear economic models to consider problems Marx raised, as we shall argue in section 5 below.

capital in so far as it is determined by its technical composition and mirrors the changes of the latter" Marx [19, p. 574]), the relative diminution of the variable part of capital, the concentration of capital, and the industrial reserve army or the relative surplus-population ("... if a surplus labouring population is a necessary product of accumulation or of the development of wealth on a capitalist basis, this surplus-population becomes, conversely, the lever of capitalistic accumulation, nay, a condition of existence of the capitalist mode of production" Marx [19, p. 592]).

The final part of Volume 1 concerns "The So-called Primitive Accumulation", which is "preceding capitalistic accumulation; an accumulation not the result of the capitalist mode of production, but its starting-point" (Marx [19, p. 667]). As Marx noted elsewhere (Marx [22, p. 43]), it is J. Steuart who "gives a great deal of attention to this *genesis* of capital" while "in Adam Smith's writings this process ... is assumed to be already completed." The final chapter of Volume 1 is Chapter 33, "The Modern Theory of Colonisation".

The second volume of *Das Kapital* consists of three parts, "The Metamorphoses of Capital and their Circuits", "The Turnover of Capital" and "The Reproduction and Circulation of the Aggregate Social Capital". Different economists may differently evaluate the importance of the first five chapters in Volume 2 on the form of circulation, as in the case of the form of value in Volume 1. Chapter 6, on the cost of circulation, is interesting from the point of view of seeing whether labor input in the circulation is considered to create values. "The general law is that *all costs of circulation which arise only from changes in the form of commodities do not add to their value*" (Marx [20, p. 152]). Genuine costs of circulation do not add to the value of commodities, while some costs of storage and costs of transportation do. Part 2 of Volume 2 is devoted to a detailed study of the turnover of capital.

Part 3 deals with the famous reproduction schema. Simple reproduction is considered in Chapter 20, where total product, and the total production of society is divided into two departments, Means of Production and Articles of Consumption, and the value of the entire product of each department consists of the part to replace the constant capital consumed in the production, another part to replace the variable capital advanced to laborers, and the surplus value. The condition for simple reproduction is that the sum of the variable capital and the surplus value in the department of the means of production must be equal to the value of the constant capital in the department of articles of consumption. Chapter 21 discusses the expanded reproduction which makes the starting point of the macro dynamics of the later Marxian economists. It has been emphasized that the schema is of a highly abstract character, since exchanges at value are assumed. The use of labor value may, however, be vindicated since

> ... it was inevitable – perhaps it still is – that macroeconomic models be built on arbitrary rigidities and aggregation rules which gloss over market price adjustments and the several principles of substitution. ... The labor theory of value provided Marxian writers with an easy ... aggregation mechanism which may have plunged them forward into macrodynamics ahead of their time. (Bronfenbrenner and Wolfson [6].)

Consisting of seven parts, the third volume of *Das Kapital*

> must locate and describe the concrete forms which grow out of the *movement of capital as a whole*. ... The various forms of capital ... approach step by step the form which they assume on the surface of society, in the action of different capitals upon one another, in competition, and in the ordinary consciousness of the agents of production themselves." (Marx [21, p. 25].)[8]

Marx starts Part 1, "The Conversion of Surplus-Value into Profit and of the Rate of Surplus-Value into the Rate of Profit", by introducing the concept of cost-price (the portion of the value of the commodity which replaces the price of the consumed means of production and labor power) and defining the rate of profit in terms of value. "The rate of surplus-value measured against the variable capital is called rate of surplus-value. The rate of surplus-value measured against the total capital is called rate of profit" (Marx [21, p. 43]). Although the surplus value is exploited from laborers by capitalists buying labor power with variable capital, individual capitalists are interested only in the rate of profit, since "surplus-value and rate of surplus-value are, relatively, the invisible and unknown essence that wants investigating, while rate of profit and therefore the appearance of surplus-value in the form of profit are revealed on the surface of the phenomenon."

The famous problem of the transformation of values into prices of production is considered in Part 2, "Conversion of Profit into Average Profit". Since the different organic composition of capital in different branches of production results in differences in the rate of profit (Chapter 8), the values of commodities must be transformed into prices of production so as to form a general rate of profit or average rate of profit (Chapter 9). What Marx did was to calculate the price of production of a commodity by summing the cost price (in terms of value) and the profit which is obtained by the use of the average

---

[8] This suggests that topics covered in *Das Kapital* are not restricted to those of the first section ("Capital in general"), but include some of the second section ("Competition"), of the first of the six books, i.e., "Capital", of Marx's original plan. See Chapter 1, section 5, Marx [25, pp. 54–55], and Rosdolsky [42, pp. 10–23].

rate of profit, the aggregate surplus value/the aggregate capital. We shall consider this transformation problem in detail in the next section. While the transformation problem is concerned with the redistribution of surplus values among capitalists of different industries, the problem of the market value (Chapter 10) is concerned with the redistribution among differently conditioned capitalists in the same industry, which will be discussed in section 6 below.

Part 3 of Volume 3 discusses "The Law of the Tendency of the Rate of Profit to Fall". Marx considered the problem in terms of value. If the rate of surplus value is constant, technical changes which make the organic composition of capital higher reduce the rate of profit (Chapter 13). Marx quickly added that increasing intensity of exploitation acts as a counteracting influence to the law (Chapter 14). We shall discuss this problem in section 5. As Blaug noted [1 p. 292], Chapters 4–6 in Part 1 should rather be read in conjunction with Part 3, particularly Chapter 5, where Marx discusses the technical changes with the economy of scale. Chapter 15 contains Marx's comments on business cycles.

After the discussion on the distribution of surplus value from industrial capital to commercial capital and money-dealing capital in Part 4, "Conversion of Commodity-Capital and Money-Capital into Commercial Capital and Money-Dealing Capital (Merchant's Capital)," in Part 5," Division of Profit into Interest and Profit of Enterprise. Interest-Bearing Capital", Marx discusses how the rate of interest is determined. "The average rate of interest prevailing in a certain country – as distinct from the continually fluctuating market rates – cannot be determined by any law. In this sphere there is no such thing as a natural rate of interest in the sense in which economists speak of a natural rate of profit and a natural rate of wages" (Marx [21, p. 362]). As we shall argue in section 4 below, this conclusion follows from the fundamental character of Marx's concept of capital. Part 5 also shows that Marx's sympathies lie with the banking school and against the currency school. Marx was against the quantity theory of money, since the value of money is determined by labor productivity in the gold production, not by the quantity of money in circulation, and the quantity of money in circulation is regulated by the value of the aggregate flow of capital.

It is evident that banks issuing notes can by no means increase the number of circulating notes at will, as long as these notes are at all times exchangeable for money. ... The quantity of circulating notes is regulated by the turnover requirements, and every superfluous note wends its way back immediately to the issuer. (Marx [21, pp. 523–524].)

Marx's theory of rent is given in Part 6 of Volume 3, "Transformation of

Surplus-Profit into Ground-Rent", where Marx discusses not only the differential rent developed by Ricardo, but also the absolute rent considered by Rodbertus. See section 4 below for the details.

The final part of *Das Kapital* is "Revenues and their Sources". Chapter 48 criticizes the trinity formula, capital–profit (profit of enterprise plus interest), land–ground rent, labor–wages, or capital–interest, land–ground rent, labor–wages (including profit of enterprise). It is written, of course, from the point of view of Marx's concept of capital.

> Capital, land, labour! However, capital is not a thing, but rather a definite social production relation, belonging to a definite historical formation of society, which is manifested in a thing and lends this thing a special social character. Capital is not the sum of the material and produced means of production.... It is the means of production monopolised by a certain section of society, confronting living labour-power as products and working conditions rendered independent of this very labour-power, which are personified through this anti-thesis in capital. (Marx [21, pp. 814–815].)

> We saw also that capital ... and the capitalist is merely capital personified and functions in the process of production solely as the agent of capital ... in its corresponding social process of production, pumps a definite quantity of surplus-labour out of the direct producers, or labourers; capital obtains this surplus-labour without an equivalent, and in essence it always remains forced labour ... no matter how much it may seem to result from free contractual agreement. (Marx [21, p. 819].)

2. Some linear models

Let us consider a most simple linear model of Marx's economics.[9] Suppose the economy produces two goods, i.e., a producer's good (good 1) and a wage good (good 2). Assuming constant returns to scale, let us denote by a_i and l_i, respectively, the input coefficient of producer's good and the labor input coefficient in the production of good i, $i = 1, 2$. Then the embodied labor value of good i, v_i, can be obtained, as the sum of the value transferred from the producer's good consumed and the input of living labor, from

$$v_i = a_i v_1 + l_i, \quad i = 1, 2. \tag{1}$$

---

[9] For linear economic models applied to Marx's economics, see, among others, Morishima [27], Morishima and Catephores [28], Nikaido [30], [31], Okishio [32], [33], Roemer [40], and Steedman [49]. The following is a drastically simplified version of models used in Morishima [27] and Morishima and Catephores [28], which were also considered by Nikaido [30], [31].

Suppose the unit of labor power which can generate one unit of labor can be reproduced by the consumption of w units of the wage good. Then, the rate of surplus value e is identical in two sectors.

$$e = ((l - a_1)v_1 - wl_1v_2)/wl_1v_2 \tag{2}$$

$$= (v_2 - a_2v_1 - wl_2v_2)/wl_2v_2 = (l - wv_2)/wv_2$$

and (1) can be rewritten as

$$v_i = a_iv_l + wv_2l_i + ewv_2l_i, \quad i = 1, 2, \tag{3}$$

where the first, second and third terms in the right-hand side are respectively called the constant capital, the variable capital and the surplus value.[10]

For the economy to be able to generate surplus products, the input matrix

$$A = \begin{bmatrix} a_1 & a_2 \\ wl_1 & wl_2 \end{bmatrix} \tag{4}$$

must be productive in the sense that there exists a positive column vector $x = (x_1, x_2)$ such that $x > Ax$, where x_i can be taken as the level of the output of the good i. Let g be any positive low vector, and consider

$$y = yA + g. \tag{5}$$

Since A is productive,

$$x = Ax + f \tag{6}$$

has a non-negative, non-zero solution x, for any column vector f which is non-negative, non-zero (Morishima [27, p. 22]). By premultiplying (6) by y, and by postmultiplying (5) by x, we have $yf = gx$. By making only the ith component of f as 1, the other being zero, we can make $y_i = yf = gx > 0$ for all i. At such $y > 0$, $y > yA$ from (5). Then, $y' > A'y'$ where A' is the transposed matrix of A and y' is the transposed vector of y. Thus the productiveness of A implies that of A' and vice versa.

While Marx was exclusively concerned with values and the rate of surplus value in Volume 1 of *Das Kapital*, he transferred them into prices of production and the rate of profit in Volume 3. Since relative prices p_1/p_2 and the rate of profit r can be directly obtained from

$$p_i = (1 + r)(a_ip_l + wl_ip_2), \quad i = 1, 2, \tag{7}$$

---

[10] Therefore, the equality of the rate of surplus value need not be assumed independently, if labor mobility is assumed so that the real wage is equal among different industries. See, however, Blaug [1, pp. 246, 292–293.]

however, the process of transformation can be called a process of rejection of
values and replacement by prices. "Transforming from values to prices can be
described logically as the following procedure: (1) Write down value relations;
(2) take an eraser and rub them out; (3) finally write down the price relation
– thus completing the so-called transformation process" (Samuelson [44, p.
311]). But it cannot be concluded that values have nothing to do with prices.
The bridge connecting values and prices is constructed by the so-called
Fundamental Marxian Theorem.[11]

According to Okishio and Morishima, the proof of the theorem is as follows.
Suppose every industry earns positive profits, so that

$$p_1 > a_1 p_1 + w l_1 p_2 \tag{8}$$

$$p_2 > a_2 p_1 + w l_2 p_2 \tag{9}$$

where the price of the good i, p_i's are all positive. This implies that the input
matrix A is productive. Therefore there are positive output vector $x=(x_1,x_2)$
such that

$$x > Ax. \tag{10}$$

By premultiplying (10) by the positive value vector (v_1,v_2) and taking (3) into
account, we have

$$v_1 x_1 + v_2 x_2 - v_1(a_1 x_1 + a_2 x_2) - v_2(w l_1 x_1 + w l_2 x_2)$$
$$= e(w l_1 x_1 v_2 + w l_2 x_2 v_2) > 0 \tag{11}$$

from which the rate of surplus value e is found to be positive. Exploitation is
the source of profits, since it is impossible for each and every industry to earn
positive profits simultaneously unless $e>0$.

Conversely, let us assume $e>0$. From (3) we have

$$v_1 > a_1 v_1 + w l_1 v_2 \tag{12}$$

$$v_2 > a_2 v_1 + w l_2 v_2. \tag{13}$$

By putting $p_1 = k v_1$, $p_2 = k v_2$, where k is any positive number, we can see at
once that they are all positive and satisfy the conditions for positive profits, (8)
and (9). When there is exploitation, it is possible for all industry to earn positive
profits. This accomplishes the proof of the Fundamental Marxian Theorem
that there exists a set of prices fulfilling (8) and (9) if and only if the real wage
rate w is given such that the rate of surplus value e is positive. It is asserted that

[11] See Morishima and Seton [29], Okishio [33], and Morishima [27, pp. 46–71]. For the
theorems which do not assume the no-joint output, see Morishima and Catephores [28, pp.
22–58].

the exploitation of laborers by capitalists is necessary and sufficient for the existence of prices yielding positive profits, or, in other words, for the possibility of conserving the capitalist economy (Morishima [27, pp. 53–54]).

In his process of the transformation of values into prices, Marx considered (1) that "the sum of the prices of production of all commodities produced in society – the totality of all branches of production – is equal to the sum of their values" (Marx [21, p. 159–160]) and (2) that "surplus-value and profits are identical from the standpoint of their mass" (Marx [21, p. 167]). If these two conditions are satisfied, it is natural to calculate, as Marx did, the rate of profit by dividing the aggregate surplus values by the aggregate value of capital. While the rate of surplus value and values are determined by a_i, l_i and w in (1) and (2) and therefore independent of the level of output of different goods, however, the rate of profit computed by Marx is different from r and depends on the level of output of different goods. In general, it is impossible to satisfy two conditions Marx considered for the given combination of the level of output of different goods. Morishima vindicated Marx, however, by showing that Marx was right for a particular but very important combination of levels of output.

Writing price determined equations (7) in matrix form,

$$p = (1 + r)pA \tag{14}$$

where $p = (p_1, p_2) > 0$. If A is a non-negative matrix, we can show (Morishima [27, p. 67]) that there is a non-negative vector $y = (y_1, y_2)$ such that

$$y = (1 + r)Ay. \tag{15}$$

Actually $y > 0$ in our case, since A is a positive matrix. By multiplying (3) by y_1 and y_2 respectively and then adding them up, and by premultiplying (15) by $v = (v_1, v_2)$, we can obtain the so-called Morishima–Seton equation (Morishima and Seton [29]),

$$r = eV/(C + V), \tag{16}$$

where $V = v_2 wl_1 y_1 + v_2 wl_2 y_2$ is the aggregate variable capital and $C = v_1 a_1 y_1 + a_2 v_1 y_2$ is the aggregate constant capital. Equation (16) shows that Marx's calculation of the rate of profit is consistent with r obtained in (7), if the level of outputs of different goods satisfy condition (15).

Such levels of output correspond to those along the balanced equilibrium growth path, which is called the golden age path. The rate of growth is identical to the rate of profit in such a case, since laborers are assumed not to save and capitalists are assumed not to consume (Morishima [27, p. 68]).

In his process of the transformation of value into prices, Marx computed the price of production of a commodity by multiplying $(1+r)$ to the cost price of the commodity which is given in terms of value.

$$p=(1+r)vA \tag{17}$$

where p and v are respectively the vector of the price of production and that of the value. This procedure is criticized by Bortkiewicz [4], who said that it only transformed outputs from value to price, retaining inputs intact. Marx was, however, well aware of the problem.

> We had originally assumed that the cost-price of a commodity equalled the *value* of the commodities consumed in its production. But for the buyer the price of production of a specific commodity is its cost-price, and may thus pass as cost-price into the price of other commodities. Since the price of production may differ from the value of a commodity, it follows that the cost-price of a commodity containing this price of production of another commodity may also stand above or below that portion of its total value derived from the value of the means of production consumed by it. It is necessary to remember this modified significance of the cost-price, and to bear in mind that there is always the possibility of an error if the cost-price of a commodity in any particular sphere is identified with the value of the means of production consumed by it. Our present analysis does not necessitate a closer examination of this point. (Marx [21, pp. 164–165].)

Morishima and Caterphores [28, pp. 160–166] considered an iteration process

$$p_{t+1}=(1+r)p_t A, \quad t=0,1,2,\ldots \tag{18}$$

and noted that $\lim_{t\to\infty} p_t = p$ such that

$$p=(1+r)pA \tag{14}$$

since the matrix $(1+r)A$ can be considered as a primitive Markov matrix, that is, a non-negative matrix whose largest positive characteristic root is unity. Marx is vindicated that with (17) he considered the first step of the iteration (18) by making $p_0 = v$, and that he could approach the true prices of production p if he proceeded with the iteration process.

The equilibrium rate of profit and relative price obtained from (7) or (14) are actually to be established through the competition among capitalists in pursuit of a higher rate of profit. Nikaido [30], [31] is concerned with the stability problem of this process towards the equilibrium rate of profit and relative price, in other words, whether they can eventually be established through capital mobility across sectors in pursuit of a higher rate of profit.

If M_i and x_i are the existing level of money and real capitals in the ith sector, they are related by

$$M_i = (p_1 a_i + p_2 w l_i) x_i = q_i x_i, \quad i = 1, 2 \tag{19}$$

where q_i is the price of the ith sector's capital, i.e., the value of one unit of the capital consisting of a_i units of the producer's good and wl_i units of the wage good at their prices. When the current relative price (p_1/p_2) is higher than its equilibrium level determined in (7) or (14), the rate of profit is higher in the first sector than in the second, so that money capital moves from the second to the first sector, i.e., dM_1/dt is positive and dM_2/dt is negative, where t denotes time, and vice versa. If there is no movement of real capitals, we have from (19)

$$dM_i/dt = x_i dq_i/dt, \quad i = 1, 2 \tag{20}$$

and

$$dq_i/dt = a_i dp_1/dt + wl_i dp_2/dt, \quad i = 1, 2. \tag{21}$$

By substituting (21) into (20), we obtain

$$m_1 = a_1 x_1 dp_1/dt + wl_1 x_1 dp_2/dt \tag{22}$$

$$m_2 = a_2 x_2 dp_1/dt + wl_2 x_2 dp_2/dt \tag{23}$$

where $m_i = dM_i/dt$. Equations (22) and (23) can be solved for dp_i/dt, i.e.,

$$dp_1/dt = (m_1 wl_2 x_2 - m_2 wl_1 x_1)/x_1 x_2 |A| \tag{24}$$

$$dp_2/dt = (m_2 a_1 x_1 - m_1 a_2 x_2)/x_1 x_2 |A| \tag{25}$$

where $|A|$ is the determinant of the input matrix A. The sign of $|A|$ characterizes how both sectors differ from each other in organic composition of capital, a_i/wl_i, since

$$|A| = wl_1 l_2 ((a_1/l_1 w) - (a_2/l_2 w)). \tag{26}$$

It is positive (negative) if the organic composition is higher (lower) in the first sector than in the second.

Suppose that the first sector is higher in organic composition than the second so that the denominator is positive in the right-hand side of (24) and (25). If the relative price p_1/p_2 is currently higher than the equilibrium level, p_1/p_2 deviates farther from the equilibrium to widen the profit rate differentials, since m_1 is positive and m_2 is negative in (24) and (25). Similarly, if the current p_1/p_2 is lower than the equilibrium, (24) and (25) imply further deviation downward of p_1/p_2 away from the equilibrium to widen the profit rate differentials. Suppose next that the first sector has lower organic composition than the second, so that $|A|$ is negative. In this case, according to (24) and (25), prices change in the direction to lessen the deviation from the equilibrium toward equalization of profit rates.

If we introduce the movement of real capitals x_1, x_2 through net real investment, the resultant changes in them must satisfy the following condition, provided that capital is fully used. The demand for investment and consumption must equal the net supply, i.e.,

$$A(dx/dt) + c = (I - A)x \qquad (27)$$

where $x = (x_1, x_2)$, $(dx/dt) = (dx_1/dt, dx_2/dt)$, $c = (0, c_2)$ and c_2 denotes the capitalists's constant demand for the second good. The behavior of x_1 and x_2 as the solution of (27) depends on the characteristic roots and vectors of the matrix $(I - A)^{-1}A$, and therefore on the sign of $|A|$. There is a further difficulty that changes in x_1 and x_2 determined by (27) may not satisfy the requirement that x_1 increases if p_1/p_2 is higher than the equilibrium level, and so on.

Although we cannot go into the details of Nikaido's analysis, we believe that readers are already ready to accept his conclusion that in the process of capital movement motivated solely by the higher profit rate seeking the equalization of rates of profit is not a universal tendency, but a phenomenon conditional on such a casual property of technology as the organic composition of capital of the producer's good sector relative to that of the wage good sector.

3. On exploitations

In terms of the embodied labor value, Marx defined the surplus value as "the difference between the value of the product and the value of the elements consumed in the formation of that product, in other words, of the means of production and the labour-power" (Marx [19, p. 201]). This surplus value is exploited from labor by capital, since

> ... that portion of the commodity-value making up the surplus-value does not cost the capitalist anything simply because it costs the labourer unpaid labour. Yet, on the basis of capitalist production, after the labourer enters the production process he himself constitutes an ingredient of operating productive capital, which belongs to the capitalist. Therefore, the capitalist is the actual producer of the commodity. (Marx [21, p. 26].)

It has often been argued that "when labor is the only primary factor – that is, if all other inputs in the economy are produced – then one can define the total embodied labor contents of commodities" (Burmeister [7, p. 134]). To show that the surplus labor value is the appropriation of the unpaid labor, however, labor (power) cannot be regarded as the primary factor of production, but must be considered to be (re)produced by the consumption of the wage goods which are, in return, produced by the use of labor. The relations between labor (power) and wage goods are, then, reciprocal and symmetric in this circular production relation. As far as formal logic is concerned, therefore, we may define value not in terms of labor, but in terms of wage goods. If the theory of exploitation is not independent of this redefinition of values, we have to conclude that exploitation is merely a matter of definition.

To make the story simple, let us consider an economy composed of labor (power) and a single wage good, where land is not scarce and can be disregarded economically. Let us assume that a unit of the wage good has to be consumed to reproduce a unit of labor power which we assume can generate a unit of labor service, the length of a working day being an institutionally given constant. Dismissing the fixed capital, let us suppose that two units of the wage good can be produced from the input of a unit of labor. Of course, laborers have no stock of wage goods and have only labor power to sell, while capitalists have a stock of wage goods which can be advanced as a variable capital.

Marx's explanation of exploitation is as follows. Since both the wage good and labor power are labor products, directly or indirectly, exchanges are made according to embodied labor value. The value of one unit of the wage good is 0.5 since two units of the wage good can be produced from the input of one unit of labor, while the value of one unit of labor power is also 0.5, since it can be reproduced by the consumption of one unit of the wage good. Suppose 100 units of labor power and 100 units of wage good are exchanged between laborers and capitalists at the beginning of the period. At the end of the period, 100 units of labor power are reproduced, while 100 units of wage good advanced are reproduced and, in addition, another 100 units of the wage good are appropriated by capitalists as the surplus products.

Since both labor power and the wage good can also be regarded as the products produced from the input of wage good, directly and indirectly, we may also consider that they are exchanged according to the embodied contents of the wage good. If we define values in terms of the wage good, one unit of labor power has value 1, since it can be reproduced from the consumption of one unit of the wage good, while the value of one unit of the wage good is 0.5, since two units of it can be produced from the input of one unit of labor. At the beginning of the period, laborers and capitalists exchange 200 units of the wage good and 100 units of labour power according to the embodied wage good value, and 200 units of the advanced wage good are just replaced and 200 units of labor power are produced at the end of the period. While surplus population is created, no surplus is made in the production of the wage good, so that exploitation of labor by capital is impossible. Exploitation appears only if value is defined in terms of embodied labor.[12]

Even if we stick to the definition of value in terms of labor, furthermore, there is another difficulty. In Chapter 1, Volume 1 of *Das Kapital*, Marx argued that commodities – say, a coat and 10 yards of linen – are exchanged according to the value, i.e., the embodied quantities of labor, by reducing tailoring and weaving labors to the abstract human labor (Marx [19, pp. 50–51]). This is possible if and only if the labor is perfectly mobile between tailoring and weaving. Otherwise, we cannot compare tailoring labor with weaving labor, and in general it is not true that commodities are exchanged according to the embodied quantities of respective labors. Can we say, then, that capitalists exploit laborers on the grounds that the value of labor products produced by the hired laborers is larger than the value of labor power which is paid by the capitalists? Such a statement can be made if and only if the labor embodied in the labor products in question and the labor embodied in the wage goods, i.e., the means of subsistence bought by laborers with wages, are reduced to the homogeneous abstract human labor.

These two labors are, however, differently dated, since the latter labor is the past labor already expended, while the former is going to be expended. Except in the world of science fiction, labor is not perfectly mobile through time, since we cannot use future labor in the present. Differently dated labors cannot be reduced to the abstract human labor. Since all productions are not instantaneous and wages have to be advanced by capitalists, therefore, we cannot accept Marx's theory of exploitation of labor by capital in the case of equal labor quantity exchange.

This is essentially the point raised by Böhm-Bawerk against Marx, not in his famous *Karl Marx and the Close of his System* (1896) but in his criticism of the exploitation theory of interest in *Capital and Interest, The History and Critique of Interest Theories* (1884). Böhm-Bawerk attacked Rodbertus's exploitation theory of interest on the grounds that future and present goods are wrongly considered identical, and stated that the same argument can be applied to Marx's theory. Even though surplus value is produced by labor alone, it accrues only after the passage of time. There is no exploitation if workers receive at present the entire present value of their future output which is smaller than the future value, since the physically same goods located at

---

[12] In other words, surplus appears, by definition, only in the production of commodities which are not used to define values.

different time points are not identical in view of the existence of the rate of interest. Böhm-Bawerk considered the following example.

Suppose a single worker spends five years to complete independently from start to finish a steam engine, which commands, when completed, a price of $5,500. There is no objection to giving him the whole steam engine or $5,500 as the wage for five years' continuous labor. But when? Obviously it must be at the expiration of five years. It is impossible for him to have the steam engine before it is in existence. He cannot receive the steam engine, valued at $5,500 and to be created by him alone, before he has created it. His compensation is the whole future value at a future time.

But the worker, having no means of subsistence, cannot and will not wait until his product has been fully completed. Suppose our worker wishes, after the expiration of the first year, to receive a corresponding partial compensation. The worker should get all that he has labored to produce up to this point, say, a pile of unfinished ore, or of iron, or of steel material, or the full exchange value which this pile of material has now. The question is how large will that value be in relation to the price of the finished engine, $5,500. Can it be $1,100, since the worker has up to this time performed one-fifth of the work?

Böhn-Bawerk said "No". One thousand one hundred dollars is one-fifth of the price of a completed, present steam engine, which is different from what the worker has produced in the first year, i.e., one-fifth of an engine which will not be finished for another four years. The former fifth has a value different from that of the latter fifth, in so far as a complete present machine has a different value from that of an engine that will not be available for another four years. Our worker, at the end of a year's work on the steam engine that will be finished in another four years, has not yet earned the entire value of one-fifth of completed engine, but something smaller than it. Assuming a prevailing interest rate of 5 per cent, Böhm-Bawerk concluded that our worker should get the product of the first year's labor, which is worth about $1,000 at the end of the first year (Böhm-Bawerk [2, pp. 263–265]).

Böhm-Bawerk used the rate of interest to discount the value of future goods in his arguments against the exploitation theory of interest, while Marx applied a zero rate of discount to the value of the future goods to compare it with that of the present goods in his theory of exploitation of labor by capital.[13] There seems to be no reason why Böhm-Bawerk is wrong and Marx

---

[13] Weizsäcker [54] proposes to use the rate of growth to discount the value of the future goods to the present. Since it falls short of the rate of interest if capitalists consume part of the profit, his position with respect to the possibility of capitalist exploitation is located between Marx and Böhm-Bawerk.

is right. To vindicate his theory of exploitation, Marx had to show why there is no difference between identical goods located at different time points.

One may rightly argue that physically same but differently dated goods can be regarded as identical in a stationary state, which Marx calls a simple reproduction, since exactly identical activities are repeated in every period and inputs and outputs can be synchronized in spite of the existence of the period of production. Since Marx assumes the subsistence wage to be just sufficient to reproduce labor power so that laborers remain laborers and cannot become capitalists, capitalists to be assumed to remain capitalists forever. A stationary state is possible, then, if and only if capitalists consume the whole profit and keep their capital unchanged. Since the level of consumption as well as the social milieu around them is unchanged, the marginal rate of substitution between consumptions in different periods is equal to 1 for rational capitalists who do not underevaluate future wants. If the rate of profit is positive, however, they can increase their consumption in the future by more than what they reduce their consumption today by saving and investing their profit. A stationary state cannot be maintained, therefore, unless the rate of profit is zero and there is no exploitation.

One may wrongly hope that physically same but differently dated goods can be regarded identical in a von-Neumann like balanced growth path where relative prices and relative quantities remain unchanged. Suppose the rate of profit is 100 per cent, so that the rate of growth is also 100 per cent, since all the profit is reinvested. Comparing the output of a wage good, say, wheat in 1984, and the wheat wages paid in 1983, Böhm-Bawerk would discount the former by the rate of profit (100 per cent) and conclude that there is no exploitation at all, while Marx would not discount the former and insist that the rate of exploitation is 100 per cent. One bushel of wheat in 1983, however, produces four bushels in 1985, while a bushel in 1984 produces only two bushels in 1985. To regard the 1983 wheat and the 1984 wheat identical is, therefore, to make four bushels of wheat identical to two bushels of wheat in 1985.[14]

Marx considered not only the exploitation of labor by capital in the case of equal labor quantity exchange, but also the exploitation of a poor country by a rich one through unequal labor quantity exchanges. He argued that the richer country with higher productivity and higher money (not real) wages

---

[14] See Chapter 3, section 3, in the above for the difficulties Marx's definition of the value of labor power has with the balanced economic growth. If there is no industrial reserve army, there is no balanced growth, since wages are at subsistence level, corresponding only to reproduction of labor power expended in the production. Introduction of a reserve army, however, generates the difficulty that relative quantities do not remain unchanged, let alone the problem that excess labor supply is inconsistent with exchanges according to values.

exploits the poorer one with lower productivity and lower money wages, in the sense that three days of labor of the latter country are exchanged against one day of labor of the former country (Marx [19, p. 525]; [24, pp. 105–106]). How can Marx make such a statement? Here Marx is implicitly assuming that the labor of different countries is identical. Since labor is not mobile between countries, this assumption of an international abstract human labor cannot, in general, be justified. Unlike the case of the immobility through time that means that future goods cannot be consumed in the present, however, at least internationally traded goods are mobile between countries. We may argue, therefore, that physically identical labor, i.e., labor of the same intensity and equally trained, of different countries is socially and economically identical, if the quantities of internationally traded goods directly and indirectly necessary to reproduce the labor power are identical between countries.

Let us construct a simple model of a two-country three-goods economy. The first good is a non-wage good and the last two goods are wage goods, while the first two goods are internationally tradable and the last good is a local or non-traded good. By taking units properly, we can assume that a unit of labor power can be reproduced by the consumption of a unit of the second good and of a unit of the third good. By choosing the first good as *numéraire*, we denote the price of the second good, that of the third good in the first country, and that of the third good in the second country by p, w, and v, respectively. Finally, let us denote by a_{ij} the quantity of labor necessary to produce a unit of the jth good in the ith country, and assume that the first country has the comparative advantage in the first good, i.e., $a_{11}/a_{12} < a_{21}/a_{22}$.

The price-cost equations are

$$1 = (1 + r)a_{11}(w + p) \tag{1}$$

$$p = (1 + s)a_{22}(v + p) \tag{2}$$

$$w = (1 + r)a_{13}(w + p) \tag{3}$$

$$v = (1 + s)a_{23}(v + p) \tag{4}$$

where r and s are the rate of profit in the first and second countries, respectively. The first and the third goods are produced in the first country, where the rate of wage is $w + p$, while the second and third goods are produced in the second country, where the rate of wage is $v + p$.

Let us denote by x_i the quantity of the second good directly and indirectly necessary to reproduce one unit of labor power in the ith country, and by y_i the quantity of the second good directly and indirectly necessary to produce one unit of the third good in the ith country. Since one unit of labor power can be reproduced by the consumption of one unit of the second and the third goods,

$$x_i = 1 + y_i, \quad i = 1, 2. \tag{5}$$

Since the input of a_{i3} labor is necessary to produce one unit of the third good in the ith country,

$$y_i = a_{i3} + a_{i3} y_i, \quad i = 1, 2. \tag{6}$$

To make the labors in different countries identical, we must have $x_1 = x_2$. Therefore, we see that $a_{13} = a_{23}$ by solving x_i from (5) and (6).

Without losing the generality, let us suppose that the second country is the richer one, with higher productivity, i.e., $a_{11} > a_{21}$ and $a_{12} > a_{22}$. Then we have

$$p \geqq a_{22}/a_{21} > a_{22}/a_{11} \tag{7}$$

since

$$a_{22}/a_{21} \leqq p \leqq a_{12}/a_{11} \tag{8}$$

from the principle of comparative costs.

Between two countries, p units of the first good, which contains $p\,a_{11}$ units of labor of the first country, are exchanged against one unit of the second good, which contains a_{22} units of labor of the second country. Therefore, $p > a_{22}/a_{11}$ implies that " the richer country exploits the poorer one, even where the latter gains by exchange" (Marx [24, p. 106]), as the theory of comparative costs shows. Since real wages are identical between countries, it is the rate of profit that is higher in the richer country. In other words, capitalists exploit capitalists.

Since $a_{13} = a_{23}$, we have from (1) to (4)

$$p = a_{22} v / a_{11} w. \tag{9}$$

In view of (7), therefore, this implies that $v > w$. The money wage is, as Marx argued, higher in the richer country, since we can assume that the gold (money) is (a part of) the first good. In other words, "the relative value of money will, therefore, be less in the nation with more developed capitalist mode of production than in the nation with less developed" (Marx [19, p. 525]), since it is a_{22}/p in the former, depending on the value (not physical) productivity of its export industry, while it is a_{11} in the latter, and $p > a_{22}/a_{11}$.[15]

We can, therefore, accept Marx's labor theory of international value, and international exploitation through unequal labor quantity exchange, which

[15] Ricardo and Senior are Marx's predecessors in this respect. See Ricardo [38, p. 146], Senior [45, p. 15], and Bowley [5, p. 223].

unfortunately Marx could not develop fully,[16] although we agree with Böhm-Bawerk that Marx's theory of capitalists' exploitation of labor does not make sense.

4. Marx's dichotomy of distribution

Marx dichotomized the problem of distribution into that of the exploitation of surplus products and that of the redistribution of surplus products. The distribution of income between property owners and wage earners is considered in Volume 1 of *Das Kapital* by the use of the labor theory of value, while the redistribution among property owners (different capitalists, land-owners) is left to be analyzed in Volume 3 by the theory of prices of production, the theory of rent and the theory of the interest rate.

> The capitalist who produces surplus-value, i.e., who extracts unpaid labour directly from the labourers, and fixes it in commodities, is, indeed, the first appropriator, but by no means the ultimate owner, of this surplus-value. He has to share it with capitalists, with landowners, etc., who fulfil other functions in the complex of social production. Surplus-value, therefore, splits up into various parts. Its fragments fall to various categories of persons, and take various forms, independent the one of the other, such as profit, interest, merchants profit, rent, etc. It is only in Book III that we can take in hand these modified forms of surplus-value. ... We treat the capitalist producer as owner of the entire surplus-value, or better perhaps, as the representative of all the shares with him in the booty. (Marx [19, pp. 529–530].)

If successful, such a two-step approach, i.e., the dichotomy, is certainly useful since we can separate a simpler, but more fundamental problem (exploitation of surplus products) from other more complex but secondary problems (redistribution of surplus products), and can study the former without being bothered by the latter. The success of the dichotomy depends, however, on the condition that the solution of the first step is independent of the solution of the second step. If this condition is not met, all the problems have to be solved simultaneously. In the case of Marx's dichotomy, the rate of surplus value in the labor theory of value has to be independent of the redistribution of surplus products among different capitalists and between capitalists and landowners. In other words, the labor theory of value has to

---

[16] According to Marx's unrealized plan of six books, international trade is the topic to be treated in the fifth book, while *Das Kapital* is a part of the first book. See Marx [25, pp. 54–55].

solve a part of the problem of distribution without the help of the theory of prices of production, the theory of rent and the theory of the rate of interest.

Let us first consider the dichotomy between the exploitation of surplus products and the redistribution of surplus products among capitalists of various industries, dismissing the existence of land and landowners. By the assumption of no land, we can safely assume that input coefficients are technically given constants and apply a linear economic model to the problem. For the sake of simplicity, let us consider a two-good (two-sector) economy, dismissing the existence of durable capital and joint production.

The input–output relation is

$$x_1 = a_{11}x_1 + a_{12}x_2 + y_1 \tag{1}$$

$$x_2 = a_{21}x_1 + a_{22}x_2 + y_2 \tag{2}$$

where x_i, y_i and a_{ij} denote respectively the gross output of the ith good, net output of, or final demand for, the ith good, and the constant input coefficient of the ith good in the production of the jth good. The dual value system to (1) and (2) is

$$v_1 = a_{11}v_1 + a_{21}v_2 + L_1 \tag{3}$$

$$v_2 = a_{12}v_1 + a_{22}v_2 + L_2 \tag{4}$$

where v_i and L_i are respectively the value of the ith good and the constant labor input coefficient in the production of the ith good.

The total employment of labor is defined as

$$L = L_1 x_1 + L_2 x_2 \tag{5}$$

and it is easily seen that

$$L = v_1 y_1 + v_2 y_2, \tag{6}$$

which indicates that the value of net output is equal to the input of living labor. Wage is assumed to be equal to the real reproduction cost of labor power,

$$v = c_1 v_1 + c_2 v_2 \tag{7}$$

where c_1 and c_2 are physiologically or socially given constants.

The distribution of a newly created value L between wage earners and the representative capitalist is denoted by the rate of surplus value

$$e = (L - vL)/vL = (1 - v)/v, \tag{8}$$

which indicates the ratio of surplus products exploited and the wage paid, both given in terms of value. In view of (3), (4) and (7), it remains constant, provided that input coefficients in the production, including the reproduction of labor power, are constant.

Surplus products exploited by the representative capitalist are, then, redistributed among industrial capitalists so that the rate of profit r is equalized between two sectors. This is done by transforming values v_i into price of production p_i, so that

$$p_1 = (1+r)(L_1 w + a_{11} p_1 + a_{21} p_2) \tag{9}$$

$$p_2 = (1+r)(L_2 w + a_{12} p_1 + a_{22} p_2) \tag{10}$$

are satisfied where

$$w = c_1 p_1 + c_2 p_2. \tag{11}$$

The pattern of demand depends, in general, on the pattern of distribution, as Marx clearly pointed out that

> ... the social demand, i.e., the factor which regulates the principle of demand, is essentially subject to the mutual relationship of the different classes and their respective economic position, notably therefore to, firstly, the ratio of total surplus-value to wages, and secondly, the relation of various parts into which surplus-value is split up (profit, interest, ground-rent, taxes, etc.). (Marx [21, p. 181].)

In particular, the pattern of capitalists' demand depends on the distribution among different capitalists, i.e., on whether the rate of profit is equalized between different sectors or not. In other words, the final demand y_i in (1) and (2), which is the sum of the demand from laborers $c_i L$ and the demand from capitalists, is not independent of the determination of p_1, p_2 and r and of the different patterns of demand of capitalists in different sectors.

Changes in y_1 and y_2 are, however, absorbed into changes in x_1 and x_2 in (1) and (2). Values are determined in (3) and (4) independently of the pattern of the final demand. The determination of the rate of surplus value e is, therefore, independent of the redistribution of surplus products among capitalists. We can now conclude as the proposition that Marx's dichotomy does work between the theory of value and the theory of prices of production.[17] The distribution between wage earners and capitalists in value terms is indepen-

---

[17] It should be emphasized that this conclusion depends on the assumption of constant returns to scale. If Marx's consideration of increasing returns to scale is to be emphasized (as will be done in the next section), the dichotomy does not work even between theory of value and theory of price of production.

dent of the redistribution among capitalists. In other words, Marx's labor value is useful as the aggregator (weights of goods in aggregation) in the macroeconomic theory of distribution between capitalists and wage earners (Morishima [27, p. 10]).

The next problem to be considered is the dichotomy between the theory of value and the theory of rent, i.e., the distribution of surplus products between capitalists and landowners. Marx's theory of rent consists of the theory of differential rent and that of absolute rent. Let us first consider the case of differential rent. Marx's discussion of differential rent is much more complicated but essentially identical to Ricardo's, in the sense that both intensive and extensive margins of cultivation are considered.[18] For our purpose, however, it suffices to consider the former, under the assumption that the land is homogeneous.

Since the existence of the limited land is admitted, input coefficients in agriculture are no longer constants but are assumed variable and an increasing function of the level of output of agricultural products, i.e., the first good. We assume constant input coefficients for non-agricultural goods which are aggregated and called manufactured goods, i.e., the second good. Introducing diminishing returns on land, we have to replace the linear input–output relation (1) and (2) by a non-linear one,

$$x_1 = A_{11}(x_1)x_1 + a_{12}x_2 + y_1 \qquad\qquad (12)$$

$$x_2 = A_{21}(x_1)x_1 + a_{22}x_2 + y_2 \qquad\qquad (13)$$

where A_{11} and A_{21} are average input coefficients of the first good and the second good in the production of the first good and increasing functions of x_1. Other notations are identical to those in (1) and (2).

Values are determined, on the other hand, by

$$v_1 = a_{11}(x_1)v_1 + a_{21}(x_1)v_2 + L_1(x_1) \qquad\qquad (14)$$

$$v_2 = a_{12}v_1 + a_{22}v_2 + L_2 \qquad\qquad (4)$$

where a_{11}, a_{21} and L_1 are marginal, not average, input coefficients of the first good, the second good and the labor in the production of the first good, and all increasing functions of x_1, while other notations are identical to those in (3) and (4). This is because values are determined by direct and indirect inputs of the average social labor when labor is not particularly assisted by the fertility of the soil at the margin of cultivation while within the margin "the exceptionally productive labour operates as intensified labour; it creates in

---

[18] Differential rent I (Marx [21, pp. 649–673]) is concerned with extensive margin while differential rent II (Marx [21, pp. 674–737]) is concerned with intensive margin. See, however, Blaug [1, p. 299].

equal periods of time greater values than average social labour of the same kind" (Marx [19, p. 302]).

Total employment of labor is defined as

$$L = W_1(x_1)x_1 + L_2 x_2 \tag{15}$$

where W_1 is the average, not marginal, labor input coefficient in the production of the first good and an increasing function of x_1. From (12), (13), (14), (4), and (15), then, it is derived that

$$v_1 y_1 + v_2 y_2 = L + (a_{11} - A_{11})v_1 x_1 + (a_{21} - A_{21})v_2 x_1 + (L_1 - W_1)x_1, \tag{16}$$

which indicates that the value of the net output is larger than the input of living labor, since marginal input coefficients are larger than average ones in the production of the first good. The difference has to be called "a false social value" (Marx [21, p. 661]), since it is created by labor assisted by land and not the contribution of labor but that of land, which the labor theory of value eliminated from the consideration.

Wage is defined again as (7) in terms of value so that the surplus value obtained by capitalists $v_1 y_1 + v_2 y_2 - vL$ is larger than the exploited value from L, i.e., $L - vL$, by the same difference as the value of the net output is larger than the input of living labor. This difference is called extra-surplus-value (Marx [19, p. 301]). The distribution of newly created value between wage earners and capitalists is denoted by the rate of surplus-value

$$e = (v_1 y_1 + v_2 y_2 - vL)/vL, \tag{17}$$

which indicates the ratio of surplus-value including extra-surplus-value to the wage paid, both in terms of value. From (14), v_i's are not independent of x_i's, and therefore not independent of the demand pattern of capitalists through (12) and (13). In view of (16), then, e defined in (17) is also not independent of the demand pattern of capitalists.

Let us now turn to the problem of the redistribution of surplus-value obtained by capitalists between capitalists and landowners, i.e., the theory of differential rent. To simplify the story, let us dismiss the problem of prices of production and consider the rent in terms of the so-called market value rather than the market price of production, since the differential rent "arises from the law of market value, to which the products of the soil are subject," and which "asserts itself on the basis of capitalist production through competition" (Marx [21, p. 661]).

While a capital invested at the margin of cultivation obtains no extra-surplus-value, capitals invested within the margin can enjoy it, as the past and living labor they employ are intensified by the fertility on the land. Through the competition of capitalists and landowners in agriculture then, extra-surplus-value must be transferred to landowners as the differential rent, so that the rate of surplus-value is equalized to e defined in (8) for any capital invested in agriculture.[19] Since the demand pattern of landowners is different from that of capitalists, this redistribution of surplus-value changes the final demand. This induces changes in the equilibrium values of x_i through (12) and (13) and therefore those of v_i through (14) and (4). In view of (16), then, the distribution in the theory of value of newly created values between wage earners and capitalists who also represent landowners, indicated by e in (17), is no longer independent of the redistribution of surplus products between capitalists and landowners in the theory of differential rent. In other words, Marx's dichotomy between Volume 1 and Volume 3 fails between theory of value and theory of differential rent. Unless land cannot be ignored, value and rent should be considered simultaneously. The labor theory of value cannot solve even a part of the problem of distribution, i.e., the distribution between wage earners and non-wage earners, without the help of the theory of rent. This is no wonder, since the labor theory of value starts with the elimination of land rent, as in the case of Ricardo, by considering the marginal land, the location of which is left to be considered in the theory of rent. This is the reason why Ricardo, unlike Smith and Marx, put his chapter on land rent just after that on value, i.e., before those on wages and profit (Chapter 4, section 1).

Incidentally, the above argument is somewhat based on the so-called production theory of differential rent which is insisted on by Liubimov.[20] According to his theory, differential rent is a part of the surplus-value created in agriculture, i.e., exploited from agricultural laborers. On the other hand, according to the so-called circulation theory of differential rent, which is, for example, proposed by Bulgakov, the origin of the differential rent is the surplus-value produced in manufacturing and circulated into agriculture. The difficulty with this theory is, among others, that it cannot explain the rent in a purely agricultural society.

Absolute rent is the rent which is paid even by the marginal investment which does not pay the differential rent. It was insisted on by Rodbertus and Marx followed it critically.[21] Marx explained the reason of the existence of

---

[19] For an excellent discussion on extra surplus value and its relation to land rent, see Hirase [14, pp. 170–188]. Of course, extra surplus value is defined originally with respect to extra value due to the new method of production, which is to be eliminated by competition. As far as it exists, however, its nature is not different from extra value to be transformed to differential rent.

[20] For the production theory and circulation theory of differential rent, see Liubimov [17, Chapter 40].

[21] See Marx [21, pp. 748–772], Rodbertus [39], and Marx [23, Chapter 8]. Absolute rent is different from monopoly rent (Ricardo [38, pp. 250–251]), since the price of agricultural products cannot exceed their value in the former, though the following arguments can be applied also to the case of monopoly rent. See Marx [21, pp. 762–764].

absolute rent as follows.

> If capital meets an alien force which it can but partially, or not at all, overcome, and which limits its investment in certain spheres, admitting it only under conditions which wholly or partly exclude that general equalisation of surplus-value to an average profit, then it is evident that the excess of the value of commodities in such spheres of production over their price of production would give rise to a surplus-profit, which could be converted into rent and as such made independent with respect to profit. Such an alien force and barrier are presented by landed property, when confronting capital in its endeavour to invest in land, such a force is the landlord vis-a-vis the capitalist. (Marx [21, pp. 761–762].)

To dismiss the problem of the extra-surplus-value and the differential rent, let us suppose that homogeneous land is not scarce and that input coefficients are constant even in the agriculture. Values are, then, defined in (3) and (4) and independent of the changes of the level of output. Suppose the organic composition of capital is higher in manufacturing than in agriculture. The rate of profit in terms of value is then higher in agriculture than in manufacturing. Transformation of values into prices of production may be prevented from the equalization of the rate of profit in terms of prices, however, if the land-ownership limits the investment in agriculture.

The price–cost equations in such a case are

$$p_1 = (1 + r_1)(L_1 w + a_{11} p_1 + a_{21} p_2) \tag{18}$$

$$p_2 = (1 + r_2)(L_2 w + a_{12} p_1 + a_{22} p_2) \tag{19}$$

where w is given in (11) and r_1 and r_2 are respectively the rate of return (profit and absolute rent) in agriculture and the rate of return (profit) in manufacturing. Since the rate of profit is equalized at r_2, the absolute rent is $(r_1 - r_2)p_1 x_1$ and the total profit is $r_2(p_1 x_1 + p_2 x_2)$.

The transformation of values into prices and the transfer of a part of the profit from capitalists to landowners as absolute rent certainly changes the pattern of the final demand, which in return causes changes in the level of output. Since values are independent of changes in the level of output, however, the rate of surplus-value e defined in (8) is not changed by this redistribution of surplus-value. We can conclude as a proposition that Marx's dichotomy does work between the theory of value and the theory of absolute rent. The distribution between wage earners and property owners in value terms is independent of the distribution between capitalists and landowners, if the latter takes only the form of absolute rent.

As even a leading Marxian economist admitted (Hidaka [12, p. 423]), unfortunately, the absolute rent has a conceptual difficulty, which can be seen in the following definition of absolute rent given by Marx.

> Just as it is the monopoly of capital alone that enables the capitalist to squeeze surplus-labour out of the worker, so the monopoly of landowner-ship enables the landed proprietor to squeeze that part of surplus labour from the capitalist, which would form a constant excess profit. (Marx [23, p. 94].)

It should be noted that the word "monopoly" is interpreted here, not in the modern sense that capitalists or landowners act jointly so as to maximize common gains, but in the classical sense that the supply of capital or land is limited (at least in the short-run) so that it is scarce, or in the Marxian sense that capital (land) is owned exclusively by capitalists (landowners). The monopoly of capital, therefore does not exclude the competition among capitalists. Otherwise, there would be no equality of the rate of profit. Similarly, the monopoly of landownership does not exclude the possibility that each landowner acts independently. Though Marx made some confusing statements (Bortkiewicz [3, p. 432]), it is clear that he did not have the joint action of all the landowners in mind. For a single landowner, then, there is no reason not to invite additional investment on land when there is absolute rent, i.e., the price of the agricultural product exceeds the price of production. The joint result of such individual actions is, however, the reduction of absolute rent due to an increase in the supply of agricultural products, which continues until the absolute rent disappears.

Finally, let us consider the division of profit into profit of enterprise and interest. "Interest flows to the money-capitalists, to the lender, who is the mere owner of capital, ... while the profit of enterprise flows to the functioning capitalist alone, who is non-owner of the capital" (Marx [21, p. 374]). If we regard capital as capital goods, as in neo-classical economics, and consider entrepreneurs and capital goods as two different factors of production, the profits of enterprise and interest are quasi-rents to be imputed respectively to entrepreneurs and capital goods. Division of the surplus-value into the profit of enterprise and interest causes, through the different demand patterns of industrial capitalists (entrepreneurs) and of money capitalists (lenders), changes in the rate of surplus-value, as in the case of the division of the surplus-value into profit and differential land rent. Marx's dichotomy does not work, then, between the theory of value and the theory of interest.

However, Marx refuses to consider that capital is a thing (Marx [21, p. 815]). "As Marx frequently reminds his readers, capital is a social relation, not a thing. The term is often a rough proxy for the capital–labour relation" (Elliott [10]).

> Two entirely different elements – labor-power and capital – act as determinants in the division between surplus-value and wages, which division essentially determines the rate of profit .... We shall see later that the same occurs in the splitting of surplus-value into [land] rent and profit. Nothing of the kind occurs in the case of interest. (Marx [21, p. 364].)

In other words, the division of products into wages, profit and land rent is a result of a mutual relation between labor, capital and land in the process of production. In the division of profit into profit of enterprise and interest, however,

> ... the same capital appears in two roles – as loanable capital in the lender's hands and as industrial, or commercial, capital in the hands of the functioning capitalists. But it functions just once, and produces profit just once. In the production process itself the nature of capital as loanable capital plays no role. (Marx [21, p. 364].)

Since it is not a result of the process of production, "there is no such thing as natural rate of interest" and "the average rate of interest prevailing in a certain country cannot be determined by any law" (Marx [21, p. 362]). For the same reason, how the rate of interest is determined has no influence on the rate of the surplus-value, which is firmly determined by the capital–labor relation in the process of production. Marx's dichotomy works, therefore, between the theory of value and the theory of interest rate.

Unlike neo-classical economists, Marx did not consider that the natural rate of interest is determined as the quasi-rent to capital goods. He rather thought that the rate of interest depends on the expectations of borrowers and lenders. In this sense, there is a striking similarity with Keynes's analysis of the rate of interest in Chapter 15 of *The General Theory of Employment, Interest and Money* (Panico [37]).

5. The falling rate of profit

As we saw in Chapter 4, section 2, Ricardo insisted that the rate of profit falls and the total land rent rises as the result of increased population and the accumulation of capital. The reason is, of course, that the supply of land is limited. Marx insisted that a falling rate of profit is due to a rising organic composition of capital, however, without taking the problem of land into consideration.

> The gradual growth of constant capital in relation to variable capital must necessarily lead to *a gradual fall of the general rate of profit*, so long as the rate of surplus-value, or the intensity of exploitation of labour by capital, remain the same. (Marx [21, p. 212].)

> Proceeding from the nature of the capitalist mode of production, it is thereby proved a logical necessity that in its development the general average rate of surplus-value must express itself in a falling general rate of profit. Since the mass of the employed living labour is continually on the decline as compared to the mass of materialised labour set in motion by it, i.e., to the productively consumed means of production, it follows that the portion of living labour, unpaid and congealed in surplus-value, must also be continually on the decrease compared to the amount of value represented by the invested total capital. Since the ratio of the mass of surplus-value to the value of the invested total capital forms the rate of profit, this rate must constantly fall. (Marx [21, p. 213].)

According to the first quotation above, since the rate of profit in terms of value r is defined as

$$r = S/(C+V) = (S/V)/[C/V)+1],\tag{1}$$

where C, V and S are respectively the aggregate constant capital, variable capital and surplus-value, r falls as the organic composition of capital C/V rises, if the rate of surplus-value S/V remains unchanged. Sweezy [50, pp. 100–102] argued, however, that a rise in the organic composition of capital goes hand in hand with increasing labor productivity and that we have Marx's own word for it that higher productivity is invariably accompanied by a higher rate of surplus-value.

According to the second quotation from Marx given in the above, on the other hand, Tomizuka [52] and Rosdolsky [41] considered that the upper limit of the rate of profit falls, since

$$r = S/(C+V) < (V+S)/(C+V) < (V+S)/C\tag{2}$$

and the living labor $V+S$ is continually on the decline as compared to the materialized labor C. The fall of the upper limit of the rate of profit does not, of course, exclude the possibility of a temporal rise in the rate, but there is certainly a tendency of the rate to fall in the long run.

What is more important is, however, to recognize that such a technical change as raising the organic composition of capital or the ratio of past labor to living labor can be realized in a capitalist economy if and only if it is favorable for capitalists to adopt such a technique as with higher organic composition or a higher ratio of past to living labors. If we assume that capitalists who make decisions on the choice of technique are competitive in the sense that they take market prices as constant, a new technique, whether it raises the organic composition or not, can be adopted if and only if it can reduce the cost of production calculated at the given current prices.

For the sake of simplicity, let us consider a two-good economy where the price of the first good, the producer's good, is denoted by p and the second good, the wage good, plays the role of *numéraire* with the unitary price. For the production of a unit of the ith good, $i=1, 2$, the input of a_{i1} unit of the producer's good is necessary, while the unit of labor power is properly defined so that its reproduction requires the consumption of a unit of the wage good, and the input of a_{i2} unit of labor is necessary to produce a unit of the ith good. The price of the producer's good p and the rate of profit r are determined from

$$p=(1+r)(a_{11}p+a_{12}) \tag{3}$$

$$1=(1+r)(a_{21}p+a_{22}), \tag{4}$$

since the wage in terms of the wage good has to be paid so that the labor can be reproduced.

Suppose a new technique is adopted in the production of the wage good so that input coefficients a_{21} and a_{22} are changed into a'_{21} and a'_{22} respectively. For the new technique to be adopted by capitalists,

$$a'_{21}p+a'_{22}<a_{21}p+a_{22} \tag{5}$$

must be satisfied at p which is determined in (3) and (4), since the cost of production must be reduced when it is calculated at the current price. After the introduction of the new technique, the price of the producer's good p' and the rate of profit r' are determined from

$$p'=(1+r')(a_{11}p'+a_{12}) \tag{6}$$

$$1=(1+r')(a'_{21}p'+a'_{22}). \tag{7}$$

Comparing (3) and (6), we see from

$$p[1/(1+r)-a_{11}]=p'[1/(1+r')-a_{11}] \tag{8}$$

that $p'>p$ if $r'>r$ and $p'<p$ if $r'<r$, i.e., the rate of profit always changes in the same direction as the price of the producer's good, i.e., the good produced under the unchanged technique. Next, comparing (4) and (7) and taking note of

(5), we have

$$(1+r)(a'_{21}p+a'_{22})<(1+r')(a'_{21}p'+a_{22}).\qquad(9)$$

From (9), we see that $p'>p$ if $r'<r$, i.e., the price of the producer's good rises if the rate of the profit falls. But this is clearly a contradiction. Therefore, we have to conclude that $r'>r$, i.e., the rate of profit has to rise.

The introduction of a new technique which reduces the cost of production calculated at the current prices, i.e., satisfies (5), necessarily raises the rate of profit, even if it is with higher organic composition of capital, i.e., $a'_{21}>a_{21}$, and $a'_{22}<a_{22}$. This is the so-called Shibata–Okisio theorem.[22] Does this mean, then, that Marx's law of falling rate of profit does not hold, if capitalists are assumed to behave rationally? Not necessarily, since the model of an economy used to prove the Shibata–Okishio theorem is too strait a jacket for Marx. The theorem started with Shibata's study, which tried to solve the problems raised by Marx by using a simplified model of an economy developed by the Lausanne school of economics. The model is a static one, which is developed, like recent models of Marx after Sraffa, under the assumption of constant cost (returns to scale) and perfect competition, in the neo-classical sense that firms face infinitely elastic demand curves.

Marx's description of the process of dynamic rivalry among capitalists which leads to the falling rate of profit suggests to us, however, a world of diminishing cost (internal economy of scale) and firms facing demand curves downwardly sloping, i.e., Chamberlin's DD and dd curves [8, pp. 90–91].

> A capitalist working with improved but not as yet generally adopted method of production sells below the market-price, but above his individual price of production; his rate of profit rises until competition levels it out (Marx [21, p. 231].)

> Under competition, the increasing minimum of capital required with the increases in productivity for the successful operation of an independent industrial establishment .... No capitalist ever voluntarily introduces new method of production, no matter how much more productive it may be, and how much it may increase the rate of surplus-value, so long as it reduces the rate of profit. Yet every such new method of production cheapens the commodities. Hence, the capitalist sells them originally above their price of production .... His method of production stands above social average. But competition makes it general and subject to the general law. There follows

[22]See Shibata [46], [47, pp. 236–242], [48], Okishio [32], [34, pp. 111–148, especially pp. 111–114], and [35, pp. 250–252]. See also Roemer [40, pp. 87–133].

a fall in the rate of profit which is, therefore, wholly independent of the will of the capitalist. (Marx [21, pp. 262, 264–265].)

It is, of course, true that free competition is assumed throughout Marx's *Das Kapital*. As Sylos–Labini [51] emphasized, however, in the case of classical economics competition implies merely a free entry and, unlike in the case of neo-classical perfect competition, not necessarily an infinitely elastic demand curve for an individual supplier. This can be clearly seen from Marx's following arguments on extra surplus value and market price or value.

The working-day of 12 hours is, as regards him, now represented by 24 articles instead of 12. Hence, in order to get rid of the product of one working-day the demand must be double what it was, i.e., the market must become twice as extensive. Other things being equal, his commodities can command a more extended market only by a diminution of their prices. (Marx [19, p. 301].)

If one produces more cheaply and can sell more goods, thus possessing himself of a greater place in the market by selling below the current market-price, or market-value, he will do so, and will thereby begin a movement which gradually compels the other to introduce the cheaper mode of production … . (Marx [21, p. 194].)

If the demand curve for an individual supplier is infinitely elastic, he can sell whatever amount he likes without reducing the price. What Marx had in mind, therefore, must be a demand curve for an individual supplier under free entry, which is infinitely elastic for quantities smaller than the current sale, but downwardly sloping for quantities larger than it.[23] This is exactly the case considered by Adam Smith, as we discussed in Chapter 3, section 4.

The internal economy of scale is also not foreign to Marx.

The battle of competition is fought by cheapening of commodities. The cheapness of commodities depends, *ceteris paribus*, on the productiveness of labour, and this again on the scale of production. Therefore, the larger capitalists beat the smaller. It will further be remembered that, with the development of the capitalist mode of production, there is an increase in the minimum amount of individual capital necessary to carry on a business under its normal conditions. (Marx [19, pp. 586–587].)[24]

---

[23] For Japanese literature on Marx on competition, see Hirase [13, pp. 22, 102] and Hishiyama [15].
[24] See also Hishiyama [15], though he considered not merely internal scale economy but rather a U-shaped cost curve.

But why does the productiveness of labour depend on the scale of production? This is, at least partly, due to the diminishing overheads cost. Marx emphasized the role of fixed capital in the process of a falling rate of profit due to higher organic composition.

> Owing to the distinctive methods of production developing in the capitalistic system the same number of labourers, i.e., the same quantity of labour-power set in motion by a variable capital of a given value, operate, work up and productively consume in the same time span an ever-increasing quantity of means of labour, machinery and fixed capital of all sorts, raw and auxiliary materials – and consequently a constant capital of ever-increasing value. (Marx [21, p. 212].)

In addition to its durability aspect, we have to notice the overheads cost aspect of fixed capital, which Marx did clearly.

> The simultaneous employment of a large number of labourers effects a revolution in the material conditions of the labour-process. The building in which they work, the store-houses for the raw material, the implements and utensils used simultaneously or in turn by the workmen; in short, a portion of means of production, are now consumed in common. ... When consumed in common, they give up a smaller part of their value to each single product; partly because the total value they part with is spread over a greater quantity of products ... . (Marx [19, p. 307].)

> Another rise in the rate of profit is produced, not by savings in the labour creating the constant capital, but by saving in the application of this capital itself. On the one hand, the concentration of labourers, and their large-scale co-operation, saves constant capital. The same buildings, and heating and lighting appliances, etc., cost relatively less for the large-scale than for small-scale production. The same is true of power and working machinery. Although their absolute value increases, it falls in comparison to the increasing extension of production ... . (Marx [21, p. 82].)

The above extract from *Das Kapital* suggests to us a resulting dynamic model of rivalry among capitalists which leads to a falling rate of profit due to increasing fixed or overhead capital. Since Chamberlin's *dd* curve drawn under the assumption that other firms in the same industry keep price unchanged is less steep, those firms which first adopt a new technique can enjoy economy of scale and extra profit by selling large amounts. Eventually, however, the new technique prevails and it turns out that economy of scale is less than expected, since Chamberlin's *DD* curve drawn under the assumption that all the firms charge the same price is very steep. The result is a lower rate of profit.

An equilibrium *E* of the representative firm in an industry is described in Figure 6.1, where the curve *AA* shows the average cost including the normal profit calculated from the general rate of profit and the curve *Ed* is Chamberlin's *dd* demand curve. Consider the introduction of a new technique with a higher organic composition of capital, such that the total fixed capital (assumed as constant capital) is increased, but the circulating capital (assumed as variable capital) per unit of output is decreased. As in Figure 6.1, when *Ed* is not steep, the curve *AA* can be shifted to a curve like *BB*, which is located below *Ed* for sufficiently large output, even though it is located above *Ed* at the level of the original equilibrium output *OX*. In words, a profit maximizing firm adopts such a technique if it considers that sufficiently large amounts of output can be sold without much price reduction.

When many other firms adopt the new technique and try to sell larger amounts, however, the necessary price reduction turns out to be much larger than expected. Chamberlin's *DD* curve is drawn as *ED*, which is much steeper than the *Ed* curve. The new average cost curve *BB* fails to shift below the *ED* curve. The result is that the price of the product falls and the rate of profit for all the firms in the industry must be lower than the general rate of profit, which was used to draw curves *AA* and *BB*. For those firms which have not followed the adoption of the new technology yet, it is profitable to move to other

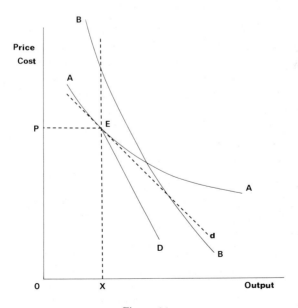

Figure 6.1.

industries where the rate of profit is higher, i.e., at the normal level. As the result of such a capital movement, however, the rate of profit is equalized among industries and the rate of profit itself is reduced throughout the economy.

One may argue. like Steedman, that

... unless the previously adopted technique is no longer available, even if new invention should lead many capitalists mistakenly to adopt it, as soon as it is found to be less profitable than the previously used technique, all capitalists will revert to the latter. Since technical knowledge has seldom, if ever, been lost beyond recovery within the capitalist era. (Steedman [49, pp. 126–129].)

This is certainly true in a static problem of the choice of two techniques. In a dynamic capitalist economic process, however, another technique will become available which has still higher organic composition of capital than the currently prevailing one. Then, the choice is not between the previously used technique, with organic composition lower than the currently prevailing one, and the currently prevailing technique. It should be between the previously used technique and the newest technique, which has not been used and has the highest organic composition. For a single firm it may be possible that the adoption of the newest one is more profitable than to revert to the previously used one.

Nor can one blame the myopic behavior of individual firms which adopt such a technique that eventually results in a falling rate of profit. Since future profits have to be discounted to be compared with current profits, for a pioneering firm the lower rate of profit in the future can be compensated by the current extra profit. It is logically possible, therefore, to have a never-ending, repeating process of adopting techniques with higher organic composition which result in a lower rate of profit.

Finally, however, we have to admit that this possibility of the falling rate of profit is inconsistent with Marx's argument that "the fall in commodity-prices and the rise in the mass of profit on the augmented mass of these cheapened commodities is but another expression for the law of the falling rate of profit" (Marx [21, p. 231]). As we have already seen, the rate of profit always changes in the same direction as the relative price of the good produced under the unchanged technique, provided that the good is produced under constant returns to scale. In other words, the falling rate of profit raises the relative price of the good which is produced under a new technique with higher organic composition of capital. Of course, the price of this good falls if the ED curve is relatively less steep than the BB curve in Figure 6.1, so that the latter curve is located below the former for a sufficiently large output. In this case, however, the rate of profit has to rise. A falling rate of profit is possible if and only if the economy of scale achieved by each firm is rather less than expected when all the firms adopted the new technique.

6. On market values

While the theory of prices of production is concerned with distribution among capitalists in different industries, the theory of market values considers distribution among different capitalists in the same industry. Marx's theory of market values has been regarded as one of the most difficult parts of *Das Kapital*, and interpretations are divided and confused among Marxian economists. Marx defined market value as, strictly speaking, an average value of commodities produced in a single industry, while Uno [53, p. 93] and Ouchi [36, p. 496] judged Marx's explanation to be unsatisfactory and seriously doubted the significance of such a definition. Marx further argued that market value differs from the individual value of the commodities produced under average conditions if demand or supply is greater than, or drops below the usual level. Grigorovici [11, p. 37] insisted, however, that market value is exclusively determined by technical conditions and has nothing to do with demand. Yamamoto [55] insisted, furthermore, that Marx was wrongly confused between market price and market value in this so-called "obscure part" of Chapter 10, Volume 3, of *Das Kapital*.[25]

In our opinion, it seems that these confusions are due to the fact that the difference in the nature of demand and supply equilibria corresponding to market price and to market value is not fully recognized by Marxian economists. Market price corresponds to a Marshallian temporary or very short-run equilibrium with industrial supply an arbitrary given, while market value corresponds to a Marshallian short-run or long-run equilibrium where industrial supply is changeable but does not change, at least not instantaneously. Since market value is concerned with the situation where different producers in an industry produce commodities under different conditions, it is worth considering the problem of market value from the point of view of the

---

[25] "Der Marktwert der Waren Steht in keinem Zusammenhange mit dem gesellschaftlichen Bedurfnisse nach diesen Waren. Der Marktwert wird ausschliesslich durch das technische Moment bestimmt ..." (Grigorovici [11, p. 37]). See Rosdolsky [42, p. 93], for a critical review of Grigorovici. For an excellent survey of the Japanese literature on market value, see Itoh [16, pp. 80–92].

Marshallian theory of a normal supply price with a representative firm and normal profit.[26]

Marx argued that

> ... there is also the *market-value* to be distinguished from the individual value of particular commodities produced by different producers. The individual value of some of these commodities will be below their market-value while that of others will exceed the market-value. On the one hand, market-value is to be viewed as the average value of commodities produced in a single sphere, and, on the other, as the individual value of the commodities produced under average conditions of their respective sphere and forming the bulk of the products of that sphere. (Marx [21, p. 178].)

Even if commodities produced under average conditions form the bulk of the product, it is clear that the average value may differ in general from the individual value of products produced under average conditions. Marx seems to insist that market value is, strictly speaking, the average value but that it coincides with the individual value of the product of average producers ordinarily, since he argued that "it is only in extraordinary combinations that commodities produced under the worst, or the most favourable, conditions regulate the market-value" (Marx [21, p. 178]).

Ouchi [36] doubted seriously the significance of Marx's definition of market value in terms of average value, and, following Uno [53, p. 83], insisted that market value is regulated by the individual value of the product of average producers who can accommodate the additional demands. It is understandable that the most favorable producers cannot accommodate additional demand, since their capacity, though expanding, may still be limited. As for the least favorable producers, Ouchi argued that they are to be weeded out. Additional demand can, however, also be accommodated by slowing down the weeding out of the least favorable producers.[27]

The most serious problem with the definition of market value in terms of the individual value of the products of average producers is that there is then no assurance of the equality of demand and supply at the market price equalized to market value, since Marx clearly admitted that "supply and demand coincide when their mutual proportions are such that the mass of commodities

---

[26] For Marshall's theory of stationary state, normal supply price, representative firm, and so forth, see Chapter 10, section 3 of this book. Market value corresponds to Marshall's normal supply price including the normal profit of the representative firm which is the miniature of the industry, and the individual value of different producers' products corresponds to Marshall's supply price of individual firms which are expanding or reducing output even in the stationary state of the industry.

[27] Ouchi [36, pp. 464–505, particularly 477, 494, 496, and 497].

of a definite line of production can be sold at their market-value, neither above nor below it" (Marx [21, p. 189]). Suppose that the supply from the least favorable producers, who are unable to realize a portion of the surplus-value, is shrinking more rapidly than the supply from the most favorable producers with extra-surplus-value is expanding. Even if we start from the situation where demand and supply coincide, they deviate instantaneously unless the market price deviates from the market value. Average producers can certainly accommodate excess demand if the market price is higher than the market value which is equal to their individual value, but there is no incentive for them to expand if the market price is equal to the market value. The equilibrium of demand and supply can, therefore, not be maintained, if the market value is defined merely as the individual value of the product of average producers who can accommodate the additional demand.

Marx further argued as follows in the so-called "obscure part" of Chapter 10, Volume 3 of *Das Kapital*.

If the demand is so great that it does not contract when the price is regulated by the value of commodities produced under the least favourable conditions, then these determine the market value. This is not possible unless demand is greater than usual, or if supply drops below the usual level. Finally, if the mass of the produced commodities exceeds the quantity disposed of at average market-values, the commodities produced under the most favourable conditions regulate the market-value. (Marx [21, p. 179].)[28]

Should demand be weaker than supply, the favourably situated part, whatever its size, makes room for itself forcibly by paring its price down to its individual value. The market-value cannot ever coincide with this individual value of the commodities produced under the most favourable conditions, except when supply far exceeds demand. (Marx [21, pp. 184–185].)

If the supply is too small, the market-value is always regulated by the commodities produced under the least favourable circumstances and, if the supply is too large, always by the commodities produced under the most favourable conditions ... therefore it is one of the extremes which determines the market-value. (Marx [21, p. 185].)

It should be emphasized that Marx never abandoned his definition of

---

[28]"Average market-values" here is "mittlern Markt-werten" in the original German (Marx [18, III, p. 204]) and clearly implies the individual values of products produced under average conditions rather than the average value of the products of all the producers.

market value in terms of average value in these arguments. It is merely insisted on that market value may differ from the individual value of the products of average producers. Ouchi [36, pp. 495–496] argued, however, that Marx abandoned his definition in terms of average value, on the basis of the following argument of Marx.

> Suppose that the total mass of the commodities in question brought to market remains the same, while the value of the commodities produced under less favourable conditions fails to balance out the value of commodities produced under more favourable conditions, so that the part of the mass produced under less favourable conditions forms a relatively weighty quantity as compared with the average mass and with the other extreme. In that case, the mass produced under less favourable conditions regulates the market, or social, value. (Marx [21, p. 183].)

It seems to us that this argument does not contradict the definition of market value in terms of average value, either. It merely points out that commodities produced under average conditions may not form the bulk of the product.[29]

Let us construct a simple model of an industry to show that Marx's definition of market value is satisfactory, even if we suppose, following Ouchi [36], that producers under favorable conditions are expanding their production and producers under unfavorable conditions are reducing the level of output. Consider a Marshallian stationary state where the level of industrial output remains constant, although some producers are expanding while others are being weeded out. Let us use x to denote the individual value of commodities produced by different producers and v to denote the market value of the product of the industry. A producer increases his output if v is larger than his x, and decreases it if v is smaller than x. It is assumed that the rates of change in output are proportional to the difference between v and x. The different producers may have an identical value of x or different values of x. Let $y(x)$ be the total output of producers with the same value of x. Furthermore, let $D(x)$ denote changes (increases if positive, decreases if negative) in y. Then, from the assumption,

$$D(x)/y(x) = (v - x). \qquad (1)$$

Since the industrial output remains unchanged, i.e.,

$$\int y(x)\mathrm{d}x = \text{constant}, \qquad (2)$$

---

[29] See the comments of Rozenberg [43, pp. 349–351], on market value and demand and supply in Chapter 10, Volume 3 of *Das Kapital*.

from (1),

$$\int D(x)\mathrm{d}x = \int (v-x)y(x)\mathrm{d}x = 0. \tag{3}$$

If we define the proportion of the total output $y(x)$ of producers with individual value x to the total industrial output as

$$f(x) = y(x)/\int y(x)\mathrm{d}x, \tag{4}$$

we have, in view of (4),

$$v = \int x f(x)\mathrm{d}x, \tag{5}$$

since from the right-hand side of (3)

$$v \int y(x)\mathrm{d}x = \int xy(x)\mathrm{d}x. \tag{6}$$

From the definition (4),

$$\int f(x)\mathrm{d}x = 1. \tag{7}$$

Therefore, (5) implies that the market value of the product of the industry is exactly the average value of commodities produced by the industry, i.e., the definition given by Marx.

Thus the market value of the product of the industry v is dependent on the distribution of industrial output over different producers, and in general not independent of the level of demand for the industry, particularly when producers with some value of x have limited capacity, or the individual value of a producer changes as his level of output changes.

Suppose the individual value of commodities produced by a producer remains unchanged up to the capacity limit. We may further assume that those producers with x lower than v are operating at full capacity, and those producers with x higher than v only, then, can accommodate the additional demand. In general, an increase in demand seems to raise v. The relation between changes in v and changes in the demand is, however, not so simple, since distribution of demand is arbitrary over those producers with x higher than v. The market value v may not rise, if the distribution of demand to producers with the highest x is reduced, in spite of the increased demand for the industry as a whole.

To make the story simple, let us suppose that producers in the industry are grouped into only three, i.e., those producing under the least favorable conditions, average conditions, and the most favorable conditions. Under each type of condition, the individual value of commodities produced by a producer is constant with respect to the level of output up to the capacity limit which, for the sake of simplicity, is assumed to be the limit of the ability of the capitalist to oversee laborers. Since producers whose product's individual value is lower than the market value are assumed to be operating at the full capacity, the increase in the output of such producers proportional to the difference between the market and individual values is due to the entry of new producers, while the decrease proportional to such a difference in the output of producers whose product's individual value is higher than the market value is due both to the exit of producers and to the reduction of output of the remaining producers.

Suppose the aggregate demand for the industry is given and unchanged. The market value should be defined so that the industrial supply can be maintained to be equal to the industrial demand. In other words, it should be the average of individual values, so that the increase in the output of producers with lower individual value products is cancelled out by the decrease in the output of producers with higher individual value products.

In the ordinary case, we may assume, like Marx, that the average value is equal to the individual value of the products produced under average conditions, though Marx assumed further, unnecessarily, that the bulk of commodities is produced under average conditions.

Now suppose that the bulk of these commodities is produced under approximately similar normal social conditions, so that this value is at the same time the individual value of the individual commodities which make up this mass. If a relatively small portion of these commodities may now have been produced below, and another above, these conditions, so that the individual value of one portion is greater, and that of the other smaller, than the average value of the bulk of the commodities, but in such proportions that these extremes balance one another, so that the average value of the commodities at these extremes is equal to the value of commodities in the centre, then the market value is determined by the value of commodities produced under average conditions. The value of the entire mass of commodities is equal to the actual sum of the values of all individual commodities taken together produced under average conditions, or under conditions above or below the average. In that case, the market-value, or social value, of the mass of commodities – the necessary labour-time contained in them – is determined by the value of the preponderant mean mass. (Marx [21, pp. 182–183].)

Clearly what is necessary for the equality of market value and the individual value of products produced under average conditions is the balance of the value of output produced under the least favorable conditions and that produced under the most favorable conditions, and not the assumption that the bulk of commodities is produced under average conditions. Even if the latter assumption is satisfied, it is possible that the individual value of products produced under average conditions is different from the market value which is the average of the individual value of the products of all the producers. What is more interesting is the assumption that producers working under average conditions are not operating at full capacity and can accommodate additional demand. The individual value of products produced under average conditions can then remain as the market value, even if demand for the industry is changed. If demand is increased against the given supply, the market price deviates upward from the market value. This causes an increase in supply from producers working under average conditions, which is more reliable and much quicker than increases from other sources, since the latter involve entry and re-entry of producers and the temporal reversal of adjustments currently being made. The same applies to reduction of demand. In this sense the market value is likely to be independent of changes in demand, which gives a limited support to the so-called technology theory that market value is determined mainly by the present state of technology.

As Marx noted, however, this is possible only in the ordinary case. Suppose demand is extraordinarily large relative to supply, so that not only producers working under the most favorable conditions but also producers working under average conditions are operating at full capacity. It is possible, then, that the output produced under the least favorable conditions is so large that the market value, i.e., the average value of the product of all the producers in the industry, is higher than the individual value of the product produced under average conditions, and that the decrease in the output produced under the least favorable conditions, which is proportional to the difference between the individual value and the market value of the product, is balanced with the increase in the output produced under the most favorable and average conditions, which are proportional to the difference between the market value and individual values.

The individual lots of commodity-value produced at the two extremes do not balance one another. Rather, the lot produced under the worse conditions decides the issue. Strictly speaking, the average price, or the market-value, of each individual commodity, or each aliquot part of the total mass, would now be determined by the total value of the mass as obtained by adding up the values of the commodities produced under different conditions, and in accordance with the aliquot part of this total value falling to the share of each individual commodity. The market-value thus obtained would exceed the individual value not only of the commodities belonging to the favourable extreme, but also of those belonging to the average lot. Yet it would still be below the individual value of those commodities produced at the unfavourable extreme. How close the market-value approaches, or finally coincides with, the latter would depend entirely on the volume occupied by commodities produced at the unfavourable extreme of the commodity sphere in question. (Marx [21, p. 184].)

Similarly, let us suppose that demand is extraordinarily small relative to supply so that even producers working under the most favorable conditions are not operating at full capacity. It is possible, then, that the market value is lower than the individual values of the product of producers working under both the average and the least favorable conditions and that their decrease in output proportional to the difference of individual and market values balances with the increase in output of the producers working under the most favorable conditions. Marx [21, p. 184] argued

If the lot of commodities produced at the favourable extreme occupies greater place than the other extreme, and also the average lot, then the market-value falls below the average value. The average value, computed by adding the sums of values at the two extremes and at the middle stands here below the value of the middle, which it approaches, or vice versa, depending on the relative place occupied by the favourable extreme.[30]

For the market value being lower than the individual value of the products produced under average conditions, however, the output of the producers working under the most favorable conditions need not be large compared with the output of the producers working under average conditions, since the producers working under the least favorable conditions may not produce at all at the market value lower than the individual cost price which cannot yield any positive surplus value to them.

If we consider Marx's market value as Marshall's normal supply price of an industry in a stationary state, the so-called obscurity of the theory of market value seems to have cleared. The market value is to be defined as the average of individual values. In general it may differ from the individual value of products produced under average conditions and the individual value of the bulk of

---

[30]The first "average value" in this quotation is "mittlern Wert" and the second one is "Durchschnittswert" in the original German (Marx [18, III, p. 210]). The first one should rather be translated as the value of the products of the average producers.

the products of the industry, while these two individual values may also differ from each other. Marx rightly defined the market value and recognized the role of demand and supply which causes the market value to deviate from the individual value of products produced under average conditions, although he wrongly emphasized the unnecessary assumption that market value coincides with the individual value of the bulk of the industrial product.

The reason why the market value is the average of individual values is that it is the conditions necessary to keep the industrial supply equalized with the given demand for the industry, when producers with products of lower individual value expand their output and producers with products of higher individual value reduce their output. In other words, it is the condition necessary to keep the industrial structure proper so that the demand and supply are kept equalized and the market price does not deviate from the market value.

References

[1] Blaug, M., *Economic Theory in Retrospect*, Cambridge University Press, 1978.
[2] Böhm-Bawerk, E.V., *Capital and Interest, The History and Critique of Interest Theories*, G.D. Hunke and H.F. Sennholz, tr., Libertarian Press, 1959.
[3] Bortkiewicz, L.V., "Die Rodbertus'sche Grundrententheorie und die Marx'sche Lehre von der absoluten Grundrente", Zweiter Artikel, *Archiv für die Geschichte des Sozialismus und der Arbeiterbewegung*, 1(1911), pp. 389–434.
[4] Bortkiewicz, L.V., "On the Correction of Marx's Fundamental Theoretical Construction in the Third Volume of Capital", *Karl Marx and the Close of his System*, pp. 197–221, P.M. Sweezy, ed., Kelly, 1949.
[5] Bowley, M., *Nassau Senior*, George Allen and Unwin, 1937.
[6] Bronfenbrenner, M., and M. Wolfson, "Marxian Macrodynamics and the Harrod Growth Model", *History of Political Economy*, 16(1984), pp. 175–186.
[7] Burmeister, E., *Capital Theory and Dynamics*, Cambridge University Press, 1980.
[8] Chamberlin, E.H., *The Theory of Monopolistic Competition*, Harvard University Press, 1948.
[9] Ekelund, R.B. Jr., and R.F. Hébert, *A History of Economic Theory and Method*, McGraw-Hill, 1983.
[10] Elliott, J.E., "Continuity and Change in the Evolution of Marx's Theory of Alienation; from the Manuscripts through the Grundrisse to Capital", *History of Political Economy*, 11(1979), pp. 317–362.
[11] Grigorovici, T., *Die Wertlehre bei Marx und Lassalle*, Ignaz Brand, 1910.
[12] Hidaka, S., *Jidaironkenkyu* (A Study of Rent Theory), Jichosha, 1962.
[13] Hirase, M., *Keizaigaku Yottsu no Miketsu Mondai* (Four Unsettled Questions in Economics), Miraisha, 1967.
[14] Hirase, M., *Shihonron Gendaiko* (*Das Kapital* Considered from a Contemporary Viewpoint), Miraisha, 1983.
[15] Hishiyama, I., "Daikiboseisan to Shijokinko (Large Scale Production and Market Equilibrium)", *Keizaigaku niokeru Koten to Gendai* (Classics and Moderns in Economics), Committee on Festschrift for Dr. Kishimoto, ed., Nihon–Hyoron, 1965.
[16] Itoh, Makoto, *Value and Crisis, Essays on Marxian Economics in Japan*, Monthly Review Press, 1980.

[17] Liubimov, L., *Ocherki teorii zemelinoi renty*, Moscow National Publishing House, 1930.
[18] Marx, K., *Das Kapital*, Marx–Engels–Lenin Institut, 1932–1933.
[19] Marx, K., *Capital*, I, Progress Publishers, 1954.
[20] Marx, K., *Capital*, II, Progress Publishers, 1956.
[21] Marx, K., *Capital*, III, Progress Publishers, 1959.
[22] Marx, K., *Theories of Surplus Value*, I, Foreign Language Publishing House, 1963.
[23] Marx, K., *Theories of Surplus Value*, II, Progress Publishers, 1968.
[24] Marx, K., *Theories of Surplus Value*, III, Progress Publishers, 1971.
[25] Marx, K., *Grundrisse, Foundations of the Critique of Political Economy* (Rough Draft), M. Nicolaus, tr., Allen Lane (Penguin Books), 1973.
[26] Mawatari S., The Uno School: a Marxian Approach in Japan", *History of Political Economy*, 17 (1985), pp. 403–418.
[27] Morishima, M., *Marx's Economics*, Cambridge University Press, 1973.
[28] Morishima, M., and G. Catephores, *Value, Exploitation and Growth*, McGraw-Hill, 1978.
[29] Morishima, M., and F. Seton, "Aggregation in Leontief Matrices and the Labour Theory of Value", *Econometrica*, 29 (1961), pp. 203–220.
[30] Nikaido, H., "Marx on Competition", *Zeitschrift für Nationalökonomie*, 43 (1983), pp. 337–362.
[31] Nikaido, H., "Dynamics of Growth and Capital Mobility in Marx's Scheme of Reproduction", *Zeitschrift für Nationalökonomie*, 45 (1985), pp. 197–218.
[32] Okishio, N., "Technical Changes and the Rate of Profit", *Kobe University Economic Review*, 7 (1961), pp. 85–99.
[33] Okishio, N., "A Mathematical Note on Marxian Theorem", *Weltwirtschaftliches Archiv*, 91 (1963), pp. 287–299.
[34] Okishio, N., *Shihonseikeizai no Kisoriron* (Basic Theory of Capitalist Economy), Sobunsha, 1965.
[35] Okishio, N., *Marx Keizaigaku* (Marxian Economics), Chikuma, 1977.
[36] Ouchi, T., *Keizaigenron* (Principles of Economics), University of Tokyo Press, 1982.
[37] Panico, C., "Marx's Analysis of the Relationship between the Rate of Interest and the Rate of Profit", *Keynes's Economics and the Theory of Value and Distribution*, J. Eatwell and M. Milgate, eds., Duckworth, 1983.
[38] Ricardo, D., *On the Principles of Political Economy and Taxation*, Cambridge University Press, 1951.
[39] Rodbertus, J.C., *Sociale Briefe an von Kirchmann*, Dritter Brief, Widerlegung der Ricardo'schen Lehre von der Grundrente und Begrundung einer neuen Rententheorie, 1851.
[40] Roemer, J., *Analytical Foundations of Marxian Economic Theory*, Cambridge University Press, 1981.
[41] Rosdolsky, R., "Zur neueren Kritik des Marxschen Gesetzes der fallenden Profitrate", *Kyklos*, 9 (1956), pp. 208–226.
[42] Rosdolsky, R., *The Making of Marx's 'Capital'*, P. Burgess, tr., Pluto Press, 1977.
[43] Rozenberg, D.I., *Kommentarii ko btoromu i tretbemu tomam "Kapitala" K. Marksa*, Moskva, SOCEKGIZ, 1961.
[44] Samuelson, P.A., *The Collected Scientific Papers*, III, R.C. Merton, ed., MIT Press, 1972.
[45] Senior, N.W., *Three Lectures on the Cost of Obtaining Money*, Murray, 1830.
[46] Shibata, K., "On the Law of Decline in the Rate of Profit", *Kyoto University Economic Review*, 9 (1934), pp. 61–75.
[47] Shibata, K., *Riron Keizaigaku* (Economic Theory), I, Kobundo, 1935.
[48] Shibata, K., "On the General Profit Rate", *Kyoto University Economic Review*, 14 (1939), pp. 40–66.
[49] Steedman, I., *Marx After Sraffa*, NLB, 1977.
[50] Sweezy, P.M., *The Theory of Capitalist Development*, Oxford University Press, 1942.
[51] Sylos-Labini, P., "Competition: the Product Markets", *The Market and the State*, pp. 200–232, T. Wilson and A.S. Skinner, eds., Oxford University Press, 1976.

[52] Tomizuka, R., "Rijunritsu no Keikotekiteika no Hosoku to Kyoko no Hitsuzensei Nikansuru Ichishiron (An Essay on the Law of the Tendency of the Rate of Profit to Fall and the Necessity of Crisis)", *Shogakuronshu* (Journal of Commerce, Economics and Economic History of Fukushima University), 22–5 (1954), pp. 99–149.

[53] Uno, K., *Principles of Political Economy*, T. Sekine, tr., Harvester, 1980.

[54] Weizsäcker, C.C., "Modern Capital Theory and the Concept of Exploitation", *Kyklos*, 26 (1973), pp. 245–281.

[55] Yamamoto, F., "Shijokachi to Shijokakaku (Market Value and Market Price)", (4) *Rikkyo Keizaigakukenkyu* (St. Paul's Economic Review), 8–1 (1954), pp. 59–124.

CHAPTER 7

WALRAS AND THE GENERAL EQUILIBRIUM THEORY

1. Augustin Cournot

Of the four greatest economists in the world, according to Schumpeter, three were French, i.e. François Quesnay, Augustin Cournot and Léon Walras (Samuelson [26, pp. 1501, 1502, 1556]). However, this is not the only reason why we should consider Cournot in this section before our discussion, in the rest of this chapter, of Walras, one of the three big stars of the marginal revolution, the initiator of the general equilibrium theory and the author of *Eléments d'économie politique pure*, the Bible of modern neo-classical economics. The so-called Walras's law, which signifies the self-compactness or closedness of an economic system, was already suggested in Cournot's discussion of the exchanges. The Walrasian view of competitive market prices, quite distinct from those of Menger and Jevons, can be considered as having developed under the strong influence of Cournot's view.

Antoine Augustin Cournot was born in 1801 at Gray, in Haute-Saone, France. He studied mathematics at the Ecole Normale in Paris, and became Professor of Mathematics at Lyons in 1834, with the help of the great physicist and statistician, Poisson. He also served as Rector of the Academy at Grenoble, Inspecteur General des Etudes, and Rector of the Academy at Dijon. Cournot published extensively on mathematics, philosophy and economics, before he died in 1877. The most important book on economics, is, of course, *Recherches sur les principes mathématiques de la théorie des richesses* (1838), in which he applied differential calculus for the first time in economics. Although this book is usually regarded as a classical treatise on such topics as monopoly and oligopoly, its significance is by no means limited to them, from the point of view of modern economic theory as well as from that of the history of economic thought.

Cournot first considers the mutual interdependence of countries in a world economy in his theory of exchanges (Chapter 3).

To find the equations of exchange, we will suppose, to begin with, that the cost of exchange is less than the cost of transportation, or that the exchange takes place without any real transportation of money, without any change in the distribution of the precious metals between the commercial centres. (Cournot [5, p. 30].)

The rate of exchange of currencies of different countries (commercial centers) should be freely adjustable so that there is no transportation of money. If there are r countries, the number of the rate of exchange can be considered as $r(r-1)$. But it can be reduced to $r-1$, if arbitrages between two and three countries are carried out freely. The equations to determine $(r-1)$ unknown rates of exchange are obtained from the condition that what one country owes to all the others is of precisely the same value as what all the others owe to it, since there is no actual transportation of money. These equations are in number r, but one of them is not independent from others. "Adding all these equations together except the first, and eliminating from each member the terms which cancel, we obtain again the first equation. Thus there are only just as many distinct equations as there are independent variables" (Cournot [5, p. 34]).

This is essentially identical to Walras's discussion of the existence of a general equilibrium in an r good economy to the effect that the number of unknown relative prices is $r-1$ while the number of independent conditions of the equality of demand and supply is also $r-1$, in view of the so-called Walras's law that the value of aggregate demand for all goods is identically equal to the value of the aggregate supply of all goods.

As for the theory of monopoly, Cournot (Chapter 5) obtained the condition for the maximization of profit, which is essentially identical to the equality of marginal revenue and marginal cost. Assuming the law of indifference (the law of one price for one good), Cournot considers that the demand $F(p)$ is a continuous function of the market price p. To maximize the net receipts, obtained by subtracting the cost of production from the gross receipts, Cournot maximizes $pF(p) - \phi\ [D(p)]$ with respect to p, where the cost of production is considered as a continuous function $\phi(D)$ of the quantity to be supplied D and the demand and supply equilibrium $D = F(p)$ is assumed. The condition for the maximization of the net receipts is

$$D + (p - d\phi/dD)dD/dp = 0. \tag{1}$$

Cournot considered the duopoly next (Chapter 7). The condition for the equality of demand and supply is $D_1 + D_2 = F(p)$, where D_1 and D_2 are respectively quantities to be supplied from two firms. It is convenient to consider the inverse demand function $p = f(D_1 + D_2)$. The net receipts of the first firm are

$$f(D_1 + D_2)D_1 - \phi(D_1) \tag{2}$$

and those of the second firm are

$$f(D_1+D_2)D_2-\phi(D_2). \tag{3}$$

In words, the net receipts of a firm are a function not only of its own supply but also of the supply of the other firm. Cournot considers that each firm will independently maximize its net receipts, assuming that the supply of the other is unchanged. The equilibrium of duopoly is therefore a Nash solution of non-cooperative game, and the conditions for it are obtained by the differentiation of (2) and (3) respectively with respect to D_1 and D_2,

$$f(D_1+D_2)+D_1 f'(D_1+D_2)-\phi'(D_1)=0 \tag{4}$$

and

$$f(D_1+D_2)+D_2 f'(D_1+D_2)-\phi'(D_2)=0 \tag{5}$$

where f' and ϕ' denote the derivatives of f and ϕ.

Since two firms are enjoying entirely identical conditions, we should have $D_1=D_2$ at equilibrium. By adding (4) and (5) together, therefore, we have

$$2f(D)+Df'(D)-2\phi(D/2)=0 \tag{6}$$

where $D=D_1+D_2$.

Similarly, in the case of oligopoly[1] of n firms, the ith firm's net receipts are

$$f\left(\sum_i D_i\right)D_i-\phi(D_i), \quad i=1,\ldots,n, \tag{7}$$

where $D_i, i=1,\ldots,n$, is the supply of the ith firm. The condition to maximize (7) with respect to D_i is given as

$$f\left(\sum_i D_i\right)+D_i f'\left(\sum_i D_i\right)-\phi'(D_i)=0, \quad i=1,\ldots,n, \tag{8}$$

if the other firms' supplies $D_j, j=i$, are considered unchanged. Conditions are identical for all firms, and we should have $D_1=D_2=\ldots=D_n$ in (8). Adding n conditions together in (8), then, we have

$$nf(D)+Df'(D)-n\phi'(D/n)=0, \tag{9}$$

where $D=\sum_i D_i$.

Being based on (9), Cournot insists that the price p is equalized to the

---

[1]Cournot did not use the term "oligopoly". According to Schumpeter [27, p. 305], it was first used by Thomas More in his *Utopia*. See, however, Friedman [9, pp. 20–21]. I owe this footnote to Mr. Jun-ichi Tominaga of the University of Tokyo.

marginal cost ϕ' when the number of firms is sufficiently large and the competition is unlimited, i.e., the case of perfect competition (Chapter 8). To see this, let us simplify the story by assuming that the demand function is linear and that the marginal cost is constant. By substituting $p = f(D) = a - bD$ and $\phi'(D/n) = c$, where a, b and c are positive constants, into (9), we obtain

$$D = n(a - c)/b(n + 1).\tag{10}$$

The substitution of (10) into $p = a - bD$ yields

$$p = (a + nc)/(n + 1).\tag{11}$$

If n gets sufficiently larger, then, the price p approaches the marginal cost c. The competitive price is a limit of oligopoly prices when the number of oligopoly firms becomes infinitely large.

This limit theorem of Cournot's is a pioneering contribution to the theory of a large economy (an economy with an infinitely large number of participants) which is a central topic of modern mathematical economics. It is very interesting to compare this with another classical limit theorem, Edgeworth's limit theorem, which we shall examine in Chapter 9. In the latter theorem, the law of indifference is established only at the limit where the allocation of goods is that of perfect competition. As we saw, Cournot assumed the law from the beginning so that there exists a unique market price p even when the number of firms is small and p is not a perfectly competitive price. This difference may be worth recognizing, since Cournot with respect to this assumption is a pioneer to Walras and therefore it is also the difference between Walras on one hand and Edgeworth and his pioneer Jevons on the other.

In view of Cournot's limit theorem, we have to admit that the existence of an infinite number of firms is a sufficient condition for perfect competition in which a single firm perceives an infinitely elastic demand curve. It is, however, by no means a necessary condition. Even for the case of $n = 2$, that is, a duopoly, Bertrand and Fellner argued that the price will be equalized to the marginal cost if each duopolist assumes that the other will keep his price (not supply) unchanged and identical average as well as marginal costs are constant.[2] If the price is higher than the cost, each firm will undercut its rival by a very small margin because it will monopolize the market and obtain maximum profit by undercutting infinitesimally. This process continues until the price is equalized to the marginal cost. In other words, a Bertrand-type duopolist behaves as if he perceived an infinitely elastic demand curve.

[2] See Bertrand [4] and Fellner [8, pp. 77–86]. Edgeworth [7, pp. 111–142] and Fellner [8, pp. 79–82] argued that price oscillation appears if cost functions are different for different firms and/or there is an upper limit for the capacity of firms.

Bertrand's assumption can be criticized, of course, since duopolists will know, when they are out of equilibrium or when they decide to test their assumption, that their assumption is incorrect; their rivals do not keep their prices constant. But Cournot's assumption is also subject to the same criticism, and we cannot accept Cournot and at the same time reject Bertrand.

The basic assumption of Cournot's theory of duopoly (and oligopoly) is that each firm changes its supply assuming that the supply of the other firm is unchanged. In other words, each firm adjusts its supply to the given supply of the other. In Bowley's terminology, conjectural variations are both zero. Stackelberg called such behavior of firms "followership". If a firm acts as a follower, however, the other firms can make a larger profit (net receipts) by taking advantage of it. Suppose the first firm chooses D_1 in accordance with (4) when D_2 is given. The second firm can make its conjectural variation

$$\mathrm{d}D_1/\mathrm{d}D_2 = (f' + D_1 f'')/(\phi'' - D_1 f'' - 2f') \tag{12}$$

by differentiating (4), where f'' and ϕ'' are second derivatives of f and ϕ. The second firm's supply to maximize its profit is then obtained by the substitution of (12) into

$$f(D_1 + D_2) + D_2 f'(D_1 + D_2) + D_2 f'(D_1 + D_2)\mathrm{d}D_1/\mathrm{d}D_2 - \phi'(D_2) = 0 \tag{13}$$

and by the replacement of (5) with (13). Stackelberg called such active behavior of a firm "leadership". While Cournot's duopoly equilibrium is follower–follower equilibrium, a leader–follower equilibrium is certainly a possible alternative. If both firms act as leader, however, there is no equilibrium. This is the problem of Stackelberg's disequilibrium.[3]

A recent development is to consider a multi-period model of duopoly which allows for collusion without requiring the firms to make binding agreements (Friedman [9, pp. 123–124]). Consider the maximization of the joint profit of two identical firms. The condition for it is

$$f(2D) + 2Df'(2D) - \phi'(D) = 0 \tag{14}$$

where D signifies the supply of a single firm, f is the inverse demand function and ϕ is a common cost function. Let us denote the value of D which satisfies (14) by D^m and the maximized joint profit by π^m. Similarly, let us denote Cournot solution which satisfies (4) and (5) by $D_1 = D_2 = D^c$ and the corresponding profit of each single firm by π^c. Certainly $\pi^m/2 > \pi^c$.

Suppose the time horizon of two firms is infinite and the second firm openly

---

[3] For conjectural variation and the leader–follower problem, see Hicks [11] and Fellner [8, pp. 71–72, 98–119]. Ono [24] is an interesting recent contribution to this area.

announces the following strategy. In the first period, the second firm supplies D^m, and it continues to do so in the future provided that the first firm also supplies D^m in each period. If the first firm does not supply D^m in any period, the second firm supplies D^c in the future. For the first firm, there are two alternative reactions possible. Firstly, it can supply D^m in the first period and also in the future, so that it can enjoy profit $\pi^m/2$ in all periods. Secondly, given the supply D^m of the second firm in the first period, the first firm may maximize its profit in the first period, the condition for which is

$$f(D_1 + D^m) + D_1 f'(D_1 + D^m) - \phi'(D_1) = 0. \tag{15}$$

The profit of the first firm corresponding to D_1 which satisfies (15) is larger than $\pi^m/2$. The first firm, however, can expect no more profit than π^c in the future since the second firm supplies D^c in this case. Unless the rate of the time preference of the first firm is very high, therefore, it is possible to have a case of tacit collusion of duopoly firms or self-enforcing agreements between them.

2. Eléments d'économie politique pure

Marie-Esprit Léon Walras was born in 1834 at Evreux, in Normandy, France. His father was Antoine Auguste Walras, an economist who suggested *rareté* as the true source of value, rejecting utility and labor. His mother was Louise Aline of Sainte-Beuve. Having twice failed in the examination to enter the Ecole Polytechnique, Léon Walras was admitted to the Ecole des Mines. Since he was not interested in engineering, however, he turned to literature, philosophy and history. In 1858, he published his principal novel, *Francis Sauveur*, which, however, enjoyed no real success. He was then persuaded by his father to devote himself to the development of economics, and in 1860 wrote his first work on economics, *L'économie politique et la justice, Examen critique et réfutation des doctrines économiques de M. P.-J. Proudhon*. Before he obtained an academic position, however, he had to work as a journalist, a clerk in a railway office, a managing director of a bank for co-operatives, a newspaper editor, etc. Walras's interest in taxation and social justice led him to participate in an international taxation congress at Lausanne in Switzerland in 1860. Because he made an excellent impression there, he was appointed "professeur extraordinaire" at the University of Lausanne when a chair in political economy was established in 1870.

According to his "Notice autobiographique" (Walras [32, p. 5]), the selection committee consisted of three notable persons of the district and four professors of economics. While the former group was for Walras, three of the latter were against. The fourth professor, Professor Dameth of Geneva, voted for Walras, considering that it would be useful to have Walras for the development of economics, even though he himself was against Walras's ideas. In 1871, Walras was promoted to "professeur ordinaire". After publishing "Principe d'une théorie mathématique de l'échange" (1873), "Equations de l'échange" (1875), "Equations de la production" (1876) and "Equations de la capitalisation et du crédit" (1876) in rapid succession, Walras completed the first edition of *Eléments d'économie politique pure* (1874–1877). It was followed by *Théorie mathématique de la richesse sociale* (1883) which contains mathematical discussion of bimetallism, and *Théorie de la monnaie* (1886). Walras retired from the University of Lausanne in 1892 and was succeeded by his disciple, Vifredo Pareto. However, Walras continued his research and revealed his system of economics by publishing *Etudes d'économie social* (1896) and *Etudes d'économie politique appliquée* (1898). In 1896, Walras published the third edition of *Eléments*, which contains his article on marginal productivity, "Note sur la réfutation de la théorie anglaise du fermage de M. Wicksteed". And after "Equations de la circulation" (1899), it was followed by the fourth edition of *Eléments*, which is actually the definitive edition. Walras died in 1910 at Clarens, near Lausanne.

Walras's system of economics consists of pure economics, applied economics and social economics. This is based on the fact that social wealth is defined as all things, material or immaterial, that are scarce, that is to say, useful to us and only available to us in limited quantity, and that such useful things, limited in quantity, are valuable and exchangeable, can be produced and multiplied by industry, and are appropriable (Walras [31, pp. 65–67]).

> From what point of view shall we study it [social wealth]? Shall we do it from the point of view of *value in exchange*, that is, from the point of view of the influences of purchase and sale to which social wealth is subject? Or shall we do it from the point of view of *industrial production*, that is, from the point of view of the conditions which favour or hinder the increase in quantity of social wealth? Or, finally, shall we do it from the point of view of *property*, the object of which is social wealth, that is to say, from the point of view of the conditions which render the appropriation of social wealth legitimate or illegitimate? (Walras [31, p. 68].)

Pure economics, applied economics and social economics study social wealth respectively from the point of view of value in exchange, industry and property.

Walras insists that "wheat is worth 24 francs a hectolitre" is a natural phenomenon which "does not result either from the will of the buyer or from the will of the seller or from any agreement between the two" (Walras [31, p. 69]). If two things have a definite value in exchange with respect to each other, it is because they are more or less scarce, that is, more or less useful and more or less limited in quantity, but both of these conditions are natural phenomena. Value in exchange is also a mathematical fact. Pure economics, that is, the theory of exchange and value in exchange is, therefore, a physico-mathematical science which uses mathematical method. Since

> the mathematical method is not an *experimental* method; it is a *rational* method, ... the pure science of economics should then abstract and define ideal-type concepts in terms of which it carries on its reasoning. The return to reality should not take place until the science is completed and then only with a view to practical applications. (Walras [31, p. 71].)

Pure economics must precede applied economics, just as pure mechanics ought to precede applied mechanics.

Industry is defined "as the sum total of relations between persons and things designed to subordinate the purpose of things to the purpose of persons" (Walras [31, p. 73]). Industrial production pursues a twofold aim, firstly, to increase social wealth, that is, useful things limited in quantity, and secondly, to transform it, that is, to transform things with indirect utility, like wool, into things with direct utility, like cloth. This twofold aim is pursued through two distinct classes of operations, technical operations and the economic organization of industry under a system of the division of labor. The two phenomena are both human and not natural, and they are both industrial and not social. The theory of the economic production of social wealth, that is, of the organization of industry under a system of the division of labor is thus an applied science or a theory of policy. Therefore, Walras called it applied economics.

> The appropriation of scarce things or of social wealth is a phenomenon of human contrivance and not a natural phenomeon. It has its origins in the exercise of the human will and in human behavior and not in the play of natural forces. ... Moreover, the appropriation of things by persons or the distribution of social wealth among men in society is a moral and not an industrial phenomenon. It is a relationship among persons. (Walras [31, pp. 76–77].)

In other words, it is within our power to determine a way in which the appropriation is carried on, though this power does not belong to each of us individually but to all of us taken collectively. If the mode of appropriation is good, justice will rule and there will be a mutual coordination of human destinies. If the mode of appropriation is bad, injustice will prevail and the destiny of some will be subordinated to that of others. What mode of appropriation is compatible with the requirement of moral personality is the problem of property which Walras defined as consisting of fair and rational or rightful appropriation. While appropriation itself is a pure and simple objective fact, property is a right which is a phenomenon involving the concept of justice. "Between the objective fact and the right, there is a place for moral theory" (Walras [31, p. 78]). While appropriation is a moral phenomenon, the theory of property must be a moral science. Since justice is defined as rendering to each that which is properly his, the science of the distribution of social wealth must espouse justice as its guiding principle. Walras designates this science social economics.

In the terminology of modern economics, pure economics is a positive science of market mechanism, applied economics is a normative science of optimal allocation of resources, and social economics is a normative science of optimal distribution of income. It should be emphasized that the economics of Walras consists not only of pure economics but also of applied and social economics and that Walras made a very clear distinction between these three branches of economics.

Although its implications are not necessarily clear, Walras insisted that pure economics proved the principle of *laissez-faire, laissez-passer*, that is, the attainment of maximum utility through free competition.[4] The principle of free competition must be applied, therefore, in applied economics which considers the relation between persons and things in the organization of agriculture, industry and trade from the point of view of material well-being. Walras warned, however, that the application should be limited to the cases where his proof is established.

> The principle of free competition, which is applicable to the production of things for private demand, is not applicable to the production of things where public interest is involved. Are there not economists, however, who have fallen into the error of advocating that public services be brought within the fold of free competition by turning these services over to private industry? (Walras [31, p. 257].)

Walras also argued that the principle of free competition can be applied in applied economics which is the economics of the industry, but that it cannot be

---

[4] Without the concept of Pareto optimality, it is impossible to demonstrate the possibility of optimal resource allocation through competition. See, however, Jaffé [15, pp. 326–335]. See also Walker [29].

applied in social economics which is the economics of the property right.

> Though our description of free competition emphasizes the problem of utility, it leaves the question of justice entirely to one side, since our sole object has been to show how a certain distribution of services gives rise to a certain distribution of products. The question of the [original] distribution of services remains open, however. And yet, are there not economists who, not content with exaggerating the applicability of *laisser-faire*, *laisser-passer* to industry, even extend it to the completely extraneous question of property? Such are pitfalls into which a science stumbles when treated as literature. (Walras [31, p. 257].)

As for the problem of property rights, it is well known that Walras insisted on the nationalization of landed property.

Only pure economics, however, was developed systematically by Walras, i.e., in his *Eléments d'économie politique pure*. As for applied economics and social economics, Walras gave up his plan to develop them systematically and left instead *Etudes d'économie politique appliquée* and *Etudes d'économie sociale*, which are merely collections of independent essays. From the point of view of the influence Walras had on latter-day economists, only *Eléments* is important. Furthermore, we can see in *Eléments* what Walras had in mind on the relation between pure economics and applied and social economics, on the limit of pure economics, and on the whole system of economics he was planning. The first part of *Eléments* is entitled "Object and Divisions of Political and Social Economy", and gives a bird's-eye view of Walras's system of economics, which consists of pure economics, applied economics and social economics.

The second part of *Eléments*, "Theory of Exchange of Two Commodities for Each Other", is based on Walras's article, "Principe d'une théorie mathématique de l'échange" (1873). To develop his theory of pure economics mathematically, Léon Walras starts with the concept of demand curves suggested by Cournot, an old friend of Léon's father, Auguste Walras. Firstly, the supply curve of one commodity is derived from the demand curve of the other commodity. The equilibrium price ratio is then determined at the intersection of the demand and supply curves of a commodity. Secondly, demand curves of commodities are shown to be derived from each party's utility or want curves for these commodities and the given initial stock which each party possesses, through the law of the equality of the ratio of marginal utility to price. In other words, by the use of the maximization of utility Walras theoretically explained demand curves, which Cournot assumed to be given empirically. As for marginal utility, Léon Walras followed his father Auguste to use the term *rareté* and sharpened its definition as "the intensity of the last want satisfied by any given *quantity consumed* of a commodity" (Walras [31, p. 119]).

One of the contributions made by Walras in *Eléments* is certainly the discovery or rediscovery of the principles of marginal utility, which he shares with Menger and Jevons. It is, however, by no means Walras's greatest contribution. What made Walras's fame eternal is "to establish for the first time general conditions of the economic equilibrium," as is enscribed on the bronze commemoration medal in the corridor of the University of Lausanne.[5] In *Eléments*, the theory of general equilibrium is developed through the successive solutions of four major problems of pure economics, i.e., the general equilibrium of exchange, the general equilibrium of production, the general equilibrium of capitalization and credit, and the general equilibrium of circulation and money.

Being based on the article "Equations de l'échange" (1875), the theory of the general equilibrium of exchange, i.e., "Theory of Exchange of Several Commodities for the One Another", is studied in the third part of *Eléments*. Equations to determine the equilibrium of exchange are, firstly, equations which show that individuals' demand and supply of commodities depends on the market prices of all commodities, and, secondly, they are equations which require the equality of demand and supply in all markets. The former is a pioneering study of modern theory of consumers' behavior. Commodities are simply assumed to exist and there is no problem of production in the theory of exchange. Nor is any special commodity called money which serves as a medium of exchange. Instead, an arbitrary ordinary commodity is chosen as the *numéraire*, i.e., "the commodity in terms of which the prices of all the others are expressed" (Walras [31, p. 161]).

The general equilibrium of production was first studied in the article "Equations de la production" (1876) and then developed in detail in the fourth part of *Eléments*, "Theory of Production". While the law of supply (offer) and demand is formulated in the theory of exchange, the law of the cost of production or of cost price is to be added in the theory of production. Capital in general is defined as "all durable goods, all forms of social wealth which are not used up at all or are used up only after a lapse of time, i.e., every utility limited in quantity which outlasts its first use, or which, in a word, can be used more than once, like a house or a piece of furniture" (Walras [31, p. 212]). It consists, therefore, of landed capital, personal capital and capital goods proper. The entrepreneur "leases land from landowners on payment of a rent,

---

[5] Jaffé insisted that Walras proceeded from general equilibrium to marginal utility, instead of climbing up from marginal utility to general equilibrium. See Jaffé [15, pp. 25, 312–313].

hires the personal faculties of workers on payment of wages, borrows capital from capitalists on payment of interest charges" (Walras [31, p. 227]) and combines productive services of landed capital, personal capital and capital goods proper in a certain ratio to produce consumers' goods. "In a state of equilibrium in production, entrepreneurs make neither profit nor loss" (Walras [31, p. 225]). The conditions for the equilibrium of production are, therefore, (1) equality of demand from entrepreneurs and supply from landowners, workers and capitalists in the markets of factors of production, (2) equality of demand from landowners, workers and capitalists and supply from entrepreneurs in the markets of consumers' goods, and (3) equality of selling prices of products and the cost of the services employed in making them.

The ratios of factors of production to be combined, or the coefficients of production, are determined by the marginal productivity of factors. The theory of marginal productivity "shows the underlying motive of the demand for services and the offer of products by entrepreneurs, just as *the theory of final utility* shows the underlying motive of the demand for products and offer of services by landowners, workers and capitalists" (Walras [31, p. 385]). Walras's consideration of the theory of marginal productivity starts with "Note sur la réfutation de la théorie anglaise du fermage de M. Wicksteed" (1896) and is developed into Lesson 36 in the seventh part of *Eléments*.

In the theory of production only the production of consumers goods is explicitly considered, since the case of application of raw materials can be reduced to the case of the direct combination of productive services alone (Walras [31, p. 240]). Capital goods proper are simply assumed to exist, as in the case of landed capital. In the article "Equations de la capitalisation et du crédit" (1876) and the fifth part of *Eléments*, "Theory of Capital Formation [Capitalisation] and Credit", however, Walras takes into consideration the production of new capital goods and saving. Walras's theory of capital is, in short, a theory of fixed capital, although he tries to consider circulating capital in this theory of circulation and money. It stands in sharp contrast to the theory of circulating capital of classical economics, Marxian economics and Austrian economics.[6] As we shall see in section 5, however, the modern theory of economic dynamics and economic growth has been developed, not on the basis of Austrian theory, but on the basis of the Walrasian theory of capital.

As Walras himself indicated in his Preface to the fourth edition of *Eléments*, [31, pp. 38–39], his theory of money underwent several important changes between 1876 and 1899. In the first edition of *Eléments*, it was a "Fisherian"

---

[6] For a comparison of Walras's concept of capital with that of the classical and Austrian schools, see Eagly [6, pp. 7–8, 127–131]. See also Yasui [35, pp. 173–278].

equation of exchange based on the concept of the aggregate demand for money required to subserve the circulation of goods. It was replaced by a "Cambridge" equation based on the concept of the individual demand for desired cash balance in *Théorie de la monnaie* (1886). Then it was further developed, through "Equations de la circulation" (1899), into the sixth part of the fourth edition of *Eléments*, "Theory of Circulation and Money". In this last theory of general equilibrium, a special commodity called money is finally introduced and its value is explained by the application of the theory of marginal utility. In other words, the theory of money is now combined with the theory of relative prices. This is the final contribution made by Walras in more than fifty years' research on economics.

In each of his considerations of the problems of equilibrium of exchange, production, capitalization and credit, and circulation and money, Walras repeatedly tries two different solutions, i.e., a theoretical or a mathematical solution and an empirical or a practical solution.

The former solution is to confirm the equality of the number of unknowns, like the equilibrium prices, and the number of equations, like the conditions of equilibrium of supply and demand. For example, suppose the number of consumers' goods is m and the number of factors of production is n in the theory of production. The number of unknowns is $2n+2m-1$, i.e., (1) n equilibrium quantities of supply of factors, (2) n equilibrium prices of factors in terms of the mth consumers' good, *numéraire*, (3) m equilibrium quantities of demand for consumers' goods, and (4) $m-1$ equilibrium prices of consumers' goods in terms of the mth. On the other hand, there seem to be $2n+2m$ equations, i.e., (1) n supply equations of factors, (2) m demand equations for consumers' goods, (3) n conditions of the equality of the quantity of factors used in the production and the quantity of factors supplied, and (4) m conditions that the selling prices of the products are equal to the cost of the factors employed in making them. In view of the so-called Walras's law, however, one of these equations is not independent from the others. Therefore, we have $2m+2n-1$ equations to determine $2m+2n-1$ unknowns. Of course, this is by no means sufficient to prove the existence of the general equilibrium, which we shall consider in the next section.

Walras's second solution of the equilibrium problems is the famous theory of *tâtonnement*, which explains how the problems of equilibrium are empirically or practically solved in the markets by the mechanism of competition. Walras simplified the problem by assuming that exchange and therefore production can take place only when the equilibrium is established, and that productive service has to be transformed into products instantaneously once the equilibrium has been established. This assumption is not a mere simplifying one, but reflects the basic attitude of Walras who supposes "that the market is perfectly competitive, just as in pure mechanics we suppose, to start with, that machines are perfectly frictionless" (Walras [31, p. 84]). It was clearly suggested to Walras from the observation of some operations in the Paris Stock Exchange where disequilibrium transactions actually did not occur (Jaffé [15, p. 247]). However, it is very unrealistic to apply such a model of special markets to the whole economy. Thus the significance of exchange and production taken place in disequilibrium is entirely disregarded in Walras's economics and therefore in modern neo-classical economics. Even with this stringent assumption, furthermore, Walras's demonstration of the second solution was not perfect. He could not prove rigorously that the general equilibrium can be approached by the preliminary adjustments made in markets before actual exchange transactions and productions take place. We shall discuss this problem in section 4.[7]

3. The existence of a general equilibrium

Walras's theoretical or mathematical solution is not sufficient to assure the existence of a general equilibrium, since it is merely to count the number of unknowns and that of equations. If these numbers are identical, a theoretical model of an economy may be called complete or consistent, but it does not guarantee that there exists an economically meaningful solution. For example, equilibrium prices have to be real, and, in general, positive. Apart from some pioneering attempts, proofs of the existence of an economically meaningful solution in a general equilibrium model were given in 1950s by such people as K.J. Arrow, G. Debreu, L.W. McKenzie, D. Gale and F. Nikaido.[8] Mathematically, they are applications of the fixed point theorem of topology. It must be recognized, however, that important roles are played in the process of proofs by the homogeneity of demand and supply functions with respect to prices and the so-called Walras's law that the value of aggregate demand is identically equal to that of aggregate supply, both of which Walras discussed in his use of *numéraire* and to show the dependency of equations.

Unfortunately, such proofs which deal with a general case are highly technical and cannot be reproduced here in full detail. We have to be satisfied with a discussion of a very simple case like an equilibrium of exchange in

---

[7] For the life of Walras and Walras's economics in general, see Jaffé [15], Morishima [19], Walras [32, pp. 1–16] and Yasui [35].

[8] For the history of the proofs of the existence of a general equilibrium, see Weintraub [33, pp. 59–107] and Arrow and Hahn [3, pp. 51, 127–128].

a two-commodity, two-individual model of an economy. Let us consider a proof which is based on the Pareto optimality of a competitive equilibrium.[9] It is well known that resource allocation is optimal in the sense of Pareto, the successor of Walras, in a perfectly competitive equilibrium. It implies that the utility of no individual can be increased without reducing that of some others. The condition that assures the Pareto optimality is the equality of marginal rates of substitution among all individuals and all firms. This condition is satisfied in a perfectly competitive equilibrium, since marginal rates of substitution are equalized to price ratios which are common to all individuals and firms. In addition to this condition, furthermore, budget constraints of all individuals have to be satisfied in a perfectly competitive equilibrium. To prove the existence of such an equilibrium, therefore, it is sufficient to show the existence of a Pareto optimal situation in which budget constraints are satisfied when marginal rates of substitutions are interpreted as competitive price ratios.

Since one might wonder whether we can assume perfect competition in the case of a two-individual economy, let us suppose that two commodities are exchanged among $2n$ individuals for sufficiently large $n > 0$. Individuals are assumed to be grouped into two homogeneous groups of n individuals in the sense that individuals in the same group are completely identical to each other, having the same taste (utility function, indifference map) and the same initial holdings of commodities. The equilibrium of exchange among $2n$ individuals, then, can be described by the equilibrium of exchange between the representative individuals of two groups. In other words, we consider below the equilibrium of exchange between two individuals, not two isolated individuals, but the two representative individuals arbitrarily chosen respectively from different homogeneous groups of n individuals. Our model is a reduced one with the scale of one to n of the original $2n$ individual model of a competitive economy.

To consider a two-individual, two-commodity exchange equilibrium, it is convenient to use the so-called Edgeworth box diagram. Let us suppose that the first individual has an initial endowment of $\bar{X}_{11}$ units of commodity 1 and $\bar{X}_{12}$ units of commodity 2. Similarly, suppose that the second individual has an initial endowment of $\bar{X}_{21}$ units of commodity 1 and $\bar{X}_{22}$ units of commodity 2. Since there is no production, the total quantity of commodity 1 in the economy before and after exchange is given by $\bar{X}_1 = \bar{X}_{11} + \bar{X}_{21}$, and the total quantity of commodity 2 is given by $\bar{X}_2 = \bar{X}_{12} + \bar{X}_{22}$. It follows that

---

[9]See Negishi [20, pp. 12–15]. For the proofs based on the same approach of a general case involving production, see Negishi [20, pp. 15–25] and Arrow and Hahn [3, pp. 107–128].

the only possible states of the economy are those represented by a set of points contained in a rectangle having dimensions $\bar{X}_1$ by $\bar{X}_2$ (Figure 7.1), where the quantity of commodity 1 is measured horizontally, and that of commodity 2 is measured vertically. Any point in the box represents a particular distribution of the commodities between the two individuals. For example, if the distribution of commodities is given by point M, the quantities of commodity 1 and commodity 2 obtained by the first individual, x_{11} and x_{12} respectively, are measured by the coordinates of M, using the south-west corner O as the origin; the quantities obtained by the second individual, x_{21} and x_{22} respectively, are measured by the coordinates of point M, using the north-east corner O' as the origin.

The indifference map of the first individual is drawn using O as the origin, and the indifference map of the second individual is drawn using O' as the origin. The marginal rates of substitution of two individuals are equal when an indifference curve of the first individual is tangent to an indifference curve of the second individual. The locus of all such points is the contract curve CC'. The marginal rates of substitution are unequal at points not on the contract curve, say point A of the initial endowments, and it is possible to increase the utility level of both individuals by changing the existing distribution of commodities. For example, if the final position after a redistribution of commodities is in the inside of the area surrounded by two indifference curves passing A, both individuals would have gained, since both would be on higher indifference curves than at A. If a point on the contract curve is reached, it is

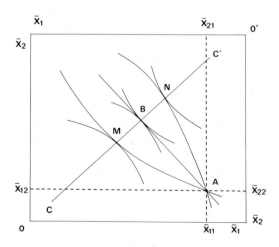

Figure   7.1

not possible to improve further the position of either person without a deterioration in the position of the other. In other words, points on the contract curve are Pareto optimal.

Suppose that two individuals are acting as price takers or quantity adjusters to the given market prices. Denoting the price ratio, i.e., the price of commodity 1 in terms of commodity 2 by p, the first individual will choose the best combination of two commodities (X_{11}, X_{12}) being subject to his budget constraint, $pX_{11} + X_{12} = p\bar{X}_{11} + \bar{X}_{12}$. Similarly the second individual will choose (X_{21}, X_{22}) being subject to $pX_{21} + X_{22} = p\bar{X}_{21} + \bar{X}_{22}$. Equilibrium conditions for each individual are (1) the equality of the marginal rate of substitution and the price ratio (i.e., the tangency of the indifference curve and the price line) and (2) the budget constraints. The market equilibrium is attained when the demand and supply of two commodities are equal, i.e., $X_{11} + X_{21} = \bar{X}_1$, $X_{12} + X_{22} = \bar{X}_2$. It should be noted that among two budget constraints and two market clearing conditions any one condition is implied by the remaining three conditions. In other words, the so-called Walras's law holds.

At any point in the box diagram market equilibrium conditions are satisfied. If the common tangent of two indifference curves is considered as the price line, the condition (1) of the equilibrium of each individual is realized at any point on the contract curve CC'. Therefore, all the conditions for the competitive equilibrium are satisfied at such a point as point B on the contract curve, where the price line BA passes the initial endowment point A, i.e., the budget constraint is satisfied for each individual.

Since markets are always cleared in the box to prove the existence of a competitive equilibrium, we have only to show that there always exist a point such as B on the contract curve CC' at which a budget constraint is satisfied. Let us first consider in Figure 7.1 the point M, i.e., the point of intersection of the contract curve and the indifference curve of the first individual passing through point A. If indifference curves are strictly convex to the origin, we have

$$F(X_{11}, X_{12}) = p(X_{11}, X_{12})X_{11} + X_{12} - p(X_{11}, X_{12})\bar{X}_{11} - \bar{X}_{12} < 0 \qquad (1)$$

at point M, where p is the marginal rate of substitution of the first individual. Budget constraint is not satisfied and M is not a competitive equilibrium. Similarly we have at point N, i.e., the point of intersection of the contract curve and the indifference curve of the second individual passing point A,

$$F(X_{11}, X_{12}) = p(X_{11}, X_{12})X_{11} + X_{12} - p(X_{11}, X_{12})\bar{X}_{11} - \bar{X}_{12} > 0. \qquad (2)$$

Budget constraint is not satisfied, and N is again not a competitive equilibrium.

If the marginal rate of substitution of the first individual p is assumed to be a continuous function of the quantity of two commodities obtained by the same individual, $F(X_{11}, X_{12})$ is also a continuous function. The movement on the contract curve from M to N can be expressed as $X_{11} = X_{11}(t)$, $X_{12} = X_{12}(t)$, $0 \leq t \leq 1$, where $[X_{11}(0), X_{12}(0)]$ are the coordinates of M, $[X_{11}(1), X_{12}(1)]$ are the coordinates of N and X_{11} and X_{12} are the continuous functions of t. Then, $F[X_{11}(t), X_{12}(t)]$ is a continuous function of t such that $F < 0$ at $t = 0$ and $F > 0$ at $t = 1$. By the theorem of intermediate values of a continuous function (Figure 7.2), we are sure that $F = 0$ at some $\bar{t}$ (possibly not unique) such that $0 < \bar{t} < 1$. The point whose coordinates from the origin O is $[X_{11}(\bar{t}), X_{12}(\bar{t})]$ is a competitive equilibrium, i.e., point B in the box diagram.

If indifference curves are not strictly convex to the origin, however, an equilibrium may not exist. Figure 7.3 shows the case of the so-called Arrow anomaly, where indifference curves of the second individual are not strictly convex and point A of the initial endowment is located on the boundary of the Edgeworth box. Curves I_1 and I_2 are indifference curves of the first individual with the origin at O and curves J_1 and J_2 are those of the second individual with the origin at O'. Note that the utility of commodity 1 is satiated for the second individual at points between O and A (including O and A), while this is not so for the first individual. Point A is clearly Pareto optimal and on the contract curve but not a competitive equilibrium, as is pointed out by Arrow [2], since there can be no price line which is tangent to both I_1 and

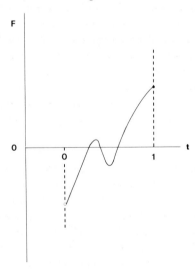

Figure 7.2

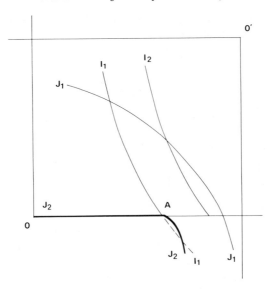

Figure 7.3

J_2 at A. Suppose the price of commodity 1 (in terms of commodity 2) is zero. The budget line through A is then horizontal and the first individual demands an infinitely large quantity of commodity 1. Suppose the price of commodity 1 is positive. The second individual demands, then, a larger quantity of commodity 2 than at A, since his budget line is not tangential to indifference curve J_2 at A, so that it is again impossible to stay in the box. Since A is also the point of the initial endowments, it is evident that there is no equilibrium, if A cannot be one. To avoid such an anomalous case, we have to assume either that indifference curves are strictly convex (utility of no commodity is satiated) or that the point of initial endowments is not located on the boundary of the box (every individual has a strictly positive quantity of every commodity).

The gist of the proof of the above for the case of a two-commodity two-individual (or two-homogeneous group of individuals of the same size) exchange economy is to find a point with budget constraints satisfied (point B) among Pareto optimal points (curve CC') by changing the weights of individuals in Pareto optimal distribution (the movement from M to N). The essentially same method of proof can be applied to the general case of m commodity n individual exchange economy, with more advanced mathematical theorems, fixed point theorems instead of the simple theorem of intermediate values of a continuous function. Consider the maximization of a weighted sum of utilities of n individuals,

$$\sum_i a_i U_i(X_{i1}, \ldots, X_{im}) \tag{3}$$

being subject to conditions of the equality of demand and supply,

$$\sum_i X_{ij} = \sum_i \bar{X}_{ij}, \quad j = 1, \ldots, m \tag{4}$$

where a_i is the given positive constant, X_{ij} is the quantity of the jth commodity to be given to the ith individual, and $\bar{X}_{ij}$ is the ith individual's given initial holding of the jth commodity. If the budget constraints

$$\sum_j p_j X_{ij} = \sum_j p_j \bar{X}_{ij}, \quad i = 1, \ldots, n \tag{5}$$

where p_j is the Lagrangean multiplier corresponding to the jth condition in (4) which is interpreted as the price of the jth commodity, are satisfied, the maximum of (3) corresponds to the perfectly competitive exchange equilibrium. To prove the existence of an equilibrium, therefore, one must find such a proper set of weights of individuals in Pareto optimal distribution (i.e., a_i's in (3)) that budget constraints are satisfied.

Similarly, the extension to the case of a production economy is also straightforward, provided that the possibility of the economy of scale is ruled out. The difficulty of the case with the economy of scale can be seen by the consideration of two-commodity one-individual one-firm (or n identical individual n identical firm) production economy. In Figure 7.4, the quantity of one of two commodities, the service of labor (time), is measured vertically, and that of the other commodity, a labor product, is measured horizontally. The curves I_1 and I_2 are indifference curves of an individual. The initial quantity of labor service held by an individual is represented by OA. It is assumed that an overhead cost is incurred to produce the product (measured horizontally), which is represented by the input AB of labor service for a firm. On the other hand, the variable cost of production of the firm is shown by the curve BC, expressing the relation between input of labor service, measured downwards from B, and the output of the product, measured to the right from O. Since the variable cost is increasing, the average cost (measured in terms of labor input) is expressed by a typical U-shaped curve. If a positive quantity of the product is produced in a competitive equilibrium, the marginal rates of substitution of individual and firm must be equal, as they are at D, to the price ratio. The price ratio of the produced commodity and labor service at D is equal to the slope of the common tangent DE of curves BC and I_1. The profit of the firm is negative,

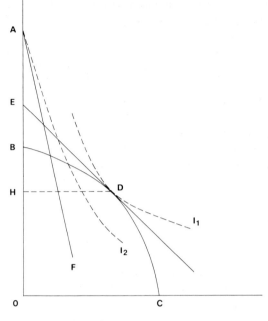

Figure 7.4

however, since the value, in terms of labor, of product DH produced from the inputs AH of labor is merely EH. If the point of no production A is a trivial equilibrium, on the other hand, the price ratio is equal to the slope of the tangent AF to the indifference curve I_2 at A. Then A cannot be an equilibrium, since it is profitable for the firm to produce a positive quantity under the price ratio AF.

This difficulty does not exist if we rule out the existence of the economy of scale by dismissing the overhead cost so that the average as well as marginal costs are increasing for any level of output. In Figure 7.4, points A and B coincide. Suppose the initial holding of labor is OB for an individual. Point D represents a competitive equilibrium in which the profit, in terms of labor, EB of a firm is distributed to an individual so that the product DH of the firm is bought by the individual with the wage income BH and the profit distributed EB.

If we suppose the trade of a firm is distributed equally to n individuals, furthermore, our model can be considered a reduced scale model of an economy consisting of n identical individuals and n identical firms. If the number n is infinitely large, then, a competitive equilibrium can exist, even if there is an economy of scale due to the existence of the overhead costs in each firm. Suppose, again, that the initial holding of labor is OA for an individual and that an overhead cost AB is incurred for a firm, in Figure 7.5, which is a reproduction of Figure 7.4. Since the number of firms is infinite, the input of labor and the output of product per firm can be at any point on the line AJ which is tangent to the curve BC representing the variable cost, if we suppose some firms are at A (no production) and the rest of the firms are at J. Then, an equilibrium exists at K, where the indifference curve I_3 of every individual is tangent to the line AJ. Since the price ratio of the product and labor service is equal to the slope of AJ, the profit of firms at J is also zero. The income of each individual is wage income only, so that AJ is his budget line. Each individual's utility is maximized at K, and the demand and supply of the product, as well as of the labor service, are equalized, since the number of individuals is equal to the number of firms.[10]

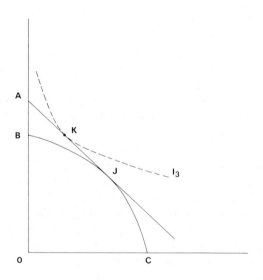

Figure 7.5

[10] For convexifying the economy in the case of a large economy, see Arrow and Hahn [3, pp. 188–195] and Hildenbrand and Kirman [14, pp. 165–169].

4. The stability of a general equilibrium

Let us consider a two-commodity exchange economy. The theoretical or mathematical solution of an exchange equilibrium is to find the equilibrium price p of the first commodity (in terms of the second commodity) which satisfies

$$E_1(p) = 0 \tag{1}$$

where E_1 denotes the excess demand (demand–supply) for the first good. If p satisfies (1), the excess demand for the second commodity E_2 is also zero, since Walras's law holds, i.e., $p_1 E_1(p) + E_2(p) \equiv 0$. The empirical or practical solution is, then, to approach such an equilibrium price through the law of supply and demand, "the commodity having an effective demand greater than its effective offer must rise in price, and the commodity having an effective offer greater than its effective demand must fall in price" (Walras [31, p. 106]). To make this solution possible, E_1 has to be a decreasing functon of p (the excess demand curve is downward sloping) so that it is negative for any p higher than the equilibrium p which satisfies (1), and positive for and p lower than the equilibrium p, which is the Walrasian stability condition for a single market or two-commodity economy.

In the empirical or practical solution, Walras made an implicit assumption that no actual exchange transactions take place at disequilibria where prices are being changed according to the law of supply and demand.[11] In other words, all the contracts made at disequilibrium prices can be cancelled so that recontracting is possible at the new price. Walras's process of *tâtonnement* (a French word meaning groping) is therefore a process of preliminary adjustment in prices (and level of production, etc.) which is made before actual transactions are carried out at equilibrium prices. The reason why we need *tâtonnement* or recontract assumption is that otherwise the empirical solution is not consistent with the mathematical solution. In Figure 7.6, the first commodity is measured horizontally, and the second is measured vertically. The equilibrium price p, i.e., the mathematical solution of (1), is indicated by the slope of the budget line AB of an individual who has initially AO of the second commodity and demands OD_1, of the first commodity at p. Suppose a purchase of OD_2 of the first commodity is actually carried out at a disequilibrium price higher than p, which is indicated by the slope of AC. If

---

[11] For the *tâtonnement* assumption, see Jaffé [15, pp. 221–266, especially p. 247], Newman [23, p. 102], and Patinkin [25, pp. 531–540, especially p. 533].

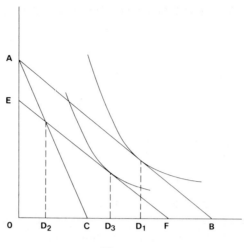

Figure 7.6

this purchase cannot be cancelled, the demand for the first commodity at the equilibrium price p obtained from the mathematical solution decreases from OD_1 to OD_3, while on the other hand there may also be a decrease in the supply of the first commodity at p from an individual who sold OD_2 at the disequilibrium price. Since there is in general no assurance that the decrease in demand is cancelled by that of supply, the excess demand is not zero at p. In other words, the original excess demand curve is shifted by the disequilibrium transactions. Without *tâtonnement* assumption, the empirical solution depends on the route followed by disequilibrium prices and on the extent of transactions made at such prices, and does not coincide with the mathematical solution.[12]

Let us now proceed to an m commodity economy. The original form of Walrasian *tâtonnement* is the process of successive adjustment in each single market (Walras [31, pp. 170–172]). Suppose the initial set of prices $(p_1, \ldots, p_{m-1})$ does not satisfy the condition of general equilibrium

$$E_j(p_1, \ldots, p_{m-1}) = 0, \quad j = 1, \ldots, m-1 \tag{2}$$

where p_j and E_j denote respectively the price of the jth commodity (in terms of the mth commodity, *numéraire*) and the excess demand in the market of the jth

[12] See Hicks [12, pp. 127–129] and Kaldor [16]. Japanese literature such as Morishima [17] and Yasui [35, pp. 353–472] has also emphasized this possibility.

commodity. We are, for example, in a situation described by

$$E_1(p_1, \ldots p_{m-1}) > 0$$

$$E_2(p_1, \ldots, p_{m-1}) < 0 \tag{3}$$

$$E_{m-1}(p_1, \ldots, p_{m-1}) > 0$$

The price of the first commodity p_1 is now adjusted by reference to its excess demand E_1, and increased in the situation (3) until an equilibrium in the first market is established, i.e.,

$$E_1(p_1', p_2, \ldots, p_{m-1}) = 0. \tag{4}$$

Here the Walrasian assumption of the stability in the single market is assumed, so that E_1 is a decreasing function of p_1, or $E_{11} < 0$, if we write the partial derivative of the excess demand function for the jth commodity with respect to the kth price by as E_{jk}.

Under the new price system $(p_1', p_2, \ldots, p_{m-1})$ the remaining $m-1$ markets may or may not be in equilibrium. If the second market is out of equilibrium, again under the assumption that $E_{22} < 0$, the price of the second commodity is changed from p_2 to p_2' so as to satisfy

$$E_2(p_1', p_2', p_3, \ldots, p_{m-1}) = 0. \tag{5}$$

Generally, this will upset the equilibrium in the first market (4). Under the price system $(p_1', p_2', p_3, \ldots, p_{m-1})$, then, the price of the third commodity p_3 is adjusted if the third market, where $E_{33} < 0$, is out of equilibrium, upsetting the equilibrium in the second market (5) just established. In this way the last, $m-1$th market, where $E_{m-1,m-1} < 0$, is eventually cleared by changing the price system from $(p_1', \ldots, p_{m-2}', p_{m-1})$ into $(p_1', \ldots, p_{m-2}', p_{m-1}')$ so as to satisfy

$$E_{m-1}(p_1', \ldots, p_{m-2}', p_{m-1}') = 0. \tag{6}$$

By this time all the markets except the last, which were once cleared successively, have generally been thrown out of their respective equilibria again. Neither the price system we have just arrived at, $(p_1', \ldots p_{m-1}')$, nor the initial system $(p_1, \ldots, p_{m-1})$, is a general equilibrium one. The question is, then, which of the systems is closer to a general equilibrium that satisfies (2). Walras [31, p. 172] argued that the former price system is closer to equilibrium than the latter since, for example, $E_1(p_1', \ldots, p_{m-1}') \neq 0$ is closer to 0 than $E_1(p_1, \ldots, p_{m-1}) \neq 0$. The reason for this, according to Walras, is that the change from p_1 to p_1' which established (4) exerted a direct influence that was invariably in the direction of zero excess demand as far as the first commodity is concerned. But the subsequent changes from p_2 to $p'_2, \ldots, p_{m-1}$ to p'_{m-1}, which jointly moved the first excess demand away from zero, exerted only indirect influences, some in the direction of equilibrium and some in the opposite direction, at least as far as the excess demand for the first commodity is concerned. So, up to a certain point, they cancelled each other out. Hence, Walras concluded, by repeating the successive adjustment of $m-1$ markets along the same lines, i.e., changing prices according to the law of supply and demand, we can move closer and closer to a general equilibrium.

Walras's argument for the convergence of the *tâtonnement* process to a general equilibrium was, as we just saw, merely an argument for the plausibility of such a convergence and cannot be considered as a rigorous demonstration of the stability of a general equilibrium. Whether the indirect influence of the prices of other commodities on the excess demand of a given commodity cancel each other out will certainly depend on substitutability and complementarity between commodities. For example, indirect influences are not cancelled out and the excess demand of a commodity is increased if the prices of all gross substitutes are raised and the prices of all gross complements are lowered. In addition to the Walrasian stability condition for a single market, i.e., $E_{jj} > 0$ for all j, therefore, some conditions on the cross-effects of prices on excess demands, i.e., on $E_{jk}, j \neq k$, have to be imposed to demonstrate the convergence of *tâtonnement* or the stability of a general equilibrium.

It was Allais [1, pp. 486–489], who first demonstrated the convergence of Walrasian *tâtonnement* by assuming gross substitutability, i.e., $E_{jk} > 0$ for all $j \neq k$. To see whether the price system moves closer and closer to a general equilibrium, which he assumes to be at least locally unique, Allais defines the distance D of a price system from the equilibrium price system as the sum of the absolute values of the value of excess demand for all commodities, including the *numéraire*. The convergence of *tâtonnement* is then demonstrated by showing that this distance D is always decreased by changes in prices that are made in accordance with the law of supply and demand. His demonstration may be reformulated in our notation as follows.

The distance to the general equilibrium is defined as

$$D = \sum_j |p_j E_j| \tag{7}$$

where the summation runs from $j = 1$ to $j = m$, and E_j is defined as a function of $p_1, \ldots, p_{m-1}$ as in (2). In view of Walras's law

$$\sum_j p_j E_j \equiv 0, \tag{8}$$

D can be replaced either by the summation of positive excess demands

$$D^+ = \sum_j p_j \max (0, E_j) \tag{9}$$

or by the summation of negative excess demands

$$D^- = -\sum_j p_j \min (0, E_j) \tag{10}$$

where $\max (0, E_j)$ denotes E_j if it is positive and 0 if E_j is negative, and $\min (0, E_j)$ denotes E_j if it is negative and 0 if E_j is positive. From (7), i.e., $D^+ - D^- = 0$, it is evident that

$$D = 2D^+ = 2D^- \tag{11}$$

so that whether D is increasing or decreasing can be seen by checking whether D^+ or D^- (whichever is more convenient) is increasing or decreasing.

Suppose E_1 to be positive as in (3) and that p_1 is raised following the law of supply and demand. From (10), we have

$$\partial D^- / \partial p_1 < 0 \tag{12}$$

since $E_{j1} > 0$ for any j such that $E_j < 0$, from gross substitutability. In other words, a change in the price of the first commodity from p_1 to p_1' to satisfy (4) decreases the sum of negative excess demands D^- and therefore the distance D to the general equilibrium. Suppose next that $E_2(p_1', p_2, \ldots, p_{m-1})$ is negative and p_2 is lowered to p_2' so as to satisfy (5). From (9) this time, we have

$$\partial D^+ / \partial p_2 > 0 \tag{13}$$

since $E_{j2} > 0$ for any j such that $E_j > 0$ from gross substitutability. In other words, a decrease in the price of the second commodity from p_2 to p_2' decreases the sum of positive excess demand D^+ and therefore the distance D to the general equilibrium.

Generally, if E_j is positive and p_j is raised, D is decreased, which can be seen from the fact that D^- is decreased. Similarly, if E_j is negative and p_j is lowered, again D is decreased, which can be seen from consideration of the behavior of D^+. Out of the general equilibrium, D remains positive and there exists at least one non-*numéraire* commodity with non-zero excess demand, so that its price is changing. The distance to general equilibrium always decreases out of equilibrium, and therefore we can move closer and closer to that equilibrium by changing prices according to the law of supply and demand, provided that gross substitutability is assumed. The process terminates only when all the excess demands are zero, i.e., at the general equilibrium.

Although Walras discussed the behavior of the process of successive adjustment, he was not against the consideration of simultaneous adjustment processes in all markets (Uzawa [28]; Jaffé [15, p. 253]). If we assume that adjustments take place not only simultaneously but also continuously, the *tâtonnement* process that the rate of change of price is governed by excess demand can be described by a set of differential equations

$$dp_j/dt = a_j E_j(p_1, \ldots, p_{m-1}), \quad j = i, \ldots, m-1 \tag{14}$$

where t denotes time and the a_j's are positive constants signifying the speed of adjustment in the jth market. Study of the behavior of the solutions of (14), i.e., prices as functions of t, which was initiated by Samuelson [26, p. 551], has been extensively carried out by many modern mathematical economists (Arrow and Hahn [3, pp. 263–323]; Negishi [20, pp. 191–206]). It is well known that gross substitutability is also a sufficient condition for the convergence of adjustment process such as (14) and that the homogeneity of excess demands with respect to prices of all commodities and Walras's law play essential roles in the proof of the stability of equilibrium through the process (14).

5. Capital and money

5.1

The time element is ignored by Walras in the theory of production by the assumption of instantaneous production. In the theory of capitalization and credit, however, it has to play an essential role. There are two alternative ways to introduce the time element into the Walrasian theory of general equilibrium. One is to consider Hicks's temporary equilibrium, as Morishima did [18], [19, pp. 70–81]). The other is to insist, like Yasui [35, pp. 173–278]), that the Walrasian equilibrium should be a stationary equilibrium. The latter approach can be developed into the theory of balanced growth based on von-Neumann's model.

As a matter of fact, Walras himself declared that he would only consider the case of a progressive economy in which net investment is positive (Walras [31, p. 269]). Walras called an economy static if, within a given period of time, no change is allowed in the data, such as the propensities to save and to consume, and the new capital goods still play no part in the production, even though the economy is progressive (Walras [31, pp. 269, 283]).[13] Since Walras's static

---

[13] The French word "*statique*" on pp. 244 and 260 in Walras [30] was translated as "stationary" on p. 269 and "static" on p. 283 in Walras [31].

economy implies that it only remains unchanged in the single period under consideration, it is similar to the concept of Hicks's temporary equilibrium. It is not easy to interpret Walras's equilibrium as a stationary equilibrium in which consumption, saving, the productivity of capital, etc., remain unchanged through periods, so that the economy's rate of growth is zero.

Yasui insists, however, that the equilibrium in Walras's theory of capitalization and credit should be the equilibrium of a stationary state. The reason is that only in such a stationary state does the price of the service of capital goods remain unchanged indefinitely into the future, which Walras assumed in his equations of the equality between the selling price of consumers' and new capital goods and their costs of production, and equations of the uniformity of the rate of net income for all capital goods proper. Of course, the factors of production can have the same relative values or prices in the future as they have at present, not only in a stationary state but also in a progressive economy of balanced growth. As Wicksell [34, pp. 226–227] pointed out, however, the latter case is inconceivable, "as the sum of natural forces cannot be increased." The stationary state is, therefore, the only remaining possibility. Incidentally, for an equilibrium of the stationary state to be possible, we cannot regard the existing quantity of capital goods as data, and we cannot consider the supply of their services as functions of prices based only on the given taste of their owners. These are unknowns to be determined so that the value of depreciation of capital goods is equalized to the gross saving. As Yasui pointed out, therefore, Walras's original theory of capitalization and credit has to be modified to be interpreted as the theory of a stationary economy.[14]

We have to note that the assumption of perfect foresight on prices in the future is responsible for the conclusion that the only logical possibility is the stationary state. Without such an assumption, therefore, we can interpret Walrasian equilibrium as a temporary equilibrium which is based on the given arbitrary subjective expectations of individuals and firms. Following Morishima, we can consider a temporary equilibrium, assuming that expectations on future prices are static, i.e., the elasticity of expectation is 1. The original Walrasian idea of a progressive economy can be revived, since the quantity of capital goods can be increased through the changing temporary equilibria of successive periods.

Since the original Walrasian system of equations of capitalization and credit is too complicated to describe, let us consider a drastically simplified version of

---

[14] Yasui pointed it out as early as 1936. See Yasui [35, p. 248] and also Garegnani [10, Part 2, Chapter 2]. The fact that the stock of existing capital goods cannot be arbitrarily given is, however, not a defect of the Walrasian theory of capital. It is also the case with the classical theory of the stationary economy.

a two-good (consumers' and capital goods) two-factor (labor and capital) economy.[15] Two goods are produced from the input of labor service and the service of capital goods under constant returns to scale. Labor is the sole primary factor of production and there is no inventory investment, nor is there money.

Let X_1 and X_2 be the level of output of the consumers' and new capital goods, respectively. The aggregate income of laborers and capitalists is

$$Y = w(a_1 X_1 + a_2 X_2) + q(b_1 X_1 + b_2 X_2) \tag{1}$$

where w denotes the rate of wage, q denotes the price of the service of capital goods, a_1 and a_2 are the labor input coefficients in the production of the consumers' and capital goods and b_1 and b_2 are the capital input coefficients in the production of consumers' and capital goods, respectively.[16]

At the equilibrium, there is no profit for entrepreneurs, so that

$$p_1 \equiv w a_1 + q b_1 \tag{2}$$

$$p_2 = w a_2 + q b_2 \tag{3}$$

where p_1 and p_2 are respectively the price of the consumers' and capital goods. Since markets for two goods have to be cleared,

$$D(p_1, p_2, w, q, Y) = X_1 \tag{4}$$

$$H = X_2 \tag{5}$$

where D denotes the demand for consumers' goods and H stands for the demand for new capital goods. Factor markets have also to be cleared so that

$$a_1 X_1 + a_2 X_2 = L \tag{6}$$

$$b_1 X_1 + b_2 X_2 = K \tag{7}$$

where L and K are respectively the given existing labor force and the given existing stock of capital goods. Since there is no money, suppose capitalists own capital goods and lend them to entrepreneurs or sell the service of capital goods to them. If gross saving is defined as the excess of income over consumption, then, capitalists save in kind or purchase new capital goods with

---

[15] This is a simplified version of the model given in pp. 108–112 of Morishima [19]. We cannot, however, agree with the interpretation of the model in pp. 112–122 of Morishima [19]. See Negishi [22].

[16] Input coefficients are functions of factor prices.

saving, so that

$$p_2 H = S(p_1, p_2, w, q, Y) \tag{8}$$

where S denotes the aggregate gross saving.

If equations (1) to (8) are interpreted as the description of a temporary equilibrium, there are eight equations to determine seven unknowns, Y, w, q, X_1, X_2, p_2, H, since we can choose the consumers' goods as *numéraire* so that $p_1 = 1$. The eight equations are not independent, however, and one of the equations can be derived from the other equations and Walras's law

$$Y \equiv p_1 D + S. \tag{9}$$

In the determination of consumption and saving, capitalists assume that goods and service of factors have the same prices in the future as they have at the present moment, and the difference between the resultant gross saving and the value of the depreciation of capital goods, i.e., the net saving, can be either positive or negative. If it is positive, we have the case of a progressive economy which Walras wished to consider. The capital stock K is larger in the next period than in the current period, so that temporary equilibrium prices in the former are in general different from those in the latter, even though capitalists in the current period expected unchanged prices through periods.

The assumption of a saving in kind is not necessary if we follow Walras to introduce a commodity E, consisting of a perpetual net income of a unit of *numéraire*, the price of which is the inverse of the rate of the perpetual net income or the rate of interest i (Walras [31, p. 274]). If this commodity is sold by entrepreneurs or firms wishing to buy new capital goods, and is purchased by capitalists wishing to save, the clearance of the market of this commodity through changes in i implies that aggregate gross saving equals "aggregate excess of income over consumption = aggregate demand for $(E) \times$ price of $(E) =$ aggregate demand for new capital goods $\times$ price of capital goods" (Walras [31, p. 21]). Therefore,

$$p_2 H = S(p_1, w, i, Y) \tag{8}'$$

instead of (8) since capitalists are now concerned, not with p_2 and q, but with i in the determination of consumption and saving. Similarly, (4) may be replaced by

$$D(p_1, w, i, Y) = X_1. \tag{4}'$$

At equilibrium, the rate of net income for capital goods has to be equalized for the rate of net income for the commodity E,

$$(q/p_2) - d = i \tag{10}$$

where d denotes the technically given rate of depreciation of capital goods. Since the introduction of a new unknown i is matched by the introduction of an additional equation (10), we still have equality between the number of unknowns and that of equations.

Entrepreneurs and capitalists fail to predict future prices correctly in a progressive economy, since changes in prices are induced by changes in K in a series of successive temporary equilibria. The expectation of unchanged prices can be correct only in the case of a stationary state in which K remains unchanged through periods. The condition for a stationary state is that the aggregate gross saving is equal to the value of depreciation of capital goods, or

$$H = dK \tag{11}$$

in view of (8) or (8)'. Since the number of equations is increased by the addition of (11), then, one more unknown should be introduced. The existing stock of capital goods K is, therefore, no longer an arbitrary given quantity, and has to be solved jointly with other unknowns from equations of general equilibrium. Then, we have nine unknowns, $K, i, Y, w, q, X_1, X_2, p_2$ and H, to be solved from any nine equations from ten equations (1) to (3), (4)', (5) to (7), (8)', (10), and (11), since $p_1 = 1$ and one of the equations is not independent in view of (9).

Two alternative interpretations of Walras's theory of capitalization and credit, that is, temporary equilibrium and stationary state, correspond to two methods of economic dynamics in the modern economic theory, that is, the temporary equilibrium method and the growth equilibrium method, distinguished in Hicks's *Capital and Growth* (Hicks [13, p. 28]). Also, it is well known that Walras's theory of capital gives the microeconomic foundation to the so-called neo-classical macro growth theory developed by Solow, Swan, Meade and Uzawa. The criticism made by Cambridge, England of the macro production function and macro theory of marginal productivity, however, does not affect the original Walrasian general equilibrium theory of capital, although it made certain points for the neo-classical macro growth theory.

5.2

In his theory of circulation and money, Walras tried to develop the general equilibrium theory of a cash-balance equation from the point of view of the marginal utility theory, although Patinkin [25, pp. 541–572] criticized Walras, saying that Walras cannot be credited with having presented a cash-balance theory, which is different from a cash-balance equation. Walras introduced money in his theory of general equilibrium as circulating capital rendering a service of storage. People demand money, therefore, for the reduction of costs of transaction and inconveniences in the process of circulating. Strictly speaking, this requires the existence of a lack of synchronization between the receipt of income and its outlay, and the existence of some uncertainties in the process of transactions and/or some imperfectness in credit markets. While criticizing Walras's mechanical application of marginal utility theory, Patinkin [25, Chapters V–VII] developed Walrasian theories of money by explicitly introducing such imperfections. Such attempts seem to succeed, however, to the extent that they are in conflict with the basic structure of Walras's general equilibrium theories. It is very difficult to introduce money into the original Walrasian system of general equilibria in a satisfactory way.

The reason for this difficulty is that Walras's theory of money is heavily handicapped by the place it occupies in the system of general equilibria. Walras insisted that complicated phenomena can only be studied if the rule of proceeding from the simple to the complex is always observed. He first breaks down a complicated economy of the real world into several fundamental components, such as consumer-traders, entrepreneurs, consumers' goods, factors of production, newly produced capital goods, and money. A very simple model of a pure exchange economy is then composed from a very limited number of such components, i.e., individual consumer-traders and consumers' goods, where the existence of all other components is simply disregarded. In order to travel from this simple model to the complex, the excluded components are added one by one, i.e., entrepreneurs and factors of production first in the theory of production, then newly produced capital goods in the theory of capitalization, and finally money in the theory of circulation and money.

From our standpoint we must emphasize that all exchanges have to be non-monetary (i.e., direct exchanges of goods for goods) in all the Walrasian theories of exchange, production and capitalization and credit, since money has not yet been introduced. Relative prices (including the rate of interest) and hence consumption and production activities are determined in non-monetary real models without using money, while the role of the model of circulation and money lies only in the determination of the level of absolute prices by the use of money (Morishima [19, pp. 170–184]; Negishi [21, pp. 9–35]). Thus Walrasian economics is completely dichotomized between non-monetary real theories and monetary theory, in the sense that all non-monetary real variables are determined in the former and money is neutral, i.e., it does not matter for the determination of such variables. "That being the case, the equation of monetary circulation, when money is not a commodity, comes very close, in reality, to falling outside the system of equations of (general) economic equilibrium" (Walras [31, pp. 326–327]). This dichotomy is, of course, designed to show the fundamental significance of the non-monetary, real mechanism of the economy, which underlies the behavior of a modern monetary economy.

In each of his non-monetary theories Walras tried to show the establishment of a general equilibrium in its corresponding self-compact closed model. General equilibrium is, of course, a state of the economy in which not only each individual consumer-trader (entrepreneur) achieves the maximum obtainable satisfaction (profit) under given conditions, but also demand and supply are equalized in all markets. In a large economy, how can we make such a situation possible without introducing money? Even in the most simple case of an exchange economy, it seems in general almost impossible to satisfy all individual traders by barter exchanges, unless mutual coincidence of wants accidentally prevails everywhere. Walras ingeniously solved this difficult problem by his *tâtonnement*, a preliminary process of price (and quantity) adjustment which precedes actual exchange transactions and/or the making of effective contracts.

Prices change in the process of *tâtonnement* of a competitive economy and it is generally impossible for a single trader to purchase or sell whatever amount he wishes at going prices. Nevertheless, each trader behaves on the assumption that prices are unchanged and that unlimited quantities of demand and supply can be realized at the current prices. This conjecture is justified by the very fact that no exchange transactions are made and no trade contracts are in effect during the *tâtonnement*, until a general equilibrium is established where prices are no longer changed, and every trader can purchase and sell exactly the amount he wishes at the going prices. The idea of *tâtonnement* was clearly suggested to Walras from the observation of how business is done in some well-organized markets in the real world, like the stock exchanges, commercial markets, grain markets and fish markets. *Tâtonnement* is therefore not entirely unrealistic as a model of adjustment in such special markets.

However, it is certainly very unrealistic to apply such a model of special markets to the whole economy of the real world, since preliminary adjustments are not usually made before exchange transactions and effective contracts take place, even in markets where competition, though not so well organized, functions fairly satisfactorily. In such a monetary economy of the real world, where, of course, at least some exchange transactions actually take place before general equilibrium is established, even a competitive trader without power to control prices has to expect price changes and to try to sell when the price is high and to buy when the price is low, although he may not always succeed in doing so. This leads to the separation of sales and purchases, a separation which is made possible only by the use of money as the unit of account, the medium of exchange and the store of value. Other commodities cannot be used as the medium of exchange, since their prices are, in general, changing in disequilibrium. In Walrasian non-monetary real models where the *tâtonnement* assumption is made, on the other hand, sales and purchases are synchronized when general equilibrium is established, so that there is no need for money, since only relative prices matter and any commodity can be used as *numéraire*. Even if sales and purchases are not synchronized in a single market period after the general equilibrium is established, furthermore, there is no reason why the role of medium of exchange should be exclusively assigned to a single item called money. Since equilibrium prices are already fixed and unchanged, almost any non-perishable commodity can be used, if a medium of exchange is necessary.

Walras even considered *tâtonnement* in his final model of the general equilibrium of economy, i.e., that of circulation and money. Since disequilibrium transactions are thus excluded and there is no uncertainty, there is no room here for money as a store of value. We have to assume, therefore, that people only demand money for the sake of convenience in transactions. Since all actual transactions are carried out at general equilibrium after the preliminary *tâtonnement* is over, however, this rationale for the demand for money is not at all convincing. The only role left for money is to determine its own price, i.e., the general level of absolute prices.[17]

While money plays a limited role in Walras's *tâtonnement* economics, it is interesting to see that the introduction of money is necessary in so-called non-*tâtonnement* models. When exchange transactions are carried out at disequilibrium, only traders on the short side (i.e., suppliers if there is excess demand, demanders if there is excess supply) can realize their plan of demand or supply fully. This short-side principle is, however, not consistent with the rule of voluntary exchange or no overfulfillment that no traders are forced to buy or sell more of any commodity than they wish. Money can, however, be exempt from this rule, since, after the sale of a commodity and before the purchase of the other, people often have more money than they wanted to keep ultimately. The introduction of money is necessary, therefore, to reconcile the short-side principle with the rule of voluntary exchange (Negishi [21, pp. 22–23]). Money can play its essential role only in a non-Walrasian world where transactions take place out of equilibrium.

---

[17]One may argue that there is a Keynesian speculative demand if the Walrasian model is interpreted as that of a temporary equilibrium. Even so, almost any non-monetary commodity can be used for such a demand. I owe this footnote to Mr. T. Oginuma of the University of Tokyo.

Paradoxically, the significance of Walras's theory of money lies in its demonstration that the Walrasian theory of general equilibrium is not "almighty", since it is based on the *tâtonnement* assumption. By absorbing various non-Walrasian theories, Walrasian economics developed into the modern neo-classical economic theory. The dichotomy between real and monetary aspects remains intact, however, through the development of Walrasian economics into neo-classical economics. In other words, the role of money in exchange transactions is not properly recognized in neo-Walrasian economics. Various attempts are being made to correct this defect of modern economic theory. We may call such attempts non-Walrasian economic theories. Incidentally, the theory of exchange and money considered by C. Menger, who shares the fame of being a founding father of modern economic theory with Walras, is in sharp contrast to that of Walras, as we shall see in the next chapter. Non-Walrasian economics begin with Menger.

References

[1] Allais, M., *Traite d'économie pure*, 2, Paris: Imprimerie Nationale, 1943.

[2] Arrow, K.J., "An Extension of the Basic Theorems of Classical Welfare Economics", *Proceedings of the Second Berkeley Symposium on Mathematical Statistics and Probability*, pp. 507–532, J. Neyman, ed., University of California Press, 1951.

[3] Arrow, K.J., and F.H. Hahn, *General Competitive Analysis*, Holden Day, 1971.

[4] Bertrand, J., Review of Walras: *Théorie mathématique de la richesse sociale* and Cournot: *Recherches sur les principes mathématiques de la théorie des richesses*, *Journal des Savants*, 1883, pp. 449–503.

[5] Cournot, A., *Researches into the Mathematical Principles of the Theory of Wealth*, N.T. Bacon, tr., Macmillan, 1897.

[6] Eagly, R.V., *The Structure of Classical Economic Theory*, Oxford University Press, 1974.

[7] Edgeworth, F.Y., *Papers Relating to Political Economy*, 1, Macmillan, 1925.

[8] Fellner, W., *Competition Among the Few*, Kelley, 1965.

[9] Friedman, J., *Oligopoly Theory*, Cambridge University Press, 1983.

[10] Garegnani, P., *Il Capitale nelle Teorie della Distribuzione*, Giuffrè, 1960.

[11] Hicks, J.R., "Annual Survey of Economic Theory: The Theory of Monopoly", *Econometrica*, 3(1935), pp. 1–20.

[12] Hicks, J.R., *Value and Capital*, Oxford University Press, 1946.

[13] Hicks, J.R., *Capital and Growth*, Oxford University Press, 1965.

[14] Hildenbrand, W., and A.P. Kirman, *Introduction to Equilibrium Analysis*, North-Holland, 1976.

[15] Jaffé, W., *Essay on Walras*, D.A. Walker, ed., Cambridge University Press, 1983.

[16] Kaldor, N., "A Classificatory Note on the Determinateness of Equilibrium", *Review of Economic Studies*, 1(1933–4), pp. 122–136.

[17] Morishima, M., *Dogakuteki Keizai Riron* (Dynamic Economic Theory), Kobundo, 1950.

[18] Morishima, M., "Existence of Solution to the Walrasian System of Capital Formation and Credit", *Zeitschrift für Nationalökonomie*, 20(1960), pp. 238–243.

[19] Morishima, M., *Walras' Economics*, Cambridge University Press, 1977.

[20] Negishi, T., *General Equilibrium Theory and International Trade*, North-Holland, 1972.

[21] Negishi, T., *Microeconomic Foundations of Keynesian Macroeconomics*, North-Holland, 1979.
[22] Negishi, T., Review of Morishima: *Walras' Economics, The Economic Review* (Hitotsubashi University), 31(1980), pp. 89–91.
[23] Newman, P., *The Theory of Exchange*, Prentice Hall, 1965.
[24] Ono, Y., "The Equilibrium of Duopoly in a Market of Homogeneous Goods", *Economica*, 45(1978), pp. 287–295.
[25] Patinkin, D., *Money, Interest and Prices*, Harper and Row, 1965.
[26] Samuelson, P.A., *The Collected Scientific Papers*, J.E. Stiglitz, ed., MIT. Press, 1966.
[27] Schumpeter, J.A., *History of Economic Analysis*, Oxford University Press, 1954.
[28] Uzawa, H., "Walras' Tatonnement in the Theory of Exchange", *Review of Economic Studies*, 27(1960), pp. 182–194.
[29] Walker, D.A., "Walras and His Critics on the Maximum Utility of New Capital Goods", *History of Political Economy*, 16(1984), pp. 529–544.
[30] Walras, L., *Eléments d'économie politique pure*, R. Pichon and R. Durand-Auzias, 1926.
[31] Walras, L., *Elements of Pure Economics*, W. Jaffé, tr., Irwin, 1954.
[32] Walras, L., *Correspondence and Related Papers*, 1, W. Jaffé, ed., North-Holland, 1965.
[33] Weintraub, E.R., *General Equilibrium Analysis*, Cambridge University Press, 1985.
[34] Wicksell, K., *Lectures on Political Economy*, 1, E. Classen, tr., Kelly, 1967.
[35] Yasui, T., *Walras o megutte* (Essay on Walras), Sobunsha, 1970.

CHAPTER 8

MENGER AND THE AUSTRIAN SCHOOL

1. Menger's marketability

1.1

The Austrian school of economics was founded by Carl Menger (1840–1921) and developed by, among others, Friedrich von Wieser (1851–1926) and Eugen von Böhm–Bawerk (1851–1914). Its contributions to the development of economic science are substitutes for as well as complements to neo-classical orthodoxy, or Walrasian economics. As some recent neo-Austrians argue, the Austrian school differentiates itself by its emphasis on subjectivism, not confined to preference but extended to expectations, time as the dimension of changes, fragmented information and the process of learning.[1] An excellent example is provided by Menger's non-Walrasian theory of market and money, which will be discussed in this section after a brief sketch of Menger's life and works. Some contributions made by the Austrian school can, however, be considered as most valuable additions to the neo-classical general equilibrium theory, for example, Wieser's theory of value and allocation (to be discussed in section 2) and Böhm–Bawerk's theory of capital and interest (to be discussed in sections 3 and 4). Incidentally, it is interesting to know that Menger rejected Böhm–Bawerk's theory of capital.[2]

Born in 1840 at Galicia in Austria (now in Poland), Carl Menger studied at the Universities of Vienna and Prague, with his two brothers, Anton, later the well-known writer on the right to the whole product of labor, and Max, who became a famous politician. Carl took his doctorate at the University of Cracow and devoted himself first to journalism, then to the Civil Service. It is reported that one of his duties was to write surveys of the state of the markets

---

[1] See articles by Lachmann and Egger in Spadaro [39, pp. 1–39, particularly, 1–2, 17, 19 and 34].

[2] This is because Böhm-Bawerk's concepts of time preference and period of production do not represent all of those economically relevant aspects of time. See Spadaro [39, pp. 1–2 and Schumpeter [38, p. 847].

and he was struck by the glaring contrast between the traditional theories of price and the facts which experienced practical men considered as decisive for the determination of prices (Hayek [11]). The first edition of *Grundsätze der Volkswirtschaftslehre* was published in 1871 and, in 1872, Carl Menger qualified as a Privatdozent for political economy in the University of Vienna. In 1876 Menger was appointed one of the tutors to the Crown Prince Rudolph and accompanied him during the next two years on his extensive travels through the greater part of Europe. After his return, Menger was appointed to the chair of political economy in Vienna in 1897.

In the Preface to the first edition of *Grundsätze*, Menger states his method, which he called atomistic and which, according to Hayek, later came to be known as methodological individualism (Hicks and Weber [12, p. 8]).

> I have endeavored to reduce the complex phenomena of human economic activity to the simplest elements that can still be subjected to accurate observation, ..., to investigate the manner in which the more complex economic phenomena evolve from their elements according to definite principles. (Menger [25, pp. 46–47.)

> ... the investigation of the causal connections between economic phenomena involving products and the corresponding agents of production ... for the purpose of establishing a price theory based upon reality and placing all price phenomena (including interest, wages, ground rent, etc.) together under one unified point of view. (Menger [25, p. 49].)

While a school was being formed by economists following Menger in Austria, Schmoller's historical school had the greatest influence in Germany at that time. In Germany, therefore, Menger's work was neglected simply because it is useless from the point of view of the historical school, which insists that political economy is a historical science and not a theoretical one. Under these circumstances, it is no wonder that Menger thought it necessary to defend the method he had adopted against the claims of the historical school rather than to continue the theoretical work. He published *Untersuchungen über die Methode der Socialwissenschaften und der politischen Oekonomie insbesondere* in 1883, which initiated the *Methodenstreit* with Schmoller. In *Untersuchungen*, Menger vindicated the rights of theoretical analysis, which consists of an exact or atomistic orientation and an empirical or realistic orientation, and tried to convince historicists that some of what they were already doing was a form of theory i.e., empirical laws.

Now the significance of the *Methodenstreit* is mainly historical,[3] but what

---

[3] For *Methodenstreit*, see Schumpeter [38, pp. 814–815], White's Introduction to Menger [27], and the article by Hutchison in Hicks and Weber [12, pp. 15–37].

may still be interesting for those economists considering economic theories of institutions is Menger's view on the organic understanding of social phenomena and social institutions such as the institution of money.

> *Natural* organisms are composed of elements which serve the function of the unit in a thoroughly mechanical way.... The so-called social organism, on the contrary, simply cannot be viewed and interpreted as the product of purely mechanical force effects.... social phenomena come about as the unintended result of individual human efforts (pursuing *individual interests*) without a *common will* directed toward their establishment. (Menger [27, p. 133].)

After he published articles on capital and money in 1888, 1892, and 1900, Menger resigned from his chair in 1903 in order to devote himself entirely to his writing. His interest and scope expanded to philosophy, psychology and ethnography. In 1921 he died with his system of political economy left unfinished. *Grundsätze* was merely the "First, General Part" of his system, which deals with the general conditions which lead to economic activity, value exchange, price and money. It was planned that the second part would deal with interest, wages, rent, income, credit, and paper money, the third part was to be the applied one, on the theory of production and commerce, and the fourth part was to be a criticism of the present economic system and proposals for economic reform (Hayek [11], Menger [24, p. vi]).

Compiled from manuscripts left by Carl Menger, the second edition of *Grundsätze* was edited and published in 1923 by Karl Menger, a mathematician and the son of Carl Menger. Scholars are divided in their evaluations of this second edition. Schumpeter [38, p. 827] regarded it as the work of old age, which adds nothing essential. Translators of *Grundsätze* into English decided to use the first edition "because it was the first edition only that influenced the development of economic doctrine, because of the posthumous character of the second edition, and because the numerous differences between the two editions make a variorum translation impractical" (Menger [25, p. 39]).[4] It was, however, Karl Polanyi [32], an anthropologist, who evaluated the second edition highly on the grounds that it extended the range of inquiry to include anthropology, sociology, and economic history, and provided a definition of the economy which would satisfy the requirements of the social sciences in general.

---

[4] Menger [26] is, however, a variorum translation into Japanese. The title is changed to *Allegemeine theoretische Wirtschaftslehre*, because it was so suggested by Menger himself in material which is kept in the Menger Library of Hitotsubashi University – a fact noted first, as far as we know, by Y. Yamada [47, p. 98].

The first edition of *Grundsätze* consists of eight chapters, "The General Theory of the Good", "Economy and Economic Goods", "The Theory of Value", "The Theory of Exchange", "The Theory of Price", "Use Value and Exchange Value", "The Theory of the Commodity", and "The Theory of Money". The second edition has nine chapters; two new chapters, "The Theory of Wants", and "Human Wants and Measure of Goods", are added and one old chapter, "Use Value and Exchange Value" is dissolved. Materials from the first edition are essentially kept but enlarged so that the second edition is twice as large as the first.

As summarized by Hayek (Hicks and Weber [12, p. 7]), Menger's main achievement in the first edition is the "extension, of the derivation of the value of a good from its utility, from the case of given quantities of consumers' goods to the general case of all goods, including the factors of production." In the second edition, however, Menger's view of the economy is wider than that of scarcity, maximization and market, which he called the economizing direction of the economy. The other direction is called technical and is derived from the requirements of production, irrespective of insufficiency.

> I call these two directions that the human economy can take – the technical and the economizing – *basic*; though these appear as a rule, indeed, almost always linked with each other, they *nevertheless spring from causes that are essentially different and independent from one another*, and in some branches of the economy actually make their appearance alone.... The technical direction of the human economy is neither necessarily dependent upon an economizing one, nor is it necessarily linked with it. (Menger [24, pp. 77–78], Polanyi [32].)

As Polanyi [32] pointed out, however, Menger was content to generalize the concept of the economy and made no further attempt to consider pre-industrial non-market economies.

As for the value which is the foundation of the theory of market economy, Menger emphasizes its subjectivity.

> Value is thus nothing inherent in goods, no property of them, nor an independent thing existing by itself. It is a judgment economizing men make about the importance of the goods at their disposal for the maintenance of their lives and well-being. Hence value does not exist outside the consciousness of men. (Menger [25, pp. 120–121]; [24, p. 108]).

What is important is, then, that Menger not only insists on the principle of marginal utility of a directly consumable good (a good of lower order) but he also develops the theory of imputed value for the factors of production (goods of higher order).

Hence the value to this person of any portion of the whole available quantity of the good is equal to the importance to him of the satisfactions of least importance among those assured by the whole quantity and achieved with an equal portion.... Nor can the value of the goods of higher order already expended in producing a good of lower order be the determining factor in its present value. On the contrary, the value of goods of higher order is, in all cases, regulated by the prospective value of the goods of lower order to whose production they have been or will be assigned by economizing men. (Menger [25, pp. 132, 150]; [24, pp. 127, 147].)

In the theory of production or input–output relations, Menger recognizes the technological substitutability and complementarity among factors of production.

A given quantity of some one good of lower order can be produced from goods of higher order that stand in very different quantitative relationships with one another. In fact, one or several goods of higher order that are complementary to a group of certain other goods of higher order may often be omitted altogether without destroying the capacity of the remaining complementary goods to produce the good of lower order. (Menger [25, p. 162]; [24, p. 155].)

With reference to the principle of marginal productivity, Menger insists that

the value of a given quantity of a particular good of higher order is not equal to the importance of the satisfactions that depend on the whole product it helps to produce, but is equal merely to the importance of the satisfactions provided for by the portion of the product that would remain unproduced if we are not in a position to command the given quantity of the good of higher order. (Menger [25, p. 164]; [24, pp. 156–157]).

Unlike the value theory of classical and Marxian economics, in which it is insisted that the embodied quantity of labor (a good of higher order) determines the value of a labor product (a good of lower order), Menger considered that the value of a good of lower order is determined by its marginal utility, and that the value of a good of higher order is imputed from that of a good of lower order, on the basis of the former good's marginal productivity in the production of the latter. Menger's attempt to explain the value of everything by the utility and marginal principle was developed further by his successors such as Wieser, as we shall see in the next section.[5]

Not all the aspects of Menger's theory were, however, fully developed by his

---

[5] The marginal productivity theory of Menger and Wieser is reformulated in terms of linear programming by Samuelson [35, pp. 505–512], and Uzawa [41].

successors. For example, Menger insists that

> the process by which goods of higher order are progressively transformed into goods of lower order and by which these are directed finally to the satisfaction of human needs is ... subject, like all other process of change, to the law of causality. The idea of causality, however, is inseparable from the idea of time. (Menger [25, p. 67]; [24, p. 28].)

He emphasizes the uncertainty (*Unsicherheit*) in the determination of the value of goods of higher order from the expectations of the value of lower order goods. Streissler (Hicks and Weber [12, pp. 171–173]) evaluates such a dynamic aspect of Menger's theory highly, and considers that Menger is a precursor of Keynes.

1.2

Unlike the Walrasian theory of price, which assumes perfect, well-organized markets, Menger's theory of price is characterized by the fact that he mainly considered more realistic, imperfect markets. The result is that Menger has no notion of the existence of a deterministic market price.

> Thus commodities that can be exchanged against each other in certain definite quantities (a sum of money and a quantity of some other economic good, for instance), that can be exchanged for each other at will by a *sale* or *purchase*, in short, commodities that are *equivalents in the objective sense of the term*, do not exist – even on given markets and at a given point in time. (Menger [25, p. 193]; [24, p. 185].)

We must note, above all, that Menger distinguishes the commodity from the good and has a separate chapter on the theory of commodity in his *Grundsätze*. The commodity is defind by him as follows.

> Products that the producers or middlemen hold in readiness for sale are called *commodities*. In ordinary usage the term is limited in its application to movable tangible goods (with the exception of money). ... But in scientific discourse a need was felt for a term designating all economic goods held ready for sale without regard to their tangibility, mobility, or character as products of labor, and without regard to the persons offering them for sale. A large number of economists ... defined commodities as (*economic*) *goods of any kind that are intended for sale*. (Menger [25, pp. 238–239]; [24, pp. 219–220].

Menger explains further the relation between goods and commodities:

From the definition just given of a commodity in the scientific sense of the term, it appears that commodity-character is nothing inherent in a good, no property of it, but merely a specific relationship of a good to the person who has command of it. With the disappearance of this relationship the commodity-character of the good comes to an end. A good ceases to be a commodity, therefore, if the economizing individual possessing it gives up his intention of disposing of it, or if it comes into the hands of persons who do not intend to exchange it further but to consume it ... Commodity-character is therefore not only no property of goods but usually only a *transitory* relationship between goods and economizing individuals. Certain goods are intended by their owners to be exchanged for the goods of other economizing individuals. During their passage, sometimes through several hands, from the possession of the first into the possession of the last owner, we call them "*commodities*," but as soon as they have reached their economic destination (that is, as soon as they are in the hands of the ultimate consumer) they obviously cease to be commodities and become "*consumption goods*" in the narrow sense in which this term is opposed to the concept of "*commodity*." But where this does not happen, as in the case very frequently, for example, with gold, silver, etc., especially in the form of coins, they naturally continue to be "commodity" as long as they continue in the relationship responsible for their commodity-character. (Menger [25, pp. 240–241]; [24, pp. 221–222].

But why do some goods cease to be commodities quickly while coins never cease to be commodities? In other words, why is it that little metal disks, apparently useless as such, can be commodities and exchanged against useful things that can become consumption goods? This is because of the different degrees of saleability or marketability of commodities (*Absatzfähigkeit der Waren*). Money is the most marketable of all commodities. "*The theory of money necessarily presupposes a theory of the saleableness of goods.*"[6] Degree of marketability of commodities is defined by Menger as "the greater or less facility with which they can be disposed of at a market at any convenient time at current purchasing prices, or with less or more diminution of the same" (Menger [23]).

Behind this definition is Menger's observation that the smaller the difference between the higher buying price and lower selling price, the more

---

[6] See Menger [23], where *Absatzfähigkeit* is translated as saleableness. See also Menger [25, p. 242], where *Absatzfähig* is translated as liquid and *Absatzfähigkeit* as marketability.

marketable the commodity usually is.

> The most cursory observation of market-phenomena teaches us that it does not lie within our power, when we have bought an article for a certain price, to sell it again forthwith at that same price … The price at which any one can at pleasure buy a commodity at given market and a given point of time, and the price at which he can dispose of the same at pleasure, are two essentially different magnitudes. (Menger [23].)

Prices vary between different places, between different times, and between different people. But, as far as the difference between buying price and selling price is concerned, it is determinate rather than stochastic, in spite of Streissler's emphasis on the stochastic price variation in Menger's theory of price (Hicks and Weber [12, p. 171]).

Although Menger describes in detail the circumstances which the degree of maketability of commodities depends, what is interesting from our point of view is the fact that it depends on whether the relevant market is well organized or poorly organized.

> If the competition for one commodity is poorly organized and there is danger therefore that the owners will be unable to sell their holdings of the commodity at economic prices, at a time when this danger does not exist at all, or not in the same degree, for the owners of other commodities, it is clear that this circumstance will be responsible for a very important difference between the marketability of that commodity and all others. … Commodities for which an organized market exists can be sold without difficulty by their owners at prices corresponding to the general economic situation. But commodities for which there are poorly organized markets change hands at inconsistent prices, and sometimes cannot be disposed of at all. (Menger [25, pp. 248–49]; [24, pp. 233, 235].)

Walras assumed that the market is well organized. Menger's theory of commodity for which the market is poorly organized and for which marketability is not high suggests that Menger's is a non-Walrasian theory of market. Menger's criticism of pre-Mengerian economics, that "investigation into the phenomena of price has been directed almost exclusively to the quantities of the commodities exchanged, and not as well to the greater or less facility with which wares may be disposed of at normal prices" (Menger [23]; [25, p. 242]; [24, p. 223]), can also be applied to Walrasian or neo-classical economics. In other words, Menger's theory of the marketability of commodities is a first attempt at non-Walrasian economics.

In recent studies of non-Walrasian economics, i.e., fixprice models or quantity constraint models, an important role is played by the short-side principle that a disequilibrium transaction equals the minimum of supply and demand (Hahn and Negishi [9]; Benassy [2]). From the point of view of Menger's marketability, the short-side principle can be seen in that a commodity is highly marketable when its suppliers are on the short side of the relevant market and not so marketable when they are on the long side of the market. Unlike those recently working in non-Walrasian economics, however, Menger was not so much interested in the fixprice situation of a perfectly competitive market as in the flexprice case of an imperfectly competitive market, as was pointed out by Streissler (Hicks and Weber [12, p. 169]). In the latter type of market we can consider that suppliers are likely to be on the long side of the market in general, in the sense that they wish to sell more at the current price if there is enough demand.

This point was well recognized by Sraffa [40], a pioneer of the modern theory of imperfect competition.

It is not easy, in times of normal activity, to find an undertaking which systematically restricts its own production to an amount less than that which it could sell at the current price, and which at the same time is prevented by competition from exceeding that price. Businessmen, who regard themselves as being subject to competitive conditions, would consider absurd the assertion that the limit to their production is to be founded in the internal conditions of production in their firm, which do not permit the production of a greater quantity without an increase in cost. The chief obstacle against which they have to contend when they want gradually to increase their production does not lie in the cost of production but in the difficulty of selling the larger quantity of goods without reducing the price, or without having to face increased marketing expenses.

In Figure 8.1, we consider the case of a firm under imperfect competition. The level of output x is measured horizontally, and the price p and costs are measured vertically. A downward sloping demand curve DD is perceived by this firm, not particularly because it is monopolist, nor particularly because its product is differentiated, but more fundamentally because the market in which the commodity is sold is poorly organized, so that a larger amount of the commodity can be disposed of in the market only at a less favorable price. The equilibrium of the firm is shown to be at A, or $(\bar{p}, \bar{x})$, with the marginal revenue MR equalized with marginal cost MC at $\bar{x}$. At the current price $\bar{p}$, the firm wishes to sell as much as x', but is quantitatively constrained at $\bar{x}$, since there is not enough demand. There is an implicit excess supply AB or $x' - \bar{x}$, and the marketability of the commodity is not high. The only possible exception is the

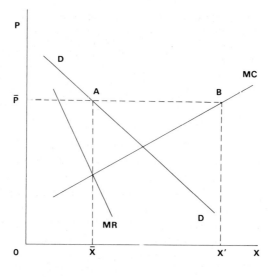

Figure 8.1

case where the firm is at full capacity and the MC curve is perpendicular at $\bar{x}$ so that A and B coincide. In a poorly organized market, therefore, the commodity is not highly marketable when firms are operating at less than full capacity.

There are two kinds of demand and supply: regular, stable demand and supply, and irregular, casual demand and supply. For example, the demand curve in Figure 8.1 is concerned with regular demand as perceived by a regular supplier. When A and B do not coincide and there exists an excess supply from a regular supplier, casual demand will be easily satisfied by regular suppliers with current price $\bar{p}$. Casual supply has to compete with regular excess supply to catch casual demand and will not be easily satisfied, unless the price is reduced. The marketability of the relevant commodity is low and the resale price of those casual suppliers who want to get rid of the commodity they just bought will be much lower than the price at which they bought as regular demanders. When, on the other hand, A and B coincide with the supply inelasticity of regular suppliers, casual suppliers do not have to compete with regular suppliers to capture demand, and their supplies will be easily satisfied. The marketability of the commodity is high and there is no gap between the resale price of those casual suppliers who wanted to get rid of the commodity they had just bought and the price at which they had bought.

Menger explains the origin of money on the basis of his theory of the marketability of commodities.[7]

> As *each* economizing individual becomes increasingly more aware of his economic interest, he is led by this *interest, without any agreement, without legislative compulsion, and even without regard to the public interest,* to give his commodities in exchange for other, more saleable, commodities, even if he does not need them for any immediate consumption purpose. (Menger [25, p. 260]; [24, pp. 248–249].)

This unintentionally increases the marketability of the latter commodities, so that they are acceptable to everyone trading and become the means of payment.

In Figure 8.1, the case of money is explained by a horizontal *DD* curve which makes *A* and *B* coincide. The suppliers of money (demanders of non-monetary commodities) are not on the long side of markets and the marketability of money is the highest. Even if the *DD* curve is not horizontal, but not very steep, however, *A* and *B* also coincide in the case where no suppliers can increase supplies – that is, the supply elasticity is zero, which Keynes [19, pp. 230–231] recognized as an essential property of money. In a well-organized market considered in Walrasian economics, the *DD* curve is horizontal so that *A* and *B* coincide. Every commodity has high marketability and, in this sense, can be accepted as a medium of exchange, even if the supply is elastic. If a special commodity called money is introduced, therefore, its role is limited in Walrasian economics. Money as a medium of exchange presupposes the low marketability of other commodities.

2. Wieser's welfare economics

Friedrich von Wieser was born in Vienna in 1851. After taking a law degree in 1875 at the University of Vienna, he studied economics at the Universities of Heidelberg, Leipzig and Jena. In 1883 Wieser became Privatdozent at Vienna, and was soon made a professor at the University of Prague. He succeeded to Menger's chair at Vienna in 1903. He also served for a while as Minister of Commerce. Wieser retired from the University in 1922 and died in 1926. His main contributions are *Der natürliche Werth* (1889) and *Theorie der gesellschaftlichen Wirtschaft* (1914), in which he followed Menger to develop the subjective theory of value statically. Schumpeter [38, p. 987] evaluated Wieser

---

[7] For recent discussions on Menger's theory of money, see Nagatani [28, pp. 118–130], O'Driscoll [30], and Hirayama [13].

highly, on the grounds that Wieser was the first to realize "that any attempt to develop a general logic of economic behavior will automatically yield a theory of the socialist economy."

In his *Theorie der gesellschaftlichen Wirtschaft*, Wieser started with a consideration of the simple economy, which is an essential prerequisite to the theory of social economy, and in which the elementary law of valuation, as developed by the consideration of a "Robinson Crusoe" economy, can be applied directly. Although the theory of the simple economy assumes that the subject is a single person whose satisfaction should be maximized, Wieser emphasized that he did

> not have in mind here the meagre economy of an isolated Crusoe. The imagined conditions of production have a breadth that is only realized in the activities of an entire nation. At the same time millions of persons are regarded as a massed unit. In the same way one contrasts humanity and nature or thinks of a people directing its great forces to some common goal. (Wieser [43, p. 9].)

We may suppose, therefore, that an aggregate of individual utilities or the utility of the model person is maximized in a rationalistic utilitarian way in the simple economy, where the influence of social and economic power is eliminated.[8]

Value established in the simple economy corresponds to the natural value defined in Wieser's *Der natürliche Werth*.

> That value which arises from the social relation between amount of goods and utility, or value as it would exist in the communist state, we shall henceforth call Natural Value. ... Natural Value shall be that which would be recognized by a completely organic and most highly rational community ... it will be excellent aid in realising what would remain out of present economy if we could think away private property, as well as all the troubles which are a consequence of human imperfection. (Wieser [45, pp. 60, 61].)

Although natural value is realized in a communist society where there exists no private property, it is, of course, also important for our present economy, if we are interested in the social judgement of value, or the estimate put upon goods by society. Price does not denote it.

> ... that point of view from which price become a social judgement of value, really amounts to a disregard of all the individual differences which emerge in purchasing power, and which separate price from natural value. A great

[8] See Wieser [43, pp. 20, 142, 165 and 398].

many theorists have thus written the value theory of communism without being aware of it, and in doing so have omitted to give the value theory of the present state. (Wieser [45, p. 61; see also p. 52].)

In the simple economy, the natural value of a consumption good is estimated according to its unstratified marginal utility. In the case of production goods which have no utility, "the consideration that, from production goods, one can obtain a return in goods which possess not only utility but value, gives production goods their value" (Wieser [45, p. 70]). In other words, value is imputed to a production good according to its productive contribution, i.e., "that portion of return in which is contained the work of the individual productive element in the total return of production. The sum of all the productive contributions exactly exhausts the value of the total return" (Wieser [45, p. 88]). In this way, values are determined by utilities and not by costs. However, "between costs and utility there is no fundamental opposition. Costs are goods valued, in the individual case, according to their general utility. The opposition between costs and utility is only that between the utility of the individual case, and utility on the whole" (Wieser [45, p. 183]).

Let us now formulate Wieser's theory of natural value in the simple economy. Suppose there are m consumption goods denoted by $j = 1, \ldots, m$, and n individuals denoted by $i = 1, \ldots, n$ in the economy. Let us denote the utility of the ith individual by $U_i(x_{i1}, \ldots, x_{im})$, where x_{ij} signifies the amount of the jth good consumed by the ith individual. If the jth good is not consumed, simply $x_{ij} = 0$. The utility to be maximized in the simple economy is a function of individual utilities denoted by $W(U_1, \ldots, U_n)$. For example, W is the utility of the model person or average person obtained from n individuals. Since the marginal use of a good is equalized everywhere in the simple economy and unstratified marginal utility signifies the natural values, we have

$$(\partial W/\partial U_i)(\partial U_i/\partial x_{ij}) = \partial U_i/\partial x_{ij} = v_j, \quad i = 1, \ldots, n, \quad j = 1, \ldots, m \quad (1)$$

where v_j is the natural value of the jth good. We can integrate (1) into

$$W = \sum_i U_i(x_{i1}, \ldots, x_{im}). \quad (2)$$

In the theory of imputation, Wieser [45, pp. 86–89] assumed the constant coefficient of production and solved for the natural value of the kth productive goods v_k, $k = 1, 2, 3$, from

$$v_h = \sum_k a_{hk} v_k, \quad h = 1, 2, 3 \quad (3)$$

where a_{hk} is the input coefficient of the kth production good in the production of the hth consumption good and v_h denotes the natural value of the hth consumption good. In view of Menger's emphasis on the substitutability of factors of production (section 1.1), we may generalize the input–output relations into production functions

$$X_j = F_j(Y_{j1}, \ldots, Y_{jr}), \quad j = 1, \ldots, m \tag{4}$$

where X_j is the output of the jth consumption good and Y_{jk} is the input of the kth production good or factor of production in the production of the jth consumption good. Then the natural values of r production goods are derived from the natural values of consumption goods by

$$v_j(\partial F_j/\partial Y_{jk}) = v_k, \quad j = 1, \ldots, m, \quad k = 1, \ldots, r \tag{5}$$

where v_j and v_k are natural values of the jth consumption good and the kth production good, respectively. If production functions (4) are assumed to be linear homogeneous, furthermore (5) implies

$$v_j X_j = v_j \sum_k (\partial F_j/\partial Y_{jk}) Y_{jk} = \sum_k v_k Y_{jk}, \quad j = 1, \ldots, m \tag{6}$$

i.e., the sum of all the productive contributions exactly exhausts the value of the total return, which is a generalization of (3).

Finally, we should have equalities of demand and supply of consumption and production goods, i.e.,

$$\sum_i x_{ij} = X_j, \quad j = 1, \ldots, m \tag{7}$$

and

$$\sum_j Y_{jk} = \bar{Y}_k, \quad k = 1, \ldots, r \tag{8}$$

where $\bar{Y}_k$ is the given supply of the kth production good.

Consider the maximization of (2) being subject to (4), (7) and (8). If we denote the Lagrangean multipliers corresponding to (7) and (8) by v_j and v_k, respectively, conditions (1) and (5) are satisfied by the conditions for the constrained maximization. In other words, natural values are derived as Lagrangean multipliers from the maximization of utilitarian social welfare function (2) being subject to resources and technological constraints (4), (7) and (8).

Armed with the theory of the simple economy and natural value, Wieser proceeds to the study of the social economy and exchange value.

The theory of exchange presupposes a social economy unhampered by interference on the part of the state. The theory of the simple economy having shown in what manner a single subject manages and calculates his economic affairs, we now show how the numerous juridical subjects, who meet in the course of exchange as they seek their economic advantage, determine prices and thus erect the structure of a social economy. Private property is presupposed. (Wieser [43, p. 10].)

The relation between the simple economy and the social economy is clear. Since "the collective private economies that are associated in the national economy are in themselves simple economies" (Wieser [43, p. 151]), both economies are identical if we assume that all the individuals have identical income, needs and valuation.

With an assumption such as this, the economic exchange value equals the unitary personal exchange value of all connected individual economies. The money computation in the national economic process has, therefore, precisely the significance it would have in the simple economy of a people. (Wieser [43, 306].)

Exchange value in the social economy is, however, different from natural value in the simple economy, if we drop such a simplifying assumption.

In natural value goods are estimated simply according to their marginal utility; in exchange value, according to a combination of marginal utility and purchasing power. In the former, luxuries are estimated far lower, and necessaries, comparatively, much higher than in the latter. Exchange value, even when considered as perfect, is, if we may so call it, a caricature of natural value; it disturbs its economic symmetry, magnifying the small and reducing the great. (Wieser [45, p. 62; see also p. 52].)

In the theory of the simple economy, the assumption is directed to the utmost possible equalization of the margin of use. In our social economy where the stratified marginal utility is decisive, the satisfaction of need is exceedingly disproportionate. (Wieser [43, p. 189].)

Since the stratified marginal utility is decisive in our social economy and goods are estimated, in exchange value, according to a combination of marginal utility and purchasing power, we may replace (1) by

$$(\partial W'/\partial U_i)(\partial U_i/\partial x_{ij}) = a_i(\partial U_i/\partial x_{ij}) = p_j, \quad i=1,\ldots,n, \quad j=1,\ldots,m \quad (9)$$

where p_j is the price or exchange value of the jth consumption good, $a_i(\partial U_i/\partial x_{ij})$ is the marginal utility stratified by the purchasing power, and W' is the social welfare function corresponding to the social exchange economy. We can integrate (9) into

$$W' = \sum_i a_i U_i(x_{i1},\ldots,x_{im}). \quad (10)$$

In the social economy, private property is presupposed, so that factors of production are privately owned by individuals, i.e.,

$$\bar{Y}_k = \sum_i \bar{Y}_{ik}, \quad k = 1, \ldots, r \tag{11}$$

where $\bar{Y}_{ik}$ is the kth factor of production owned by the ith individual. Prices of factors of production are derived, as in (5), from those of consumption goods i.e.,

$$p_j(\partial F_j / \partial Y_{jk}) = p_k, \quad j = 1, \ldots, m, \quad k = 1, \ldots, r \tag{12}$$

where p_k is the price of the kth factor of production. Then, the purchasing power of the ith individual is given by $\Sigma_k p_k \bar{Y}_{ik}$.

Each individual disposes of this purchasing power so as to maximize $U_i(x_{i1}, \ldots, x_{im})$ being subject to

$$\sum_j p_j x_{ij} = \sum_k p_k \bar{Y}_{ik}. \tag{13}$$

The conditions for this constrained maximization include

$$(\partial U_i / \partial x_{ij}) = s_i p_j, \quad j = 1, \ldots, m \tag{14}$$

where s_i is the marginal utility of the purchasing power.

Unlike in the simple economy, the allocation of goods is carried out in a decentralized way in the social economy. In view of (14), therefore, a_i's in (9) and (10) should be inversely proportional to s_i's in (14). Then, allocation of resources in a competitive social economy can be viewed as if the weighted utilitarian social welfare function (10) is maximized, being subject to (4), (7) and (8). Prices are derived as Lagrangean multipliers corresponding to (7) and (8) in the constrained maximization. As was shown in Negishi [29], to choose a_i's in (10) so that they are inversely proportional to s_i's in (14) obtained from such prices is possible under some plausible conditions, i.e., there is a general equilibrium in a competitive economy, which maximizes a properly defined social welfare function (10).

Taking (13) and (14) into consideration, we can easily see from the comparison of (1) and (9) that exchange and natural values are identical when all the individuals have identical taste and the same income. Otherwise, prices (exchange values) and natural values are generally different. Then, the marginal utility of income s_i for the rich is smaller than that for the poor, if Gossen's first law, i.e., diminishing marginal utility, is assumed so that utility function is concave. Prices of luxuries are high, relative to necessities, even though marginal utilities are low, since s_i of those who purchase them is small.

Wieser's theory of natural and exchange values can be considered as a precursor of the welfare economics of Lange [21], in which the optimality of a competitive economy is discussed by the use of social welfare functions. Lange called a_i's in our social welfare function (10) the marginal social significance of individuals. Furthermore, Lange [20] based his argument for the possibility of market socialism on the formal similarity between socialism and capitalism, which corresponds to that between natural and exchange values in Wieser's theory of simple and social economies. In the socialist calculation debate, however, Lange's position based on Walrasian or neo-classical static theory was attacked by the Austrians who believe that dynamic rivalry among capitalists and entrepreneurs is necessary for the coordinating market process which makes complex capitalist production in a monetary economy possible. It is to be emphasized that even Wieser was critical of the possibility of the socialist economy.[9]

Wieser was also against the equal distribution of income. The following argument is very interesting, from the point of view of recent theories of optimal income distribution.

> Were the task of economy to consist merely in distributing stores of goods, given without human cooperation, to the most needy, then, indeed no other distribution could be tolerated but one guided by the rational needs, as well known socialistic formula prescribes. But the most important task of economy consists in acquisition. The stores of commodities are not turned over to man by nature, ready for immediate use; they have to be procured painstakingly before they can be enjoyed. And to this principal problem of acquisition the economic law, now become a fact of history, is fittingly adjusted. It is not a simple law of enjoyments to be obtained, it is a rigorous law of acquisitions to be made.... It may well be that a system of rules, which distributes very unequally the enormous gains to which it is instrumental, is after all more beneficial to the mass of the citizens than another, doing out its much smaller proceeds according to principles of right and reason.... Society dares not withhold the higher wage from the competent worker. To do so is to risk losing the most valuable services. But when the strict rule declares against him also, who without fault of his own, lost what he had and perhaps even his working ability as well, sympathy prevails and we cannot quite approve of the rigorous discipline. So, too, the excessive income and riches which go far beyond moderate wealth, can no longer be sanctioned by the general conscience. (Wieser [43, p. 398].)

[9] For Austrians in the socialist calculation debate, see Lavoie [22, particularly, pp. 22–27]. See also Wieser [45, pp. 61, 63], [43, pp. 396–397], and Lavoie [22, pp. 80–85], for Wieser's view on the practical possibility of the communist state.

The inequalities in the distribution of income and wealth are justified, therefore, if and only if they work out to the advantage of the most unfortunate individuals, as Rawls [33, p. 78] recently insisted. Consider a two-individual economy. Suppose, in Figure 8.2, that the first individual, whose utility U_1 is measured horizontally, represents entrepreneurs and competent workers, while the second individual, whose utility U_2 is measured vertically, represents ordinary workers and those who cannot work. Let us assume that the special ability of the first individual cannot be mobilized unless there is the incentive that his utility is higher relative to that of the second individual. Line *oa* indicates equal distribution of real income while line *ob* shows the minimum required utility difference. The utility frontier, i.e., the boundary of the set of utilities possible under resources and technological constraints, is curve *cjde* when there is no incentive for entrepreneurs and competent workers. If there is a sufficient incentive for them, on the other hand, the utility frontier is shifted into curve *fgh*. Since the minimum required incentive is indicated by line *ob*, utility combinations between *f* and *g* are actually impossible. The realizable utility frontier is, therefore, considered to be *cjdgh*, having a rising portion *dg*.[10] The utility combination recommended by Wieser and Rawls is clearly *g*,

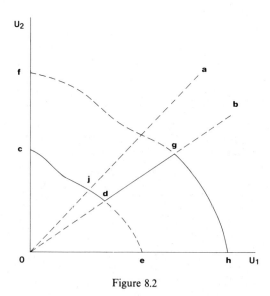

Figure 8.2

[10] Phelps [31] also uses a utility frontier with a rising portion to explain Rawls's theory of optimal distribution, although he does not discuss in detail why his utility frontier is not downward sloping.

where the higher utility of the first individual is justified on the grounds that it makes the lower utility of the second individual higher than it is otherwise, for example, at the point *j* of the equal distribution.

To make a comparison of the points in Figure 8.2, however, we have to make an interpersonal comparison of utilities. It may be made, if ever possible, by the introspection on which the Austrians in general, and Wieser in particular, put a great emphasis.

> For all actions which are accompanied by a consciousness of necessity, economic theory need never strive to establish a law in a long series of inductions. In these cases we, each of us, hear the law pronounced by an unmistakable inner voice. (Wieser [43, p. 8].)

> We can observe natural phenomena only from outside but ourselves from within.... This psychological method chooses the most advantageous position for observation. It finds for us in common experience all the most important facts of necessity.... It finds that certain acts take place in our consciousness with a feeling of necessity. What a huge advantage for the natural scientist if organic and inorganic world clearly informed him of its laws, and why should we neglect such assistance? (Wieser [44, p. 17]; see also Hutchison [15, p. 155].)

3. Böhm-Bawerk and the positive rate of interest

Eugen von Böhm-Bawerk, brother-in-law of Wieser, was born in Brünn in Austria (now in Czechoslovakia) in 1851. He first studied law at the University of Vienna, and then economics, with Wieser, in Heidelberg, Leipzig, and Jena. In 1881 he was appointed Professor of Economics at the University of Innsbruck, but in 1889 entered the Austrian Finance Department and was named Austrian Minister of Finance in 1895, 1897 and 1900. It was in 1904 that Böhm-Bawerk resigned and thereafter he devoted his life to writing and teaching economics at the University of Vienna. In his article, "Grundzüge der Theorie des wirtschaftlichen Güterwerts" (1886), Böhm-Bawerk developed the theory of value that Carl Menger had outlined. Böhm-Bawerk established that it is marginal pairs of buyers and sellers that determine price. It is the evaluations of the weakest of successful buyers and the strongest of successful sellers, coupled with the evaluations of the strongest of unsuccessful buyers and the weakest of unsuccessful sellers, that set the limit to exchange value. The greatest contribution of Böhm-Bawerk was, however, his theory of capital and interest in his *Positive Theorie des Kapitals* (1889), the second volume of

Kapital und Kapitalzins, in which he insisted that the rate of interest is positive in a stationary economy. This is a very interesting argument, since modern theories of economic growth suggest positive relations between the rate of growth and the rate of interest.

As is well known, Böhm-Bawerk adduced three causes of the existence of interest, *Kapitalzins*, i.e., a premium (agio) attached to the present consumers' goods in the exchange against future consumers' goods. They are (1) better provision for wants expected in the future than in the present, (2) under-valuation of future wants, and (3) the superiority of a more roundabout or more protracted method of production (Böhm-Bawerk [4, pp. 259–289, especially 283].) The first cause implies that the marginal utility of future consumption is lower than that of present consumption, since one is given more goods in the future than in the present. If everybody is in such a situation, a positive rate of interest is necessary, since, otherwise, everybody wishes to borrow in order to consume more in the present and nobody will lend to consume more in the future. The second cause insists, on the other hand, that the marginal utility of future consumption is lower than that of present consumption, even if one is provided equally in the future as in the present. In other words, the rate of interest is positive, since people are myopic and consume more in the present unless the rate of interest is positive. The second cause alone, therefore, assures a positive rate of interest in a stationary state. While the first two causes are both concerned with the supply of capital or saving, finally, the third cause implies that the capital or saving is demanded even if the rate of interest is positive, since a more roundabout and more capital-using method of production is technically superior to a less round-about and less capital-using one.

Böhm-Bawerk's explanation runs as follows for his first cause of the interest:

A first principal cause capable of producing a difference in value between present and future goods is inherent in the difference between the relation of supply to demand as it exists at one point in time and that relation as it exists at another point in time.... If a person suffers in the present from appreciable lack of certain goods, or of goods in general, but has reason to hope to be more generously provided for at a future time, then that person will always place a higher value on a given quantity of immediately available goods than on the same quantity of future goods. This situation occurs with very great frequency in our economic life. [Of course,] it must be admitted that the counterpart is no rarity in economic life. There are people who at the moment are relatively well provided for and for whom there will presumably be less provision in the future. [However,] most goods are durable, especially money, which with its aspect of non-particularization is capable of representing all classes of goods, hence they can be reserved for the service of the future. (Böhm-Bawerk [4, pp. 265–268].)

On average, therefore, people expect their wants to be better provided for in the future than in the present.

The situation can be shown in Figure 8.3. Present goods are measured horizontally, and future goods are measured vertically. Line *Oa* has slope 1 and indicates an equal provision for wants in the present as in the future. If a person is provided with *Od* amount of present goods and expects to be provided with *Oe* amount of future goods, the indifference curve passing point *b* which has slope −1 at *f* (no undervaluation of future wants) has slope less than −1 at *b* (the curve is steeper at *b* than at *f*) indicating a positive rate of interest, since the marginal utility of future goods is less than that of present goods.

The situation in which Böhm-Bawerk's second cause exists can also be seen at point *c* in Figure 8.3. Since future wants are systematically undervalued (Böhm-Bawerk [4, pp. 268–273]), the slope of the indifference curve at point *c* is less than −1. The rate of interest is positive, even if there is no "difference between the relation of supply to demand as it exists at one point in time and

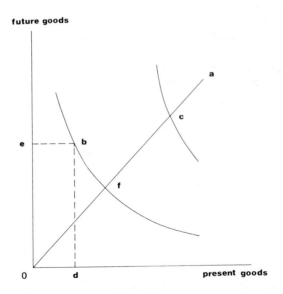

Figure 8.3

that relation as it exists at another point of time." The second cause is independent of the first cause and can explain by itself the positive rate of interest in a stationary state. It is clear that the second cause is also independent of the third cause, since the second cause is independent of the relative availability of future goods with respect to present goods, which is caused by the technical superiority of a more roundabout method of production. It is also clear that the first cause is independent of the second cause, and can explain by itself the positive rate of interest in a growth situation. The first cause is, however, not independent of the third cause, since the latter can create the relative abundance of future goods compared with present ones.

As for the third cause of the interest, Böhm-Bawerk had two different models, i.e., the model of circulating capital and the period of production, which he explained by his famous numerical examples (Böhm-Bawerk [4, pp. 356–358]), and the model of fixed capital and the capital–labor ratio, for which he gave some examples, such as a boat and net in fishing and a sewing machine in tailoring.[11] In view of his detailed exposition of the circulating capital model using numerical examples, it is clear that Böhm-Bawerk put the utmost emphasis on the third cause, i.e., the superiority of roundabout production. Following Böhm-Bawerk, Wicksell [42, pp. 172–184] developed a stationary state model in which a positive rate of interest is explained by the marginal productivity of the period of production in the sense of Jevons [16, p. 246]. In such a one-sided productivity model, however, there is one equation missing, since the supply or the maintaining of capital is not assured. This can be solved independently either by consideration of the first cause i.e., the better provision of future wants, or by the introduction of the second cause i.e., the undervaluation of future wants. While recent theories of capital and interest rely too heavily on the second cause,[12] it should be noted that the third cause can explain a positive rate of interest without the help of the second cause, since the third cause itself generates and works through the first cause, as Böhm-Bawerk admitted in the controversy with I. Fisher and Bortkiewicz (Böhm-Bawerk [5, pp. 192–193]. From the point of view of economic theory as well as that of the history of economic thought, then, it seems more natural to demonstrate positive interest in a stationary state by a combination of the

---

[11] For example of a boat and net, which is originally due to Roscher, see Böhm-Bawerk [4, pp. 280–281]. The example of a sewing machine is discussed in [4, p. 83].

[12] See, for example, Hirshleifer [14]. It is true that the first cause is introduced implicitly along with the second cause in Bernholz, Faber and Reiss [3]. In the case of a stationary state where net investment is zero, however, the positive rate of interest is still explained by the second cause. See also Faber [7, pp. 111–130].

third cause and the first cause, which necessarily follows from the third cause, rather than by a combination of the second and third cause, whose coexistence is regarded by Böhm-Bawerk as accidental.

As Arvidsson [1] pointed out, we have to consider a life-cycle model of individual members of the economy, in which people live for finite periods, having rising incomes, and consume their life-incomes, to apply the first cause in a stationary state where the economy as a whole is equally provided for in the future as well as in the present.[13] The life-cycle model is not alien to Böhm-Bawerk, since he considered the case of "all the indigent beginners in every calling, especially the budding artist or jurist, the first year medical student, the civil servant or business man just breaking in", as examples of those who expect future wants to be better provided for than present ones, and who value future goods less, and admitted also the counterpart, "a clerk in an office, for instance, who is fifty years old and is earning sixty dollars a week must face the prospect that in ten or fifteen years he will have nothing of his own but a few hundred dollars a year from an annuity, perhaps, that he purchased from an insurance company" (Böhm-Bawerk [4, p. 266]).

Let us consider an economy of stationary population, where each individual lives for two periods, so that the size of the young and working population and that of the old and retired population are equal in each period. In the first period, each individual works for a given number of hours but consumes less than he earns and lends his saved capital to firms, while he not only consumes yield from his capital but also dissaves all his capital in the second period. The second cause, i.e., time preference, is dismissed, so that

$$U_1(c_1, c_2)/U_2(c_1, c_2) = 1, \quad \text{if } c_1 = c_2, \tag{1}$$

where $U = U(c_1, c_2)$ is the utility of the representative individual, c_1 and c_2 denote respectively the amount of consumers' goods he consumes in the first and second periods, and U_1 and U_2 are partial derivatives of U with respect to c_1 and c_2, i.e., marginal utilities of the first and second period consumption.

The life-time budget equation for the representative individual is

$$p c_1 + p c_2/(1 + r) = w\bar{L}/b \tag{2}$$

where $p, w, r, \bar{L}, b$ are, respectively, the price of consumers' goods, wage, rate of interest, given total labor supply and the scale ratio of the representative individual and the whole economy. If the life-time utility $U(c_1, c_2)$ is

---

[13] We are indebted to Professor G.O. Orosel for the suggestion that the life-cycle model should be used, while we owe to Professor M. Faber the reference to Arvidsson [1].

maximized being subject to (2),

$$U_1(c_1, c_2)/U_2(c_1, c_2) = 1 + r \tag{3}$$

should be satisfied. Since time preference is assumed away, the left-hand side of (3) is 1, if $c_1 = c_2$ from (1). When r is positive, therefore, c_2 should be larger than c_1 from the usual assumption of the quasi-concavity of U, which implies that the future want is better provided for than the present one (the first cause). In Figure 8.4, c_1 is measured horizontally, and c_2 is measured vertically. The budget equation (2) is represented by the line fg whose slope is such that tan $a = 1 + r$. Condition (3) is satisfied at b, where an indifference curve whose slope is -1 at c (i.e., when $c_1 = c_2$) is tangent to the budget line fg. As b in Figure 8.3, b in Figure 8.4 also indicates that the future want is better provided for than the present one.

The possibility for the better provision of future want is assured by the third cause, i.e., the superiority of a more roundabout method of production. In the circulating capital model, the third cause implies that the labor productivity is an increasing function of the period of production, i.e.,

$$Y = f(t) L, \quad f'(t) > 0 \tag{4}$$

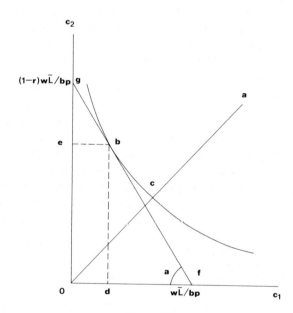

Figure 8.4

where Y is the volume of output of a consumers' good, L is the labor input and t is the time interval between Y and L, i.e., the period of production. Wages have to be advanced at the time of labor input since laborers are stripped of any means of subsistence, though wages can be higher than the subsistence level so that capital can be accumulated out of wage income. Capital in this model is heterogeneous, composed of past labor inputs of different dates or of semi-finished goods at different stages, and its value is

$$K = \sum w\bar{L}(1+r)^s \qquad (5)$$

where the summation runs from $s=0$ to $s=t-1$, and w, r and $\bar{L}$ denote respectively the rate of wage, the rate of interest, and the given total supply of labor.

Since the maximization of r with respect to t gives

$$f(t)/f(t-1) \geqq 1 + r \geqq f(t+1)/f(t), \qquad (6)$$

$r > 0$ in a stationary state, where r is defined by

$$p\,Y = (1+r)^t w\,L. \qquad (7)$$

There is, however, no assurance that the period of production chosen by firms is shorter than the life-span of an individual person. If the period of production is not shorter than the life-span, the value of existing capital, i.e., labor inputs in the past which have not yet matured into output, is larger than the value of the saving made in the past by the retired generation in the present. In a stationary state the representative individual cannot dissave all his capital at the end of his life but must leave the capital to the next generation, the value of which is equal to that of what he inherited at the beginning of his life. Because of the inherited capital, of course, he can consume more than what he earned in his life-time, if he wishes to do so. As his life-time consumption is related to the capital inherited at the beginning of his life, so the life-time consumption of the next generation is related to the capital he is going to have at the end of his life. A positive rate of interest is, therefore, impossible in a stationary state, unless the representative individual undervalues the consumption of the next generation in comparison with his own consumption. This seems, however, to re-introduce Böhm-Bawerk's second cause through the back door.[14]

We can get rid of the difficulty with respect to the problem of bequest and inheritance in the case of the fixed capital model in which a more roundabout method of production is regarded as a more capital intensive method

[14] Discussion with Professor Makoto Yano of Yokohama National University was very useful in this respect.

with higher capital–labor ratio. In view of the difficulty with respect to the concept of the period of production (Faber [7, pp. 29–33]), this model of Böhm-Bawerk's seems to be more acceptable to contemporary economists than his circulating capital model.[15] Let us consider that consumers' goods can be produced instantaneously from labor and capital goods while it takes a unit period to produce capital goods. "The sewing by machine is only a portion – and indeed the smallest portion – of the circuitous capital path. The principal length of that path is covered by the making of the sewing machine" (Böhm-Bawerk [4, p. 83]; [5, pp. 57, 59]). If we dismiss the durability aspect of capital goods and suppose that the life-span of capital goods is also a unit period, we can get rid of the problem of bequest and inheritance, so that the second cause is completely dismissed.

It might seem that Böhm-Bawerk's second cause is inherent in a life-cycle model in which an individual lives for a finite period.[16] This is certainly true if the problem of the bequest and inheritance of capital is dismissed, even though the life-span of capital goods is longer than that of individuals. By considering its own utility only, each generation of individuals underevaluates the wants of future generations completely, which implies the existence of a variety of the second cause. In our case, however, such a second cause does not exist, since the possibility of bequest and inheritance is ruled out by the assumption that the life-span of capital goods is shorter than that of individuals. The latter assumption is, of course, highly unrealistic. But our purpose is not so much to construct a realistic model as to make conceptual experiments by separating the different causes of a positive rate of interest.

The superiority of a more roundabout method of production is defined such that production with higher capital–labor ratio requires a smaller amount of labor directly and indirectly necessary to produce a given amount of consumers' goods. The capital–labor ratio is chosen by firms to maximize the rate of return or the rate of interest. We shall assume, at first for the sake of simplicity, that capital goods are produced by labor alone and show a positive rate of interest in a stationary state assured by the first and the third causes, by combining the life-cycle model and the capital–labor ratio model.

Suppose the production function of a consumers' good industry is

$$X = F(L, K) \tag{8}$$

where X, L, K are respectively the output, labor input, and capital input, and

---

[15] For example, see Kaldor [17] and Hawtrey [10, p. 31]; the reference to the latter we owe to Professor Ryuichiro Tachi of Aoyamagakuin University.

[16] See Samuelson [35] where Turgot's fructification theory of interest is considered using a life-cycle model.

F is homogeneous of degree one with respect to L and K. By defining capital–labor ratio a as

$$a = K/L \tag{9}$$

we can reduce (8) into

$$X = Lf(a) \tag{8$'$}$$

where $f(a) = F(1, a)$. Capital goods are assumed to be putty-clay, in the sense that a can be variable when capital goods are to be produced, but a remains unchanged once capital goods are installed.

If we assume that the amount of labor necessary to produce a unit of capital good with given a is $N(a)$ such that $N'(a) > 0$, the total amont of labor directly and indirectly necessary to produce X is given as

$$W(X, a) = L + K\, N(a) = L + LN(a)a = X(1 + N(a)a)/f(a). \tag{10}$$

The superiority of a more roundabout method of production, i.e., the third cause, is defined such that for given X, W is a decreasing function of a, which requires that

$$f(a)N(a) + aN'(a)f(a) - f'(a) - f'(a)N(a)a < 0. \tag{11}$$

The rate of return or the rate of interest r is implicitly defined by

$$F(L, K) - wL = wN(a)K(1 + r) \tag{12}$$

or

$$f(a) - w = w\, N(a)a(1 + r) \tag{13}$$

where w is the rate of wage in terms of consumers' good. Competitive firms producing capital goods choose a to maximize r, when w is given. By differentiating (13) with respect to a and r to obtain $dr/da = 0$, we have

$$f'(a) - wN(a)(1 + r) - wN'(a)a(1 + r) = 0. \tag{14}$$

By eliminating w from (13) and (14), r can be expressed as a function of a,

$$\begin{aligned} r = & (-f'(a) - f'(a)N(a)a + f(a)N'(a)a + f(a)N(a)) \\ & /(f'(a)N(a)a - f(a)N(a) - f(a)N'(a)a). \end{aligned} \tag{15}$$

The numerator of the right-hand side of (15) is negative in view of (11), while the denominator is also negative since $N'(a) > 0$ and $f(a) > f'(a)a$. This assures a positive rate of interest in a stationary state.

More generally, we can determine six variables w, r, a, L, c_1 and c_2 from six equations, which are, in addition to (13) and (14),

$$c_1 + c_2/(1+r) = w\bar{L}/b \tag{2}$$

$$U_1(c_1, c_2)/U_2(c_1, c_2) = 1 + r \tag{3}$$

$$b(c_1 + c_2) = Lf(a) \tag{16}$$

$$\bar{L} = L + LN(a)a \tag{17}$$

where c_1 and c_2 are the consumption of the representative individual when he is young and when he is old, $\bar{L}$ is the given total supply of labor and b is the scale ratio of the representative individual and the whole economy. Equations (2) and (3) are already explained, although we made $p = 1$ (consumers' good is *numéraire*) here. The demand and supply of consumers' goods are equalized in equation (16). The right-hand side of (17) is, finally, the demand for labor, i.e., that from the production of consumers' goods and that from the production of the capital goods, since $aL = K$.

The assumption that capital goods are produced by labor alone may be typically Austrian, but it is certainly unrealistic. Let us next consider the case that capital goods are also necessary to produce capital goods. To produce X consumers' goods, we need L labor and $K = aL$ capital goods. To produce aL capital goods, $N(a)aL$ labor is necessary, as already assumed. If we consider that the capital–labor ratio is identical in the production of consumers' goods and in the production of capital goods, $N(a)aL$ labor has to be combined with $aN(a)aL$ capital goods. To produce $N(a)a^2L$ capital goods, $N(a)^2a^2L$ labor is necessary, which has to be combined with $N(a)^2a^3L$ capital goods, and so on.

The total amount of labor directly and indirectly necessary to produce X consumers' goods is then

$$V(X, a) = L + N(a)aL + N(a)^2a^2L + \cdots = X/(1 - N(a)a)f(a) \tag{18}$$

in view of (8)'. The condition for the convergence in (18), i.e., $aN(a) < 1$, is natural, since it does not make sense to use $N(a)a^2L$ capital goods to produce aL capital goods, unless $aN(a) < 1$. The superiority of a more roundabout method of production is that V is a decreasing function of a, given X. From (18), it requires that

$$-f'(a) + N(a)f(u) + f'(a)aN(a) + af(a)N'(a) < 0. \tag{19}$$

The rate of return or the rate of interest r is implicitly defined in

$$F(L, K) - wL = (1+r)wN(a)K + (1+r)aN(a)K(F(L, K) - wL)/K \tag{20}$$

since capital goods have to be equally rewarded in the production of consumers goods and in the production of capital goods, i.e., $(F(L, K) - wL)/K$, and to produce K capital goods we need $N(a)K$ labor and $aN(a)K$ capital goods. In view of (8)' and (9), (20) is reduced to

$$f(a)N(a)a(1+r)-f(a)+w=0. \tag{21}$$

Competitive firms producing capital goods choose a so that r is maximized, when w is given. By differentiating (21) with respect to a and r to obtain $dr/da=0$, we have

$$f'(a)N(a)a(1+r)+f(a)N(a)(1+r)+af(a)N'(a)(1+r)-f'(a)=0 \tag{22}$$

from which r can be expressed as a function of a,

$$r=(f'(a)-f'(a)N(a)a-f(a)N(a)-af(a)N'(a))$$
$$/(f'(a)N(a)a+f(a)N(a)+af(a)N'(a)). \tag{23}$$

The numerator of the right-hand side of (23) is positive in view of (19), while the denominator is clearly positive. This assures a positive rate of interest in a stationary economy.

We can determine seven variables w, r, a, L, c_1, c_2 and the total amount of capital goods $\bar{K}$ in a stationary state from seven equations, which are, in addition to (2), (3), (16), (21) and (22),

$$\bar{L}=L+\bar{K}N(a) \tag{24}$$

$$\bar{K}=La+\bar{K}N(a)a. \tag{25}$$

Equation (24) states that the given total supply of labor $\bar{L}$ is equal to the demand for labor, L in the production of consumers' goods and $\bar{K}N(a)$ in the production of capital goods since $\bar{K}$ has to be reproduced in each period. Equation (25) shows the equality of the supply of capital goods $\bar{K}$ and demand for capital goods $K=aL$ in the production of consumers goods and $\bar{K}N(a)$ a in the production of capital goods.

4. Böhm-Bawerk versus Schumpeter

In the previous section we argued for the existence of a positive rate of interest in a stationary state on the basis of Böhm-Bawerk's first and third causes, the latter cause being interpreted as meaning that labor productivity can be increased by making the capital–labor ratio higher. However, we had to admit that the existence of the third cause in this sense in a stationary state requires fairly stringent conditions concerning the technological nature of production functions. Unfortunately, our conditions, i.e., (11) and (19) in the previous section, are somewhat complicated and their implications are not necessarily clear. It may be desirable, therefore, to consider what restriction is imposed on the form of production function in a drastically simplified model.

We are still considering the two-period life-cycle generation model of an economy with a stationary population given in the previous section. To make the story simple, however, let us specify the utility function of the representative individual $U(c_1, c_2)$ as

$$U(c_1, c_2) = \log c_1 + \log c_2 \tag{1}$$

where c_1 and c_2 denote, of course, the amount of goods he consumes in the first and second periods, respectively. The life-time budget equation for the representative individual is

$$p_1 c_1 + p_2 c_2/(1+r) = w\bar{L}/b \tag{2}$$

where $p_1, p_2, w, r, \bar{L}$ and b are, respectively, the price of the present good, that of the future good, wage, rate of interest, the given total labor supply and the scale ratio of the representative individual and the whole economy. The maximization of (1) under the condition (2) requires

$$c_2/c_1 = (1+r)p_1/p_2. \tag{3}$$

When r is positive in a stationary state where $p_1 = p_2$, c_2 should be larger than c_1, which implies that the future want is better provided for than the present one (Böhm-Bawerk's first cause of interest). Perhaps it may be convenient to decompose the lifetime budget equation (2) into single period equations

$$p_1 c_1 + p_1 S/b = w\bar{L}/b \tag{4}$$

and

$$p_2 c_2 = (1+r)p_1 S/b \tag{5}$$

where S denotes the total amount of capital to be saved.

We dismiss the distinction between consumers' goods and capital goods and consider a homogeneous and malleable good which can be used in both consumption and production. It is further assumed that the life-span of goods used as capital goods is a unit period. The aggregate production function is assumed to be of the Cobb–Douglas type,

$$Y = K^a L^{(1-a)} \tag{6}$$

where Y, K and L are respectively the total output, total capital input and total labor input. Since capital has to be invested one period earlier, the rate of interest r is implicitly defined in

$$p_1 Y - wL = (1 + r)p_0 K \qquad (7)$$

where p_0 is the price of the good in the previous period.

Competitive firms choose K and L to maximize r, when p_1, p_0 and w are given. By substituting (6) into (7) and solving $dr/dK = 0$, we have

$$ap_1 Y = (1 + r)p_0 K \qquad (8)$$

and

$$(1 - a)p_1 Y = wL. \qquad (9)$$

If we consider a stationary state, and make the produced homogeneous good *numéraire*, we have $p_2 = p_1 = p_o = 1$. Since markets for labor, capital, and the produced good have to be cleared,

$$L = \bar{L} \qquad (10)$$

$$K = S \qquad (11)$$

$$bc_1 + bc_2 + K = Y. \qquad (12)$$

Of the ten equations (3) to (12), only eight are independent, since (7) can be derived from (8) and (9), and (12) can be derived from (4), (5), (8), (9), (10) and (11). These eight independent equations can determine eight unknowns, c_1, c_2, w, r, K, S, L and Y.

Consider (12), which states that the total output is distributed between the consumption of younger population, that of the older population and capital maintenance. From (5) and (11), $bc_2 = (1 + r)K$, then from (3) $bc_1 = K$, while from (8), $Y = (1 + r)K/a$. Condition (12) is, therefore, changed into

$$K + (1 + r)K + K = (1 + r)K/a \qquad (13)$$

from which we have

$$r = (3 - 1/a)/(1/a - 1). \qquad (14)$$

Since $0 < a < 1$, the denominator of the right-hand side of (14) is positive. Therefore, r can be positive if and only if $a > \frac{1}{3}$. If $a = \frac{1}{3}$, which is by no means unlikely, however, we have to admit that the rate of interest does not exist in a stationary state.

What has become of Böhm-Bawerk's third cause for interest? The superiority of a more roundabout method of production in terms of capital–labor ratio implies the positive net marginal productivity of capital,

$$dY/dK - 1 = aY/K - 1 > 0 \tag{15}$$

since labor input is given as $\bar{L}$. If $a = \frac{1}{3}$, however, $aY/K = 1$ in a stationary state, in view of (8) and (14). The third cause ceases to operate when the economy reaches a stationary state, if $a = \frac{1}{3}$. Then, the first cause for interest also ceases to operate since $c_1 = c_2$, in view of (3).

What we have to admit is, then, that the rate of interest is zero in a stationary state if a parameter in the aggregate production function takes a certain critical value, i.e., $a = \frac{1}{3}$ in the case of our simplified model. If $a > \frac{1}{3}$ in our model, we can still insist that the rate of interest is made positive in a stationary state by Böhm-Bawerk's third cause and first cause of interest, the latter being generated by the former. It is well known, however, that Joseph A. Schumpeter (1883–1950), who studied economics at Vienna as a student of Böhm-Bawerk, insisted on the zero rate of interest in a stationary state as the general proposition.

Schumpeter was born in 1883 at Triesch in Austria (now in Czechoslovakia). After graduating from the University of Vienna in 1906, he was appointed to the chair of Political Economy at the University of Czernowitz in 1909, and at the University of Graz in 1911. He published *Wesen und Hauptinhalt der theoretischen Nationalökonomie* in 1908, *Theorie der wirtschaftlichen Entwicklung* in 1912, and *Epochen der Dogmen- und Methodengeschichte* in 1914. Although he started his study of economics at Vienna, it is clear that he was much more influenced by Walras than by the Austrians. In 1919, Schumpeter was named Austrian Minister of Finance, the same office his teacher Böhm-Bawerk had held, but he resigned after six months. He then became president of the Biedermann Bank, which went bankrupt in 1924. Returning to academic life, Schumpeter was first invited to a chair at the University of Bonn and then went to Harvard in 1932, where he stayed. *Business Cycle* was published in 1939, followed by *Capitalism, Socialism and Democracy* in 1942. Schumpeter died in 1950, with the manuscript of *History of Economic Analysis* left to be published in 1954.

Schumpeter [36, p. 175] called the following three propositions the basis of his theory of interest: (1) Interest as a great social phenomenon is a product of development. (2) It flows from entrepreneurial profit. (3) It does not adhere to concrete goods. Being "a product of development", interest does not exist in a stationary state. Although Schumpeter later admitted the existence of some interest in a stationary state [37, pp. 105–106], it was from the point of view of realism, and not from the point of view of theory or principle. How, then, can Schumpeter deny the existence of the rate of interest in principle in a stationary state? His reasons can be seen from the following argument:

> It also makes no difference to an individual firm whether it produces consumption or production goods. In both cases it disposes of its products in the same way, receives, under the hypothesis of completely free competition, a payment corresponding to the value of its land or labor services, and nothing else. If we choose to call the manager or owner of a business 'entrepreneur,' then he would be an *entrepreneur faisant ni benefice ni perte*, without special function and without income of a special kind. If the possessors of produced means of production were called 'capitalists', then they could only be producers, differing in nothing from other producers, and could no more than the others sell their products above the costs given by the total of wages and rents. (Schumpeter [36, pp. 45–46].)

In the footnote to an *entrepreneur faisant ni benefice ni perte*, Schumpeter said that it is a construction of Walras. Why can a Walrasian entrepreneur make no profit at equilibrium? It is because he always expands production if there is a positive profit in *tâtonnement*. If a possessor of produced means of production similarly increases his stock whenever it has a positive net marginal productivity, there is certainly no positive rate of interest at equilibrium. A possessor of produced means of production can, however, increase his stock only by reducing his current consumption and increasing his saving. The problem is, therefore, whether the level of capital stock which makes its net marginal productivity zero is identical to the level of capital stock which individuals wish to maintain through their optimal consumption-saving behavior at the zero rate of interest. In our model given above, the level of the capital stock individuals wish to maintain at $r = 0$ is $\frac{1}{3}$ of the level of output, as is seen from the left-hand side of (12) and (13). The level of capital stock which makes the net marginal productivity zero is a times the level of output, in view of (15). They are not identical, unless a is $\frac{1}{3}$.

As we have done, Schumpeter also dismissed Böhm-Bawerk's second cause for interest. "Of the famous three reasons upon which he bases the value premium on present purchasing power, I reject only one: the "discounting" of future enjoyments, so far as Böhn-Bawerk asks us to accept it as a cause not itself requiring any explanation" (Schumpeter [36, p. 158]). If the representative individual of a stationary population has an infinite time horizon, then, his level of consumption has to be stationary in a stationary economy and a stationary state cannot be maintained with a positive rate of interest, since the positive rate of interest necessarily induces an increase in capital stock through saving. An infinite time horizon implies, however, that an individual takes into consideration not only his own utility, but also those of future generations. It is natural for a rational individual, then, to discount the significance of the utility of future generations in comparison with that of his own utility and to discount more for the more remote generations. This is, however, to re-introduce the second cause of Böhm-Bawerk. If we continue to dismiss the second cause, therefore, we have to assume that the representative individual has a finite time horizon.[17] He may not, then, increase his saving even if the rate of interest is positive, and the capital stock may remain unchanged with a positive net marginal productivity in a stationary state, in spite of Schumpeter's argument to the contrary.[18]

As far as the case of a stationary economy is concerned, therefore, we may conclude that Böhm-Bawerk was right, rather than Schumpeter. To consider the more positive aspect of Schumpeter's theory of interest, however, we have to leave the case of a stationary state and turn to the case of a growth equilibrium. Empirical investigations of the economic growth in the developed industrialized capitalist economies since the second half of the nineteenth century have found the following so-called "stylized facts" of economic growth:[19] (1) The investment–output ratio is constant. (2) The capital–output ratio is constant. (3) The capital–labor and output–labor ratios are rising at a constant rate. (4) The rate of interest is constant. (5) The real wage rate is rising. (6) The relative shares of capital and labor are constant.

Let us now introduce a growth factor into our model. Suppose that $\bar{L}$ signifies not the number of laborers but the efficiency units of labor and $\bar{L}$ is assumed to increase steadily at the rate of g, not because the labor population increases but because the efficiency of labor is increased by the introduction of more efficient technology. Consider a balanced growth of all the quantities, Y, K, S, L, c_1 and c_2 at the same growth rate g while the absolute price level is assumed to be constant, so that we still have $p_0 = p_1 = p_2 = 1$ and the wage for the efficiency unit of labor, w, is kept unchanged through time. It is easily seen that all the stylized facts of economic growth are realized on such a balanced growth path.[20] All the growing quantities should now be dated as $\bar{L}(t)$, $Y(t)$,

---

[17] In spite of Haberler [8], a finite horizon does not imply the second cause of Böhm-Bawerk. It is rather an infinite horizon that is consistent with the second cause.

[18] The problem is, therefore, not whether the marginal net productivity of capital is positive for any, possibly very large, amount of capital, but whether it is positive for an equilibrium amount of capital in a stationary state.

[19] The stylized facts are originally due to Kaldor [18]. See Burmeister [6, pp. 46, 291].

[20] It is easily seen that facts (1) and (2) are realized. Since the labor population is constant, while capital and output are increasing, fact (3) is also realized. While the wage for the efficiency unit is constant, the real wage for a laborer is rising, since prices remain constant and labor efficiency is increasing, i.e., the stylized fact (5). Finally the rate of interest is constant (fact (4)), while both $w\bar{L}$ and rK increase at the rate of g, so that we observe that (6) is satisfied.

$K(t)$, $S(t)$, $L(t)$, $c_1(t)$, and $c_2(t)$ in equations (3) to (12), and the equations (6), (7), (8) and (12) should be modified into

$$Y(t) = [K(t)/(1+g)]^a L(t)^{(1-a)} \tag{6'}$$

$$Y(t) - wL(t) = (1+r)K(t)/(1+g) \tag{7'}$$

$$aY(t) = (1+r)K(t)/(1+g) \tag{8'}$$

$$bc_1(t) + bc_2(t)/(1+g) + S(t) = Y(t), \tag{12'}$$

since $K(t-1) = K(t)/(1+g)$ and $c_2(t-1) = c_2(t)/(1+g)$. Still (7)′ can be derived from (8)′ and (9), and (12)′ can be derived from (4), (5), (8)′, (9), (10) and (11). Eight unknowns, $c_1(t)$, $c_2(t)$, w, r, $K(t)$, $S(t)$, $L(t)$ and $Y(t)$, are determined by eight independent equations among ten equations, (3) to (5), (6)′, (7)′, (8)′, (9) to (11) and (12)′, when $\bar{L}(t)$ is given.

While $bc_2(t) = (1+r)\ S(t)$ and $bc_1(t) = S(t)$ from (3) and (5), $Y(t) = (1+r)\ S(t)/a(1+g)$ from (8)′ and (11). Condition (12)′ is, therefore, changed into

$$(1+g) + (1+r) + (1-g) = (1+r)/a \tag{13'}$$

from which we have

$$(1+r) = 2(1+g)/(1/a - 1). \tag{14'}$$

If we assume that $1/a = 3$ so that $r = 0$ in (14), we now have $r = g > 0$ from (14)′ here.

If the rate of interest is zero in a stationary state, it is positive and identical to the growth rate in a balanced growth equilibrium induced by a steady growth of labor productivity. The reason for the existence of a positive rate of interest is that the increase in the supply of capital is constantly lagging behind the growth of the productive power of labor due to technological progress. Such an economic growth may be identified with Schumpeter's development, which is defined as follows:[21]

> By "development," therefore, we shall understand only such changes in economic life as are not forced upon it from without but arise by its own initiative, from within.... Nor will the mere growth of the economy, as shown by the growth of population and wealth, be designated here as

---

[21] If the development is financed by the creation of purchasing power by banks (Schumpeter [36, p. 73]), the price level may not be unchanged. Suppose the supply of money and therefore prices are increased at the rate i. The wage w is now dated as $w(t)$ and changes at the rate i, while prices are also dated and change at the same rate in such a way that $p_0(t)(1+i) = p_1(t)$, $p_1(t)(1+i) = p_2(t)$. From the point of view of the rate of interest, the only relevant change is that the left-hand side of (14)′ is now $(1+r)/1(1+i)$, so that the real rate of interest is equal to the rate of growth if $1/a = 3$.

a process of development. For it calls forth no qualitatively new phenomena, but only processes of adaptation of the same kind as the changes in
the natural data.... To produce means to combine materials and forces
within our reach.... Development in our sense is then defined by the
carrying out of new combinations. This concept covers the following...
cases.... (2) The introduction of a new method of production, that is one
not yet tested by experience in the branch of manufacture concerned, which
need by no means be founded upon a discovery scientifically new,....
(Schumpeter [36, pp. 63, 65–66].)

In other words, the economic growth made possible by the introduction of
new technology is definitely a Schumpeterian development, since it is not
induced by the passive adjustment of an economy to changes in data
exogenously given such as an increase in the population, but caused by active
decisions to adopt technologies that have not been used before, from the stock
of technologies newly invented or already accumulated.

Schumpeter [36, p. 83] emphasized the distinction between two types of
individuals: mere managers and entrepreneurs. "The carrying out of new
combinations we call 'enterprise'; the individuals whose function is to carry
them out we call 'entrepreneurs' " [36, p. 74]. The reason for this distinction is
that 'carrying out a new plan and acting according to a customary one are
things as different as making a road and walking along it" [36, p. 85].
Schumpeter further insisted that entrepreneurs with new combinations
compete with other managers with old combinations. "New combinations are,
as a rule, embodied, as it were, in new firms which generally do not arise out of
the old ones but start producing besides them" [36, p. 66]. This co-existence of
two methods of production leads to the appearance of entrepreneurial profit.

The looms produce a greater physical product than the services of labor and
land contained in them could produce by the previous method, although in
the case of constant prices of production goods and products this latter
method would also enable production to be carried on without loss....
Hence there arises a difference between receipts, which are determined
according to the prices which were equilibrium, that is cost prices when
hand labor alone was being used, and outlays, which are now essentially
smaller per unit of product than for other business. (Schumpeter [36, p.
131].)

The surplus is realised, ... Now to whom does it fall? Obviously to the
individuals who introduced the loom into the circular flow [the stationary
state],... And what have they done? They have not accumulated any kind of

goods, they have created no original means of production, but have employed existing means of production differently, more appropriately, more advantageously. They have 'carried out new combinations.' They are entrepreneurs. And their profit, the surplus, to which no liability corresponds, is an entrepreneurial profit. (Schumpeter [36, p. 132].)

In our growth equilibrium, which is a Schumpeterian development, however, there is a positive rate of interest but no entrepreneurial profit, while Schumpeter insists on his second proposition of interest that 'interest must flow from entrepreneurial profit" [36, p. 175]. Perhaps we may conceive that entrepreneurs are followed by all the other managers very quickly, so that "the surplus of the entrepreneur in question and of his immediate followers disappears" [36, p. 132].

Of Schumpeter's three propositions of interest [36, p. 175], we can support the first proposition that interest is a product of development, since the rate of interest is positive in a steady development, even if it is zero in the circular flow, i.e., the stationary state. The second proposition that interest flows from entrepreneurial profit is a questionable one, if it implies that the rate of interest is zero when entrepreneurial profit disappears. Similarly, the third proposition that interest does not adhere to concrete goods is also open to objections. Certainly, the entrepreneurial profit does not adhere to concrete goods. But interest is a quasi-rent to capital goods whose supply is constantly in short of demand in a growth equilibrium. It seems that, in a sense, Schumpeter himself admitted this last point.[22]

If entrepreneurs were in a position to commandeer the producers' goods which they need to carry their new plans into effect, there would still be entrepreneurs' profit, but no part of it would have to be paid out by them as interest. . . . It is only because other people have command of the necessary producers' goods that entrepreneurs must call in the capitalist to help them to remove the obstacle which private property in means of production or the right to dispose freely of one's personal sevices puts in their way. (Schumpeter [36, p. 177].)

References

[1] Arvidsson, G., "On the Reasons for a Rate of Interest", *International Economic Papers*, 6(1956), pp. 23–33.

---

[22] Schumpeter's emphasis on entrepreneurs and banks may make one feel that the role of caitalists is not properly recognized. See Yagi [46] for a critical discussion of this point.

[2] Benassy, J.P., "A Neo-Keynesian Model of Price and Quantity Determination in Disequilibrium", *Equilibrium and Disequilibrium in Economic Theory*, pp. 511–544. G. Schwodiauer, ed., D. Reidel, 1978.

[3] Bernholz, P., M. Faber, and W. Reiss, "A Neo-Austrian Two Period Multi-sector Model of Capital", *Journal of Economic Theory*, 17(1978), pp. 38–50.

[4] Böhm-Bawerk, E.V., *Capital and Interest, Positive Theory of Capital*, G.D. Hunke and H.F. Sennholz, trs., Libertarian Press, 1959.

[5] Böhm-Bawerk, E.V., *Capital and Interest, Further Essays on Capital and Interest*, H.F. Sennholz, tr., Libertarian Press, 1959.

[6] Burmeister, D., *Capital Theory and Dynamics*, Cambridge University Press, 1980.

[7] Faber, M., *Introduction to Modern Austrian Capital Theory*, Springer, 1979.

[8] Haberler, G., "Schumpeter's Theory of Interest", *Review of Economics and Statistics*, 33(1951), pp. 122–128.

[9] Hahn, F.H., and T. Negishi, "A Theorem of Non-Tâtonnement Stability", *Econometrica*, 30(1962), pp. 463–469.

[10] Hawtrey, R.G., *Capital and Employment*, Longmans, Green and Co., 1952.

[11] Hayek, F., "On Menger", *The Development of Economic Thought*, pp. 526–553, H.W. Spiegel, ed., Wiley, 1952.

[12] Hicks, J.R., and W. Weber, eds., *Carl Menger and the Austrian School of Economics*, Oxford University Press, 1973.

[13] Hirayama, A., "Quality Uncertainty, Commerce and Money", *The Economic Studies Quarterly*, 34(1983), pp. 249–258.

[14] Hirshleifer, J., "A Note on the Böhm-Bawerk/Wicksell Theory of Interest", *Review of Economic Studies*, 34(1967), pp. 191–199.

[15] Hutchison, T.W., *A Review of Economic Doctrines 1870–1929*, Oxford University Press, 1953.

[16] Jevons, W.S., *The Theory of Political Economy*, Macmillan, 1888.

[17] Kaldor, N., "Annual Survey of Economic Theory: The Recent Controversy on the Theory of Capital", *Econometrica*, 5(1937), pp. 201–233.

[18] Kaldor, N., "Capital Accumulation and Economic Growth", *Theory of Capital*, F.A. Lutz and D.C. Hague, eds., Macmillan, 1961.

[19] Keynes, J.M., *The General Theory of Employment, Interest and Money*, Macmillan, 1936.

[20] Lange, O., "On the Economic Theory of Socialism", *Review of Economic Studies*, 4(1936–1937), pp. 53–71, 123–142.

[21] Lange, O., "The Foundation of Welfare Economics", *Econometrica*, 10(1942), pp. 215–228.

[22] Lavoie, D., *Rivalry and Central Planning*, Cambridge University Press, 185.

[23] Menger, C., "On the Origin of Money", *Economic Journal*, 2(1892), pp. 239–255.

[24] Menger, C., *Grundsätz der Volkswirtschaftslehre*, 2. Aufl., Holder–Pichler–Tempsky A.G. Wien, 1923.

[25] Menger, C., *Principles of Economics*, J. Dingwall and B.F. Hoselitz, trs., Free Press, 1950.

[26] Menger, C., *Ippanrironkeizaigaku* (Allegemeine theoretische Wirtschaftslehre), K. Yagi, T. Nakamura and Y. Nakajima, trs., Misuzu, 1982–1984.

[27] Menger, C., *Investigations into the Method of the Social Sciences with Special Reference to Economics*, J. Nock, tr., New York University Press, 1985.

[28] Nagatani, K., *Monetary Theory*, North-Holland, 1978.

[29] Negishi, T., "Welfare Economics and Existence of an Equilibrium for a Competitive Economy", *Metroeconomica*; 12(1960), pp. 92–97.

[30] O'Driscoll, G.P., "Money: Menger's Evolutionary Theory", *History of Political Economy*, 18(1986), pp. 601–616.

[31] Phelps, E.S., "Taxation of Wage Income for Economic Justice", *Quarterly Journal of Economics*, 87(1973), pp. 331–354.

[32] Polanyi, K., "Carl Menger's Two Meanings of 'Economic'", *Studies in Economic Anthropology*, pp. 16–24, G. Dalton, ed., American Anthropological Association, 1971.

[33] Rawls, J., *A Theory of Justice*, Oxford University Press, 1971.
[34] Samuelson, P.A., *Collected Scientific Papers*, 1, MIT Press, 1966.
[35] Samuelson, P.A., "Land and the Rate of Interest", *Theory for Economic Efficiency*, pp. 167–185, H.I. Greenfield, A.M. Stevenson, W. Hamovitch, and E. Rotwein, eds., MIT Press, 1979.
[36] Schumpeter, J.A., *The Theory of Economic Development*, R. Opie, tr., Harvard University Press, 1934.
[37] Schumpeter, J.A., *Business Cycles*, McGraw-Hill, 1939.
[38] Schumpeter, J.A., *History of Economic Analysis*, Oxford University Press, 1954.
[39] Spadaro, L.M., ed., *New Directions in Austrian Economics*, Sheed Andrews and McMeel, 1978.
[40] Sraffa, P., "The Law of Returns under Competitive Conditions", *Economic Journal*, 36 (1926), pp. 535–550.
[41] Uzawa, H., "A Note on the Menger–Wieser Theory of Imputation", *Zeitschrift für Nationalökonomie*, 18 (1958), pp. 318–334.
[42] Wicksell, K., *Lectures on Political Economy*, 1, E. Classen, tr., Kelly, 1977.
[43] Wieser, F., *Social Economics*, A.F. Hinrichs, tr., Adelphi, 1927.
[44] Wieser, F., "Das Wesen und der Hauptinhalt der Theoretischen Nationalökonomie, Kritische Glossen", *Gesammelte Abhandlungen*, Verlag von J.C. Mohl, Paul Siebeck, 1929, pp. 10–34.
[45] Wieser, F., *Natural Value*, C.A. Malloch, tr., G.E. Stechert, 1930.
[46] Yagi, K., "Schumpeter niokeru Shihonshugikatei no Tankyu (Capitalist Process in Schumpeterian Economics)", *Keizaironso* (The Economic Review, Kyoto University), 134 (1984), pp. 59–177.
[47] Yamada, Y., ed., *Kindaikeizaigaku no Seisei* (The Formation of Modern Economics), Kawade, 1955.

CHAPTER 9

JEVONS AND EDGEWORTH

1. Hermann Heinrich Gossen

As we started Chapter 7, i.e., the chapter of Walras, with the contributions made by Cournot, we may perhaps begin this chapter with a discussion of the significance of Gossen's work. This is because Jevons clearly admitted that Gossen had completely anticipated him as regards the general principles and method of the theory of economics, although at the same time he insisted that he never saw nor so much as heard any hint of the existence of Gossen's book, published in German in 1854, before 1878, i.e., before the publication of his own book in 1871 (Jevons [13, pp. xxxviii–xli]). We wish to emphasize particularly the fact that Gossen anticipated not only the theory of marginal utility of which Jevons shared the fame with Walras and Menger, but also Jevons's theory of exchange in the market, which was based on a view of the market quite different from that of Cournot and Walras, and was succeeded and developed by Edgeworth. After Gossen's work is reviewed in this section, sections 2 and 3 are devoted to discussing, respectively, the economic theories of Jevons and Edgeworth. Finally, in section 4, we shall consider the significance of these theories to the modern theories of mathematical economics and industrial organization.

Heinrich Wilhelm Joseph Hermann Gossen was born in 1810 at Duren, a small town near Cologne, which was then part of the Napoleonic Empire. His father was a government official, a tax collector in the French Administration and also in the Prussian Government reinstated after the collapse of the French Empire. Gossen studied law and public administration at the Universities of Bonn and Berlin, as his father insisted that he, too, should be a government official. Gossen's career in public service was not successful, however, comprising misplaced effort and disappointments. This may be attributed to his predilection for abstract studies. He retired from public life after 1847. He was first occupied with projects of insurance, but afterwards with his book entitled *Entwickelung der Gesetze des menschlichen Verkehrs, und der darous fliessenden Regeln für menschliches Handeln,* which was published in

1854. Although Gossen claimed honors in economic science equal to those of Copernicus in astronomy [9, p. cxlvii], this book was ignored even in Germany during the author's life, let alone in England. Gossen died in 1858, and it was in 1879 that Jevons recognized Gossen as one of the predecessors of the marginal revolution in general and of his own theory in particular.[1]

Gossen's *Entwicklung* was not originally divided into parts or chapters. As Walras [21] saw it, however, it falls naturally into two parts of approximately equal length. The first part is devoted to pure theory and comprises the laws of enjoyment and of work, the laws of exchange and the theory of rent (Gossen [9, Chapters 1–13, pp. 1–139]). The second part is devoted to applied theory and comprises rules of conduct pertaining to desires and pleasures, and the refutation of certain social errors concerning education, money, credit and property [9, Chapters 14–25, pp. 140–299]. In the first part, Gossen began with the so-called Gossen's first law of enjoyment that "*The magnitude [intensity] of pleasure decreases continuously if we continue to satisfy one and the same enjoyment without interruption until satiety is ultimately reached*" and derived from it the so-called Gossen's second law of enjoyment that "*Man obtains the maximum of life pleasure if he allocates all his earned money* E *between the various pleasures and determines the* e *in such a manner that the last atom of money spent for each pleasure offers the same amount [intensity] of pleasure.*"[2]

Walras [21] agreed with Jevons to recognize Gossen's laws of enjoyment and his theory of exchange which follows in the first part of *Entwicklung* as one of the predecessors of the marginal revolution. Walras insisted, however, that, unlike Jevons, he could lay claim to the originality of a good part of his discoveries, since neither Gossen nor Jevons had as much as touched the problem of the determination of the equilibrium price under the mechanism of free competition with the unity of the market price. According to Walras, the competitive equilibrium price is established as a result of the equalization of demand and supply, both of which are functions of the market price, common and identical to all exchangers in the market. The second part of *Entwicklung* is also evaluated highly by Walras [21], since it contains discussions on the nationalization of land.

From the point of view of this chapter, however, what is most interesting is Gossen's theory of exchange, which can be considered as the predecessor of the theory of Jevons, and also of Edgeworth.[3] Gossen considered the case of

---

[1] See Jevons [13, pp. xxxv–xlii, particularly, p. xxxviii]. See also the introduction written by Georgescu-Roegen to Gossen [9, pp. xi–cxlv] and Walras [21].

[2] See Gossen [9, pp. 6, 108–109, and xciv]. The *e* in the statement of the second law signifies the proportion of income for a specific pleasure. See [9, p. 308].

[3] See Gossen [9, pp. 95–100]. See also Jaffé [12] and Georgescu-Roegen's exposition [9, pp. cv–cxiii].

a two-individual two-good exchange, with highly special assumptions on the shape of the marginal utility curves and on the initially available quantities of goods to each individuals. It clearly shows, however, a view of markets which is different from that of Cournot and Walras discussed in Chapter 7, and is similar to those of Jevons and Edgeworth to be discussed in the following sections.

Suppose an individual *A* has initially the quantity *ad* of good I and another individual *B* owns the quantity *a'd'* of good II. In the lower part of Figure 9.1, the line *c'b'* signifies the marginal utility for *A* of good II which is obtained through the exchange with *B*, while the kinked line *a'bc* shows the marginal

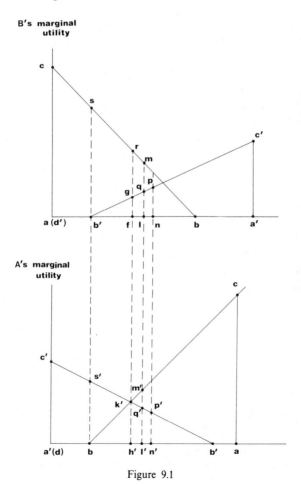

Figure 9.1

utility for A of good I which he gives up to obtain good II. It is assumed that the utility of good I is satiated for the individual A at the quantity of ab which is less than the quantity ad. Similarly, in the upper part, the line cb is the marginal utility curve for B of good I which is obtained through the exchange with A, while the kinked line $ab'c'$ signifies the marginal utility lost for b of good II which he gives to A in exchange for good I. It is assumed that the utility of good II is satiated for the individual B at the quantity of $a'b'$ which is less than the quantity $a'd'$.[4]

Gossen first assumes that one unit of good I is exchanged against one unit of good II and that each individual trades off exactly what is superfluous to him. In other words, the individual A offers the quantity bd of good I which is equal to the difference between his initial holding ad and the quantity ab at which his utility is satiated, while the individual B offers the quantity $b'd'$ of good II which is equal to the difference between his initial holding $a'd'$ and the quantity $a'b'$ at which his utility is satiated. A's utility gains from exchange can be seen in the lower part of Figure 9.1 as the area of the trapezoid $a'c's'b$, since he now has the quantity bd of good II, which is equal to the quantity $b'd'$. Similarly, in the upper part of Figure 9.1, the utility gains from exchange of B is the area of the trapezoid $acsb'$, since he now has the quantity $b'd'$ of good I, which is equal to the quantity bd.

Gossen recognizes "that the gain from barter is by no means exhausted by each individual trading off what is superfluous to him" [9, p. 97], since in Figure 9.1 it is clear that the marginal utility of the good to be received is higher, for both A and B, than that of the good to be surrendered if one more unit of good I is exchanged against one more unit of good II. From the point of view of the individual A, the most advantageous trade is at the point h' where two marginal utility lines cross, since

> up to this point, the value of the commodity given up remains smaller than what is obtained in exchange. Were the exchange to go beyond this, to the point l', the relation would be reversed.... When equal quantities are exchanged, the barter remains advantageous for A until the value of the last atoms of both objects now owned by A have become equal. (Gossen [9, p. 99].)

From the point of view of the individual B, however, the point f which corresponds to the point h' is by no means the most advantageous, since the marginal utility fr of good I is still higher than the marginal utility fg of good II.

[4] Figure 9.1 is based on Figure 7.2 on page 98 of Gossen [9]. The notations are slightly changed to simplify the exposition. Corresponding changes are also made in the quotations from Gossen [9] in the below.

B will be able to continue the equal quantity barter of two goods advantageously beyond the point at which the barter is most advantageous for *A*. "Such a continuation, however, would run contrary to the interest of *A*: yet the barter need not come to an end at *h'*. The extraordinary advantage that its continuation would bring to *B* may induce *B* to compensate *A* for the disadvantage suffered by the latter by giving up a greater quantity to *A* than *B* receives" [9, p. 99]. Suppose *A* gives up to *B*, in addition to the quantity $a'h'$ of the good I, also the quantity $h'l'$. The utility lost by this additional offer is the area of the trapezoid $h'l'm'k'$. If *A* is to receive for this quantity of good I only an equal quantity of good II, its value for *A* would be represented by the area of the trapezoid $h'l'q'k'$. In this case, *A* would clearly suffer a loss of value equal to the area of the triangle $k'q'm'$. *A* will be compensated for this loss, however, if *B*, instead of giving *A* just the quantity $h'l'$, actually gives him a quantity $h'n'$ such that the area of trapezoid $l'n'p'q' \geq$ the area of the triangle $k'q'm'$. "In the present case, *B* can proceed in this way with great advantage" [9, p. 99], since the quantity $h'n' = fn$ of good II represents for *B* the value of the trapezoid $fnpg$, while the quantity $fl = h'l'$ of good I, which *B* receives for its return, has for *B* the value represented by the area of the trapezoid $flmr$, and clearly the area of the trapezoid $gqmr$ is larger than the area of the trapezoid $lnpq$, in the upper part of Figure 9.1.

After this interesting argument that *A* and *B* can continue the process of exchange by changing the relative price of two goods, Gossen's argument becomes somewhat confused, as is pointed out by Jaffé [12] and Georgescu-Roegen (Gossen [9, p. cxi]). Then Gossen jumped to the conclusion that "after the exchange, each of the two commodities must be distributed between *A* and *B* in such a manner that the last atom one receives from the other will provide the same amount of value for both" [9, p. 100]. Unfortunately, this conclusion is neither interesting nor correct, since it does not make sense unless one admits a utilitarian interpersonal comparison of utility, and it is not necessarily possible to reach such a distribution of commodities through the process of exchange described by Gossen.

What is important, however, is that Gossen clearly offered a view of market which is different from that of Cournot and Walras, in the sense that the existence of unique market prices is not presupposed and the relative price is changing in the process of exchange even between the same pair of individuals. Of course, Gossen did not state correctly the final outcome of such a process of exchange. Nor did he make clear the relation between different views of the market. These are left to be considered by Jevons, who admitted that Gossen was his predecessor, and Edgeworth, who succeeded the Gossen–Jevons view of market, as will be seen in the following sections of this chapter.

2. Jevons's theory of exchange

William Stanley Jevons was born in Liverpool in 1835, the ninth child of Thomas, who was in the iron trade and interested in engineering innovations, and Mary Ann, a poet, who was the daughter of a learned historian, William Roscoe. He was raised in a Unitarian environment in which social and economic problems were often discussed. In 1850, he entered University College, London and studied mathematics, biology, chemistry and metallurgy. Because of the bankruptcy of his parental business, however, he accepted a position as an assayer to the mint in Sydney, where he remained for five years. In Australia, the study of meteorology attracted him strongly. As was pointed out by Keynes [14], furthermore, he was struck by the original ideas on economics that he later developed into an important part of the marginal revolution.

On his return to London in 1859, he resumed his studies at University College, but changed his specialization from mathematics and chemistry to logics and economics. Jevons sent a short paper entitled *Notice of a General Mathematical Theory of Political Economy* to Section F of the British Association for the Advancement of Science, which was read in his absence at the 1862 meeting at Cambridge, but attracted no attention and was not published. In 1866, he was appointed Professor of Logic and Mental and Moral Philosophy and Cobden Lecturer on Political Economy at Owens College, Manchester. In 1876, suffering from nervous and physical exhaustion, Jevons left Manchester, and was elected Professor of Political Economy in University College, London, a post he retained till 1880. Two years later, unfortunately, he met his death in a drowning accident.

Jevons's first book on economics is *The Coal Question; an Inquiry concerning the Progress of the Nation and the Probable Exhaustion of our Coal Mines* (1865). His natural law of social growth is based on an analogy to Malthus's law of population and, in a geometrical progression of industries, coal plays the role played in Malthus's theory by corn. The appearance of articles by Fleeming Jenkin prompted the publication of Jevons's *Theory of Political Economy* (1871), which is developed from his paper read at the 1862 meeting of the British Association. Jevons is also well known for his life-long inductive studies of commercial fluctuations and prices, which are collected in *Investigations in Currency and Finance* (1884). His sunspot theory of commercial crises integrated earlier works on economic fluctuations and prices with his life-long interest in astronomy and meteorology. Finally, Jevons wrote many books on logic, the largest of which is *The Principles of Science, A Treatise on Logic and Scientific Method* (1874).

The Theory of Political Economy [13] consists of a Preface to the first edition, a Preface to the second edition, eight chapters and two appendices. In the Preface to the first edition (1871), Jevons declared his intention "to treat Economy as a Calculus of Pleasure and Pain" [13, p. vii], while in the Preface to the second edition (1879), he stated that "the question is not so much whether the theory given in this volume is true, but whether there is really any novelty in it" [13, p. xviii], and frankly admitted the existence of his many predecessors, including Gossen. Chapter I is the Introduction, which starts with the declaration that "*value depends entirely upon utility*" [13, pp. 1–2] against the then prevailing labor theory of value. Jevons argues

> that Economics, if it is to be a science at all, must be a mathematical science, . . . , *simply because it deals with quantities.* . . . The theory consists in applying the differential calculus to the familiar notions of wealth, utility, value, demand, supply, capital, interest, labour, and all the other quantitative notions belonging to the daily operations of industry. (Jevons, [13, pp. 3–47].)

The next two chapters are respectively entitled "Theory of Pleasure and Pain" and "Theory of Utility". "Whatever can produce pleasure or prevent pain *may* possess utility" [13, p. 41]. Jevons made the distinction between total and marginal utilities. "We must now carefully discriminate between the *total utility* arising from any commodity and the utility attaching to any particular portion of it" [13, p. 49]. The marginal utility is called the *final degree of utility* and is defined "as meaning the degree of utility of the last addition, or the next possible addition of a very small, or infinitely small, quantity to the existing stock" [13, p. 55]. Then, the so-called second law of Gossen is derived in the discussion on the distribution of commodity in different uses. "We must . . . have the *final degrees of utility* in the two uses equal" [13, p. 65].

Chapter IV of Jevons's *Theory* is "Theory of Exchange". After the definition of a trading body and the argument on the law of indifference, Jevons demonstrates the proposition which is called "the keystone of the whole Theory of Exchange, and of the principal problems of Economics" [13, p. 103], by using the so-called equations of exchange which we shall discuss in detail below. The supply of labor is considered in Chapter V in terms of the painfulness of labor and the utility of the commodity produced by the application of labor. This is, therefore, not so much the theory of labor supply as the theory of production.[5] After the theory of rent is discussed in Chapter VI, Chapter VII is devoted to considering the theory of capital. The rate of

---

[5] For Jevons's theory of production, see Pagano [18, pp. 77–81] and Walras [21].

interest of capital is defined as "*the rate of increase* [*with respect to* "*the interval of abstinence*"] *of the produce divided by the whole produce*" [13, p. 267]. Chapter VIII is entitled "Concluding Remarks".

Although Jevons first believed that he discovered the concept of marginal utility, he later recognized the existence of his predecessors, such as Dupuit and Gossen. Therefore, the original contribution, if any, of Jevons should be sought, not in the theory of utility (Chapter III of his *Theory*), but in the theory of exchange (Chapter IV of *Theory*). According to Fisher [8, pp. 68, 98, 155], however, Jevons's model in his discussion on the distribution of commodity in different uses (in Chapter III of *Theory*) is the initial model with the hard core of his research programme, from which a series of other models are derived.

Let s be the whole stock of some commodity, and let it be capable of two distinct uses. Then we may represent the two quantities appropriated to these uses by x_1 and y_1, it being a condition that $x_1 + y_1 = s$. ... Let Δu_1, Δu_2, be the increments of utility, which might arise respectively from consuming an increment of commodity in the two different ways. When the distribution is completed, we ought to have $\Delta u_1 = \Delta u_2$; or at the limit we have the equation

$$du_1/dx = du_2/dy \tag{1}$$

which is true when x, y are respectively equal to x_1, y_1. We must, in other words, have the *final degree of utility* in the two uses equal. (Jevons [13, pp. 64–65].)

Soon we shall see that Jevons's model for the equations of exchange is based on this initial model for Gossen's second law, in such a way that Jevons's view of the equilibrium of exchange in the market is similar to that of Gossen but different from those of Cournot and Walras. Before considering Jevons's equations of exchange, however, we have to discuss two concepts, i.e., the trading body and the law of indifference, both of which are very important if we are to understand the true implications of Jevons's theory of exchange.

By a *trading body* I mean, in the most general manner, any body either of buyers or sellers. The trading body may be a single individual in one case; it may be the whole inhabitants of a continent in another; it may be the individuals of a trade diffused through a country in a third. England and North America will be trading bodies if we are considering the corn we receive from America in exchange for iron and other goods. The continent of Europe is a trading body as purchasing coal from England. The farmers of

England are a trading body when they sell corn to the millers, and the millers both when they buy corn from the farmers and sell flour to the bakers. (Jevons [13, pp. 95–96].)

Though some historians of economic thought are critical of Jevons's use of the term, trading body, (Blaug [2, p. 312], and Howey [11, p. 52]), similar concepts have very often been used in various fields of economic theory. For example, as Jevons himself suggested, countries are regarded as trading bodies and the utility function, or indifference map, of a country is considered in the theory of international trade.[6] Another example concerns the models used in theories of the microeconomic foundations of macroeconomics, in which the representative or aggregate household and representative or aggregate firm exchange labor services and consumers' goods (Benassy [1]; Malinvaud [16]).

The reason why Jevons uses such an artificial invention to explain exchange is that the behavior of the aggregate or average person is much more stable than that of an individual person. In other words, differential calculus can only be used for the case of the aggregate or average person.

The use of an average, or, what is the same, an aggregate result, depends upon the high probability that accidental and disturbing cases will operate, in the long run, as often in one direction as the other so as to neutralize each other. Provided that we have a sufficient number of independent cases, we may then detect the effect of any tendency, however slight. Accordingly, questions which appear, and perhaps are quite indeterminate as regards individuals, may be capable of exact investigation and solution in regard to great masses and wide averages. (Jevons [13, p. 17].)

A single individual does not vary his consumption of sugar, butter, or eggs from week to week by infinitesimal amounts, according to each small change in the price. He probably continues his ordinary consumption until accident directs his attention to a rise in price, and he then, perhaps, discontinues the use of the articles altogether for a time. But the aggregate, or what is the same, the average consumption, of a large community will be found to vary continuously or nearly so. (Jevons [13, pp. 96–97].)

The law of indifference, which insists that there is only one price for each commodity in equilibrium, is necessary, as we shall see, to derive Jevons's equations of exchange from his initial model of distribution of commodity in different uses. Jevons explains that the law is established only at the equilibrium through the arbitrage behavior of sellers and buyers. In other

[6] See Chipman [3] for conditions necessary for the existence of social indifference curves.

words, it is not to be presupposed, in the case of markets he has in mind, unlike in the case of the well-organized markets considered by Cournot and Walras.

> If, in selling a quantity of perfectly equal and uniform barrels of flour, a merchant arbitrarily fixed different prices on them, a purchaser would of course select the cheaper ones .... Hence follows what is undoubtedly true, with proper explanations, that *in the same open market, at any one moment, there cannot be two prices for the same kind of article.* (Jevons [13, pp. 98–99].)

> It follows that *the last increments in an act of exchange must be exchanged in the same ratio as the whole quantities exchanged.* Suppose that two commodities are bartered in the ratio of x for y; then every mth part of x is given for the mth part of y, and it does not matter for which of the mth parts ... even an infinitely small part of x must be exchanged for an infinitely small part of y, in the same ratio as the whole quantities. This result we may express by stating that the increments concerned in the process of exchange must obey the equation $dy/dx = y/x$. (Jevons [13, pp. 102–103].)

Behind this "statical view of the equation" there must be a dynamic process of trading. What Jevons had in mind was a piecemeal exchange process, since "dynamically we could not treat the ratio of exchange otherwise than as the ratio of dy and dx, infinitesimal quantities of commodity" [13, p. 102]. In other words, the equation of the law of indifference

$$dy/dx = y/x \tag{2}$$

is an equilibrium condition which is not established "when equilibrium is not attained."

Now we are ready to consider the proposition which contains "the keystone of the whole theory of exchange, and of the principal problems of economics." "*The ratio of exchange of any two commodities will be the reciprocal of the ratio of the final degrees of utility of the quantities of commodity available for consumption after the exchange is completed*" [13, p. 103].

> Let us now suppose that the first [trading] body, A, originally possessed the quantity a of corn, and that the second [trading] body, B, possessed the quantity b of beef. As the exchange consists in giving x of corn for y of beef, ... the quantities exchanged satify two equations, ...
>
> $$F_1(a-x)/G_1(y) = y/x = F_2(x)/G_2(b-y) \tag{3}$$
>
> ... The two equations are sufficient to determine the results of exchange; for there are only two unknown quantities concerned, namely, x and y, the quantities given and received. (Jevons [13, pp. 107–108].)

Equations (3) are the so-called Jevons's equations of exchange, in which the cumbersome notations originally used by Jevons are replaced by more ordinary ones, and F_1 and G_1, and F_2 and G_2, respectively, denote A's final degrees of utility of corn and beef, and B's final degrees of utility of corn and beef. These equations are derived from the equations of the second law of Gossen, (1), which can be rewritten in this case as

$$F_1(a-x)/G_1(y)=dy/dx \tag{4}$$

and

$$F_2(x)/G_2(b-y)=dy/dx, \tag{5}$$

since "different uses can be expanded to include exchange as a possibility (Jevons [13, pp. 107–108]; Fisher [8, p. 159]). In terms of the Edgeworth box diagram, which we shall explain in the next section, equations (4) and (5) are conditions for x and y to be located on the so-called contract curve. The equations of exchange (3) are, then, derived from these conditions and the law of indifference (2), and determine the equilibrium point (x, y) on the contract curve.

Walras's regard for Jevons's equations of exchange (3) was not high, since, in his letter to Jevons, Walras pointed out that Jevons had failed to derive "the equation of effective demand as a function of price, which ... is so indispensable for the solution of the problem of the determination of equilibrium price" (Walras [23, p. 397]; [22 pp. 205–206]). This is not surprising, since the view of market of Walras, who followed Cournot, is different from that of Jevons, who followed Gossen. Walras presupposed the existence of market prices which competitive traders always accept as data, while Jevons tried to justify this supposition by explaining market prices as the equilibrium ratio of exchange resulting from a process of freely competitive exchange.

Walras defines the equilibrium as the equality of demand and supply, both of which are functions of the given market price. Since the law of indifference is simply presupposed, all the individual traders in the market take the identical price, even in disequilibrium situations. One might suppose a well-organized, highly institutionalized market in which the specialized auctioneer determines the market price and changes it according to the excess demand or supply generated by price-taking traders, as the incarnation of the law of supply and demand.

For Jevons, on the other hand, demand and supply are trivially equal even in disequilibrium situations.

Mill's equation ... states that the quantity of a commodity given by A is equal to the quantity received by B. This seems at first sight to be a mere truism, for this equality must necessarily exist if any exchange take place at all .... We may regard x as the quantity demanded on one side and supplied on the other; similarly, y is the quantity supplied on the one side and demanded on the other. (Jevons [13, pp. 109, 110].)

Equilibrium is defined by Jevons by the law of indifference, which is established by arbitrage of different exchange ratios, which exist in a single market at disequilibrium.

One may argue that Cournot and Walras also emphasized the importance of arbitrage (Morishima [17, pp. 18–19]). In the case of three or more commodities, Walras certainly insists that "we do not have perfect or general market equilibrium unless the price of one of any two commodities in terms of the other is equal to the ratio of the prices of these two commodities in terms of any third commodity" (Walras [22, p. 157]). As Morishima admitted, however, "in the two-commodity case the arbitrage theory is trivial, because there is, of course, no arbitrage via a third commodity" [17, p. 20]. In other words, Walras only considered arbitrage among different markets and did not consider arbitrage in a single market where two commodities are exchanged.

Although Walras and Jevons viewed the process of market differently, the resulting equilibrium is identical, since the identical set of x and y is determined both by Walras's condition of demand and supply equality and by Jevons's condition of equations of exchange (3). In other words, in spite of Walras, Jevons arrived at the identical equilibrium which Walras considered, even though Jevons failed to derive the equation of effective demand as a function of price, which is, therefore, not necessarily indispensable for the solution of the equilibrium price or equilibrium exchange ratio y/x. While Walras discussed in detail the process of *tâtonnement* by which the equilibrium is established (see Chapter 7, section 4 of this book), however, Jevons unfortunately did not make clear how the equilibrium (3) is established by the process of arbitrage among traders. The problem is left to Edgeworth, whose contributions we shall consider in the next section.

3. Edgeworth's *Mathematical Psychics*

While Walras and Menger founded, respectively, the Lausanne and the Austrian schools in the marginal revolution, it has been said that Jevons, who revolted against the classical school in its home country, was isolated and established no school of his own. The problems raised by Jevons were, however, succeeded to and solved by Edgeworth, who is now regarded, with

Walras, as one of the two founding fathers of the equilibrium theory of modern mathematical economics.[7]

Francis Ysidro Edgeworth was born in 1845 in Edgeworthstown in County Longford, Ireland, where the famous family, whose name was taken from Edgeware, formerly Edgeworth, in Middlesex, had settled in the reign of Elizabeth I. His father died when he was two years old. After studying at Trinity College, Dublin, Edgeworth entered Exeter College, Oxford in 1867, and then transferred to Magdalen Hall and to Balliol, where he obtained a first class degree in *literae humaniares*. In 1877, he was called to the bar by the Inner Temple, and published his first book, *New and Old Methods of Ethics: or 'Physical Ethics' and 'Methods of Ethics'*. While applying unsuccessfully for a professorship of Greek and philosophy, he gave lectures on English language, literature, logic, the mental and moral sciences, and metaphysics. In 1881 he published *Mathematical Psychics: An Essay on the Application of Mathematics to the Moral Sciences*. Marshall reviewed this book – "one of the two only reviews which Marshall ever wrote, the other being of Jevons's *Theory of Political Economy*" (Keynes [15, p. 255]).

During the 1880s, Edgeworth worked at a considerable rate on mathematical statistics, so that he received more recognition for his statistical works than for his writings on economics. His third and final book *Metreike: or the Method of Measuring Probability and Utility* was published in 1887. In 1890, he succeeded Thorold Rogers in the Tooke Chair of Economics and Statistics at King's College, London. In the next year, 1891, he again succeeded Rogers, this time to become Drummond Professor of Political Economy at Oxford, and was elected a Fellow of All Souls, where he remained for the rest of his life. He retired from the Oxford professorship in 1922. The British Economic Association, which in 1902 became the Royal Economic Society, was founded in 1890 and the publication of *Economic Journal* was started with Edgeworth as the first editor. Edgeworth was continuously responsible for it as editor or co-editor from the first issue in 1891 to his death in 1926. For the last fifteen years, Keynes was a co-editor to Edgeworth.[8]

Although he published many articles and some monographs, such as *Mathematical Psychics*, Edgeworth never attempted to write and publish a treatise, such as Marshall's *Principles of Economics*. When Keynes "asked him why he had never ventured on a treatise he answered, with his characteristic smile and chuckle, that large scale enterprise, such as treatise

---

[7] "We show how two different approaches to the solution of the exchange problem lead, in large economies, to essentially the same result. The two approaches derive from ideas developed by Edgeworth and Walras" (Hildenbrand and Kirman [10, p. v]).

[8] For the life and work of Edgeworth, see Creedy, [4, pp. 7–22] and Keynes [15, pp. 251–266].

and marriage, had never appealed to him" (Keynes [15, p. 262]). In 1925 the Royal Economic Society published, under Edgeworth's own editorship, his *Papers Relating to Political Economy* in three substantial volumes, which comprise the whole of Edgeworth's papers – articles and reviews – on economics, which he himself wished to see preserved. The articles are grouped into six sections, "Value and Distribution", "Monopoly", "Money", "International Trade", "Taxation" and "Mathematical Economics". The reviews included are those on books written by, among others, N. Keynes, Marshall, Sidgwich, Böhm-Bawerk, I. Fisher, Bortkiewicz, Pigou and Cassel.

In his *New and Old Methods of Ethics* (1877), Edgeworth attempted first to synthesize the various approaches and then to apply mathematical techniques to the problem of determining the optimal utilitarian distribution. Creedy [4, p. 34] pointed out the important fact that Edgeworth already used Lagrangean multiplier methods and the calculus of variations extensively in this book, a fact which has been overlooked in the literature on the early history of mathematical economics. Keynes commented on this book that "quotations from the Greek tread on the heels of the differential calculus, and the philistine reader can scarcely tell whether it is a line of Homer or a mathematical abstraction which is in course of integration" [15, p. 257].

The same comment may also be applied to Edgeworth's *Mathematical Psychics* (1881). Unlike contemporary readers of Edgeworth, modern readers may find it difficult to read, not mathematically, but literarily, since Edgeworth often used Greek, and occasionally Latin, in the middle of arguments and also often quoted short passages from English literature, without giving the sources. Fortunately, however, Creedy [4, pp. 135–160] provides excellent notes on *Mathematical Psychics*, in which Greek or Latin phrases are translated into English and the sources of most of the literary quotations are traced. After a brief introductory description of the contents, Part 1 of *Mathematical Psychics* is devoted to justifying the use of mathematics in economics where numerical data are not available. Part 2 is concerned with the Calculus of Pleasure and "may be subdivided, namely Economics and Utilitarian Ethics. The economical Calculus investigates the equilibrium of a system of hedonic forces each tending to maximum individual utility; the Utilitarian Calculus the equilibrium of a system in which each and all tend to maximum universal utility" (Edgeworth [6, pp. 15–16]).

In "Economical Calculus", Edgeworth started with the definition that the first principle of "Economics is that every agent is actuated only by self interest" [6, p. 16]. Contract is defined as the species of action that the agent acts with "the consent of others affected by his actions" [6, pp. 16–17]. "The problem to which attention is specially directed ... is: *How far contract is indeterminate* – an inquiry of more than theoretical importance, if it show not only that indeterminateness tends to prevent[9] widely, but also in what direction an escape from its evils is to be sought" [6, p. 20].

Demonstrations. – The general answer is – (α) Contract without competition is indeterminate, (β) Contract with *perfect* competition is perfectly determinate, (γ) Contract with more or less perfect competition is less or more indeterminate. (α) Let us commence with almost the simplest case of contract, – two individuals, X and Y, whose interest depends on two variable quantities, which they are agreed not to vary without mutual consent. Exchange of two commodities is a particular case of this kind of contract. Let x and y be the portions interchanged, as in Professor Jevons's example. (Edgeworth [6, p. 20].)

To consider "Professor Jevons's example", Edgeworth first introduced the now famous concepts of the contract curve and indifference curves. Since "his presentation can hardly be described as transparent" and "the notation used by Edgeworth is not helpful" (Creedy [4, p. 55]), however, let us rather consider the problem by using the so-called Edgeworth box diagram, which was actually adumbrated by Pareto "twelve years after the publication of Edgeworth's *Mathematical Psychics*" (Jaffé [12]).

Jevons's equations of exchange to determine the quantities exchanged, discussed in the previous section, are satisfied at point E in Figure 9.2, the

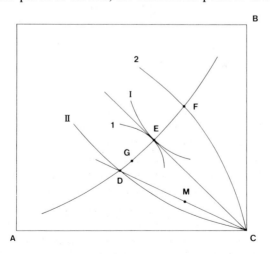

Figure 9.2

[9]"To prevent" should read "to be present". See Creedy [4, p. 138].

so-called Edgeworth box diagram, where the quantity of corn is measured horizontally, that of beef vertically, the quantities of commodity available to the trading body *A* are measured with the origin at *A*, those available to the trading body *B* with the origin at *B*, and point *C* denotes the initial allocation of commodities. Curves I, II, etc. are indifference curves of trading body *A* and curves 1, 2, etc. are those of trading body *B*. The common tangent to two indifference curves at *E* passes through point *C*, so that Jevons's equations of exchange are satisfied at *E*. The curve *DEF* is the contract curve which is a locus of points where the indifference curves of the two bodies are tangent to each other. "At what point then will they refuse to move at all? When their *lines of indifference* are coincident (and *lines of preference* not only coincident, but in opposite directions)" (Edgeworth [6, p. 22]).[10]

If each trading body consists of only a single individual, i.e., in the case of isolated exchange or bilateral monopoly, the equilibrium point is indeterminate in the sense that any point on the contract curve between *D* and *F* is a stable outcome of exchange.

> This simple case brings clearly into view the characteristic evil of indeterminate contract, *deadlock*, undecidable opposition of interest, ... It is the interest of both parties that there should be *some settlement*, one of the contracts represented by contract-curve between limits. But *which* of these contracts is arbitrary in the absence of arbitration, the interests of the two *adversâ pygnantia fronte* all along the contract curve. (Edgeworth [6, p. 29]).[11]

There is no reason why only *E* can be an equilibrium and Jevons's equations of exchange cannot always be satisfied in this case. Since Jevons said that "the trading body may be a single individual in one case" and considered the indeterminateness of equilibrium only in the case where a commodity is indivisible,[12] we have to admit that Jevons did not recognize the indeterminateness of bilateral monopoly. In view of Jevons's reason for using the trading body, i.e., the fact that the behavior of a group of persons is more stable than that of a single individual, however, Jevons should not have admitted the case of a single-individual trading body. Edgeworth was quite generous in this respect.

> ...the Jevonian 'law of indifference' has place only where there is

---

[10] The line of indifference is the slope of the indifference curve and defined on page 21 of Edgeworth [6]. "The...*line of preference*...is perpendicular to the line of indifference" (Edgeworth [6, p. 22]).

[11] "Adversâ pugnantia fronte" means "fighting face to face". Creedy [4, p. 139].

[12] See Jevons [13, pp. 96 and 130–134].

competition, and, indeed, *perfect* competition. Why, indeed, should an isolated couple exchange every portion of their respective commodities at the same rate of exchange? Or what meaning can be attached to such a law in their case? ... This consideration has not been brought so prominently forward in Professor Jevons's theory of exchange, but it does not seem to be lost sight of. His couple of dealers are, I take it, a sort of typical couple, clothed with the property of 'indifference,' whose origin in an 'open market' is so lucidly described; not naked abstractions like the isolated couples imagined by a De Quincey or Courcelle-Seneuil in some solitary region. Each is in Berkleian phrase a 'representative particular;' an individual dealer only is presented, but there is presupposed a class of competitors in the background. (Edgeworth [6. p. 109; see also p. 31].)

Having demonstrated that (α) contract without competition is indeterminate, Edgeworth proceeded to show that (γ) contract with more or less perfect competition is less or more indeterminate. Let us follow his discussions, again using Figure 9.2 and translating them into the language of the modern theory of games.[13] Suppose first that there are two identical (in taste and initial holding) individual traders in each trading body, i.e., trader A_1 and trader A_2 of type A and trader B_1 and trader B_2 of type B. It is evident that equal quantities of goods should be allocated to identical traders of the same type, after, for example, A_1 traded with B_1 and A_2 traded with B_2.

It is evident that there cannot be equilibrium unless (1) all the field is collected at one point; (2) that point is on the *contract-curve*. For (1) if possible let one couple be at one point, and another couple at another point. It will generally be the interest of the X of the one couple and the Y of the other to rush together, leaving their partner in the lurch. And (2) if the common point is not on the contract-curve, it will be the interest of *all parties* to descend to the contract-curve. (Edgeworth [6, p. 35].)

We can, therefore, still use Figure 9.2, by interpreting it as describing the trade between the representative traders of each trading body. Allocation D on the contract curve, which can be a stable outcome of exchange in the case of single individual trading bodies, can now be blocked by a coalition of A_1, A_2 and either of B_1 and B_2. Suppose A_1 and, say, B_1, who joins the coalition, keep the contract D between them while A_2 cancels the contract D with B_2, who does not join the coalition and returns to C. Thus, A_1, A_2 and B_1 can arrange by themselves in such a way that, whilst B_1 remains at point D, A_1 and A_2

---

[13] For modern expositions of Edgeworth's theorem, see Debreu and Scarf [5] and Hildenbrand and Kirman [10, pp. 18–23].

reach the mid-point M between D and C, thereby achieving a higher level of utility than at D. With some side-payments to B_1, all the traders joining the coalition (A_1, A_2, B_1) can be better off by themselves than they are at D, and the allocation D is blocked. Any allocation on the contract curve and close to D, say, G, can be blocked similarly by the same coalition. Similarly, allocation F or those allocations on the contract curve and close to F can be blocked by a coalition of both B_1 and B_2 and any one of A_1 and A_2.

It is clear that the case of two-individual trading bodies is more competitive than the case of the bilateral monopoly of a single-individual trading body. The range of possible contracts in the former is less indeterminate than in the latter, since some of the allocations possible in the latter can be blocked in the former. Allocations like H in Figure 9.3, however, cannot be blocked by the coalitions of three traders suggested by Edgeworth and belong, therefore, to the core, i.e., the set of stable allocations which cannot be blocked by coalitions of traders. The reason why H cannot be blocked is that at the mid-point between H and C traders of type A cannot achieve a higher level of utility than at H.

> In general for any number short of the *practically infinite* (if such a term be allowed) there is a finite length of contract curve ... at any point of which if the system is placed, it cannot by contract or recontract be displaced; that there are *an indefinite number of final settlements*, a quantity continually diminishing as we approach a perfect market. We are brought back again to case (β). (Edgeworth [6, p. 39].)

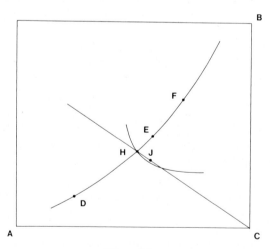

Figure 9.3

Let us now consider the case where there are infinitely many identical traders of type A and infinitely many identical traders of type B, to show that (β) contract with *perfect* competition is perfectly determinate. In this case, any allocation on the contract curve, except allocation E, can be blocked by a coalition of traders considered by Edgeworth. For example, consider the allocation H in Figure 9.3. This allocation can be blocked by a coalition formed by all the A traders and more than half but less than all the B traders. In the coalition some A traders still continue trade with B traders in the coalition and are located at H, while the rest of the A traders having no trade partners in the coalition are located at C. By increasing the number of B traders joining the coalition sufficiently and therefore increasing the number of A traders located at H, we can make the average allocation of A traders (some at H, some at C) sufficiently close to H, on the line CH, that it is located like J above the indifference curve passing through H. By reallocating among themselves, therefore, all the traders joining the coalition can be better off than they are at the allocation H, so that H is blocked by such a coalition. Similarly, any point between D and F where the common tangent to two indifference curves does not pass through the point C can be blocked by a coalition of traders, if necessary, by changing the role of A traders and B traders from those in the case of the allocation H. Obviously only the point E belongs to the core, i.e., the set of allocations which are not blocked by such a coalition, and therefore the equilibrium is determinate in this case. "Thus, proceeding by degrees from the case of two isolated bargainers to the limiting case of a perfect market, we see how *contract is more or less indeterminate according as the field is less or more affected with the first imperfection,* limitation of numbers" (Edgeworth [6, p. 42]).[14]

Since equilibrium is thus indeterminate in Edgeworth's theory of exchange except for the limiting case of infinitely large number of traders, "*competition requires to be supplemented by arbitration, and the basis of arbitration between self interested contractors is the greatest possible sum-total utility.* Thus the *economical* leads up to the *utilitarian calculus*" (Edgeworth [6, p. 56]).[15] Unlike the case of Pigou, who also considered utilitarian social welfare function,[16] in "Utilitarian Calculus", Edgeworth did not insist on equal distribution as the optimal income distribution.

[14] Besides the limitation of numbers, Edgeworth also discussed other imperfections such as the existence of combinations. Incidentally, "contract is more or less" should read "contract is less or more" in this quotation.

[15] For Edgeworth's justification of utilitarianism and its relation to contractarian neo-utilitarianism, see Creedy [4, pp. 81–85].

[16] "The economic welfare of a community is likely to be greater... the larger is the average share of the national dividend that accrues to the poor..." (Pigou [19, p. v]).

Thus *the distribution of means as between the equally capable of pleasure is* *equality; and generally is such that the more capable of pleasure shall have* *more means and more pleasure....* in the minds of many good men among the moderns and the wisest of the ancients, there appears a deeper sentiment in favour of aristocratical privilege – the privilege of man above brute, of civilized above savage, of birth, of talent, and of the male sex. This sentiment of right has a ground of utilitarianism in supposed difference of *capacity*. Capacity for pleasure is a property of evolution, as essential attribute of civilization. (Edgeworth [6, pp. 64, 77].)

4. Reflections on Edgeworth's theorem

As we saw in the previous section, Edgeworth proved a theorem that the equilibrium of exchange is determinate only in the case of perfect competition. This important theorem is called Edgeworth's equivalence theorem, since it shows the equivalence of two different approaches to the problem of exchange in the market, i.e., the Cournot-Walras approach and the Jevons-Edgeworth approach. In the Cournot-Walras approach, the law of indifference, i.e, the existence of the uniform market price, is presupposed, and competitive traders are assumed to be price takers. In the Jevons-Edgeworth approach, however, the law of indifference is established only at the equilibrium, through arbitrage activities of individual traders to take advantage of the existence of different prices in the same market. Individual traders are, therefore, not price takers, and are free to make contract at whatever price they like, to cancel it to make recontract at more favorable terms, and to organize a coalition to block existing contracts.

The assumptions made in the Cournot-Walras approach may not be realistic, unless there is an auctioneer, as in the case of well-organized markets. Edgeworth's equivalence theorem justifies Walrasian assumption, however, since it is not the assumption but the outcome that matters for a theory, and we can assume that traders behave as if they are price takers, even though traders are actually not price takers, provided that we have the same outcome as assured by Edgeworth. Walrasian theory based on the demand and supply functions can be safely applied to situations where traders are not price takers and are free to form and break coalitions in the process of bargaining as in the Jevons-Edgeworth approach, so that demand and supply functions do not, strictly speaking, make sense. Walras, who criticized Jevons for the lack of a clear concept of demand functions in the latter's equations of exchange, is thus helped by Edgeworth, who followed Jevons, to increase the relevancy of his theory.

Edgeworth's equivalence theorem is also called a limit theorem, since it is proved only for the limiting case where the number of traders is infinitely large on both sides of the market. In other words, the infinitely large number of traders is shown to be a sufficient condition for the outcome of the Jevons-Edgeworth bargaining process to be equivalent to that of perfect competition. A natural question is, then, whether it is also a necessary condition or not.

Following Farrell [7], let us consider the case of a duopoly where there are only two traders of one type and infinitely many traders of another type, although the total quantities of two goods are finite in the economy. Since equal quantities of goods should be allocated to identical traders of the same type, we can still use Edgeworth box diagrams, i.e., Figures 9.2 and 9.3, which now describe half of the economy, that of a duopolist and its infinitely many customers.

Suppose first that there are two B traders, B_1 and B_2, and infinitely many traders of type A. In Figures 9.2 and 9.3, BC is the quantity of the second good initially held by a B trader and AC is the sum of the quantities of the first good initially held by the half of A traders. Curves I, II, etc. in Figure 9.2 are aggregate indifference curves of A traders, as well as individual ones, which can be constructed if the identical individual indifference curves are homothetic, so that the marginal rate of substitution between two goods depends only on the ratio of the quantities of goods, and the Engel curve is a line through the origin (Chipman [3]).

An allocation H in Figure 9.3 can now be blocked by a coalition of one B trader and more than half but less than all of infinitely many A traders. All the A traders currently trading with the B_1 trader, who joins the coalition, also join the coalition and keep the contract H with B_1. Some A traders currently trading with B_2, who does not join the coalition, join the coalition and cancels the contract with B_2 to return to the initial point C. By sufficiently decreasing the number of the latter type A traders joining the coalitions and therefore increasing the number of A traders located at H, relative to those A traders located at C, we can make the average allocation of individual A traders in the coalition sufficiently close to that at the point H, on the line CH, so that it is like an allocation at J located above the indifference curve passing through H. By reallocating among themselves, therefore, all the A traders in the coalitions are better off than they are at the allocation H. With some side payments to B_1, who is located at H, all the traders joining the coalition can be better off than they are at H, so that H is blocked.

Suppose next that there are two A traders, A_1 and A_2, and infinitely many traders of type B. In Figures 9.2 and 9.3, then, AC is the quantity of the first good initially held by an A trader and BC is the sum of the quantities of the second good initially held by the half of B traders. Curves 1 and 2 in Figure 9.2 are the aggregate as well as the individual indifference curves of B traders. In this case an allocation H in Figure 9.3 can be blocked by a coalition of one A trader and the less than half of infinitely many B traders. Suppose A_1 joins the coalition. Those B traders also joining the coalition can keep trade with A_1 unchanged so that they can keep the same level of utility as enjoyed at the allocation H. A_1 cancels trade with those B traders who are not permitted to join the coalition, so that A_1 moves on HC from H toward C. Unless he cancels too many contracts with B traders, A_1 can be located at J above the indifference curve passing through H. By the reallocation among themselves, then, all the traders joining the coalition can be made better off than they are at the allocation H, so that H is blocked.

Similarly, any point between D and F on the contract curve where the common tangent to two indifference curves does not pass through the point C can be blocked by a coalition of traders, if necessary, by changing the roles of A traders and B traders from those in the case of the allocation H. Again, it is the point E only which belongs to the core allocation. In other words, even a duopoly market ends up with an equilibrium identical to that of perfect competition, if customers are infinitely many and free to organize coalitions.

If infinitely many customers behave as price takers so that their demand can be expressed as a function of price, duopolists will take advantage of it so that the outcome is different from that of perfect competition, as was discussed by Cournot (see Chapter 7, section1). In our case, however, even at point E where not only customers but also duopolists seem to behave as if they are price takers, customers are actually not price takers, so that there is no possibility of the price-making behavior of some traders to take advantage of the price-taking behavior of other traders, a problem that is considered by Roberts and Postlewaite [20].

Edgeworth's equivalence theorem is thus extended to the case of a duopoly in which the number of traders at one side of the market is only two, although the number of customers at the other side of the market is infinitely large. In the Jevons-Edgeworth process of bargaining, of course, it is assumed that there are no costs for traders to know about the rate of exchange in contracts made among other traders, to make contracts and to cancel them, and to organize coalitions to block contracts already established. If these costs of information, communication, transaction and organization are taken into consideration, the outcome of the Jevons-Edgeworth process may not be equivalent to that of Walrasian perfect competition. What is essential for Walrasian equilibrium with all its optimal properties is, therefore, not so much the infinity of the number of small traders on both sides of the market as the assumption of no cost for information, communication, transaction and organization.

In Cournot's model of an oligopoly (Chapter 7, section 1), an increase in the number of firms in the industry results in a lower equilibrium price and a larger consumers' surplus.[17] The allocative efficiency of the industry is, therefore, inversely related to the degree of concentration. The discussion in the above suggests, however, that the efficiency may be independent of the degree of concentration, if firms can make (and cancel) freely any type of contract directly with customers, so that customers need not behave as price takers. In other words, the above conclusion obtained from Cournot's model is a result of its too specific assumption that firms can offer only the contract of the uniform price to their customers, and can have only indirect contacts with their customers through the price of their products. This is, of course, a result of the Cournot-Walras view of the market.

To separate further Edgeworth's equivalence theorem from his limit theorem, let us return to the case where there are two traders of type A, i.e., A_1 and A_2, and two traders of type B, i.e., B_1 and B_2. Consider the allocation H on the contract curve DEF in Figure 9.4, which is essentially an identical reproduction of Figure 9.3. As we saw in the previous section, the point H cannot be blocked by the coalition of A_1, A_2 and B_1, considered by Edgeworth. We can show, however, that H is not a stable outcome of exchange of two two-individual trading bodies, if Jevons's law of indifference and his view of trading process are taken into consideration.

Jevons had in mind a piecemeal exchange process, since "dynamically we

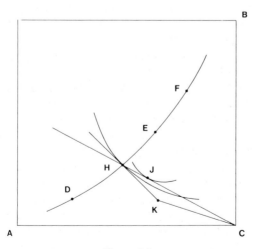

Figure 9.4

<hr />

[17] See equation (11) in Chapter 7, section 1, where p is given as a decreasing function of n.

could not treat the ratio of exchange otherwise than as the ratio of dy and dx, infinitesimal quantities of commodity" (Jevons [13, p. 102]). Let us rule out, therefore, the possibility of an indivisible lump-sum transaction and assume that each single transaction is divisible, so that every portion of a homogeneous commodity is treated indifferently, i.e., exchanged against the other commodity at the same rate of exchange. In other words, the dynamic exchange process is a piecemeal one, as considered by Jevons, and a finite, i.e., non-infinitesimal, transaction is permissible only when it is divisible.

There must be, then, at least two successive transactions and the ratio of exchange should vary in the course of exchange between C and H, in Figure 9.4, if allocation H can ever be reached by exchange starting from C. Otherwise, if there is only a single transaction and the exchange ratio remains unchanged throughout the exchange process, it must be equal to the slope of line CH and exchange must proceed on line CH, starting from C and moving toward H. Such an exchange process has to be terminated at J, however, since the transaction is divisible and it is unfavorable for A to go beyond J. Further, we can see that the variable ratio of exchange between C and H must be identical to the slope of the tangent to the indifference curve passing through H, for the last infinitesimal or finite transaction arriving at H.

Suppose, therefore, that exchange proceeds like CKH, i.e., the first transaction to be done with exchange ratio favorable to B, and unfavorable to A, like CK, and the second transaction, with exchange ratio favorable to A, and unfavorable to B, like KH, though the average ratio is CH. If we suppose that this is the case, not only with exchange between A_1 and B_1 but also with exchange between A_2 and B_2, allocation H can be blocked by the following arbitrage of different exchange ratios.[18] B_1 cancels a part of the transaction with A_1, with the ratio of exchange KH, and proposes some new transaction to A_2. Suppose, for the moment, that B_1 offers A_2 the exchange ratio CK. A_2 may accept this proposal of B_1 by cancelling a part of his transaction with B_2 at the exchange ratio CK, since "provided that A gets the right commodity in the proper quantity, he does not care whence it comes, so that we need not ... distinguish the source or destination" (Jevons [13, p. 127]). In any event, if B_1 offers A_2 an exchange ratio strictly between CK and KH, both parties can be strictly better off as a result of cancelling parts of their earlier provisional contracts. Not only B_1 but also B_2, A_1 and A_2 may take the initiative to exploit different exchange ratios.

[18] Generally, of course, the path of exchange with a varying exchange ratio may be different for different traders of the same type. Still, arbitrage is possible, since for each trader some exchange transactions are with an exchange ratio more favorable than CH and some other transactions are with an exchange ratio less favorable.

Such a coalition of, say, B_1 and A_2 to block a contract H is certainly different from the coalition of, say, A_1, A_2 and B_1 considered by Edgeworth. The latter coalition is a closed coalition so that its members can be better off by themselves than at H, irrespective of the reaction of trader B_2. The former coalition is, on the other hand, an open coalition so that its members can be better off than at H, only if non-member traders B_2 and A_1 respectively keep the transactions, which traders B_1 and A_2 do not cancel, unchanged. In view of the fact that B_2 and A_1 are, respectively, in competition with B_1 and A_2, and the assumption of divisible trade, it may be natural for the member of a coalition to expect unchanged behavior of non-member traders, when only a small part of the transactions with them is cancelled. We must, of course, admit that our discussion is based on a more stringent assumption than that of Edgeworth.[19]

Be that as it may, this kind of arbitrage activity is the basis of Jevons's law of indifference, and an allocation E, i.e., the solution of Jevons's equations of exchange, is the only allocation which is not blocked by arbitrage activities leading to the law of indifference. Thus, Edgeworth's equivalence theorem does not hold as a limit theorem, if transactions are assumed to be divisible and the competition between identical traders is assured, so as to satisfy Jevons's law of indifference. Even Edgeworth, who did Jevons more than justice insofar as the latter's concept of a trading body was generously interpreted to exclude the case of an indeterminate equilibrium of bilateral monopoly (see section 3), did Jevons less than justice here, since the implications of Jevons's law of indifference were not fully exploited in Edgeworth's equivalence theorem as a limit theorem.

References

[1] Benassy, J.P., "A Neo-Keynesian Model of Price and Quantity Determination in Disequilibrium", *Equilibrium and Disequilibrium in Economic Theory*, pp. 511–544, G. Schwödiauer, ed., D. Reidel, 1977.
[2] Blaug, M., *Economic Theory in Retrospect*, Cambridge University Press, 1985.
[3] Chipman, J.S., "A Survey of the Theory of International Trade, Part 2", *Econometrica*, 33(1965), pp. 685–760.
[4] Creedy, J., *Edgeworth and the Development of Neoclassical Economics*, Basil Blackwell, 1986.
[5] Debreu, G., and H. Scarf, "A Limit Theorem on the Core of an Economy", *International Economic Review*, 4(1963), pp. 235–246.

---

[19] In the actual world, however, closed coalition is rather rare. For example, the Second World War was fought between Axis Powers (Germany, Italy, Japan, etc.) and Allied Powers (France, U.K., U.S.A., U.S.S.R., etc.), but these two coalitions were not closed, since until the last moment diplomatic relations were kept between Japan and the U.S.S.R.

[6] Edgeworth, F.Y., *Mathematical Psychics*, Kegan Paul, 1881.

[7] Farrell, M.J., "Edgeworth Bounds for Oligopoly Prices", *Economica*, 37(1970), pp. 342–361.

[8] Fisher, R.M., *The Logic of Economic Discovery*, Wheatsheaf, 1986.

[9] Gossen, H.H., *The Laws of Human Relations and the Rules of Human Action Derived Therefrom*, R.C. Blitz, tr., MIT Press, 1983.

[10] Hildenbrand, W., and A.P. Kirman, *Introduction to Equilibrium Analysis*, North-Holland, 1976.

[11] Howey, R.S., *The Rise of Marginal Utility School*, University of Kansas Press, 1960.

[12] Jaffé, W., "Edgeworth's Contract Curve", *History of Political Economy*, 6(1974), pp. 343–359, 381–404.

[13] Jevons, W.S., *The Theory of Political Economy*, Macmillan, 1879.

[14] Keynes, J.M., "On Jevons", *The Development of Economic Thought*, pp. 489–525, H.W. Spiegel, ed., Wiley, 1952.

[15] Keynes, J.M., *Essays in Biography*, Macmillan, 1972.

[16] Malinvaud, E., *Theory of Unemployment Reconsidered*, Basil Blackwell, 1985.

[17] Morishima, M., *Walras's Economics*, Cambridge University Press, 1977.

[18] Pagano, U., *Work and Welfare in Economic Theory*, Basil Blackwell, 1985.

[19] Pigou, A.C., *The Economics of Welfare*, Macmillan, 1920.

[20] Roberts, D.J., and A. Postlewaite, "The Incentives for Price-Taking Behaviour in Large Exchange Economies", *Econometrica*, 44(1976), pp. 115–127.

[21] Walras, L., "On Gossen", *The Development of Economic Thought*, pp. 470–488, H.W. Spiegel, ed., Wiley, 1952.

[22] Walras, L., *Elements of Pure Economics*, W. Jaffé, tr., Irwin, 1954.

[23] Walras, L., *Correspondence of Leon Walras and Related Papers*, 1, W. Jaffé, ed., North-Holland, 1965.

CHAPTER 10

MARSHALL'S ECONOMICS

1. *Principles of Economics*

As we argued in the previous chapter, the contributions made by Jevons and Edgeworth to the theory of exchange are still very important from the point of view of contemporary mathematical economics. It is, however, not Jevons and Edgeworth, but Alfred Marshall (1842–1924) whose theory could be said to be dominantly influential to the development of economics in England after the marginal revolution. Unlike Jevons, who openly attacked classical economics, Marshall, who began to study economics by translating Ricardo's theory of value and distribution as expounded by J.S. Mill into differential equations, did not deny the significance of classical economics, but tried to make it more generalized.[1] This is the reason why the economics of Marshall and of his followers, the Cambridge school, were originally called the neo-classical economics, although recently many of us rather regard Walrasian tradition as neo-classical.[2] It cannot be denied, in any case, that Marshall's partial equilibrium analysis is an indispensable complement to Walras's general equilibrium analysis in forming the foundations of current mainstream economics.

To see the significance of Marshall's economics, it is convenient to make, as Hicks [10] did, a comparison of Walrasian and Marshallian economics. J.R. Hicks, who tried to combine Walrasian and Marshallian traditions in his *Value and Capital* (1939), argued as follows:

> For a quite considerable part of the way Walras and Marshall go together; and when they separate, it is a difference of interest, rather than of technique that divides them. While Walras was seeking for the general principles which underlie the working of an exchange economy, Marshall forged an analytical instrument capable of easier application to particular problems of history or experience. (Hicks [10].)

[1] See Pigou [29, pp. 20, 412], Shove [34], and Marshall [21, p. 6].
[2] See Aspromourgos [2], Spiegel [35, p. 565], Leijonhufvud [15], and Gide and Rist [7, p. 616].

Walras first decomposes a complicated economy of the real world into several fundamental components such as consumer-traders, entrepreneurs, consumers' goods, factors of production, newly produced capital goods, and money. He then starts with a simple model composed of a very limited number of such components and proceeds to more complex ones by introducing, one by one, those components so far excluded. With the exception of the last model, into which all the components of a real world economy are introduced, all Walrasian intermediate models are as unrealistic as the starting model, although they are closed and self-compact. Marshall, on the other hand, studies a whole complex of a real world economy as such. Of course, he also simplified his study at first by confining his interest to a certain limited number of aspects of the economy. But he does it not by disregarding the existence of other aspects but by assuming that other things are equal. He travels from the simple to the complex by reducing the number of aspects assumed to be equal. All the Marshallian models are realistic, although most of them are open and not self-sufficient, since other things remain unexplained and have to be exogenously given.

The most simple model of Walrasian economics is the one studied in the theory of exchange, where consumers' goods to be exchanged among individual consumer-traders are simply assumed to be endowed to them and not considered as produced at cost. No production activities exist in this hypothetical world. The corresponding simplest model of Marshall is that of the market day, in which consumers' goods to be sold are produced goods, although the amount available for sale is for the time being assumed to be constant. Production does exist in this temporary equilibrium model, although the level of output is unchanged in the very short period under consideration. In the Walrasian model considered in the theory of production, capital goods are introduced as a kind of factor of production, but the investment, i.e., the production of new capital goods, simply does not exist. On the other hand, in the Marshallian short-run theory, which is also the theory of production, investment is undertaken, although the amount of currently available capital goods remains unchanged. In Walrasian models of the theory of exchange, the theory of production and the theory of credit and capital formation, no money exists at all, until it is finally introduced in the theory of circulation and money. In Marshallian models, on the other hand, money exists from the beginning, although its purchasing power is sometimes assumed to be constant.

In other words, Walrasian models are in general not useful for practical purposes. They are designed to show the fundamental significance of such components of the real world economy as entrepreneurs and production, investment and the rate of interest, inventories and money, etc., by successively introducing them into simpler models which are then developed into more complex ones. Walras's theoretical interest was not in the solution of particular problems but in what Hicks [10] called the pursuit of the general principles which underlie the working of a market economy. On the other hand, Marshallian theories respectively correspond to special states of the real world economy. The market day (temporary equilibrium) and short-run models are as realistic as the long-run model where capitals are fully adjusted. Thus, Marshallian models are practically useful to apply to what Hicks [10] called particular problems of history or experience. "Marshall forged an analytical instrument capable of easier application." A good example is the concept of consumers' and producers' surplus which we shall discuss in section 2.

Thus, Hicks [10] insists that Walras and Marshall differ in interest, the former in principles and the latter in practical applications. Even if one is interested in principles only, however, Marshall's contributions are necessary complements to Walrasian ones. Firstly, the time structure of Marshallian equilibria (market day, short-run and long-run) clarifies the economic significance of time elements, and gives us useful suggestions on how to generalize the static and timeless Walrasian general equilibrium theory dynamically. In section 3 we shall study a problem related to a Marshallian dynamic equilibrium of the industry which is based on the biological analogy. Secondly, as we saw in section 5.2 of Chapter 7, there is an inherent difficulty in introducing money into the Walrasian general equilibrium theory. The Marshallian approach, in which the existence of money is taken into consideration from the beginning, on the other hand, can throw light on monetary aspects of the economy, which the Walrasian approach cannot do so easily. The final section of this chapter is devoted to considering the problem of trade cycles, which is a characteristic of a monetary economy, from the point of view of the Marshallian theory of market and money.

Alfred Marshall was born in Clapham, England in 1842, a son of William Marshall, a cashier at the Bank of England. Although his father hoped that his son would go into the Church, Marshall studied mathematics at Cambridge. In 1865, Lord Rayleigh was Senior Wrangler and Marshall was Second Wrangler in the Mathematical Tripos. After mathematics, Marshall studied philosophy, ethics, psychology and economics. He was elected to a Fellowship at St. John's College, and gave lectures in logic and economics for the Moral Sciences Tripos. In 1877 he married Mary Paley, a former student, and resigned his fellowship at Cambridge. Marshall left Cambridge for Bristol, where he became the first Principal of the University College and Professor of

Political Economy. While at Bristol, Marshall, in collaboration with his wife, published *The Economics of Industry* in 1879. He was then elected a Fellow of Balliol College, Oxford and lectured in economics. It was in 1885 that Marshall was elected Professor of Political Economy at the University of Cambridge. *Principles of Economics* was published in 1890. In 1903, Marshall succeeded in persuading the University of Cambridge to establish the Tripos in Economics and Politics. He retired from the chair of Professor of Political Economy in 1908 in order to devote the remainder of his life to writing. After the publication of *Industry and Trade* (1919) and *Money Credit and Commerce* (1923), Marshall died in 1924.[3]

After the first edition of *Principles of Economics* was published in 1890, Marshall continued to revise it at intervals during the remainder of his life, and the eighth and last edition appeared in 1920. According to Guillebaud, however, "the collation of different editions would not seem to support the view that there was any real evolution or development of his ideas between 1890 and 1920" (Marshall [21, p. 28]). The eighth edition consists of six books: *Preliminary Survey*; *Some Fundamental Notions*; *On Wants and their Satisfaction*; *The Agents of Production: Land, Labour, Capital and Organization*; *General Relations of Demand, Supply, and Value*; *The Distribution of the National Income*. In addition, there are twelve appendices and a mathematical appendix.

On the title page of the first edition the words "Vol. I." were written, but they were replaced by the words "An introductory volume", from the sixth edition (1910) onwards, which shows that Marshall changed his plan (Marshall [20, p. xii]). On the other hand, Marshall's motto, *natura non facit saltum*, remained there from the first to the last editions. Marshall declared in the preface to the first edition that the special character of his book lies in the prominence which it gives to applications of the principle of continuity. We can also see there Marshall's ascetic attitude towards the use of mathematics. In the preface to the eighth edition, Marshall discussed his method:

> The Mecca of the economist lies in economic biology rather than in economic dynamics. But biological conceptions are more complex than those of mechanics; a volume on Foundations must therefore give a relatively large place to mechanical analogies; and frequent use is made of the term "equilibrium," which suggests something of statical analogy.... But in fact it is concerned throughout with the forces that cause movement: and its key-note is that of dynamics rather than statics.

[3] For the life of Marshall, see Marshall [21, pp. 3–7], Hutchison [13, pp. 63–69], Ekelund and Hébert [4, pp. 328–331], and Pigou [29].

The forces to be dealt with are however so numerous, that it is best to take a few at a time; and to work out a number of partial solutions as auxiliaries to our main study. Thus we begin by isolating the primary relations of supply, demand and price in regard to a particular commodity. We reduce to inaction all other forces by the phrase "other things being equal": ... In the second stage more forces are released from the hypothetical slumber that had been imposed on them: changes in the conditions of demand for and supply of particular groups of commodities come into play; and their complex mutual interactions begin to be observed. (Marshall [20, pp. xiv–xv].)

Book I, *Preliminary Survey*, explains Marshall's views of modern economy and economic science. "The fundamental characteristic of modern industrial life is not competition, but self-reliance, independence, deliberate choice and forethought.... Even constructive competition is less beneficent than ideal altrustic co-operation" [20, pp. 5, 9]. "The chief motives of business life can be measured indirectly in money." Although "the significance of a given price is greater for the poor than the rich, ... the greater number of the events with which economics deals affect in about equal proportions all the different classes of society; so that if the money measures of the happiness caused by two events are equal, it is reasonable ... to regard the amounts of the happiness in the two cases as equivalent" [20, pp. 14, 19, 20]. Appendix A, "The growth of free industry and enterprise", and Appendix B, "The growth of economic science", were originally in Book I, but moved to the appendices from the fifth edition (1907) onwards. This shows Marshall's early interest in historical studies and may also imply that the criticism of a historian (Cunningham) caused Marshall's gradual abandonment of his historical work (Hutchison [13, pp. 66 69–70]).

Book II explains *Some Fundamental Notions* such as wealth, production, consumption, labor, necessities, income and capital. Definitions of capital are also explained in Appendix E.

Marshall admitted, in Chapter I of Book III, *On Wants and their Satisfaction*, that "until recently the subject of demand or consumption has been somewhat neglected" but warned that "the reaction against the comparative neglect of the study of wants by Ricardo and his followers shows signs of being carried to the opposite extreme" [20, pp. 84, 85]. In spite of Jevons, it is not true that the theory of consumption is the scientific basis of economics since the formation of consumers' preferences is much influenced by the productive activities of the society (Chapter II). Diminishing marginal utility, the equilibrium of the consumer's household, demand price, and

demand schedule are discussed in Chapters III and V. Elasticity of demand is
defined in Chapter IV. Although Marshall made no reference to him, the
concept of the elasticity of demand had already been discussed by William
Whewell, as Hutchison pointed out [13, pp. 64–65]. Marshall discussed the
consumers' surplus in Chapter VI, which we shall consider in section 2 below.

The agents of production and supply price are defined in Chapter I of Book
IV, *The Agents of Production: Land, Labour, Capital and Organization.*
Chapters II and III are devoted to discussing land, Chapters IV, V, VI, to labor,
and Chapter VII, to saving. Industrial organization is considered in Chapters
VIII to XII. Chapter VIII discusses Adam Smith, Social Darwinism, and the
division of labor. Economies of scale are divided into external economies,
which depend on the general development of the industry, and internal
economies, which depend on the resources of the individual houses of business
engaged in it, at the end of Chapter IX, which discusses the division of labor
and the influence of machinery. Chapter X deals with external economies
which depend on the concentration of specialized industries in particular
localities. Internal economies due to production on a large scale are discussed
in Chapter XI.[4] As for the reason why the growth of firms reaping the benefit of
internal economies does not destroy competition, Marshall argues that
individual entrepreneurship is short-lived and not inherited, and that growing
firms encounter marketing difficulties. Chapter XII continues to discuss the
fact that businessmen's abilities and tastes are not always inherited and new
blood must be brought in by some method such as private partnership, or
joint-stock companies. Chapter XIII, which concludes Book IV, contains the
famous analogy between firms in industry and trees in a forest, and the
definition of the representative firm, which we shall discuss, together with the
problem of internal economies, in section 3 below.

After a short account of the concept of a market in Chapter I of Book V,
General Relations of Demand, Supply and Value, Chapter II discusses the
temporary equilibrium of demand and supply. The famous illustration from
a local corn market shows that the market adjustment process considered by
Marshall is different from that of Walrasian *tâtonnement.* We shall consider
this difference in section 4 below. Chapter III deals with the equilibrium of
normal demand and supply in the short-run. Marshall defines equilibrium in
terms of the equality of the demand and supply price. While the demand price
is the temporary equilibrium price at which each particular amount of the
commodity can find purchasers, the normal supply price is defined as the

---

[4] Chapter XI also gives an example of external economy, the growth of trade knowledge as the
result of more newspapers and technical publications (p. 284).

expenses of production, including the gross earnings of management, of a representative firm, whose economies of production are dependent on the aggregate volume of production of the commodity. As for the influences of utility and cost of production on value, Marshall argues as follows:

> We might as reasonably dispute whether it is the upper or the under blade of a pair of scissors that cut a piece of paper, as whether value is governed by utility or cost of production.... Thus we may conclude that, *as a general rule*, the shorter the period which we are considering, the greater must be the share of our attention which is given to the influence of demand on value; and the longer the period, the more important will be the influence of cost of production on value. For the influence of changes in cost of production takes as a rule a longer time to work itself out than does the influence of changes in demand. (Marshall [20, pp. 348, 349].)[5]

Investment is taken into consideration and prime and supplementary costs are distinguished in Chapter IV. What Marshall calls special, direct or prime costs are variable costs corresponding to variable factors of production, calculated per unit produced.[6] What Marshall calls supplementary costs are fixed costs calculated per unit produced, which correspond to costs independent of the short-run volume of production, such as the general cost of administration and sale, the general physical depreciation of the durable plant in which much of the capital is invested and the depreciation caused by the plant growing old. Marshall calls the sum of these two units of costs "total cost".

In Chapter V we can see the time structure of Marshallian economic theory. The famous fiction of the stationary state is introduced as the first step towards studying the influences exerted by the element of time on the relation between cost of production and value. Using an illustration from the fishing trade, Marshall explains the relation among market prices, short-run normal prices, and long-run normal prices. "Market values are governed by the relation of demand to stocks actually in the market" (Marshall [20, p. 372]). The normal supply price of a certain given rate of aggregate production

> is that the expectation of which is sufficient and only just sufficient to make it worth while for people to set themselves to produce that aggregate amount; in every case the cost of production is marginal; that is, it is the cost of production of those goods which are on the margin of not being produced at

---

[5] In Chapter III Marshall also discusses the stability of an equilibrium. For the relation between Walrasian stability and Marshallian stability, see Negishi [24, pp. 192–195] and Ekelund and Hébert [4, pp. 373–378].

[6] Prime cost includes "wear-and-tear of plant, which is immediately and directly involved by getting a little further use out of appliances which are not fully employed" [20, pp. 374–375].

all, and which would not be produced if the price to be got for them were expected to be lower. But the causes which determine this margin vary with the length of the period under consideration. For short periods people take the stock of appliances for production as practically fixed; ... In the long period they set themselves to adjust the flow of these appliances to their expectations of demand for the goods which the appliances help to produce. (Marshall [20, pp. 373–374].)

Chapters VI and VII of Book V are devoted to considering joint and composite demand and supply, while Chapters VIII to XI "are given to a study of the marginal costs of productions in relation to the values of those products on the one hand, and on the other hand to the values of the land, machinery, and other appliances used in making them" [20, p. 403]. The nature of quasi-rent is discussed in the final footnote of Chapter IX and the first few pages of Chapter X.

Chapter XII and Appendix H examine the problem of increasing returns. Marshall considers (1) external economies, (2) the life-cycle of firms and (3) difficulties of marketing to solve the dilemma of competition and increasing returns, which we shall discuss in section 3. The concept of a particular expenses curve is introduced to discuss the problem of producers' surplus. Marshall's exposition is, however, "confusing" (Blaug [3, p. 412]). We shall consider this problem in the following section. Finally, Marshall admits that long-run demand and supply curves are irreversible and that the problem is one of organic growth and not of statical equilibrium.

Perhaps it may not be out of place to discuss the relation between short-run and long-run cost curves, which is pointed out by Frisch [6]. In the case of a single particular firm, the long-run average cost curve is the envelope of the short-run average cost curve. In the case of the representative firm with external economies, which is a small replica of an industry with free entry, the long-run average cost (LAC) curve is not the envelope but the locus of the minimum point of the short-run average cost (SAC) curves. In Figure 10.1, we measure horizontally the volume of industrial output or the corresponding output of the representative firm, and we measure prices and costs vertically. Curves SAC are short-run average cost curves of the representative firm, and curves SMC are short-run marginal cost curves of the representative firm, which is also the short-run supply curve of the industry. Curves D_1, D_2, etc. are demand curves for the industry. Finally, the curve LAC is the long-run average cost curve of the representative firm, which is also the long-run supply curve of the industry.

This can be seen as follows. Suppose the demand curve is D_1, which intersects with LAC at point A. Point A signifies the long-run equilibrium of

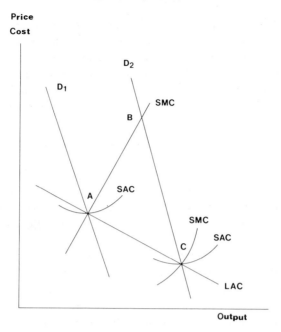

Figure 10.1

the industry. The short-run average cost of the representative firm, which corresponds to the industrial output given by the abscissa of point A, reaches the minimum at point A, so that point A is also on the curve SMC. Since the normal profit is included in the cost, the representative firm is earning the normal profit at point A, and the volume of the industrial output remains unchanged. "In a rigidly stationary state in which supply could be perfectly adjusted to demand in every particular, the normal expenses of production, the marginal expenses, and the average expenses (rent being counted in) would be one and the same thing, for long periods and for short" (Marshall [20, p. 497]).

If the demand curve is shifted to D_2, the equilibrium is shifted first to point B, at which D_2 intersects with the short-run supply curve SMC. Gradually, however, the cost curves of the representative firm are shifted downward by the external economies caused by the expansion of industrial output due to the price being higher than the normal supply price at point B, The long-run equilibrium is again established at point C.

We thus get at the true long-period marginal cost, falling with a gradual increase of demand.... We do not expect it to fall immediately in consequences of a sudden increase of demand. On the contrary we expect the short-period supply price to increase with increasing output. But we also expect a gradual increase in demand to increase gradually the size and the efficiency of this representative firm; and to increase the economies both internal and external which are at its disposal. (Marshall [20, p. 460].)

In Chapter XIII of Book V the doctrine of maximum satisfaction is considered, from the point of view of consumers' surplus. Marshall insists on a tax on an increasing-cost industry and a subsidy to a decreasing-cost industry. The argument is, however, not persuasive, since a tax on an increasing-cost industry cannot be justified from the point of view of the maximum satisfaction, if the producers' surplus is taken into consideration. Chapter XIV considers the theory of monopoly, also using consumers' surplus analysis. Finally, Chapter XV summarizes this long but important book beautifully.

Book VI is concerned with *The Distribution of the National Income*. While Chapter I is devoted to the explanation of the marginal productivity theory as a theory of the demand for productive agents, the supply of productive agents is discussed in Chapter II. In Appendix K, Marshall argued that workers' and savers' surpluses cannot be added to consumers' surplus, which we shall discuss critically in the following section. Chapters III to V are concerned with the problem of labor. Marshall's arguments on the peculiarities of labor as an agent of production are still useful for the contemporary economics of labor and theory of human capital. Chapter VI discusses the interest on capital. The distinction between money and the real rate of interest is explained, and Marshall's monetary theory of trade cycle is sketched. We shall return to this problem in section 4. In Chapters VII and VIII, where profits of capital and business power are considered, Marshall emphasizes the role of the fourth agent of production, organization. Chapters IX and X consider land rent and land tenure. "English features of land tenure" explain "the distinction between the quasi-rents which do not, and the profits which do, directly enter into the normal supply prices of produce for periods of moderate length" (Marshall [20, p. 636]). Chapter XI gives an excellent summary of the first ten chapters of Book VI.

In the last two chapters of Book VI, Marshall discusses economic progress. What England

has derived from the progress of manufactures during the nineteenth century has been through its indirect influences in lowering the cost of transport of men and goods, of water and light, of electricity and news: for the dominant economic fact of our own age is the development not of the manufacturing, but of the transport industry. (Marshall [20, pp. 674–675].)

In many ways

> evil may be lessened by a wider understanding of the social possibilities of economic chivalry. A devotion to public wellbeing on the part of the rich may do much, as enlightenment spreads, to help the tax-gatherer in turning the resources of the rich to high account in the service of the poor, and may remove the worst evils of poverty from the land. (Marshall [20, p. 719].)[7]

2. Consumers' and producers' surplus

The theory of consumers' and producers' surplus has been extensively applied in such fields as international trade, public finance and industrial organization. Marshall's theory of consumers' surplus [20, pp. 124–133, 841–842] is clear and straightforward, as is elucidated by Hicks [11, pp. 38–41]. His theory of producers' surplus [20, pp. 810–812, 830–832] is, however, quite ambiguous. Recently, Mishan [23] even recommended that "the term producer's surplus be struck from the economist's vocabulary." It is not unnecessary, therefore, to reconsider the theory of producers' surplus in its relation to consumers' surplus and its implications in the forms in which most recent applications are made.

The original inventor of consumers' surplus was Dupuit who was, however, criticized by Walras.

> Instead of measuring utility, as J.B. Say did, by the pecuniary sacrifice which the consumer actually does make once he knows the price, Dupuit measures utility by the sacrifice which the consumer is willing to make.[8] ... Thus, the measure of total utility is geometrically represented by the area under the demand curve drawn as a function of price.... Unfortunately, all these statements are erroneous.... In general, the maximum pecuniary sacrifice which a consumer is willing to make to obtain a unit of a product depends not only on the utility of the product in question, but also on the utility of all the other products in the market, and, finally, on the consumer's means.... We may, therefore, ... definitely reject all Dupuit's statements in his two memoirs which bear upon the variation of utility as price varies and as quantity demanded varies from price to price.... they rest on a confusion

---

[7] As a guide to Marshall's *Principles*, see Blaug [3, pp. 396–420]. See also Frisch [6] particularly for Book V of *Principles*.

[8] This statement of Walras is slightly unfair to Say, who distinguished, in a letter of Ricardo, "utilité naturelle fesant partie des richesses que la nature ne nous fait pas payer," from "utilité créée par l'industrie, les capitaux et les terres, utilité que nous payons et qui est la seule qui fasse partie des richesses echangeables." Say's concept of natural utility is a primitive version of that of consumers' surplus. See Rıcardo [30, pp. 31–36].

of ideas resulting from Dupuit's complete failure to distinguish between utility or want curves on the one hand, and demand curves on the other. (Walras [39, pp. 445–446].)

Marshall's theory of consumers' surplus is free from Walras's criticism of Dupuit. Along with the assumption that "equal sums of money measure equal utilities to all concerned" [20, p. 471], Marshall assumes "that the marginal utility of money to individual purchaser is the same throughout" [20, p. 842]. If one wants to measure utility in terms of money, one has to assume that each unit of money has the same utility. The length of a measure must be constant, if it can measure the length of others. Since the marginal utility of a product at equilibrium is equal to the product of its price and the marginal utility of money, the utility curve of a product coincides with the demand curve, if the marginal utility of money is assumed to be unchanged. The utility of money signifies the utility of "all the other products in the market" and also the utility of "the consumer's means."

In Figure 10.2, which is originally due to Hicks [11, p. 39], we measure the quantity of a certain product horizontally, and the quantity of money is measured vertically. Curves such as AG and BH are indifference curves of an individual person. Since the utility of money represents the utility of all the

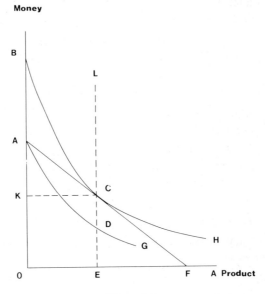

Figure 10.2

other products which can be bought by money, we have to consider the real quantity of money rather than the nominal one. These two quantities are identical, however, since the prices of all the other products are given and unchanged. Suppose the individual has initially OA amount of money, and the price of the product in question in terms of money is shown by the slope of the budget line AF. The individual chooses the point C where an indifference curve is tangent to AF. He buys OE amount of the product by paying AK amount of money. The corresponding consumers' surplus is the difference expressed in terms of money of the utility level between the indifference curve BH which passes C and the indifference curve AG which passes A. In other words, it is the vertical distance between two indifference curves, which, like AB and DC, is indeterminate in general, unless the marginal utility of money is constant.

Let us use x to denote quantity of a certain product measured horizontally in Figure 10.2, M to denote the quantity of money measured vertically, and U to denote the utility of an individual as a function of x and M. The constancy of the marginal utility of money $\partial U/\partial M$ implies that $\partial^2 U/\partial M\partial M =0$ and $\partial^2 U/\partial x\partial M =0$. In other words, the marginal utility of the product in question $\partial U/\partial x$ remains unchanged when M is changed but x is kept constant. The slope of the indifference curves between x and M remains unchanged if M only is changed, since it is the ratio of the marginal utility of money to the marginal utility of the product. In Figure 10.2, the slope of the indifference curves at points such as A and B, or D and C, which have equal abscissas, are identical. Therefore, $AB=CD$, and more generally, the vertical distance between two indifference curves is the same at any point. If the marginal utility of money is constant, therefore, U can be expressed in terms of M and the consumers' surplus is determinate. When the initial amount of money OA is changed, the equilibrium point C moves vertically on EL and there are no changes in the amount of the product purchased OE, provided that the price of the product is unchanged. In other words, the income elasticity of demand for the product is zero and there is no income effect, if the marginal utility of money is constant. This implies that the product in question is not important in the budget of consumers and the proportion of income spent upon it is a very small part of the total income.[9]

In addition to consumers' surplus, Marshall introduces other surpluses in Appendix K of his *Principles* [20], i.e., workers' and savers' surpluses, which are better seen when people are regarded as producers. Workers' surplus is, for example, explained as follows: "As a worker, he derives a *worker's surplus*, through being remunerated for all his work at the same rate as for that last

---

[9] For the details of recent theory of consumers' surplus, see Varian [37, pp. 32, 93, 209] and Takayama [36].

part, which he is only just willing to render for its reward; though much of the work may have given him positive pleasure" [20, p. 830]. Marshall insisted, however, that these producers' surpluses cannot be added to the consumers surplus.

> These two sets of surpluses are not independent: and it would be easy to reckon them up so as to count the same thing twice. For when we have reckoned the producer's surplus at the value of the general purchasing power which he derives from his labour or saving, we have reckoned implicitly his consumer's surplus too, provided his character and the circumstances of his environment are given (Marshall [20, p. 831].)

Workers' surplus is, for example, nothing but the consumers' surplus from the consumption of their own leisure, and we have to assume the constancy of the marginal utility of money to make it determinate, as in the case of the consumers' surplus from the consumption of a certain product. Furthermore, Marshall dismisses a generalized utility function as less adapted to express the every-day fact of economic life than an additive separable utility function [20, p. 845]. The equilibrium amount of the consumption of the product in question can be obtained from the condition that its marginal utility, which is independent of the quantity of leisure, is equal to the product of its price and the marginal utility of money, while the equilibrium amount of the leisure is obtained from the condition that its marginal utility, which is independent of the quantity of the product, is equal to the product of its price, the rate of wage, and the marginal utility of income. In spite of Marshall's warning about counting the same thing twice, therefore, the consumers' surplus of a product and the producers' surplus, like the workers' surplus, are independent and can be added, provided there are many other products which can be represented by money, whose marginal utility is assumed constant. The case of Robinson Crusoe mentioned by Marshall is a highly exceptional one, since there are no products which money can represent other than the one produced by his own labor.

Marshall continues, in Appendix K, to introduce additional producers' surpluses which are different from workers' and savers' (or waiters') surpluses.

> These surpluses must be distinguished from the excess of earnings of an appliance of production over the prime cost of its works. All appliances of production, whether machinery, or factories with the land on which they are built, or farm, are alike in yielding large surpluses over the prime costs of particular acts of production to a man who owns and works them: also in yielding him normally no special surplus in the long run above what is required to remunerate him for his trouble and sacrifice and outlay in

purchasing and working them (no special surplus, as contrasted with his general worker's and waiter's surplus). But there is this difference between land and other agents of production, that from a social point of view land yields a permanent surplus, while perishable things made by man do not. (Marshall [20, pp. 831–832].)

These additional producers' surpluses which factors of production specific to firms yield in the short-run can be represented by the area *SAF* in Figure 10.3, which is given by Marshall in Appendix H of his *Principles* [20, p, 811]. The producers' surplus like the workers' surplus, is not included, since the curve *SS'* is not a true supply curve but is what Marshall calls a particular expenses curve in Figure 10.3, in which the prices and costs of a product are measured vertically, the volume of industrial output is measured horizontally, and the curve *DD'* is an ordinary demand curve. "Now the difference between the particular expense curve and a normal supply curve lies in this, that in the former we take the general economies of production as fixed and uniform throughout, and in the latter we do not. The particular expenses curve is based throughout on the assumption that the aggregate production is *OH*" [20, p. 811]. The rate of wage rises, for example, as the industrial output expands. *PM*, however, represents the expenses of production calculated by the rate of wage prevailing when the industrial output is not *OM* but *OH*. The workers' surplus is, therefore, not included in the area *SAF* but in the area *OSAH*.

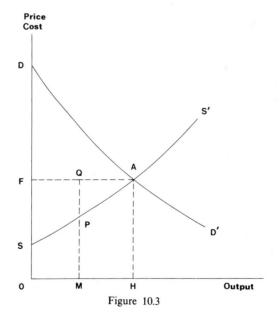

Figure 10.3

Let us now introduce the producers' surplus into Figure 10.2. In Figure 10.4, as in Figure 10.2, we measure horizontally the volume of a certain product, and we measure vertically the real amount of money which represents all the other goods. Curve *BH* is a social indifference curve and curve *DG* is the production frontier which shows the amount of all the other goods to be sacrificed to produce the given amount of the product in question. The marginal utility of money is assumed to be constant. The equilibrium point is *C*, and *OE* of the product in question is produced and consumed. If this product is not produced, *OD* of other goods is produced, but now only *OK* of other goods is available. Since the money price of the product in question is given by the slope of the line *AF*, the aggregate income of consumers is *OA*, *AK* of it is spent on the product in question and *OK* of it is spent on the other goods. Since the level of aggregate utility represented by the indifference curve *BH* is *OB* in terms of money, however, *AB* is the consumers' surplus, which represents the increase in utility caused by the consumption of the product in question. If the product is not produced, on the other hand, the aggregate income is *OD*. *AD* is, therefore, the producers' surplus, which represents the increase in utility or in income caused by the production of the product in question.[10]

In the short-run, we may consider that the product in question is produced from the input of a mobile factor of production (labor) and the input of immobile factors of production (capital and land) which are specific to particular firms. Since the distribution of the latter factors among firms is given, the marginal productivity of the former factor diminishes, in the production of the product in question, as more of it is transferred from the production of other goods. Thus, curve *DG* is concave to the origin. Since the price line *AF* and the production frontier *DG* are tangent to each other at the equilibrium point *C*, the price of the product is equalized to its marginal cost of production. In other words, the price of the mobile factor of production is equalized to its value marginal product in the production of the product in question.

Suppose that the mobile factor is one of all the other goods, so that its price in terms of money remains unchanged. In Figure 10.4, the input of the mobile factor is *DK* to produce *OE* or *KC* of the product in question. Since the money value of *KC* of the product is *AK*, however, the difference of *AK* and *DK*, i.e., *AD*, is the profit or rent to be imputed to the immobile factors of production. If we consider the curve *SS'* in Figure 10.3 as the marginal cost curve, which

---

[10] Mishan [23] argues, in an appended note, that the division of the welfare gain into consumers' surplus and producers' surplus is quite arbitrary, since it can also be made differently on the horizontal axis. Mishan seems to forget the fact that surplus can be measured only vertically in terms of money whose marginal utility is assumed to be constant.

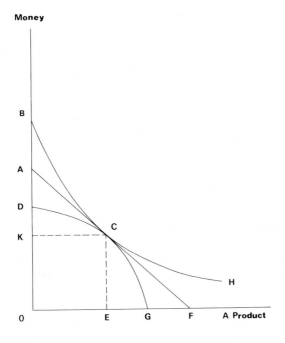

Figure 10.4

shows the diminishing marginal productivity of the mobile factor, then, the area *SAF* represents the producers' surplus which factors specific to firms yield in the short-run. In this case, the workers' surplus is not included in the area, not because the curve *SS'* is not a true supply curve but a specific expenses curve. The workers' surplus is simply dismissed, since the scale of the industry is assumed to be small relative to that of the economy and the rate of wage is assumed to be unchanged as the industry expands. This is the implication of the assumption that the mobile factor (leisure) is one of all the other goods which are represented by money and that the marginal utility of money is constant.

In the long-run, all the factors of production are mobile, and there is no factor of production which is specific to firms. Suppose other goods represented by money include all the factors of production. In Figure 10.4, curve *DG* is now a straight line and coincides with the price line *AF*. No producers' surplus which is imputed to firms exists, since *A* and *D* coincide with each other. In Figure 10.3, the supply curve *SS'* must be horizontal so that the area *SAF* vanishes. As in the case of the two-good two-factor model in the theory of international trade, however, it is sometimes considered that the production frontier DG in Figure 10.4 is concave to the origin, even in the long-run. In such a case, the producers' surplus AD does not vanish. It is, of course, not the surplus imputed to firms, but the net increase in rents imputed to factors of production, whose aggregate supply is assumed to be constant in the long-run.[11]

In the long-run, we consider only such primary factors of production as land and labor. Capital goods whose supply is perfectly variable in the long-run are merely intermediate goods and can be decomposed into primary factors of production. In Figure 10.4, suppose that money, the volume of which is measured vertically, does not represent factors of production. In other words, the volume of a certain product is measured horizontally and that of money, which represents all the other products, is measured vertically. It is assumed that factors of production have no direct utility, so that there is no reservation demand for factors, and their aggregate supplies are given constants. All the products are produced under constant returns to scale (production functions are linear homogeneous). Without loss of generality, we may assume that the product in question (measured horizontally) is relatively labor intensive, while all the other products (measured vertically) are relatively land intensive.

Let us start from point D in Figure 10.4 and increase the output of the product in question, which is measured horizontally. At first we can do it easily without sacrificing much of the other products. This is because the product in question can be produced by the intensive use of labor, which is not used intensively in the production of other goods and therefore is not so scarce. As we move along the curve DG towards G further, however, the output of the product in question is increased relative to other products, so that the scarcity of labor rises. We have to sacrifice a larger amount of other products to increase the given amount of the product in question. The curve DG is, therefore, concave to the origin. As we move along DG from D to G, the price of the product in question rises in terms of money, which represents other products. The reason is that the rate of wage rises, since labor is intensively used in the production of the product in question, and that the rent of land declines, since land is intensively used in the production of other products. The difference between the increase in wage income and the decrease in rent income is measured as AD in terms of money when the production is carried out at point C.

In the long-run, therefore, the producers' surplus AD in Figure 10.4 consists of, for example, the workers' surplus caused by the production of the product

---

[11] We are following Marshall to assume a stationary state.

in question, net of the decrease in land rent. Since the aggregate supply of labor as well as that of land are assumed to be constant, we may say that it is the net increase in (quasi-) rent imputed to the primary factors of production. In Figure 10.3, the curve SS' and the area SAF correspond respectively to the curve DG and the line segment AD in Figure 10.4. In other words, the curve SS' is now a true supply curve which shows how marginal cost changes as the output of the product in question is increased. The specific expenses curve is now a horizontal straight line FA, which shows the cost of production calculated by the rate of wage and the rate of rent, which are realized when the output of the product is OH.

3. Life-cycle theory and internal economies

3.1

Marshall offered three different solutions for the compatibility of increasing returns or diminishing cost and competitive equilibrium (Robertson [31]; Hague [8]):

(1) Individual firms face a downward sloping demand curve even in a competitive market, unless the market is ideally organized like a Walrasian one:

> There are many trades in which an individual producer could secure much increased "internal" economy by a great increase of his output; and there are many in which he could market that output easily; yet there are few in which he could do both. And this is not an accidental, but almost a necessary result. For in most of those trades in which the economies of production in a large scale are of first-rate importance, marketing is difficult. (Marshall [20, p. 286].)

> When we are considering an individual producer, we must couple his supply curve – not with the general demand curve for his commodity in a wide market, but – with the particular demand curve of his own special market. And this particular demand curve will generally be very steep; perhaps as steep as his own supply curve is likely to be, even when an increased output will give him an important increase of internal economies. (Marshall [20, p. 458].)[12]

[12] See also Marshall [20, pp. 457, 459] and Chapter 10, section 4 of this book.

In this sense, it is also possible to argue that Marshall was a pioneer of the modern theory of imperfect competition after Sraffa.

(2) Increasing returns may be due to external economies rather than to internal economies. We have already shown that the long-run average cost curve can be downward sloping in Figure 10.1 of section 1 of this chapter. As Robinson [32, pp. 337–343] argued, however, this does not solve the problem, if the external economies of an industry are due to increasing returns in other industries which are based on economies either internal or external to individual firms there. Nor can we rely on a Smith-Young specialization of firms in an industry, the extent of which is dependent on the general development of the industry, since there is no reason why such specialization is impossible from the beginning, when the scale of the industry is small, unless there are internal economies in individual firms. Increasing returns due to division of labor cannot be compatible with competition, unless individual demand curves are, at least partially, downward sloping, as is argued in Chapter 3, section 4. The only remaining possibility, therefore, for external economies seems to be the supply of public factors of production or public intermediate goods, which is favorable to larger industries.[13]

(3) Internal economies may not be fully exploited by an individual firm since its life-span is limited. Like an individual tree in a forest, an individual firm in an industry grows and decays, although the forest and the industry remain stationary.

> Rapid growth of firms in some trades which offer great economies to production on a large scale... But long before this end [monopoly] is reached, his [a new businessman's] progress is likely to be arrested by the decay, if not of his faculties, yet of his liking for energetic work. (Marshall [20, pp. 285–286].)

> A tendency to Increasing Return prevails: that is, an increasing output can generally be produced at a diminishing rate of cost. It is obvious that, under this tendency a firm, which had once obtained the start of its rivals, would be in a position to undersell them progressively, provided its own vigour remained unimpaired, and it could obtain all the capital it need ... under the law of Increasing Return, there might have seemed to be nothing to prevent the concentration in the hands of single firm of the whole production of the world .... The reason why this result did not follow was simply that no firm

[13] According to the voluntary theory of public finance, the level of public expenditure is determined by individual beneficiary/tax payers seeking to maximize their net gains. Large industry is surely one of the most influential individual beneficiary/tax payers. See Negishi [25].

ever had a sufficient long life of unabated energy and power of initiative for the purpose. (Marshall [17, pp. 315–316].)

Marshall put the main burden of solving the problem of the compatibility of increasing returns and competitive equilibrium on this life-cycle theory of private firms. Since this theory is based on Marshall's theory of a long-run equilibrium of an industry in which individual firms are at disequilibria, we shall first consider the latter theory in general in this subsection, and then try to rehabilitate the former theory in the next subsection so that it can be applied in a modified form to the modern economy where the life-span of firms is not necessarily limited.

Just as Marx considered market value in the case where different producers are under different conditions in the same industry (see Chapter 6, section 6), Marshall also considered the long-run normal supply price in the case where "some businesses will be rising and others falling" (Marshall [20, p. 378]). Marshall considered the relation between an industry and its firms to be like the relation between a forest and its trees.

We may read a lesson from the young trees of the forest as they struggle upwards through the benumbing shade of their older rivals. Many succumb on the way, and a few only survive; those few become stronger with every year, they get a larger share of light and air with every increase of their height, and at last in their turn they tower above their neighbours, and seems as they would grow on for ever, and for ever become stronger as they grow. But they do not. One tree will last longer in full vigour and attain a greater size than another; but sooner or later age tells on them all. Though the taller ones have a better access to light and air than their rivals, they gradually lose vitality; and one after another they give place to others, which, though of less material strength, have on their side the vigour of youth. And as with the growth of trees, so was it with the growth of business as a general rule. (Marshall [20, pp. 315–316].)

As his first step "towards studying the influences exerted by the element of time on the relations between cost of production and value," Marshall considered the stationary state of an industry (Marshall [20, p. 366].)

Of course we might assume that in our stationary state every business remained always of the same size, and with the same trade connection. But we need not go so far as that; it will suffice to suppose that firms rise and fall, but that the representative firm remains always of about the same size, as does the representative tree of a virgin forest. (Marshall [20, p. 367].)

The representative firm is defined in this way as the miniature of an industry and, as Frisch [6] emphasized, is a construction of the mind, so that there may not be an actual firm which may be picked out as representative in the industry. It is, however, a very convenient device to consider the normal supply price of an industry composed of firms behaving differently under different conditions. The normal supply price is assumed to be the normal expenses of production (including normal profit) of the representative firm.

This is the price the expectation of which will just suffice to maintain the existing aggregate amount of production; some firms meanwhile rising and increasing their output, and others falling and diminishing theirs; but the aggregate remaining unchanged. A price higher than this would increase the growth of the rising firms, and slacken, though it might not arrest, the decay of the falling firms; with the net result of an increase in the aggregate production. On the other hand, a price lower than this would hasten the decay of the falling firms, and slacken the growth of the rising firms; and on the whole diminish production. (Marshall [20, p. 343].)

Why do some firms increase their output while others diminish theirs? Marshall considered, of course, that young firms, like young trees, grow while old firms, like old trees, decay, on the basis of his life-cycle theory of firms. We may, furthermore, consider that a young (an old) firm increases (decreases) its output since its normal expenses of production (including normal profit) falls short of (exceeds) that of the representative firm, i.e., the normal supply price of the industry.[14] In our stationary state, of course, the demand price is equalized to the normal supply price of the industry, while the supply price of each firm is considered to be its normal expenses of production, including normal profit.

When . . . the amount produced is such that the demand price is greater than the supply price, then sellers receive more than is sufficient to make it worth their while to bring goods to market to that amount; and there is at work an active force tending to increase the amount brought forward for sale. On the other hand, when the amount produced is such that demand price is less than the supply price, sellers receive less than is sufficient to make it worth their while to bring goods to market on that scale; so that those who were just on the margin of doubt as to whether to go on producing are decided not to do so, and there is an active force at work tending to diminish the amount brought forward for sale. (Marshall [20, p. 345].)

---

[14] In other words, the short-run average cost including normal profit is higher (lower) than the normal supply price of the industry for the contracting (expanding) firms, while the short-run marginal cost is equal to the normal supply price of the industry for all firms.

Let us use x to denote the supply price of a firm and p to denote the supply price of the industry. A firm increases its output if p is higher than x, and decreases it if p is lower than x. It is assumed that the rate of change in output is proportional to the difference between p and x. The different firms may have an identical value of x or a different value of x. Let $y(x)$ be the total output of firms with the same value of x. Furthermore, let $D(x)$ denote changes (increases if positive, decreases if negative) in y. Then, from the assumption,

$$D(x)/y(x)=(p-x). \tag{1}$$

Since the industrial output remains unchanged, i.e.,

$$\int y(x)\,dx = \text{constant}, \tag{2}$$

from (1),

$$\int D(x)\,dx = \int (p-x)y(x)\,dx = 0. \tag{3}$$

If we define the proportion of the total output $y(x)$ of firms with the supply price x to the total industrial output as

$$f(x)=y(x)\Big/\int y(x)\,dx \tag{4}$$

we have, in view of (4),

$$p=\int xf(x)\,dx \tag{5}$$

since from the right-hand side of (3)

$$p\int y(x)\,dx = \int xy(x)\,dx. \tag{6}$$

From the definition (4),

$$\int f(x)\,dx = 1. \tag{7}$$

Therefore, (5) implies that the normal supply price of the industry or its representative firm is the average of the supply prices of the individual firms in the industry.

If internal economies exist and the supply price of an individual firm is a decreasing function of its output, there is no limit for the expansion of a young firm with the lowest individual supply price, until the whole industrial output is concentrated in its hands so that its supply price coincides with the industrial supply price. To prevent the concentration of the whole industrial output in the hands of a single firm, Marshall emphasized that the life-span of private firms is limited and that expanding young firms are eventually changed into shrinking old firms long before such concentration is actually realized.

Although Marshall's life-cycle theory of firms gives a realistic picture of nineteenth-century industry, however, the question remains as to its relevancy after the great development of joint-stock companies. Marshall himself was well aware of this problem: "As with the growth of trees, so was it with the growth of business as a general rule before the great recent development of vast joint-stock companies, which often stagnate, but do not readily die" (Marshall [20, p. 316]).[15] "A private firm without great vigour is sure to die; a large joint-stock company has special advantages, many of which do not materially dwindle with age" (Marshall [17, p. 316]). Since Marshall put the main burden of solving the problem of the compatibility of diminishing cost and competitive equilibrium on his life-cycle theory of the firm, however, it is worthwhile to consider whether the theory can be revived in a somewhat modified form, even without the assumption that the life-span of an individual firm is limited.[16]

Instead of Marshall's supposition that the life-span of an individual firm is limited, we may consider that a capital asset with embodied technology has a limited life, since wages rise as a result of technical progress. In other words, we may replace Marshall's theory of the life-cycle of a firm with a theory of the life-cycle of technology. Although Marshall "exclude[s] from view any economies that may result from substantive new inventions" (Marshall [20, p. 460]), we can argue that the balanced growth equilibrium with technical progress is not so foreign from his "modification of the fiction of a stationary state" which will "bring us nearer to real life and help to break up a complex problem (Marshall [20, p. 368]).[17]

The stationary state has just been taken to be one in which population is

---

[15] It was in the sixth edition of *Principles* (1910) that Marshall first added a reservation clause on joint-stock companies. See Marshall [21, p. 343].

[16] Instead of a regular cycle of the birth, growth, decay and death of firms, Shove [33], Wolfe [42], Newman [27], and Newman and Wolfe [28] introduced random influences on cost curves and considered the statistical long-run equilibrium of the industry – that is, the size distribution of firms.

[17] See Whitaker [40, pp. 305–316], for Marshall's unpublished notes on the theory of economic growth, in which changes in the art of production are taken into consideration. Unfortunately, Marshall did not inquire "into the qualitative properties of solutions for secular growth paths: indeed the models as they stand are much too complex and unrestricted to lend themselves readily to such analysis."

stationary. But nearly all its distinctive features may be exhibited in a place where population and wealth are both growing, provided they are growing at about the same rate .... For in such a state by far the most important conditions of production and consumption, of exchange and distribution will remain of the same quality, and in the same general relations to one another, though they are all increasing in volume. (Marshall [20, p. 368].)

While Marshall considers here economic growth with both population and wealth growing but technology unchanged, we are going to consider the growth of physical wealth with technical progress and unchanged population. In view of the so-called stylized facts of economic growth that the real wage and capital-labor ratio are rising while the relative shares of capital and labor remain unchanged,[18] however, it is evident which plan will "bring us nearer to real life and help to break up a complex problem."

3.2

To make the story simple, let us assume that capital goods do not depreciate physically. Given a set of capital goods k, the short-run average variable cost of output y produced by the use of k and some primary factor of production such as labor is denoted by $c(y, k)$. The short-run marginal cost of y is increasing, since k is given. The average cost curve is U-shaped, therefore, first diminishing with respect to y, due to the diminishing average constant cost, and then increasing with respect to y, due to the increasing marginal cost. Marshallian internal economies are, however, not concerned with the short-run diminishing average cost under the given capital k. Marshallian internal economies imply that the average cost is diminishing, not with y, but with k.

"The tendency to increasing return does not act quickly," wrote Marshall [20, p. 455]. "We expect the short-period supply price to increase with increasing output. But we also expect a gradual increase in demand to increase gradually the size and efficiency of this representative firm, and to increase the economies both internal and external which are at its disposal" [20, p. 460]. In other words, Marshallian internal economies are concerned with the long-run average cost of individual firms.

In Marshall's stationary state, technical progress does not exist, and all the prices and wages remain unchanged through time. Unlike Marshall, however, we consider that the life-span of a firm is not limited. Since capital goods do not

---

[18] For the stylized facts of economic growth, see Chapter 8, section 4 of this book and the literature mentioned there.

depreciate physically as well as morally, investment is carried out so that the condition that the rate of profit is indefinitely normal, that is,

$$py - c(y, k)y = rqk \tag{8}$$

is satisfied, where p, q and r denote, respectively, the price of the output, the price of a set of capital goods, and the normal rate of profit. By dividing by the level of output y, we have

$$p = c(y, k) + (rqk/y) \tag{9}$$

which implies that the price is equalized to the average cost, including normal profit in the long-run equilibrium. "The normal supply price of any amount of that commodity may be taken to be its normal expenses of production (including gross earnings of management)" according to Marshall [20, pp. 342–343].

In the long-run equilibrium defined by condition (8), furthermore, the excess profit

$$E = py - c(y, k)y - rqk \tag{10}$$

which vanishes at the equilibrium, must be the maximized one with respect to the level of output y and the amount of capital k. The following conditions are, therefore, necessary.

$$\partial E/\partial y = p - c(y, k) - y\partial c(y, k)/\partial y = 0 \tag{11}$$

and

$$\partial E/\partial k = -y\partial c(y, k)/\partial k - rq = 0 \tag{12}$$

Condition (11) is nothing but the condition that the short-run marginal cost of output, $c + y\partial c/\partial y$, is equalized to the price, and can be satisfied easily from our supposition that the competitive price is constant and the marginal cost is increasing. Condition (12), on the other hand, requires that there should be no unexhausted internal economies remaining at the equilibrium, in the sense that the average cost including normal profit, $c + (rqk/y)$ can no longer be decreased by increasing k.

Provided that the long-run average cost including normal profit is falling, in other words, there cannot be a long-run competitive equilibrium, since investment in capital assets is expanded indefinitely. Internal economies are not compatible with competition in a stationary equilibrium, if the life-span of the firm and its capital is unlimited. While Marshall solved this problem by limiting the life-span of the firm, let us do it by introducing technical progress and limiting the life-span of capital goods morally in the balanced growth equilibrium with technical progress. The possibility of a steady-state growth equilibrium with technical progress can be seen by considering the following simplified aggregate model of a growing economy where technical progress is embodied in capital.

Suppose the investment–saving relation is simply

$$K(t) = sY(t) \tag{13}$$

where $Y(t)$ denotes the aggregate level of malleable output which can be either consumed or invested, at time t, $K(t)$ denotes the aggregate level of investment at t, and s is a positive constant less than 1. Because capital does not depreciate physically, $K(t)$ also denotes the amount of the existing capital produced at t. The capital–output ratio is assumed to be such a technical constant that one unit of capital always produces one unit of output. If capitals up to T-years-old are actually utilized in the production, then, the aggregate output available is

$$Y(t) = K(t) + K(t-1) + \ldots + K(t-T). \tag{14}$$

The capital–labor ratio is also assumed to be technically constant in such a way that a unit of $K(t)$ requires a^t units of labor to be operated, where a is a positive constant less than 1. Technical progress can be seen from the fact that less labor is required by newer capital to produce the same output. Since the labor market must be cleared,

$$L = K(t)a^t + K(t-1)a^{t-1} + \ldots + K(t-T)a^{t-T} \tag{15}$$

where L denotes the stationary supply of labor.

By solving (15) for $K(t)$, we can easily see that the steady-state growth rate is $1/a$ in this vintage capital model with fixed coefficients. Both the aggregate output and newly produced capital grow at the rate of $1/a$, with capitals up to T-years-old always being in use. By eliminating $Y(t)$ from (13) and (14), then, we can see that T and s vary inversely. While the supply of labor remains stationary, the level of real wage $w(t)$ rises also at the rate of $1/a$, since the condition

$$1 = a^{t-T}w(t) \tag{16}$$

must be nearly satisfied if t changes almost continually. In other words, one cannot expect profit from the use of the oldest capital of that actually used. In view of (16), profits obtained from the use of capitals less old than T,

$$1 - a^{t-s}w(t) = 1 - a^{T-s}, \quad s < T \tag{17}$$

are independent of t.[19]

---

[19] See Allen [1, pp. 299–303] for the details of this fixed coefficient model.

Generally, of course, the capital–output ratio and the capital–labor ratio are not technically constant but are functions of real wage, so that the model would be much more complicated. In view of the results obtained from the simple model considered above, however, we may suppose that, in general, the real wages and relative prices of the primary factors of production whose supplies are given continue to rise as a result of technical progress, while the rate of profit remains unchanged. Even though the capital assets do not depreciate physically, they depreciate morally, since the cost of the product resulting from them, combined with the labor and other primary factor input, increases as time goes on. The economic life-span of capital assets is limited and there is a life-cycle, not of a firm, but of technology embodied in capital, or of a branch or sector of a firm – that is, a set of capital assets. A set of newly produced capital assets, being the most efficient ones, produce a larger than normal profit, although in the next period, being old and less efficient, they produce smaller than normal profit, even a negative one, but may still replace the variable cost. Finally, say, from the third period onwards, being unable to replace even the variable cost, they cease to be utilized. In the long-run equilibrium, we can say that, not only the industry, but also firms (unlike Marshall [20, p. 367]) are in equilibrium, although different sections of a firm are constantly changing through the process of birth, growth, decay and death.

Let us consider whether an internal economy remains unexhausted in a section of a competitive firm when the economy grows with technical progress, and the wages of labor and prices of other primary factors of production continue to rise, but other prices and the normal rate of profit are stationary. Although the capital goods do not depreciate physically, they now depreciate morally, since they have to compete with newer, more efficient capital goods. Suppose a section of a firm is newly created and investment is done there in the period 0, so that capital assets k can be used in the period 1 and on. In period 1 a larger than normal profit can be produced by the use of k, since k, being the most efficient capital, the average variable cost $c(y, k)$ of output y is much lower than the given price p of output y. In period 2, however, only a smaller than normal profit can be produced by the use of k, since the average variable cost $c'(y, k)$ is much higher than $c(y, k)$, due to higher wages of labor and prices of other primary factors of production caused by the use of more efficient capital goods in the other parts of the economy. Since the capital cost is sunk, nevertheless, k is still used in period 2, provided that c' is somewhat lower than the unchanged p. Finally, in the period 3, k ceases to be used at all and this section of the firm has to be dissolved, since the average cost $c''(y, k)$ is now higher than p, due to still higher wages of labor and prices of other primary factors of production.

Since capital goods now depreciate morally, we have to take the depreciation into consideration in the calculation of average cost to be compared to price in each period. To simplify the story by avoiding this complicated problem as far as possible, however, let us simply assume that old capital assets have no scrap value and that depreciation quotas to two periods, D_1 and D_2, are such constants as $D_1(1+r)+D_2=1$, where r denotes the rate of normal profit, which is a given constant to competitive firms.

Since free entry is assumed, the level of investment in the period 0 satisfies

$$(py-c(y,k)y)/(1+r)+(py'-c'(y',k)y')/(1+r)^2 = qk \qquad (18)$$

where p, y, y', q and r denote, respectively, the unchanged price of output, the level of output in period 1 and that in period 2, the unchanged price of capital assets k, and the unchanged rate of normal profit. Condition (18) states that the sum of the discounted revenues expected is equalized with the cost of k in the period 0. It can be changed into

$$E=(py-c(y,k)y-rqk-D_1qk)+(py'-c'(y',k)y'-rqk-D_2qk)/(1+r)$$
$$=0 \qquad (19)$$

which corresponds to (10) in the case of no technical progress, where the average cost remains unchanged so that k can be used for production indefinitely. Condition (19) states that the excess profit is zero or the total profit is normal, with the profit in period 1 higher and the profit in period 2 lower than normal.

The competitive firm tries to maximize the excess profit E, which actually vanishes at equilibrium, with respect to y, y' and k. The following conditions are, therefore, necessary.

$$\partial E/\partial y = p - c(y,k) - y\partial c(y,k)/\partial y = 0 \qquad (20)$$
$$\partial E/\partial y' = p - c'(y',k) - y'\partial c'(y',k)/\partial y'$$
$$=0 \qquad (21)$$

and

$$\partial E/\partial k = (-y\partial c(y,k)/\partial k - rq - D_1q) + (-y'\partial c'(y',k)/\partial k - rq - D_2q)/(1+r)$$
$$=0. \qquad (22)$$

Conditions (20) and (21) are nothing but the condition that the marginal cost of output is equalized to the price in each period.

Figure 10.5, in which the level of output in each period is measured horizontally and the cost and price are measured vertically, shows how cost

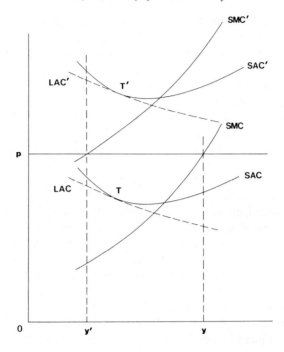

Figure 10.5

curves are shifted between two periods. The curve SAC shows the short-run average cost including normal profit in the period 1, $c(y, k) + (D_1 qk/y) + (rqk/y)$, and curve SMC, the short-run marginal cost in the period 1, $c(y, k) + y\partial c(y, k)/\partial y$. The profit here being higher than normal, SAC must be increasing at y, which satisfies (20). The dashed curve LAC is the envelope for SAC curves with different k's and the SAC curve is shifted rightwards when k is increased. Since the envelope, which is the long-run average cost curve, is downward sloping, an internal economy exist and the averge cost at y can be reduced by increasing k, since the SAC curve is higher than the envelope at y, satisfying (20), which is located to the right of the tangential point T of two curves. This implies that the first term of $\partial E/\partial k$ in (22) is positive.

   In the period 2, on the other hand, cost curves are shifted upwards. Since the profit here is now lower than normal, the short-run average cost curve SAC' must be decreasing at y', which satisfies (21). The average cost at y', $c'(y', k) + (D_2 qk/y') + (rqk/y')$, must be increased by increasing k, and y' must be located to the left of the tangential point T' of SAC' and the long-run average cost curve LAC', since the second term of $\partial E/\partial k$ in (22) must be negative.

Unlike in the case of condition (12), which corresponds to condition (22) when there is no technical progress, condition (22) can be satisfied with finite k, with the first term in (22) being positive and the second, negative, even though the long-run average cost curve is downward sloping and the minimum (with respect to y and y') of the short-run average cost, including normal profit $c(y, k) + (D_1 qk/y) + (rqk/y)$ and $c'(y', k) + (D_2 qk/y') + (rqk/y')$, decreases as k increases. This is because a further increase in k diminishes the average cost at the actually chosen level of output in period 1, but increases such average cost in period 2. In other words, the competitive equilibrium is possible, even if an internal economy remains unexhausted and the average cost, including normal profit, diminishes as the amount of capital is increased.

The internal economy remains unexhausted simply because capital input cannot be changed, unlike the case of labor, in each period. If capital goods can be sold at the end of period 1, the use of capital will be increased in period 1 in so far as its value marginal productivity is higher than the normal rate of profit and internal economy cannot be compatible with competition. By definition, however, capital goods are something which, once installed, cannot be disposed of so easily. If they are not disposed of at the end of period 1, furthermore, they have to be used rather than thrown away in period 2, even though the value marginal productivity of capital falls short of the normal rate of profit. Investment in period 0 has to be stopped, therefore, before the value marginal productivity of capital in period 1 is equalized to the normal rate of profit.

4. From Marshall to Keynes

John Maynard Keynes (1883–1946) was a son of John Neville Keynes, the author of *The Scope and Method of Political Economy* (1890), and was educated at Eton and Cambridge. In 1905, Marshall wrote to J.N. Keynes, "Your son is doing excellent work in Economics. I have told him that I should be greatly delighted if he should decide on the career of a professional economist."[20] The greatest contribution of J.M. Keynes as a professional economist is certainly *The General Theory of Employment, Interest and Money* (1936), in which he showed the possibility of an equilibrium with involuntary unemployment in a modern monetary economy. From his *Tract on Monetary Reform* (1923), through *Treatise on Money* (1930), to *General Theory*, however, Keynes constantly emphasized the importance of the monetary aspects of the

[20] See Harrod [9, p. 107] and Ekelund and Hébert [4, p. 432]. For Marshall's letters to J.M. Keynes himself, see Pigou [29, pp. 479–483].

modern economy. In his contribution to a Festschrift for Spiethoff, entitled "A monetary theory of production," which played an important role in his movement from *Treatise* to *General Theory*, Keynes argued that a monetary economy, rather than a real-exchange economy, should be considered to study phenomena such as booms and depressions.

> The main reason why the problem of crises is unsolved, or at any rate why this theory is so unsatisfactory, is to be found in the lack of what might be termed a *monetary theory of production* . . . . An economy, which uses money but uses it merely as a neutral link between transactions in real things and real assets and does not allow it to enter into motives or decisions, might be called . . . a *real-exchange economy.*The theory which I desiderate would deal, in contradiction to this, with an economy in which money plays a part of its own and affects motives and decisions and is, in short, one of the operative factors in the situation, so that the course of events cannot be predicted, either in the long period or in the short, without a knowledge on the behaviour of money between the first state and the last. And it is this which we ought to mean when we speak of a *monetary economy* . . . it is my belief that the far-reaching and in some respects fundamental differences between the conclusions of a monetary economy and those of the more simplified real-exchange economy have been greatly underestimated by the exponents of the traditional economics; with the result that machinery of thought with which real-exchange economics has equipped the minds of practioneers in the world of affairs, and also of economists themselves, has led in practice to many erroneous conclusions and policies . . . . I am saying that booms and depressions are phenomena peculiar to an economy in which money is not neutral. (Keynes [14, pp. 408–411].)

Walrasian theory as a whole may be called a theory of a real-exchange economy in the sense of Keynes, since, as we saw in Chapter 7, section 5.2, it is based on the dichotomy between real and monetary theories and money, even if introduced, remains neutral. While money is introduced after relative prices are determined in a Walrasian system, in a Marshallian system money does exist from the beginning, but its purchasing power is assumed constant when relative prices are considered. Because of this assumption, Keynes argued that Marshallian theory is also a theory of a real-exchage economy.

> Most treatises on the principles of economics are concerned mainly, if not entirely, with a real-exchange economy; and – which is more peculiar – the same thing is also largely true of most treatises on the theory of money. In particular, Marshall's *Principles of Economics* is avowedly concerned with a real-exchange economy . . . Marshall expressly states . . . that he is dealing

with *relative* exchange values. The proposition that the prices of a ton of lead and a ton of tin are £15 and £90 means no more to him in this context than that the value of a ton of tin in terms of lead is six tons. "We may throughout this volume," he explains, "neglect possible changes in the general purchasing power of money. Thus the price of anything will be taken as representative of its exchange value relative to *things* in general." ... In short, though money is present and is made use of for convenience, it may be concerned to cancel out for the purposes of most of the general conclusions of the *Principles* ... Now the conditions required for the "neutrality" of money, in the sense in which this is assumed in Marshall's *Principles of Economics*, are I suspect, precisely the same as those which still insure that crises *do not occur.*[21]

Since Marshall gave an explicit and extensive account of the trade cycle by emphasizing changes in relative prices caused by changes in the purchasing power of money, however, one cannot argue that Marshall's economics as a whole is a theory of a real-exchange economy. Marshall's theory of the trade cycle was first developed in *Economics of Industry* (jointly with his wife). He made use of it in his testimony before the Depression of Trade and Industry Commission, reproduced it in *Principles of Economics*, and repeated it in *Money, Credit and Commerce.*[22] Although, in Marshall's *Principles of Economics*, the general purchasing power of money is assumed to be constant, as one of other things which are constant, even there we find the following argument:

> When we come to discuss the causes of alternating periods of inflation and depression of commercial activity, we shall find that they are intimately connected with those variations in the real rate of interest which are caused by changes in the purchasing power of money. For when prices are likely to rise, people rush to borrow money and buy goods and thus help prices to rise; business is inflated and is managed recklessly and wastefully; those working on borrowed capital pay back less real capital than they borrowed, and enrich themselves at the expense of the community. When afterwards credit is shaken and prices begin to fall, everyone wants to get rid of commodities, and get hold of money which is rapidly rising in value; this makes price fall all the faster, and the further fall makes credit shrink even more, and thus for a long time prices fall because prices have fallen. (Marshall [20, pp. 594–595].)

---

[21] See Keynes [14, pp. 409–411]. For the reference to Marshall, see Marshall [20, pp. 61–62].
[22] See Marshall and Marshall [22, pp. 150–167], Marshall [20, pp. 710–711], [18, Book IV], and [19, pp. 1–16].

Thus Marshall's economics consists of two parts. The first is that of a real-exchange economy in the sense of Keynes, where the general purchasing power of money is assumed to be constant, money is neutral, and crises do not occur. The second is that of a monetary economy in the sense of Keynes, where the general purchasing power of money changes, money is not neutral, and crises do occur. If Marshall's economics. as a whole is the economics of a monetary economy in the sense of Keynes, furthermore, it has to be able to explain changes in aggregate output and employment, since Keynes argued that "the divergence between the real-exchange economics and my desired monetary economics is, however, most marked and perhaps most important when we come to the discussion of the rate interest and to the relation between the volume of output and amount of expenditure" [14, p. 410]. While Marshall considered the trade cycle as changes in the purchasing power of money and the real rate of interest, he was, of course, aware of a suspension of industry and unemployment induced by changes in relative prices.

The connection between a fall of prices and a suspension of industry requires to be worked out ... when prices are rising, the rise in the prices of the finished commodity is generally more rapid than that in the price of the raw material, always more rapid than that in the price of labour; and when prices are falling, the fall in the price of the finished commodity is generally more rapid than that in the price of raw material, always more rapid than that in the price of labour. And therefore when prices are falling the manufacturer's receipts are sometimes scarcely sufficient even to repay him for his outlay on raw material, wages, and other forms of Circulating capital; they seldom give him in addition enough to pay interest on his Fixed capital and Earnings of Management for himself ... We conclude, then, that manufacturing cannot be carried on, except at a low rate of profit or at a loss, when the prices of finished goods are low relatively to those of labour and raw material, or prices are falling.[23]

I agree with the general opinion that a steady upward tendency in general prices conduces a little more to the general well-being than does a tendency downwards, because it keeps industry somewhat better employed ... people of all classes, and especially of the working classes, spend their income more wisely when prices and money-wages are falling, and they think themselves worse off than they are, than when a rise of prices and money-wage lends them to exaggerate their real incomes and to be careless about their expenditure. (Marshall [19, p. 9].)

[23] See Marshall and Marshall [22, pp. 155–156], Marshall [19, pp. 7–8] and [21, pp. 714–716].

Thus Marshall explained changes in aggregate output and employment by changes in relative prices which are induced by changes in the purchasing power of money. In the recent development of Keynesian economics, on the other hand, prices are considered as fixed in the sense of Hicks, and changes in output and employment are explained directly by changes in the effective demand.[24] Marshall's theory of a trade cycle cannot, therefore, be the foundation of such a model of Keynesian economics. It is, however, rather isomorphic to recent monetarist or equilibrium macroeconomics explanations of employment. For example, Friedman [5] describes the effects of a decrease in the rate of money growth in a long-run equilibrium when prices have been stable. The prices of products respond to an unanticipated decrease in nominal demand faster than the prices of factors of production, while, for example, the supply of labor is temporarily decreased by the reduction in wages to below the anticipated normal level. Therefore, real wages actually received go up, although real wages anticipated by employees go down, since at first they tend to evaluate the wages offered at the unchanged price level. This simultaneous rise *ex post* in real wages to employers and fall *ex ante* in real wages to employees enables unemployment to increase. The former effect is clearly the one emphasized by Marshall when he wrote that "the price of finished goods are low relatively to those of labour," while Marshall also grasped somewhat vaguely the latter effect when he commented that employees "think themselves worse off than they are."

Although Marshall's theory of a trade cycle with variable purchasing power of money belongs to a tradition different from the recent fixprice models of Keynesian macroeconomics, it is somewhat ironic that Marshall's price theory with constant purchasing power of money, which is a real-exchange economics in the sense of Keynes, can be microeconomic foundation of fixprice Keynesian macroeconomics. The reason is, firstly, that, unlike Walrasian price theory, it is a non-*tâtonnement* theory and, secondly, that it suggests the possibility of kinked demand curves faced by individual firms.

In Walrasian *tâtonnement*, no actual transactions are carried out in any market until the demand and supply are equalized at the equilibrium price. It is impossible, therefore, to consider the Keynesian underemployment equilibrium in which some laborers are actually employed while others are involuntarily unemployed and excess supply remains in the labor market. As we saw in Chapter 7, section 5.2, the assumption of *tâtonnement* was necessary for Walras to solve the equilibrium problems without introducing money.

---

[24] "It is not implied by the description Fixprice method that prices are never to be allowed to change – only that they do not necessarily change whenever there is demand – supply disequilibrium" (Hicks [12, p. 78]). See Malinvaud [16, pp. 1–80] and Negishi [26, pp. 53–72].

Marshall's price theory can be non-*tâtonnement* theory in which actual transactions are carried out at disequilibria, therefore, since money does exist in the Marshallian economic system, even when relative prices and the allocation of real resources are considered.

The fact that Marshall's price theory is a non-*tâtonnement* theory can be seen in his consideration of the temporary equilibrium in the corn market (Marshall [20, p. 332]). According to demand and supply schedules given by Marshall, at the prices of 37 shillings, 36 shillings, and 35 shillings, holders will be willing to sell, respectively, 1,000 quarters, 700 quarters, and 600 quarters, and buyers will be willing to buy, respectively, 600 quarters, 700 quarters, and 900 quarters. The price of 36 shillings is, of course, the Walrasian equilibrium price that is established by *tâtonnement* and announced by the auctioneer to individual dealers. Marshall considered, however, a non-*tâtonnement* market where actual transactions are carried out at a disequilibrium price among dealers, without the perfect knowledge of the equilibrium price.

It is not indeed necessary for our argument that any dealers should have a thorough knowledge of the circumstances of the market. Many of the buyers may perhaps underrate the willingness of the sellers to sell, with the effect that for some time the price rules at the highest level at which any buyers can be found: and thus 500 quarters may be sold before the price sinks below 37 shillings. But afterwards the price must begin to fall and the result will probably be that 200 more quarters will be sold, and the market will close on a price of about 36 shillings. For when 700 quarters have been sold, no seller will be anxious to dispose of any more except at a higher price than 36 shillings, and no buyer will be anxious to purchase any more except at a lower price than 36 shillings. In the same way if the sellers had underrated the willingness of the buyers to pay high price, some of them might begin to sell at the lowest price they would take, rather than their corn left on their hands, and in this case much corn might be sold at a price of 35 shillings; but the market would probably close on a price of 36 shillings and a total sale of 700 quarters. (Marshall [20, p. 334].)

Why is the same price of 36 shillings reached by Walras's *tâtonnement* as well as Marshall's non-*tâtonnement* process? Why is the equilibrium price considered to be independent of how transactions at disequilibria are carried out? The reason is Marshall's assumption of the constant marginal utility of money, which we already found useful for consumers' and producers' surplus analysis (section 2).

We tacitly assumed that the sum which purchasers were willing to pay, and which sellers were willing to take, for the seven hundredth quarter would not be affected by the question whether the earlier bargains had been made at a high or a low rate. We allowed for the diminution in the buyers' need of corn (its marginal utility to them) as the amount bought increased. But we did not allow for any appreciable change in their unwillingness to part with money (its marginal utility); we assumed that that would be practically the same whether the early payment had been at a high or a low rate. (Marshall [20, pp. 334–335].)

In the Marshallian temporary equilibrium, the level of output is constant, and therefore the total gross supply of corn is constant. As was pointed out by Hicks [11, pp. 127–129], the assumption of the constant marginal utility of money implies no income effect on the demand for corn, with the result that the total gross demand for corn, including the reservation demand for suppliers, is independent of the transactions carried out at disequilibria, provided that all buyers and sellers remain in the market until the equilibrium is reached, or at least return to the market whenever there is a change in the price (Williams [41]). It is clear, then, that the final equilibrium price reached by any non-*tâtonnement* process is identical to the one established by *tâtonnement*. Strictly speaking, however, there is no reason, contrary to what Marshall thought, that the cumulative volume of transactions in any non-*tâtonnement* process would also be equal to 700 quarters, since, as was emphasized by Walker [38], the individual net demands and supplies are not independent of the disequilibrium transactions.

If an excess supply of labor does not cause a change in the rate of wage and therefore is not cleared in a non-*tâtonnement* fixprice economy, laborers are quantity-constrained in the labor market and adjust their consumption demand to the level of income lower than that of the full employment. Similarly, if an excess supply is not cleared by a change in the price of a product, firms must face a quantity constraint in their product market and adjust their demand for labor to a level lower than that of the full capacity, which is defined by the equality of the marginal productivity of labor and the rate of real wage. To consider a Keynesian equilibrium by the use of such a fixprice method, it is necessary to explain why prices do not necessarily change, at least in the short-run, when there are excess supplies. One possible explanation is to assume that suppliers perceive kinked demand curves in excess supplied markets.[25] In this respect, it is interesting to consider the following view of Marshall on competitive markets which are not homogeneous and very imperfect.

---

[25] See Malinvaud [16, p. ix] and Negishi [26, pp. 87–98]. See also Chapter 3, section 4 of this book.

Everyone buys, and nearly every producer sells, to some extent, in a *"general"* market, in which he is on about the same footing with others around him. But nearly everyone has also some *"particular"* market; that is, some people or groups of people with whom he is in somewhat close touch; mutual knowledge and trust lead him to approach them, and them to approach him, in preference to strangers. A producer, a wholesale dealer, or a shopkeeper, who has built up a strong connection among purchasers of his goods has a valuable property. He does not generally expect to get better prices from his clients than from others. But he expects to sell easily to them because they know and trust him: and he does not sell at low prices in order to call attention to his business, as he often does in a market where he is little known. (Marshall [17, p. 182].)

The demand curve perceived by the individual producer considered by Marshall should be downward sloping and kinked at the point of the current price and current sale. It is very steep for a quantity larger than the current sale, since the producer has to sell not only in his own special or particular market but also in a wide general market, "a market where he is little known," and has to "sell at low price in order to call attention to his business." For a quantity not larger than the current sale, on the other hand, demand is very elastic at the level of the current price, since the producer in his own particular market "does not generally expect to get better price from his clients than from others" in the general market. In this sense, it is Marshall's theory of market that can supply a firm microeconomic foundation to Keynesian economics.

References

[1] Allen, R.G.D., *Macro-Economic Theory*, Macmillan, 1967.
[2] Aspromourgos, T., "On the Origins of the Term 'Neoclassical'", *Cambridge Journal of Economics*, 10(1986), pp. 265–270.
[3] Blaug, M., *Economic Theory in Retrospect*, Cambridge University Press, 1985.
[4] Ekelund, R.B., and R.F. Hébert, *A History of Economic Theory and Method*, McGraw-Hill, 1983.
[5] Friedman, M., "The Role of Monetary Policy", *American Economic Review*, 58(1968), pp. 1–17.
[6] Frisch, R., "Alfred Marshall's Theory of Value", *Quarterly Journal of Economics*, 64(1956), pp. 495–524.
[7] Gide, C., and C. Rist, *Histoire des doctrines économiques*, Recueil Sirey, 1926.
[8] Hague, D.C., "Alfred Marshall and the Competitive Firm", *Economic Journal*, 68(1958), pp. 673–690.
[9] Harrod, R.F., *The Life of John Maynard Keynes*, Macmillan, 1951.
[10] Hicks, J.R., "Leon Walras", *Econometrica*, 2(1934), pp. 338–348.
[11] Hicks, J.R., *Value and Capital*, Oxford University Press, 1946.
[12] Hicks, J.R, *Capital and Growth*, Oxford University Press, 1965.

[13] Hutchison, T.W., *A Review of Economic Doctrines 1870–1929*, Oxford University Press, 1953.

[14] Keynes, J.M., *Collected Writings, XIII, The General Theory and After*, Part I, Macmillan, 1973.

[15] Leijonhufvud, A., "Schools, 'Revolutions' and Research Programmes in Economic Theory", *Method and Appraisal in Economics*, pp. 65–108, S.J. Latsis, ed., Cambridge University Press, 1976.

[16] Malinvaud, E., *The Theory of Unemployment Reconsidered*, Basil Blackwell, 1985.

[17] Marshall, A., *Industry and Trade*, Macmillan, 1921.

[18] Marshall, A., *Money, Credit and Commerce*, Macmillan, 1923.

[19] Marshall, A., *Official Papers*, Macmillan, 1926.

[20] Marshall, A., *Principles of Economics*, I, Text, Macmillan, 1961.

[21] Marshall, A., *Principles of Economics*, II, Notes, Macmillan, 1961.

[22] Marshall, A., and M.P. Marshall, *The Economics of Industry*, Macmillan, 1879.

[23] Mishan, E.J., "What is Producer's Surplus?", *American Economic Review*, 58(1968), pp. 1269–1282.

[24] Negishi, T., *General Equilibrium Theory and International Trade*, North-Holland, 1972.

[25] Negishi, T., "The Excess of Productive Public Expenditure", *Zeitschrift für National-öconomie*, 36(1976), pp. 85–94.

[26] Negishi, T., *Microeconomic Foundations of Keynesian Macroeconomics*, North-Holland, 1979.

[27] Newman, P., "The Erosion of Marshall's Theory of Value", *Quarterly Journal of Economics*, 74(1960), pp. 587–600.

[28] Newman, P., and J.N. Wolfe, "A Model for the Long-Run Theory of Value", *Review of Economic Studies*, 29(1961), pp. 51–61.

[29] Pigou, A.C., ed., *Memorials of Alfred Marshall*, Macmillan, 1925.

[30] Ricardo, D., *Works and Correspondence*, IX, Cambridge University Press, 1952.

[31] Robertson, D.H., "The Trees of the Forest", *Economic Journal*, 40(1930), pp. 80–89.

[32] Robinson, J., *The Economics of Imperfect Competition*, Macmillan, 1933.

[33] Shove, G.F., "The Representative Firm and Increasing Returns", *Economic Journal*, 40(1930), pp. 94–116.

[34] Shove, G.F., "The Place of Marshall's Principles in the Development of Economic Theory", *Economic Journal*, 52(1942), pp. 294–329.

[35] Spiegel, H.W., *The Growth of Economic Thought*, Duke University Press, 1983.

[36] Takayama, A., "Consumer's Surplus, Path Independence, Compensating and Equivalent Variation", *Zeitschrift für die gesamte Staatswissenschaft*, 140(1984), pp. 593–625.

[37] Varian, H.R., *Microeconomic Analysis*, Norton, 1978.

[38] Walker, D.A., "Marshall's Theory of Competitive Exchange", *Canadian Journal of Economics*, 2(1969), pp. 590–598.

[39] Walras, L., *Elements of Pure Economics*, W. Jaffé, tr., Irwin, 1954.

[40] Whitaker, J.K., *The Early Economic Writings of Alfred Marshall, 1867-1890*, Macmillan, 1975.

[41] Williams, P.L., "A Reconstruction of Marshall's Temporary Equilibrium Pricing Model", *History of Political Economy*, 18(1986), pp. 639–654.

[42] Wolfe, J.N., "The Representative Firm", *Economic Journal*, 64(1954), pp. 337–349.

POSTSCRIPT

Throughout this book, we have emphasized the coexistence of many different paradigms in economics. The currently dominating mainstream theory is not the only possible theory, and there are many past theories which are of great significance to the advancement of economic theory in the present situation, or will be in the near future. The study of the history of economic theory is important, therefore, not only from the heretical point of view, to show how and why the current mainstream theory is wrong, but also from the mainstream point of view, to spur on the development of its thinking.

Although our aim is to construct foundations on which the comparative study of different competing economic theories can eventually be made, our immediate concern in this book was not the study of contemporary neo-classical (neo-Walrasian), neo-Austrian, or neo-Ricardian economic theories, but the study of the economics of Walras, Menger, and Ricardo.

In the last four chapters, therefore, we confined ourselves to the study of Walras, Menger, Jevons, Marshall and their immediate followers, and refrained from discussing contributions made by such scholars as, among others, Pareto, Wicksell, I. Fisher, Hicks, Samuelson, Mises, Hayek, and Pigou – let alone Sraffa and J. Robinson. The reason is that the contributions of these scholars should still be considered as a part of the contemporary economic theory rather than in the history of economic theory. For example, the theory of imperfect or monopolistic competition developed by Robinson and Chamberlin should, in our opinion, rather be studied in connection with the contemporary general equilibrium theory, newly developing theories of applied microeconomics, and the new developments in industrial organization.[1] It should, therefore, be left to other volumes of the Advanced Textbooks in Economics series.

Our discussion on the economics of Keynes in Chapter 10 is merely marginal, since the aim of the chapter is to show the significance or relevance of

---

[1] See, for example, O.D. Hart, "Imperfect Competition in General Equilibrium: An Overview of Recent Work", *Frontiers of Economics*, K.J. Arrow and S. Honkapohja, eds., Blackwell, 1984; E. Helpman and P.R. Krugman, *Market Structure and Foreign Trade*, MIT Press, 1985; R. Schmalensee, "The New Industrial Organization and the Economics Analysis of Modern Markets", *Advances in Economic Theory*, W. Hildenbrand, ed., Cambridge University Press, 1982; and G.P. O'Driscoll, "Competition as a Process: a Law and Economics Perspective", *Economics as a Process*, R.N. Langlois, ed., Cambridge University Press, 1986.

the economics of Marshall to contemporary economics, including Keynesian economics. Since it is an important part of contemporary economics, a study of the economics of Keynes as such is beyond the scope of this book. Therefore, we discussed it merely in its relation to the economics of mercantilism (Chapter 1), Malthus (Chapter 4) and Marshall. In addition to this, of course, the economics of Keynes should be studied from the point of view of the monetary theories of Menger and Wicksell, and the Cambridge, Swedish and Austrian theories of trade cycles, as well as in conjunction with contemporary equilibrium and disequilibrium macroeconomics.[2]

This is also the case with Schumpeter in Chapter 8. Schumpeter's disequilibrium theory of interest was considered there from the point of view of the equilibrium theory of Böhm-Bawerk, since the aim of the discussion was to show the tangency point of two theories of interest, rather than to do full justice to Schumpeter. Although he regarded Walrasian general equilibrium theory very highly, Schumpeter can still be called an Austrian, since he emphasized dynamic rivalry among entrepreneurs and managers in the theory of interest. As is seen from the fact that his *Business Cycles* (1939) was subtitled *A Theoretical, Historical, and Statistical Analysis of the Capitalist Process*, however, Schumpeter regarded theory as only a small part of economics. He emphasized the importance of the historical approach and evaluated the economics of Schmoller very highly.[3]

---

[2] In this respect, some interesting literature is: E. Stressler, "Menger's Theories of Money and Uncertainty – a Modern Interpretation", *Carl Menger and the Austrian School of Economics*, J.R. Hicks and W. Weber, eds., Oxford University Press, 1973; S. Fujino, *Money, Employment, and Interest*, Kinokuniya, 1987; J.-P. Benassy, *The Economics of Market Disequilibrium*, Academic Press, 1982; E. Malinvaud, *The Theory of Unemployment Reconsidered*, Basil Blackwell, 1985; and K. Iwai, *Disequilibrium Dynamics*, Yale University Press, 1981.

[3] See J.A. Schumpeter, "Gustav v. Schmoller und die Probleme von heute", *Dogmenhistorische und Biographische Aufsatze*, J.C.B. Mohr, 1954; and T. Ohno, *Schumpeter Taikeikenkyuu* (A Study in Schumpeter's System), pp. 59–111, Sobunsha, 1971.

AUTHOR INDEX

Akhtar, M.A., 131
Allais, M., 266
Allen, R.G.D., 371
Anderson, R.K., 43
Appleyard, D.R., 177, 179, 180
Aquinas, T., 6
Aristotle, 6
Arrow, K.J., 95, 188, 254, 255, 262, 268
Arvidsson, G., 301
Aspromourgos, T., 345

Bacon, F., 31
Balassa, B.A., 170
Barkai, H., 82, 125, 126
Barna, T., 48, 55, 56, 57, 58, 59
Bauer, S., 51
Baumol, J.W., 171
Becker, G.S., 171
Benassy, J.-P., 287, 327, 386
Bentham, J., 156
Bernholz, P., 300
Bertrand, J., 244
Blaug, M.,
    on classical economics, 74, 81, 112, 144, 148
    on institutionalism, 19, 20
    on Jevons and Marshall, 327, 352, 355
    on Marx, 194, 199, 201, 216
    on mercantilism, 9
    on Quesnay, 52, 53
    on Schoolmen, 6
Bloomfield, A.I., 94
Böhm-Bawerk, E., 26, 100, 279
    on capital and time, 100, 279
    on causes of interest, 298, 307
    on fixed capital, 300, 304
    Kapital und Kapitalzins, 26, 208, 298, 332
    life sketch, 297
    on Marx, 208, 209
Bortkiewicz, L., 23, 204, 220, 300, 332
Bowley, A.L., 245
Bowley, M., 33, 34, 74, 100, 212
Boyle, R., 31
Breit, W., 186
Brems, H., 109, 121
Bronfenbrenner, M., 3, 5, 7, 198
Burmeister, D., 206, 312

Cairnes, J.E., 189
Caldwell, 4
Cannan, E., 97
Cantillon, R., 41, 48, 88, 109, 112
Casarosa, C., 109, 119, 136
Cassel, G., 332
Catephores, G., 192, 200, 202, 204
Cesarano, F., 5
Chamberlin, E.H., 27, 224, 227, 385
Chipman, J.S., 43, 113, 177, 180, 327, 339
Cochrane, J., 109
Coleridge, S.T., 157
Colie, R.L., 34
Commons, J.R., 19
Comte, A., 157
Corry, B.A., 144, 147
Cournot, A., 24, 26, 27, 91, 241, 323, 326, 330, 338, 340
Creedy, J., 331, 332, 337
Cunningham, W., 349

Darwin, C., 19
Debreu, G., 254, 335
Dome, T., 148
Dornbusch, R.S., 43
Dupuit, J., 25, 155, 326, 355

Eagly, R.V., 46, 52, 55, 137, 140, 144, 252
Easlea, B., 4
Edgeworth, F.Y., 27, 331
    on duopoly, 244
    equivalence theorem, 331, 335, 338
    on Jevons, 319, 323, 343
    life sketch, 331
    marginal revolution, 27, 345
    on market concept, 244, 338
    Mathematical Psychics, 27, 331, 332
    on J.S. Mill, 177
    on perfect competition, 335
    on utilitarianism, 337
Egger, J.B., 279
Ekelund, R.B., 11, 53, 162, 167, 192, 348, 351, 375
Elliott, J.E., 192, 220
Eltis, W.A., 48, 58, 59, 61, 64, 141, 144
Emmanuel, A., 24, 138

Engels, F., 21, 51, 155, 192, 193

Faber, M., 300, 301, 304
Farrell, M.J., 92, 339
Fellner, W., 244, 245
Feyerabend, P., 4
Fisher, I., 28, 252, 300, 332
Fisher, R.M., 326
Fisher, S., 43
Foley, V., 50
Friedman, D.D., 6
Friedman, J., 243, 245
Friedman, M., 29, 108, 379
Frisch, R., 352, 355, 366
Fujino, S., 386
Fukagai, Y., 171

Galbraith, J.K., 19
Gale, D., 254
Garegnani, P., 269
Georgescu-Roegen, N., 320, 323
Gide, C., 345
Gossen, H.H., 25, 319, 323, 326
Grigorovici, T., 229
Guillebaud, C.W., 348

Haberler, G., 312
Hague, D.C., 363
Hahn, F.H., 141, 188, 254, 255, 262, 268, 287
Harrod, R., 375
Hart, O.D., 168, 385
Harwitz, M., 178
Hatori, T., 34, 37
Hawtrey, R.G., 304
Hayek, F.A., 27, 152, 157, 280, 282
Hébert, R.F., 53, 162, 192, 348, 351, 375
Heckscher, E.F., 9, 24
Helpman, E., 385
Hicks, J.R., 27, 109, 245, 264, 268, 272, 280, 345, 355, 379, 381
Hidaka, S., 220
Hildenbrand, B., 16
Hildenbrand, W., 262, 331, 335
Hilferding, R., 22
Hirase, M., 218, 225
Hirayama, A., 289
Hirshleifer, J., 300
Hishiyama, I., 53, 64, 225
Hollander, S., 77, 83, 90, 97, 109, 144, 148, 156, 166
Howey, R.S., 327
Hume, D., 28, 31, 40, 41, 47, 72
Hutchison, F., 72
Hutchison, T.W., 10, 280, 297, 348, 349, 350

Ingram, J.C., 177, 179, 180
Itoh, M., 23, 193, 194, 229
Iwai, K., 386

Jaffé, W., 72, 249, 251, 254, 263, 268, 320, 323, 333
Jenkin, F., 324
Jevons, W.S., 25, 27, 324
  on capital, 300
  on equations of exchange, 329, 333
  on Gossen, 319, 323
  on law of indifference, 27, 327, 334, 343
  life sketch, 324
  marginal revolution, 25, 319, 330, 345, 349
  on market concept, 244, 326, 330, 338, 341, 343
  Theory of Political Economy, 25, 324, 331

Kaldor, N., 264, 304, 312
Kalecki, M., 4
Kamm, J., 157
Kautsky, K., 21, 192
Kemp, M.C., 43
Keynes, J.M., 28, 375, 385
  on Edgeworth, 331, 332
  General theory of Employment, Interest and Money, 28, 170, 221, 375
  on Jevons, 324
  and Malthus, 4, 5, 28, 108, 139, 143, 144, 145, 151
  and Marshall, 108, 376, 379
  on mercantilism, 9
  post-Keynesians, 108, 155
  and Ricardo, 108, 144
Keynes, J.N., 332, 375
Kimura, T., 74
Kirman, A.P., 262, 331, 335
Klein, L.R., 141
Kobayashi, N., 10, 11, 33, 95, 102
Kojima, K., 138
Knies, K., 16
Kregel, J.A., 108, 155
Krugman, P.K., 385
Kuczynski, M., 50, 61
Kuhn, T.S., 2

Lachmann, L.M., 18, 279
Lakatos, I., 3
Lange, O., 80, 143, 295
Lavoie, D., 295
Law, J., 34
Leibenstein, H., 21
Leigh, A.H., 34, 37
Leijonhufvud, A., 108, 170, 345

Lenin, V.I., 23, 193
Leontief, W., 77
Levy, D., 109
List, F., 10, 16
Liubimov, L., 218
Locke, J., 31, 33, 37
Luxemburg, R., 22

Malinvaud, E., 327, 379, 386
Malthus, T.R., 12, 138
  on effectual demand, 147, 152
  on glut, 139, 146
  and Keynes, 4, 5, 28, 151
  letter from Say, 145
  life sketch, 138
  on motives to produce, 146, 147
  on optimal saving, 143, 148
  and Ricardo, 139, 144, 145, 146, 147
  on Say's law, 16, 141, 181
Marshall, A., 27, 345
  book reviews, 331
  on consumers' surplus, 354, 356
  on economic growth, 368, 369
  on increasing returns, 352, 363, 369
  influence of Ricardo, 27, 107
  and Keynes, 108, 375, 376
  on life cycle of firms, 365, 368
  life sketch, 347
  marginal revolution, 27, 345
  on market concept, 380, 382
  neoclassical economics, 345
  on normal supply price, 230, 351, 370
  Principles of Economics, 27, 107, 331, 348, 355, 376
  on producers' surplus, 354, 358, 359
  on representative firm, 352, 366
  on trade cycle, 354, 377
  and Walras, 346
Marx, K., 21, 22, 191
  on capital concept, 200, 201, 220
  on competition, 224, 225
  on distribution, 213
  on economy of scale, 196, 199, 224
  on exploitation, 206, 209, 213, 214
  on international value, 210, 212, 213
  Das Kapital, 21, 22, 191, 192, 198, 201, 213, 225, 226, 229, 231
  on labor theory of value, 6, 71, 83, 194, 208
  on land rent, 199, 216
  life sketch, 192
  Manifest der Kommunistischen Partei, 155, 192
  on market value, 199, 229, 365
  his Plan, 21, 198, 213
  on Quesnay, 48, 51, 59
  on rate of profit, 199, 221
  and Ricardo, 107
  and Smith, 71, 80, 89
  on surplus value, 195, 217
  Theorien über den Mehrwert, 21, 83, 192
  on transformation problem, 198, 201
Mawatari, S., 23, 156, 193, 194
McCulloch, J.R., 8, 41
McKenzie, L., 254
Meade, J.E., 272
Meek, R.L., 48, 50, 51, 55, 56, 59, 61, 83, 144
Mehta, G., 3
Melvin, J.R., 178
Menger, C., 5, 25, 26, 279
  Grundsätze der Volkswirtschaftslehre, 25, 282
  life sketch, 279
  marginal revolution, 25, 319, 330
  on marketability of commodities, 26, 285
  on money, 26, 289
  on organic theory, 17, 281
  Untersuchungen über die Methode, 280
  on value, 282, 292, 297
Menger, K., 281
Mill, J., 156
Mill, J.S., 12, 155
  on business cycles, 156, 175
  on equilibrium, 33, 156, 180, 181, 329
  Essays on Some Unsettled Questions of Political Economy, 155, 160, 171
  influence to Marshall, 27, 107, 345
  on international trade, 15, 138, 176
  life sketch, 156
  on market concept, 171
  Principles of Political Economy, 12, 155, 157, 162, 170, 189
  on Say's law, 170
  on Smith, 95, 97
  on value, 13, 15
  on wages fund, 6, 162
Mirabeau, V.R., 50, 56, 59
Mises, L.E., 5, 27
Mishan, E.J., 355, 360
Mitchell, W.C., 19
Modigliani, F., 141
More, T., 243
Morishima, M.,
  on Marx, 23, 115, 192, 200, 201, 202, 203, 204, 216
  on Walras, 141, 254, 264, 268, 270, 273, 330
Morita, K., 138
Mun, T., 8, 41
Mussa, M., 43

Myrdal, G., 19

Nagatani, K., 289
Negishi, T.,
  on classical economics, 93, 131, 132, 141,
    162, 186, 188
  on marginal revolution and after, 255, 268,
    270, 273, 287, 294, 351, 364, 379
Neumann, J.V., 88, 268
Newman, P., 263, 368
Newton, I., 72
Nikaido, H., 23, 200, 204, 254

O'Driscoll, G.P., 289, 385
Oginuma, T., 275
Ohlin, B., 24, 137
Ohno, T., 386
Okada, J., 74
Okishio, N., 23, 200, 202, 224
Ong, N.P., 128
Ono, Y., 245
Orosel, G.O., 301
Oswald, J., 42
Ouchi, T., 229, 230, 232

Pagano, U., 325
Paniko, C., 221
Pareto, V., 25, 247
Pasinetti, L., 109, 116, 124, 131
Patinkin, D., 28, 35, 171, 263, 272
Perelman, M., 87
Petty, W., 14, 49, 112
Phelps, E.S., 296
Phillips, A., 53
Pigou, A., 27, 332, 337, 345, 348, 375
Polanyi, K., 281, 282
Popper, K.R., 2
Postlewaite, A., 92, 340
Proudhon, P.J., 246

Quesnay, F., 12, 31, 48, 56, 241
  life sketch, 49
  physiocracy, 12, 61
  Tableau Économique, 51, 59

Rawls, J., 296
Reiss, W., 300
Ricardo, D., 12
  on capital, 134
  dichotomy, 131, 137
  on distribution, 106, 124, 126
  on foreign trade, 15, 45, 106, 132, 138
  influence of, 5, 27, 107, 192, 212, 345, 349

  on labor theory of value, 13, 49, 71, 83, 119,
    128
  on land rent, 14, 105, 124, 218
  life sketch, 105
  on machinery, 121
  and Malthus, 139, 144, 146, 147
  Principles, 12, 105, 119, 121, 126
  on rate of profit, 124, 221
  and Say, 355
  and Smith, 71, 75, 82, 95, 97, 105, 106
  on value, 127
Richardson, G.B., 91
Rist, C., 345
Roberts, D.J., 92, 340
Robertson, D.H., 363
Robinson, J., 27, 91, 364, 385
Rodbertus, J.C., 200, 208, 218
Roemer, J., 23, 200, 224
Rogers, T., 331
Roncaglia, A., 113, 114, 115
Roscher, W.G.F., 16, 300
Rosdolsky, R., 22, 198, 222, 229
Rousseau, J.J., 41
Rozenberg, D.I., 232

Saint-Simon, C.H. de R., 157
Samuelson, P.A.,
  on land theory of value, 49, 110
  on Marx, 23, 77, 202
  on Menger and Wieser, 283
  on Quesnay, 62
  on Ricardo, 77, 109, 118
  on Schumpeter, 241
  on Smith, 77, 84
  on specie-flow, 43
  on stability, 268
  on Turgot, 304
Sargent, T.J., 156, 176
Say, J.B., 16, 75, 141, 145, 156, 158, 170, 181,
  355
Scarf, H., 335
Schmalensee, R.L., 385
Schmitt, H.O., 3, 11
Schmoller, G., 10, 16, 18, 280
Schumpeter, J.A., 26, 386
  on Böhm-Bawerk, 279
  on the dawn of economics, 5, 8
  on development, 26, 313
  on entrepreneur, 26, 314
  on French economists, 241
  on historical school, 17, 18, 386
  on land theory of value, 49, 112
  life sketch, 310
  on Methodenstreit, 280

on More, 243
on Ricardo, 107
on Smith, 75, 81, 84
on Wieser, 290
Schwartz, P., 164, 166
Senior, N.W., 212
Seton, F., 23, 202, 203
Shibata, K., 23, 68, 224
Shitovitz, B., 92
Shove, G.F., 107, 345, 368
Sidgwick, H., 332
Sismondi, J.C.L., 175, 181
Smith, A., 12, 71
    on capital, 10, 45, 95, 98, 134
    on division of labor, 90, 98, 364
    on economic growth, 83, 88
    on effectual demand, 75, 147
    on human capital, 87
    on increasing returns, 91
    on international trade, 94, 102
    life sketch, 71
    on mercantilism, 8, 76, 131
    on natural price, 12, 74, 86, 147
    on natural wage, 86
    The Wealth of Nations, 12, 41, 71, 73, 77, 83,
        86, 95, 98, 105
Solow, R.M., 272
Sombart, W., 18
Spadaro, L.M., 279
Spencer, H., 19
Spengler, J.J., 86
Spiegel, H.W., 33, 34, 345
Sraffa, P., 5, 13, 24, 27, 77, 93, 105, 117, 118,
    224, 287
Stackelberg, H., 245
Staley, C.E., 42, 47
Stalin, J., 193
Steedman, I., 23, 200, 228
Steuart, J., 10, 49
Stigler, G.J., 13, 144
Streissler, E., 284, 287, 386
Swan, T.W., 272
Sweezy, P., 222
Sylos-Labini, 92, 225

Tachi, R., 304
Takayama, A., 43, 357
Taussig, F.W., 27
Tawney, R.H., 2
Taylor, H., 157
Thomson, H.F., 72
Thornton, W.H., 156, 164, 182
Thunen, J.H.V., 24, 113
Tollison, R.D., 11

Tominaga, J., 243
Tomizuka, R., 222
Triffin, R., 28
Turgot, A.R.J., 304

Uno, K., 23, 193, 229, 230
Uzawa, H., 268, 272, 283

Varian, H.R., 357
Vaughn, K.I., 31, 37, 39
Veblen, T.B., 19, 20
Viner, J., 6, 7, 42, 47, 72

Walker, D.A., 19, 20, 249, 381
Walras, A., 246, 250
Walras, L., 25, 75, 241, 254
    on capital, 252, 268
    on Dupuit and Say, 355
    Elément d'économie politique pure, 25, 250
    on existence of equilibrium, 254
    on Gossen, 320
    on Jevons, 329
    life sketch, 246
    marginal revolution, 25, 319, 330
    on market concept, 244, 286, 323, 326, 330,
        338
    and Marshall, 346
    on money, 272
    neoclassical economics, 345
    on stability of equilibrium, 263
Watanabe, T., 68
Watarai, K., 109
Weber, M., 16, 18
Weber, W., 280
Weintraub, E.R., 254
Weizsäcker, C.C., 209
Whewell, W., 109, 350
Whitaker, J.K., 368
White, L.H., 280
Wicksell, K., 26, 27, 269, 300
Wicksteed, P.H., 247, 252
Wieser, F., 26, 279, 289
Williams, P.L., 381
Wolfe, J.N., 368
Wolfson, M., 198
Wordsworth, W., 157

Yagi, K., 315
Yamada, Y., 281
Yamamoto, H., 229
Yano, M., 303
Yasui, T., 252, 254, 264, 268, 269
Yokoyama, M., 53
Young, A.A., 89, 91, 100, 364

SUBJECT INDEX

absolute rent, 218
abstract human labor, 208, 211
agriculture, 11, 51, 61, 68, 96, 100, 163
alienation, 192
anthropology, 20, 281
arbitrage, 330, 337
Arrow anomaly, 258
astronomy, 2, 72, 320
auction, 182
Austrian school, 5, 26, 279, 330

biology, 347, 348
blood circulation, 50
business cycles (*see also* trade cycles), 27, 156, 176

Cambridge School, 345
capital, 76, 375
  classical economics on, 45, 97, 134
  Marx on, 200, 201, 220
  Mill on, 158, 173
  organic composition of, 196, 222
  Quesnay on, 12
  Walras on, 137, 251, 252
capital formation and credit,
  Walras's theory of, 252, 268, 346
capital movement, 24, 135
catallactics, 159
circulation and money,
  Walras's theory of, 253, 275, 346
classical economics, 12, 21, 27, 71, 105, 155, 192, 283, 330, 345
Colbertism, 11
collusion, 245
commodity, 194, 284
  basic, 117, 118
  marketability of, 26, 285
comparative cost (advantage), 15, 95, 106, 132, 160, 176
competition,
  classical economics on, 92, 159, 225
  imperfect, 27, 287, 364
  and increasing returns, 91, 363
  neo-classical concept, 91
  perfect, 91, 244, 245, 333, 335
conjectural variation, 245
conjecture and refutation, 1
consumers' surplus, 350, 354, 355, 367
contract, 332

contract curve, 256, 333, 335
cost,
  of circulation, 197
  of transaction, 340
  and utility, 26, 27, 291, 351

demand curve
  Chamberlin's, 224, 226, 227
  inelastic, 164, 167, 183
  kinked, 93, 225, 381
development (Schumpeter), 26, 313
dichotomy,
  between real and monetary theory, 131, 137, 156, 274, 376
  Marx's, 213
  Vebren's, 19
differential calculus, 327
differential rent, 14, 216
diminishing cost (*see also* economies, increasing returns), 224, 363
disequilibrium, 28, 122, 181, 188, 254, 287
distribution, 124, 213, 295, 337
division of labor, 73, 100, 172, 364
  and capital, 95, 98
  and market, 82, 89
duopoly, 242, 339
dynamic economics, 27, 160, 226, 295

economic development, 14, 56
economic growth, 7, 14, 61, 68, 83, 85, 312, 368, 369
Economic Journal, 331
The Economics of Industry (Marshall), 348, 377
economies (*see also* increasing returns),
  external, 350, 364
  internal, 350, 364, 367, 369, 375
economy of scale (*see also* increasing returns), 225, 260
Edgeworth box diagram, 255, 333
effective demand, 4, 9, 28
effectual demand, 75, 147
elasticity, 350
Eléments d'économie politique pure (Walras), 25, 241, 247, 250
entrepreneur,
  Schumpeter on, 26, 314
  Walrasian, 251, 311
entry, 92, 225

Entwicklung der Gesetze des menschlichen Verkehrs (Gossen), 25, 319
equation of exchange (Fisher), 28, 252
equations of exchange (Jevons), 326, 329, 333
equilibrium,
    Edgeworth, 337
    existence of, 177, 180, 188, 242, 253, 255
    Jevons, 326, 329
    Marshall, 229, 350, 365
    Mill, 33, 156, 162, 189
    multiple (indeterminate), 6, 180, 183, 337
    natural, 119
    Smith, 75
    stability of, 266, 351
    temporary, 268, 272, 346
    Walras, 250, 252, 320, 329
equilibrium analysis,
    general, 24, 25, 38, 75, 77, 241, 251, 345, 347
    partial (*see also* other thing being equal), 345
equilibrium (balanced) growth, 87, 210, 272, 371
equivalence theorem (Edgeworth), 338, 343
Essay on the Influence of a Low Price of Corn (Ricardo), 105, 119
Essays on some Unsettled Questions (Mill), 155, 162, 171
exchange (*see also* market), 255
    Gossen's theory of, 320
    Jevons's equations of, 326, 329, 333
    Jevons's theory, 319, 325, 338
    Walras's theory of, 248, 338, 346
exchange value (Wieser), 292
exploitation, 195, 206, 208, 209, 210
exporters and importers, 45, 46
external economies, 350, 364

fixed point theorem, 254
fixprice method, 287, 379, 381
forced saving, 123
foreign exchange,
    rate of, 142
foreign trade, *see* international trade
fundamental Marxian theorem, 191, 202

The General Theory of Employment, Interest and Money (Keynes), 9, 28, 170, 221, 375
glut, 4, 16, 146, 160
Gossen's laws, 320
Grundsätze der Volkswirtschaftslehre (Menger), 25, 280

hard core, 4, 29

historical school, 16, 280
history,
    materialistic interpretation of, 21
history of economics, 1
hoarding, 145
homogeneity, 268
human capital, 87

Idealtypus, 18
imperfect (monopolistic) competition, 27, 287, 364
imputation, 26, 291
income policy, 7
increasing returns (*see also* economies, diminishing cost), 82, 89, 352, 363
    and competition, 91, 363
indifference curve, 333
industrial organization, 385
industrial reserve army, 197, 210
Industry and Trade (Marshall), 348, 381
infant industry, 162
institution,
    Menger's organic theory of, 17, 281
Institutionalism, 19
interest,
    Böhm-Bawerk's three causes of, 298
    exploitation theory of, 208
    fructification theory of, 304
    liquidity preference thoery of, 145
    loanable funds theory of, 141, 145
    Marx on, 199, 220
    natural rate of, 199, 221
    Schumpeter's propositions on, 310
internal economies, 350, 364, 367, 369, 375
international trade,
    classical theory of, 45
    Mill's theory of, 15, 176
    neo-classical theory of, 24, 45, 46, 95, 137, 176
    in Quesnay, 12, 59
    Ricardo's theory of, 15, 131, 132, 138
    Smith's theory of, 93, 102
investment,
    natural order of, 76, 96
    and saving, 28, 144
invisible hand, 12, 77

joint-stock company, 368
just price, 3, 5, 6

Das Kapital (Marx), 21, 191, 192, 193, 213, 229, 231
Kapital und Kapitalzins (Böhm–Bawerk), 26, 208, 298

Keynesian Economics, 2, 28, 50, 144, 156, 382
kinked demand curve, 93, 225, 381

labor power, 195, 206, 210
labor theory of value, 6, 12, 21, 49, 74, 109,
  119, 155, 192, 194
labor value,
  commandable, 74, 83
  embodied, 74, 83, 200, 206, 210
Lagrangean multiplier, 80, 260, 292, 294
laissez-faire, 11, 12, 76, 249
land theory of value, 48, 112
large economy, 27, 244
Lausanne school, 25, 247, 330
law of indifference, 27, 172, 242, 244, 327, 330,
  338
life-cycle, 301, 365, 368, 372
limit theorem, 244, 339, 343
linear economic models, 24, 54, 191, 196, 200
linear programming, 24, 54, 80, 113, 114, 283
liquidity preference theory, *see* interest
loanable fund theory, *see* interest
long-run, 15, 162, 347, 352, 361, 365, 369

machinery problem, 121
Malthusian law of population, 13, 79, 82, 139
manufacture, 51, 68, 97, 101
marginal productivity, 25, 247, 252, 283
marginal revolution, 2, 24, 241, 320, 330
marginal utility, 25, 251, 282, 291, 293, 319,
  325, 326
  of money, 356, 380
market (*see also* exchange),
  Marshall on, 380, 381
  Menger on, 26, 286
  Mill on, 171
  Walras on, 26, 28, 253, 274, 286
marketability of commodity, 26, 285
market value, 217, 229, 236
Marxian economics, 4, 21, 155, 191, 283
Marx's plan, 21, 198, 213
Mathematical Psychics (Edgeworth), 27, 331,
  332
mercantilism, 3, 5, 8, 28, 41, 76, 131
Methodenstreit, 17, 280
methodological individualism, 280
micro-foundations of macroeconomics, 28, 93,
  182, 327, 379
model, 1
monetarism, 4, 29, 379
monetary dynamics, 26
monetary economy, 144, 274, 376
money,
  Aquinas on, 6

Keynes on, 289
  in Marshall, 346
  Marx on, 194, 199
  Menger's theory of, 26, 281, 285, 289
  neutral, 144, 156, 273, 376
  quantity theory of, 4, 28, 32, 37
  in Walras, 252, 272, 347
Money Credit and Commerce (Marshall), 348,
  377
money illusion, 176
monopolistic competition, *see* imperfect
  competition
monopoly, 92, 242
moral sentiments, 72
motives to produce (Malthus), 147

Nash solution, 243
natural equilibrium, 119
natural law, 11, 12, 16
natural price, 12, 75, 86, 147
natural rate of interest, 108, 199
natural rate of wage, 13, 82, 83, 86, 88, 119,
  135, 162
natural value (Wieser), 290
neo-classical economics, 20, 24, 71, 191, 224,
  241, 254, 272, 279, 345
neo-Ricardians, 5, 13, 24, 114, 155
neutral money, 144, 156, 273, 376
new classical macroeconomics, 156, 175
non-cooperative game, 243
non-linear programming, 177
non-tâtonnement, 275, 380
nontraded (domestic) good, 44
normal supply price, 230, 236, 350, 366, 370
numéraire, 251

oligopoly, 243, 341
*On the Principles of Political Economy and
  Taxation* (Ricardo), 12, 105, 119
optimum propensity to consume, 143, 148
organic composition of capital, 196, 222
organic theory, 17, 281
other things being equal (*see also* equilibrium
  analysis, partial), 346, 349, 377

paradigm, 2, 20, 29, 155
Pareto optimality, 249, 255
particular expenses curve, 352, 359
perfect competition, 244, 255, 333, 335
period of production, 152, 163, 300, 303
Physiocracy, 11, 48, 61, 68
post-Keynesians, 108, 155
praxeology, 27
price of production, 198, 204, 215

primitive accumulation, 10, 197
Principles of Economics (Marshall), 27, 107, 331, 348, 355, 376
Principles of Political Economy (Malthus), 12, 139, 146
Principles of Political Economy (Mill), 12, 155, 156, 162, 170, 189
private property, 294
producers' surplus, 355, 358
production,
  classical theory of, 46
  Jevons's theory of, 325
  Menger's theory of, 283, 292
  Walras's theory of, 251, 346
productive labor, 76, 140, 146
produit net, 12, 51
profit, 12, 52, 57, 73, 76, 106, 147, 148
  rate of, 13, 83, 85, 87, 117, 199, 215
protective belt, 4, 28, 29, 162
public finance,
  voluntary theory of, 364
purchasing power, 293, 313
  of money, 346, 377, 379

quantity theory of money, 4, 28, 32, 37
quasi-rent, 352

rate of profit, 13, 83, 85, 87, 117, 199, 215
  falling, 106, 118, 221
  international difference in, 134
  and wage, 13, 119, 128
real-exchange economy, 274, 376
Recherches sur les principes mathématiques de la théorie des richesses (Cournot), 24, 241
reciprocal demand, 15, 132, 160, 176
rent,
  absolute, 218
  differential, 14, 216
  quasi-, 352
  Ricardo's theory of, 14, 105, 113
  share of, 125
rent seeking, 11
representative firm, 230, 352, 366
reproduction, 197
research programmes, 4, 20, 28, 29, 162, 326
Ricardian economics,
  influence of, 5, 107
  mathematical models of, 109
  Pasinetti's model of, 116
roundabout production, 100, 298, 300
  circulating capital model of, 300, 302
  fixed capital model of, 300, 303

Saving and investment, *see* investment

Say's law, 16, 141, 156, 158, 170
Shibata–Okishio theorem, 224
short-run, 15, 29, 122, 162, 346, 351, 352, 360
short-side principle, 275, 287
simple economy (Wieser), 290
social economy (Wieser), 294
social welfare function, 292, 295, 337
socialist economy, 26, 290, 295
Sozialpolitik, 18
specie-flow mechanism, 8, 9, 41, 48
stability, 266, 351
Stackelberg disequilibrium, 245
stationary state, 14, 121
  and interest, 298, 301, 310
  Marshall on, 230, 236, 351, 365
  Mill on, 160
  and Quesnay, 52
  simple reproduction, 89, 197, 210
  and Smith, 83, 85
  and Walras, 268, 269
steady-state equilibrium growth, 88, 120, 313, 371
subsistence wage, 77, 162
surplus-value, 195, 206, 213
  extra-, 217
  rate of, 201, 214

Tableau Économique, 12, 50, 51, 59
tâtonnement, 253, 263, 274, 379
  non-tâtonnement, 275, 380
technical progress, 122, 314, 371
temporary equilibrium, 268, 272, 346, 380
terms of trade, 15, 24, 43, 64, 132
Theory of Political Economy (Jevons), 25, 325, 331
trade cycles (*see also* business cycles), 354, 377
trade union, 16, 165
trading body, 326, 334
transformation problem, 198, 201

uncertainty, 284
unemployment, 20, 28, 175, 375
unequal exchange, 24, 210
Uno school, 23, 193
unpaid labor, 206
unproductive labor, 76, 140, 146
Untersuchungen über die Methode (Menger), 280
utilitarianism, 294, 332, 337
utility and cost, *see* cost

value,
  Austrian theory of, 283, 297
  difficulty of production (Ricardo), 127, 128

exchange (Wieser), 292
international value, 212
invariable measure of, 13
labor theory of, 6, 12, 21, 49, 74, 109, 119, 155, 192, 194
land theory of, 48, 112
Locke on, 32
market, 217, 229, 236
natural (Wieser), 290
surplus, 195, 206, 213
vent, 33, 93
voluntary theory of public finance, 364

von–Neumann model, 88, 210, 268

wage,
natural rate of, 82, 83, 86, 88, 119, 135, 162
and rate of profit, 13, 119, 128
subsistence, 77, 162
wages fund doctrine, 15, 81, 156, 162
Mill's recantation of, 16, 162, 164, 183
Walras' law, 170, 241, 242, 253, 257, 268
The Wealth of Nations (Smith), 12, 73, 83, 95, 98, 105
Wertfreiheit, 18